# HUMAN RIGHTS WATCH BOOKS

Iraq and Iraqi Kurdistan

Boundary of the Kurdistan Autonomous Region (1975)

Current cease-fire line between Kurdish and Iraqi forces

© 1994 Michael S. Miller

Area of detail at right

# IRAQ'S
## CRIME OF
## GENOCIDE

## THE ANFAL CAMPAIGN
## AGAINST THE KURDS

## HUMAN RIGHTS WATCH / MIDDLE EAST

Yale University Press    New Haven and London

Research into the Anfal campaign was made possible
by grants from Herbert and Marion Sandler, George and Susan Soros,
Rosalind Whitehead, and Medico International.

Human Rights Watch and Yale University Press express their appreciation to the
J. M. Kaplan Fund for making this joint publishing program possible.

*Iraq's Crime of Genocide* was first published in different form
by Human Rights Watch, copyright © July 1993.
Human Rights Watch/Middle East was established in 1989 to monitor
and promote the observance of internationally recognized human rights
in the Middle East and North Africa.

Set in Times Roman by The Composing Room of Michigan, Inc.
Printed in the United States of America by BookCrafters, Inc., Chelsea, Michigan.

*Library of Congress Cataloging-in-Publication Data*

Iraq's crime of genocide : the Anfal campaign against the Kurds /
Human Rights Watch / Middle East.
     p.   cm. — (Human Rights Watch books)
Includes bibliographical references and index.
ISBN 0-300-06427-6 (alk. paper)

   1. Kurds—Iraq.   2. Iraq—Ethnic relations.   3. Massacres—Iraq.
4. Genocide—Iraq.   I. Human Rights Watch/Middle East.   II. Series.
DS70.8.K8I37   1995
305.89159—dc20                                              94-34779

The paper in this book meets the guidelines for permanence and
durability of the Committee on Production Guidelines for Book
Longevity of the Council on Library Resources.

10   9   8   7   6   5   4   3   2   1

# ABOUT HUMAN RIGHTS WATCH

Human Rights Watch conducts regular systematic investigations of human rights abuses in some seventy countries around the world. It addresses the human rights practices of governments of all political stripes, of all geopolitical alignments, and of all ethnic and religious persuasions. In internal wars it documents violations by both governments and rebel groups. Human Rights Watch defends freedom of thought and expression, due process, and equal protection of the law; it documents and denounces murders, disappearances, torture, arbitrary imprisonment, exile, censorship, and other abuses of internationally recognized human rights.

Human Rights Watch began in 1978 with the founding of its Helsinki division. Today, it includes five divisions, covering Africa, the Americas, Asia, and the Middle East, as well as the signatories of the Helsinki accords. It also includes five collaborative projects on arms transfers, children's rights, free expression, prison conditions, and women's rights. It maintains offices in New York, Washington, Los Angeles, London, Brussels, Moscow, Belgrade, Zagreb, Dushanbe, and Hong Kong. Human Rights Watch is an independent nongovernmental organization supported by contributions from private individuals and foundations worldwide. It accepts no government funds, directly or indirectly.

The staff includes Kenneth Roth, executive director; Cynthia Brown, program director; Holly J. Burkhalter, advocacy director; Gara LaMarche, associate director; Juan Méndez, general counsel; Susan Osnos, communications director; and Derrick Wong, finance and administration director.

The regional directors of Human Rights Watch are Abdullahi An-Na'im, Africa; José Miguel Vivanco, Americas; Sidney Jones, Asia; Jeri Laber, Helsinki; and Christopher E. George, Middle East. The project directors are Stephen Goose (acting), Arms Project; Lois Whitman, Children's Rights Project; Gara LaMarche, Free Expression Project; Joanna Weschler, Prison Project; and Dorothy Q. Thomas, Women's Rights Project.

The members of the board of directors are Robert L. Bernstein, chair; Adrian W. DeWind, vice chair; Roland Algrant, Lisa Anderson, Peter D. Bell, Alice L. Brown, William Carmichael, Dorothy Cullman, Irene Diamond, Edith Everett, Jonathan Fanton, Alan Finberg, Jack Greenberg, Alice H. Henkin, Harold

# CONTENTS

In the Name of God, the Merciful, the Compassionate

The Venerable Chief and Leader, the Honorable Saddam Hussein (May God Protect Him), President of the Republic and Head of the Honorable Revolutionary Command Council:

Struggling Comrade, I greet you. And I present myself to you as a devoted citizen.

I implore you in the name of Ba'athist Justice to hear my plight, which has deprived me of sleep night and day. For I lost all hope and when I had no one left to turn to except yourselves, I came to you with my problem, which may be of some concern to you.


Sir:

I, the undersigned, Assi Mustafa Ahmad, who returned as a prisoner of war on 24 August 1990, am a reserve soldier, born in 1955. I participated in the Glorious Battle of Saddam's Qadissiyat in the sector of al-Shoush and was taken prisoner on 27 March 1982. I remained a prisoner until the day that the decision to exchange prisoners of war was issued. Then I returned to the homeland and kissed the soil of the Beloved Motherland and knelt in front of the portrait of our Victorious Leader and President, Saddam Hussein. In my heart I felt a tremendous longing to return to my family. They would delight at seeing me, and I would delight in seeing them, and we would all be caught up in an overwhelming joy that could not be described.

However, I found my home completely empty. My wife and my children were not there. What a catastrophe! What a horror! I was told that the whole family had fallen into the hands of the Anfal forces in the Anfal operation conducted in the Northern Region, under the leadership of Comrade Ali Hassan al-Majid. I know nothing of their fate. They are:

1. Azimah Ali Ahmad, born 1955, my wife
2. Jarou Assi Mustafa, born 1979, my daughter
3. Faraydoun Assi Mustafa, born 1981, my son
4. Rukhoush Assi Mustafa, born 1982, my son

I have thus come to you with this petition, hoping that you would take pity on me and inform me of their fate. May God grant you success and protect you. You have my thanks and respect.

[Signature]
Former Prisoner of War
Reserve Soldier Assi Mustafa Ahmad
Without home or shelter in Suleimaniyeh,
Chamchamal, Bekas Quarter, Haji Ibrahim Mosque
4 October 1990

The Reply

In the Name of God, the Merciful, the Compassionate

Republic of Iraq

Office of the President

Reference No.: Sh Ayn/B/4/16565

Date: 29 October 1990

Mr. Assi Mustafa Ahmad

Suleimaniyeh Governorate

Chamchamal District

Bekas Quarter

Haji Ibrahim Mosque

With regard to your petition dated 4 October 1990. Your wife and children were lost during the Anfal Operations that took place in the Northern Region in 1988.

Yours truly,

[Signature]

Saadoun Ilwan Muslih

Chief, Office of the President

# FOREWORD TO THE 1995 EDITION

This book is the result of almost three years of research carried out by Human Rights Watch/Middle East (formerly known as Middle East Watch) in northern Iraq and at the National Archives in Washington, D.C., in 1991–94. It combines findings from forensic missions (conducted jointly with Physicians for Human Rights), eyewitnesses, extensive interviews, and the study of eighteen metric tons of Iraqi state documents in arguing that the 1988 Anfal campaign against the Kurds in northern Iraq constituted genocide.

Between 1992 and 1994, HRW/Middle East published five reports about the Anfal campaign. *Genocide in Iraq* combines and expands on the information provided in the first three reports: one on land mines, one on mass graves, and the third on two villages that suffered during the Anfal campaign—one endured a mass execution, the other a chemical attack. An earlier version of the book was published in the summer of 1993 by the Middle East division under the same title. Appendix E of the present edition includes the documentary evidence of genocide that was published in February 1994 in *Bureaucracy of Repression: The Iraqi Government in Its Own Words*.

Since publication of *Bureaucracy*, Human Rights Watch has made substantial progress in the analysis of the Iraqi state files. By the end of May 1994, it had screened close to 70 percent of the documents for evidence of genocide and other human rights abuses by the government of Iraq against its Kurdish population during the 1980s. The project has been scheduled to be completed by the end of September 1994.

JOOST R. HILTERMANN
*Iraqi Documents Project Director*
Human Rights Watch/Middle East

# PREFACE

Occasionally, opportunity can grow out of tragedy. For Human Rights Watch/ Middle East, the first opportunity to carry out human rights research in northern Iraq came unexpectedly, in the wake of the tumultuous, heart-wrenching events of early 1991 that are familiar to most of us from our television sets. As Iraqi government troops fell back in the face of advancing allied troops and Kurdish *peshmerga* fighters returning with civilian refugees from the Turkish and Iranian borders, it became evident that Baghdad's long-standing ban on access to the Kurdish region by independent investigators had been broken—by a force majeure. How long the window of opportunity would stay open no one could predict.

This debilitating uncertainty remains. For the Iraqi Kurds, their future as an often-threatened minority is at risk, as are their lives. At this writing, a severe economic squeeze, from a combination of United Nations sanctions against Iraq and an internal blockade imposed by government forces, threatens to produce mass starvation among the 3.5 million inhabitants of the Kurdish rebel– controlled enclave. Government troops amassed along a cease-fire line could easily reconquer the region before the West could come to the aid of the Kurds.

For the Middle East division of Human Rights Watch, a driving consideration over the past two years has been whether there would be time to gather reliable information both to convince international public opinion and, later, to satisfy a court of law. Although interim reports have been released about the 1988 extermination campaign known as Anfal (see Bibliography), with the publication of this book, the first objective has been accomplished. There is persuasive evidence that virtually all the many tens of thousands Kurdish civilians who disappeared at the hands of government forces in 1988 are dead, yet whether their fate can be definitively settled anytime soon remains to be seen. Much depends on the future course of internal Iraqi politics.

Allegations about enormous abuses against the Kurds by government security forces had been circulating in the West for years before the events of 1991; Kurdish rebels had spoken of 4,000 destroyed villages and an estimated 182,000 disappeared persons in 1988 alone. The phenomenon of the Anfal— the official military code name used by the government in its public pronouncements and internal memoranda—was well known inside Iraq, especially in the Kurdish region. As all the horrific details emerge, this name has seared itself into the popular consciousness—much as the Nazi German Holocaust has in the world's consciousness. The parallels are apt and are often chillingly close.

Fragmented by their mountainous geography, their own political fractiousness, and the divide-and-rule policies of regional governments at the time, few Kurds appreciated the highly organized and comprehensive nature of the Anfal. And for obvious reasons, before October 1991, when Kurdish rebel leaders unexpectedly found themselves the temporary masters of much of their traditional lands, there were few hard facts for external organizations to rely on.

In its February 1990 report, *Human Rights in Iraq,* HRW/Middle East reconstructed what had taken place from exile sources, with what in retrospect turned out to be great accuracy. Even so, some of the larger claims made by the Kurds seemed too fantastic to credit. In fact, the process of discovery has been a humbling lesson for the foreigners who follow Kurdish affairs from abroad. Western reporters, relief workers, human rights organizations, and other visitors to Iraqi Kurdistan have come to realize that the overall scale of the suffering inflicted on the Kurds by their government was by no means exaggerated.

With this latest report, painstakingly compiled over eighteen months, HRW/Middle East believes it can now demonstrate convincingly a deliberate intent on the part of the government of President Saddam Hussein to destroy, through mass murder, part of Iraq's Kurdish minority. The Kurds are indisputably a distinct ethnic group, separate from the majority Arab population of Iraq, and they were targeted during the Anfal as Kurds. (Anthropologically, they are an Indo-European people, speaking a language that is related to Persian, albeit with a large admixture of Arabic and Turkish, varying according to the countries they inhabit.) Two government instruments—the October 1987 national census and the declaration of "prohibited areas," which covered more and more of the Kurdish countryside in a crazy-quilt pattern, were the institutional foundations of this policy. These instruments were implemented against the background of nearly two decades of a government-directed policy of "Arabization," by which mixed-race districts or lands that Baghdad regarded as desirable or strategically important saw their Kurdish population guarded by government troops and diluted by Arab migrant farmers provided with incentives to relocate.

The Kurds bear arms as a matter of course and have regularly resorted to them when thwarted in their demands for greater political and cultural autonomy. Indeed, the Anfal cannot be understood without an awareness of the half century of Kurdish armed struggle against the central government of Iraq through various political regimes. In the early 1970s, the Ba'athists, still uncertain about their hold on power, went much further than their predecessors had in recognizing those demands, offering a substantial level of self-government and recognizing the Kurds' separate identity in a new constitution, which was called the Provisional Constitution. That constitution is still in force, and Baghdad still maintains the fiction that *its* autonomous region, with its own Kurdish administration, is in force. This puppet administration sits in government-controlled Kirkuk and regularly denounces the "foreign-backed usurpers" in the Kurdish rebel-run territory.

The logic of the Anfal, however, cannot be divorced from the Iran-Iraq War. After 1986, both the Patriotic Union of Kurdistan (PUK) and the Kurdistan Democratic Party (KDP), the two major Iraqi parties, received support from the Iranian government and sometimes took part in joint military raids against Iraqi government positions; the KDP also had a rear base inside Iran. That Baghdad was entitled to engage in counterinsurgency action to wrest control over Iraq's northeastern border region and much of the mountainous interior from rebels is undisputed. What HRW/Middle East contends is that, in doing so, the central government went much further than was required to restore its authority through legitimate military action. In the process, Saddam Hussein's regime committed a panoply of war crimes, together with crimes against humanity and genocide.

Although many readers will be familiar with the attack on Halabja in March 1988, in which up to five thousand Kurdish civilians died—the incident caused a brief international furor—they may be surprised to learn that the first use of poison gas against the Kurds by the central government had occurred eleven months earlier. All told, HRW/Middle East has recorded forty separate attacks on Kurdish targets between April 1987 and August 1988, some involving multiple sorties over several days. Each of these attacks was a war crime inasmuch as it involved the use of a banned weapon; the fact that the victims were often noncombatants adds to the offense.

By HRW/Middle East's estimate, in the Anfal at least fifty thousand and possibly as many as a hundred thousand persons, many women and children, were killed between February and September 1988. Their deaths did not come in the heat of battle—as "collateral damage," in the military euphemism. Nor were they the result of acts of aberration by individual commanders whose excesses passed unnoticed or unpunished by their superiors. Rather, these Kurds were systematically put to death in large numbers by order of the central Iraqi government in Baghdad days or weeks after being rounded up in villages marked for destruction or while fleeing army assaults in "prohibited areas."

Only a minority were combatants or served as a back-up force for rebel political parties. Most of the dead were noncombatants whose deaths resulted simply because they inhabited districts declared off-limits by the Iraqi government. Underlining the deliberate, preplanned nature of the Anfal, those responsible for the murders by firing squad were usually members of elite security units unconnected to the forces responsible for the Kurds' capture. In other words, while one hand would sweep, the other would dispose of what the regime considered to be the garbage.

Two experienced field researchers, Iraqi Documents Project director at HRW/ Middle East Joost Hiltermann and Human Rights Watch counsel Jemera Rone, sometimes assisted by a consultant, spent six months in northern Iraq between April and September 1992 gathering testimonies about the Anfal (see Note on Methodology). Until then, a twelve-year old boy, Taymour Abdullah Ahmad, had been the only known survivor of many accounts that Kurds—including men, women, and children—had been trucked southward to the Arab heartland of Iraq in large numbers and then disappeared. It was assumed they had all been summarily executed, but there was no proof. During their assignment, the HRW/Middle East team located and interviewed seven other survivors of the mass executions, who recalled them in convincing detail; five had been taken away and shot during the six-month military campaign, two others were taken shortly afterward and shot.

Before now we could not safely make these assertions without fear of contradiction. A division of Human Rights Watch, the Middle East division has already devoted more resources to this ambitious project than any other undertaking in its parent organization's fifteen-year history. For those individuals and foundations that have generously supported work on the Kurds project, we are deeply grateful. The publication of this book is a milestone. Yet the end is not in sight. Only when those responsible—both the government as a whole and the individuals who masterminded and carried out the Anfal—are brought to justice will the work of Human Rights Watch end.

In the absence of an international criminal court with jurisdiction to try those responsible for the grave crimes enumerated here, three options present themselves. The first is an Iraqi national court. Under current circumstances, with President Saddam Hussein and the Ba'ath Party still in power, it is almost inconceivable that this possibility will be realized. Second, there is the prospect of an ad hoc international tribunal, charged by the United Nations Security Council to hear some, if not all, the offenses, based on evidence to be gathered by a special commission of inquiry. Although such a proposal was put on the agenda at the Security Council by the Clinton Administration in July 1993, its realization is fraught with uncertainty, subject to the fluctuating politics of the major powers of the United Nations.

Last, there is the International Court of Justice (ICJ) at The Hague, known as the World Court. Part of the United Nations system, the ICJ's raison d'être is to resolve disputes between nations over breaches of international agreements and treaties. In the case of the Iraqi Kurds, the relevant treaty is the 1951 Convention on the Prevention and Punishment of the Crime of Genocide, to which Iraq and

107 other states are parties. It is important that Iraq has also accepted the jurisdiction of the ICJ to hear cases of genocide brought against it by other state parties with similar standing. In the judgment of HRW/Middle East, this acceptance is potentially the most fruitful channel through which to achieve justice for the Anfal.

Pursuing this option does not involve abandoning other courses of action. Indeed, they could complement each other since the ICJ is empowered to adjudicate only state and not individual responsibility. Contrary to popular misconceptions, however, the ICJ can be of practical benefit to the Iraqi Kurds by, for instance, ordering provisional measures of protection (a state party or parties to the Genocide Convention would in effect be acting on behalf of the Kurds), or by demanding that the government pay damages to victims.

To date, only Bosnia and Herzegovina have ever brought a case against another state under the Genocide Convention. In those cases the ICJ swiftly granted provisional protective measures (in March 1993) but has yet to rule on the substance of the complaint. Bringing a full-fledged case against Iraq on behalf of the Kurds would thus be a momentous event in international human rights law, one that it would be imperative to win, and to win on strong legal and factual grounds. The judgment would breathe life into the moribund Genocide Convention, strengthen respect for international law, and give pause to tyrannical regimes around the world that might be tempted to undertake similar actions against a minority people.

How, then, has evidence been gathered, and why is HRW/Middle East confident that a successful action can be brought against the Iraqi government?

It was in late 1991, a month after the Iraqi Kurdistan Front (a coalition of seven parties) had established its authority in the rebel enclave, that HRW/Middle East decided to send its second mission to the region (an earlier mission had produced an authoritative survey of the widespread problem of land mines, a serious hindrance to the resettlement of refugees). This mission was a joint venture with Physicians for Human Rights (PHR)—which had already carried out groundbreaking work on Iraq's use of chemical gas in 1988 during the final Anfal—and planned to enter Iraqi Kurdistan from Turkey. Its purpose was to examine the scale of the phenomenon of mass graves then being discovered by the Kurds in various locations. The ten-day mission exhumed several mass graves in and around the major Kurdish cities of Erbil and Suleimaniyeh, containing victims of the *Amn,* the main internal security force. The team left just as the deadline for the renewal of Operation Provide Comfort, the Turkey-based allied protection operation, expired (Ankara renewed permission at the eleventh hour).

During the unsuccessful March 1991 uprising, huge quantities of Iraqi government records were captured when local Kurds stormed the secret police buildings that dominated every town and city. Much was burned or destroyed in the haste, confusion, and panic that marked those days. The Kurds were mainly seeking references to themselves, to discover how much they had been infiltrated. Few were thinking about the Anfal, despite the fact that it had ended barely thirty months earlier. Obtaining access to official records became a Holy Grail for researchers. To have the opportunity to speak to survivors of human rights violations, to dig up the bones of those who had not survived, and then to read the official account of what had taken place—all while the regime that had carried out the outrages was still in power—was unique in the annals of human rights research.

Together with the Iraqi writer Kanan Makiya (whose pseudonym is Samir al-Khalil), who wrote *Republic of Fear* and *Cruelty and Silence*), and Peter Galbraith of the U.S. Senate Foreign Relations Committee, HRW/Middle East discussed with the Kurdish parties holding these documents their transfer to the United States for safekeeping and analysis. Uncertainty surrounded the subject: Exactly how much had the Kurds seized? How useful would the documents turn out to be? Where were the caches? How could the logistical and diplomatic hurdles to getting them out of the country be overcome? Several visits to the region were required before arrangements could be made. In May 1992, some fourteen tons of documents were finally transferred to the United States on the initiative of HRW/Middle East. At all times the material remained under its control. On arrival, the Senate Foreign Relations Committee took charge of the documents, entrusting them to a safe location where they were examined by a team led by HRW/Middle East (see Methodology section for a description of how the work was conducted.)

Primarily, the records were of the *Mudiriyat al-Amn al-Ameh* (General Security Directorate), the *Mudiriyat al-Istikhbarat al-Askariyeh al-Ameh* (General Military Intelligence Directorate), and to a lesser extent, the Ba'ath Party. These documents represent a key ingredient to understanding the logic and realization of the Anfal. Spanning the early 1960s to 1991, they will be crucial in the building of a legal case against the Iraqi government. Between April 1992 and April 1993, HRW/Middle East took oral testimony from over 350 eyewitnesses or survivors of Anfal-related actions by the authorities. This information forms the heart of its understanding of the government's behavior. Even on the basis of a partial examination, the documents have filled in many gaps by corroborating testimonial accounts and proving the general reliability of witnesses.

From the material examined to date, it is evident that detailed records were kept of all Kurds rounded up, sorted, and dispatched, either to their deaths or to prison or resettlement camps. When the overlord of the Anfal, Ali Hassan al-Majid, who was subsequently promoted to defense minister, met with Kurdish leaders in May 1991 for abortive peace negotiations, he knew what he was talking about. Faced with the Kurds' demands for an explanation of what had happened to the disappeared—a number they put at 182,000—al-Majid blurted out in anger that the total number killed in the Anfal "could not have been more than a hundred thousand." It was a telling order of magnitude, not to mention an admission of guilt.

Somewhere in a Baghdad archive there exists, almost certainly, a complete dossier of the missing Kurds: some may still be alive, five years after their capture. HRW/Middle East believes that the vast majority probably ended up in remote mass graves, such as those described in this book, and calls on Iraqi authorities to provide a full accounting of those they abducted so that relatives can mourn their dead and resume their lives.

It gradually became clear from field research that although the Anfal, during which most of the disappearances took place, had lasted only six months, the main campaign of village destruction and forcible relocation of hundreds of thousands inhabiting the prohibited areas had covered a two-year span, from March 1987 to April 1989. This coincided with the period when al-Majid held extraordinary powers of life and death as secretary of the Ba'ath Party's Northern Bureau. The campaign was the culmination of twenty-five years of Arabization, mass deportations, and the destruction of villages.

HRW/Middle East also learned about variations in government actions during different phases of the campaign. In the final Anfal in late August 1988, after the cease-fire in the Iran-Iraq War, HRW/Middle East encountered one of the few known cases in which government troops massacred male villagers on the spot. (Elsewhere male villagers disappeared en masse and are presumed to have been executed in clandestine locations.) The remote former village of Koreme, in Dohuk governorate, was identified in February 1992 as containing a mass grave. A second forensic anthropological team, again in conjunction with PHR and drawing on the expertise of Latin American researchers, was sent to the region in May 1992. After a month's fieldwork at Koreme and other sites, their findings—a detailed case study of the fate of Anfal victims from one region—were published in January 1993.

After a break during the winter of 1992/93, field research for this report resumed in March 1993, enabling information gaps to be filled in. However, much remains to be done before having all the answers to the tragedy that befell the Kurds. In the absence of disclosures from Baghdad, there is a need, for instance, for a more precise estimate of the number of those who have disappeared. Some, but by no means all, of the killing sites are known; extensive research work must be done in areas of Iraq that remain under government control.

But time does not stand still, and the Ba'athist regime's threat to the Kurdish enclave is as potent as ever. Behind a military cordon diagonally across northern Iraq—a cordon that has sealed off supplies of food, fuel, medicine, and other essentials to the Kurds for the past two years—the government has amassed its troops. Seemingly, all that holds them back is the threat of retaliation from the American, British, and French aircraft that daily patrol the region of Iraq north of the 36th parallel. Every six months the ritual of seeking Ankara's permission for the continuation of Operation Provide Comfort is reenacted. Until now, it has always been granted, but given Turkish negative sentiment toward the Kurds, whether in Turkey itself or across the Iraqi border, it is unlikely that Turkey will allow the Western allies to maintain their protective shield over the budding proto-state indefinitely.

Based on the evidence contained in this report, HRW/Middle East urges the international community to recognize that genocide occurred in the mountainous region of northern Iraq during 1988. The legal obligations to act on the basis of this information, to punish its perpetrators, and to prevent its recurrence, are undeniable. For this purpose, the U.S. government, as well as other states with relevant information, should disclose what knowledge they have about the Anfal. Continued protection for the Kurds is essential if the strong threat of reprisals from the Baghdad authorities is to be thwarted. Yet in the process of safeguarding the status quo one should not lose sight of the imperative that the Iraqi government should provide a full, public accounting of all those taken into the hands of its forces before, during, and after the Anfal. Although it would be unrealistic to expect President Saddam Hussein to put himself and his closest aides and relatives on trial, a successor government in Baghdad should not shirk its responsibility to carry out a thoroughgoing investigation of these enormous crimes and to prosecute all those involved to the full extent of the law.

The Iraqi Kurds must be permitted to live in peace and security, free to speak their language and practice their customs. The killings, deportations, and widespread village clearances detailed in the following pages must not be allowed to happen again.

This report was written by George Black, a writer on human rights and other international issues. (Black's most recent book, *Black Hands of Beijing* [New York: John Wiley and Sons, 1993], is a history of the Chinese democracy movement since 1976, co-authored with Robin Munro of HRW/Asia.) Bringing it to fruition was a collaborative effort involving Black, Hiltermann, and Rone. The epilogue was written by Dr. Hiltermann. Shorsh Resool, a researcher on the Iraqi Documents Project, and Dr. Hiltermann jointly provided the translations of the documents included in the epilogue.

Overall editorial responsibility for the report lies with Andrew Whitley, former executive director of HRW/Middle East. Mr. Resool contributed to the editing process and made important suggestions and corrections. Document translation was handled by several people.

Field researchers were Dr. Hiltermann and Ms. Rone, assisted by HRW/Middle East consultant Mostafa Khezri. Their fieldwork in 1992 and 1993 represents the heart of the information contained in this book. The tireless work of Kurdish interpreters in helping to obtain this information is appreciated. HRW/Middle East also extends its thanks to the Kurdistan Human Rights Organization in Iraqi Kurdistan, including its branches in Erbil, Suleimaniyeh, and Dohuk; the Committee to Defend Anfal Victims' Rights in Suleimaniyeh; and a number of doctors, lawyers, and other professionals in Iraqi Kurdistan, who must remain anonymous for their own safety. Special recognition is due Mr. Resool for his pioneering work on the Anfal campaign in 1988–89 under arduous conditions, before he joined the staff of HRW/Middle East.

Forensic research referred to in this report was conducted by joint HRW/Middle East–Physicians for Human Rights teams led in December 1991 by Eric Stover, and in May–June 1992 by Ken Anderson. Stover is executive director of PHR; Anderson is former director of Human Rights Watch's Arms Project. Clyde Snow, a distinguished forensic anthropologist, headed the scientific teams in both these missions and participated in another visit to Iraqi Kurdistan, in February 1992.

Legal research on the standards by which the Ba'ath regime should be judged on its actions in Iraqi Kurdistan from 1987 to 1989 was undertaken by Lori Damrosch of Columbia University's Law School. Keith Highet of Curtis, Mallet-Prevost, Colt, and Mosle, provided expert advice, as did Kenneth Roth, then acting executive director of Human Rights Watch.

Peter Galbraith, then senior adviser to the U.S. Senate Foreign Relations Committee and Ambassador Charles Dunbar, formerly of the U.S. Department of State, also deserve HRW/Middle East's warm thanks for the unstinting assistance they provided to this large undertaking.

Finally, HRW/Middle East wishes to thank Susan Meiselas for her enthusiasm and commitment to a subject and a people she has come to know well. Her photographs and video recordings have been of great benefit.

ANDREW WHITLEY
*Executive Director (1990–1994)*
Human Rights Watch/Middle East

# A NOTE ON METHODOLOGY

## THE METHODOLOGICAL APPROACH TO DOCUMENTARY, TESTIMONIAL, AND FORENSIC EVIDENCE USED IN THIS REPORT

### TESTIMONIAL EVIDENCE

In large measure this report is based on testimonies obtained in Iraqi Kurdistan from eyewitnesses to, and often victims of, Anfal-related abuses. Two HRW/ Middle East researchers and a consultant spent a total of six months in Kurdish areas on three separate missions between April 1992 and April 1993, conducting approximately 350 in-depth interviews.

Before its first mission in April 1992, the research team designed a questionnaire on the basis of HRW/Middle East's understanding of Anfal, which was still limited at the time, and discussions with regional experts and statisticians. This questionnaire was constructed to facilitate the tabulation and quantification of data on the forced displacement and disappearance of Kurds during the Anfal.

The team tested the questionnaire through a small number of interviews shortly after its arrival in the area and immediately determined that the questions did not take account of several factors, including specific historical events that explain the circumstances of the Anfal, nor of the methodical nature of the operation. The team revised the questionnaire drastically and began its research, making only minor adjustments in the weeks that followed.

The purpose of the research was to find out as much as possible about the Anfal and about the people who were said to have disappeared during and after the operation. The research population was divided into three groups: (1) direct eyewitnesses to Anfal-related abuses; (2) persons active in paramilitary and military units, either Kurdish guerrillas, former military officers, or advisers *(mustashars)* of the progovernment Kurdish militias; and (3) the staff of local and international nongovernmental organizations and officials of the local Kurdish administration, all of whom were intimately familiar with the situation on the ground before, during, and after the Anfal.

Because of the particular nature of Iraqi policy vis-à-vis rural Kurds in the 1980s, most eyewitnesses to the Anfal were to be found in the large housing camps *(mujamma'at)* in the valleys of northern Iraq. After the Iraqi government withdrew from a large part of the Kurdish region at the end of October 1991, villagers in some areas began returning to their destroyed villages to farm the land and sometimes to rebuild their homes. The research team visited as many of the camps as possible, as well as some of the partially rebuilt villages. In all cases the operative question was: "Where can we find the Anfals?" (*Anfalakan,* or victims of the Anfal, in Kurdish). Local residents would then guide the team to a house where Anfalakan were said to be living. The people were questioned to determine that they were indeed Anfals—and not persons who had been relocated from their villages during earlier stages of village destruction and had not been affected directly by the Anfal. This method had a snowball effect: one family of Anfalakan would lead the team to another, until the team felt it had exhaustively covered a particular geographic Anfal area.

Essentially, the team obtained eyewitness testimonies in three ways: (1) by visiting residences randomly and asking for Anfalakan (the most frequent method); (2) by pursuing specific leads; and (3) occasionally, by responding to unsolicited requests to be interviewed. In the beginning, the sole criterion employed in deciding whether a person should be interviewed was that the person had been present in a militarily demarcated area during the Anfal and had lost relatives as a result of the campaign. In later stages of the research, when clear patterns began to emerge, the search was more specifically for people from certain Anfal areas, namely, those areas for which the team had insufficient data or those where particularly egregious abuses (such as chemical weapon attacks) had taken place. In addition, a number of interviews were conducted at that time with people who had been in Anfal areas during the Anfal but whose families had managed to escape unhurt, as well as with people who had experienced various forms of human rights abuses in the periods immediately preceding and following Anfal (1987 and 1989).

The team specifically sought one subpopulation of eyewitnesses: those who had been arrested in the Anfal and were taken to mass execution sites (then and now in areas controlled by the Iraqi government) whence they had managed to escape and return to safety. The testimonies of these execution survivors have proved crucial in the effort of HRW/Middle East to provide evidence that most of those detained during the Anfal, whose fate is officially said to be unknown, were actually killed. The team was able to locate seven such Anfal survivors, as well as one person who survived an execution three months after the Anfal. Some of these survivors did not want their identities to be known because they feared future government reprisal. One of the eight, Taymour, had already been interviewed by local Kurdish television and foreign journalists on numerous occasions. A second one, Hussein, had given testimony to the U.N. Special Rapporteur on Iraq, Max van der Stoel, during the latter's visit to the area earlier in 1992. Four were located through local peshmerga commanders who had heard of their stories. The remaining two were found through the testimony of one of the survivors who had been in the same group as they at the time of the execution.

Invariably, respondents were eager to tell the team what had happened to them. In almost all cases, these people had not been interviewed about their experiences before. All freely gave their names, and only some requested that their identities be concealed from publication. Apart from those few who requested that their names be changed, all names referred to in this report are genuine. The team taped most interviews on audiocassette and took photographs (slides) of the respondents afterward. In the case of important interviews, the team asked the respondent's permission to videotape either highlights or a full second interview (as in the case of some of the execution survivors). The team always traveled with one or more Kurdish interpreters, who were asked to provide literal translations from English to Kurdish (Surani or Kurmanji dialects) and back. Some interviews were conducted by team members directly in English or Arabic.

In virtually all cases the team interviewed a single person at a time, although close relatives were often present during the interview. The questions covered the following topics:

1. Personal history before Anfal (personal status, family members, property, occupation, religious and tribal affiliations, and so forth)
2. Information concerning the village in which the person was living before Anfal (location, size of population, main tribe, main economic activity, availability of government services and facilities, and so on)
3. Military activity in and around the village before Anfal and government policies affecting the inhabitants (presence of peshmerga, government attacks, administrative and economic blockade, casualties, 1987 population census, and so forth)
4. Events during Anfal (the nature of government attacks, circumstances of arrest, the route of transport, selection process, conditions of detention, casualties, circumstances of release, and so on)
5. Living conditions after Anfal and attempts, if any, to locate missing relatives.

Usually, topics 1 and 2 followed a fairly strict question-and-answer format, although topics 3, 4, and 5 allowed for greater flexibility: the person was asked to recount events as he or she remembered them, and the team would either (a) ask questions only for clarification about specific dates, locations, or identities; (b) pursue at some length a narrative of particular interest to the project; or (c) probe any contradictions in the testimony or between the testimony and a previous testimony.

Owing to the high rate of illiteracy in rural Kurdistan, as well as the local population's particular way of marking time, the team had great difficulty in establishing exact dates for specific events or particular chronologies on the basis of interviews with individual villagers. Dates would often be related to religious feasts, for example. On the whole, though, after numerous interviews, the team was satisfied that it had obtained an accurate picture of the separate stages of Anfal and the events that transpired within those stages. Some dates have subsequently been substantiated in documents captured by the Kurds from the Iraqi intelligence agencies during the March 1991 uprising.

Generally, the team determined the accuracy of individual accounts by their internal consistency, general consistency with overall patterns gleaned during the project—including with other types of evidence—and, in a few cases, by their specific consistency tested in a follow-up interview. For all interviews, the team sought supporting evidence, including such personal documents as "movement permits," administrative orders, and inspection reports of the sites described (for example, a prison or village that had been subjected to a chemical attack). By this procedure, a small number of interviews or segments of interviews were not used either because it was not reliable or because it could not be substantiated.

For an analysis of the Iraqi government documents referred to in this report, as well as a brief overview of the Iraqi Documents Project of Human Rights Watch/Middle East, please see the Epilogue.

## FORENSIC EVIDENCE

A team of forensic investigators was sent by HRW/Middle East and Physicians for Human Rights to Iraqi Kurdistan in December 1991 and May–June 1992. The team consisted of forensic investigators trained in forensic anthropology, archaeology, and law who had carried out exhumations of graves in several countries, including Argentina, Chile, El Salvador, and Guatemala. It carried out exhumations of graves at three sites in Iraqi Kurdistan: at the village of Koreme, the village of Birjinni, and the cemetery of a camp of Anfal survivors outside the city of Erbil.

In its investigations, the team followed internationally accepted standards set forth in the United Nations "Model Protocol for a Legal Investigation of Extra-Legal, Arbitrary and Summary Executions" (the "Minnesota Protocol," found in the *Manual on the Effective Prevention and Investigation of Extra-Legal, Arbitrary and Summary Executions, 1991*). The full results of the team's investigations are found in *The Anfal Campaign in Iraqi Kurdistan: The Destruction of Koreme,* by HRW/Middle East and Physicians for Human Rights, January 1993, and its methodology at each site is described below.

### Koreme Site

The team undertook the exhumation of a mass grave at the destroyed village of Koreme, which contained the skeletal remains of twenty-six men and boys, all of whom had died by gunfire at close range in a line, indicating execution by firing squad. The team archaeologist directed the survey of the destroyed village, mapping the village as it stood before destruction using standard archaeological survey techniques, and directed the collection and mapping of cartridge casings to determine the pattern of weapon firing at the execution site. The team's lead anthropologist directed the exhumation of the grave site at Koreme, using standard exhumation techniques to preserve the skeletons and other artifacts. Investigations were carried out at the morgue at Dohuk General Hospital to determine the number of individuals in the grave, sex, age, and other identifying marks, and the manner of death. The team's lawyers supervised interviews with survivors and other villagers to yield a narrative of events corroborated by scientific evidence.

### Birjinni Site

The team carried out archaeological surveys and exhumations of graves at the destroyed village of Birjinni, which, according to surviving villagers, had been bombed in August 1988 with chemical weapons. The team archaeologist carried out standard surveys of the ruined village. The forensic anthropologists exhumed the graves of persons reported to have died from the inhalation of chemical agents. The team's lawyers conducted interviews with surviving villagers to obtain their account of events. In addition, the team took soil and other samples from the craters where chemical weapons were reported to have impacted. In 1993, the British Ministry of Defence chemical weapons laboratory at Porton Down reported discovering degradation products of mustard gas and nerve agents in samples taken from these sites. This is the first instance of a chemical weapon attack being proved on the basis of chemical residues left at an impact site.

### Erbil Site

The team undertook exhumations at the graveyard of a camp where survivors of the Anfal were taken. The grave site was surveyed by the archaeological team in order to make determinations of the ratio of adult to child graves in the cemetery. The forensic scientists exhumed three children's graves, one reported to have been made by a survivor from the village of Koreme and containing his infant sister. The exhumation of that grave corroborated his account and contained the skeletal remains of a girl about one year old, with evidence of malnutrition.

# ABBREVIATIONS

CARDRI    Committee against Repression and for Democratic Rights in Iraq
CCC       Commodity Credit Corporation
FBIS      Foreign Broadcast Information Service
FQ45      Firqa 45, the Iraqi army's 45th Division, based in Khalifan
GA        U.N. General Assembly
GDW       Games' Designers Workshop
HAWK      (U.S.-made antiaircraft missile)
ICJ       International Court of Justice, The Hague, the World Court
KDP       Kurdistan Democratic Party
KHRO      Kurdistan Human Rights Organization
KURDS     Kurdistan Reconstruction and Development Society
MIG       (Soviet-built fighter plane)
PBS       Public Broadcasting System
PHR       Physicians for Human Rights
PKK       Turkey's Kurdistan Workers' Party
PUK       Patriotic Union of Kurdistan
RCC       Revolutionary Command Council

# INTRODUCTION

This book is a narrative account of a campaign of extermination against the Kurds of northern Iraq. It is the product of more than a year and a half of research, during which a team of HRW/Middle East researchers analyzed several tons of captured Iraqi government documents and carried out field interviews with more than 350 witnesses, most of them survivors of the 1988 campaign known as Anfal. It concludes that in that year the Iraqi regime committed the crime of genocide.

Anfal, "the spoils," is the name of the eighth *sura* of the Qur'an. It is also the name given by the Iraqis to a series of military actions that lasted from 23 February to 6 September 1988. Although it is impossible to understand the Anfal campaign without reference to the final phase of the 1980–88 Iran-Iraq War, Anfal was not merely a function of that war. Rather, the winding-up of the conflict on Iraq's terms was the immediate historical circumstance that gave Baghdad the opportunity to bring to a climax its longstanding efforts to bring the Kurds to heel. The Iraqi regime's anti-Kurdish drive dated back fifteen years or more, well before the outbreak of hostilities between Iran and Iraq.

Anfal was also the most vivid expression of the special powers granted to Ali Hassan al-Majid, a cousin of President Saddam Hussein and secretary general of the Northern Bureau of Iraq's Ba'ath Arab Socialist Party.[1] From 29 March 1987 to 23 April 1989, al-Majid was granted power that was equivalent in Northern Iraq to that of the president himself, with authority over all agencies of the state. Al-Majid, who is known to this day to Kurds as Ali Anfal or Ali Chemical, was the overlord of the Kurdish genocide. Under his command, the central actors in Anfal were the First and Fifth Corps of the regular Iraqi army, the General Security Directorate (Mudiriyat al-Amn al-Ameh, or Amn) and Military Intelligence (Istikhbarat). The progovernment Kurdish militia known as the National Defense battalions, or *jahsh,* assisted in important auxiliary tasks.[2] The integrated resources of the entire military, security, and civilian apparatus of the Iraqi state were deployed, in al-Majid's words, "to solve the Kurdish problem and slaughter the saboteurs."[3]

The campaigns of 1987–89 were characterized by the following gross violations of human rights:

- Mass summary executions and the mass disappearance of many tens

1

of thousands of noncombatants, including large numbers of women and children, and sometimes the entire population of villages.

- The widespread use of chemical weapons, including mustard gas and the nerve agent GB, or Sarin, against the city of Halabja as well as dozens of Kurdish villages, killing many thousands of people, mainly women and children.
- The wholesale destruction of two thousand villages, which are described in government documents as having been burned, destroyed, demolished, and purified, as well as at least a dozen larger towns and administrative centers (*nahyas* and *qadhas*).
- The wholesale destruction of civilian objects by army engineers, including all schools, mosques, wells, and other nonresidential structures in the targeted villages, and some electricity substations.
- The looting of civilian property and farm animals on a vast scale by army troops and progovernment militia.
- The arbitrary arrest of all villagers captured in designated "prohibited areas" (*manateq al-mahdoureh*), even though these were their own homes and lands.
- The arbitrary jailing and warehousing for months, in conditions of extreme deprivation, of tens of thousands of women, children, and elderly people, without judicial order or any cause other than their presumed sympathies for the Kurdish opposition. Many hundreds of them were allowed to die of malnutrition and disease.
- The forced displacement of hundreds of thousands of villagers upon the demolition of their homes, release from jail, or return from exile. These civilians were trucked into areas of Kurdistan far from their homes and were left there by the army with only minimal governmental compensation, if any, for their destroyed property, and no provision for relief, housing, clothing, or food; they were forbidden to return to their villages of origin on pain of death. Under these conditions, many died within a year of their forced displacement.
- Destruction of the rural Kurdish economy and infrastructure.

Like Nazi Germany, the Iraqi regime concealed its actions in euphemisms. While Nazi officials spoke of "executive measures," and "special actions," as well as "resettlement in the east," Ba'athist bureaucrats spoke of "collective measures," a "return to the national ranks," and "resettlement in the south." Beneath the euphemisms, however, Iraq's crimes against the Kurds amount to genocide, the "intent to destroy, in whole or in part, a national, ethnical, racial or religious group, as such."[4]

The campaigns of 1987–89 are rooted deep in the history of the Iraqi Kurds.

Since the earliest days of Iraqi independence, the country's Kur
number more than 4 million—have fought either for indep
meaningful autonomy, but they have never achieved the resull

In 1970, the Ba'ath Party, anxious to secure its precarious holc
offer the Kurds a considerable measure of self-rule, far greater tha
in neighboring Syria, Iran, or Turkey. The regime, however, de1
distan Autonomous Region in such a way as deliberately to exclude the vast oil
wealth that lies beneath the fringes of the Kurdish lands. The Autonomous
Region, rejected by the Kurds and imposed unilaterally by Baghdad in 1974,
comprised the three northern governorates of Erbil, Suleimaniyeh, and Dohuk.
Covering some 14,000 square miles—roughly the combined area of Massa-
chusetts, Connecticut, and Rhode Island—this area was only half the territory
that the Kurds considered rightfully theirs. Still, the Autonomous Region had
real economic significance since it accounted for fully half the agricultural
output of a largely desert country that is sorely deficient in domestic food
production.

In the wake of the autonomy decree, the Ba'ath Party embarked on the
"Arabization" of the oil-producing areas of Kirkuk and Khanaqin and other
parts of the north, evicting Kurdish farmers and replacing them with poor Arab
tribespeople from the south. Northern Iraq did not remain at peace for long. In
1974, the long-simmering Kurdish revolt flared up once more under the leadership of the legendary fighter Mullah Mustafa Barzani, who was supported in the
effort by the governments of Iran, Israel, and the United States. The revolt
collapsed precipitately in 1975 when Iraq and Iran concluded a border agreement and the Shah withdrew his support from Barzani's Kurdistan Democratic
Party (KDP). After the KDP fled into Iran, tens of thousands of villagers from the
Barzani tribe were forcibly removed from their homes and relocated to barren
sites in the desert south of Iraq. There, without any form of assistance, they had
to rebuild their lives from scratch.

In the mid- and late 1970s, the regime again moved against the Kurds,
forcibly evacuating at least a quarter of a million people from Iraq's borders
with Iran and Turkey, destroying their villages to create a cordon sanitaire along
these sensitive frontiers. Most of the displaced Kurds were relocated into *mujamma'at* (plural), crude new settlements located on the main highways in
army-controlled areas of Iraqi Kurdistan. The word literally means "amalgam-
ations" or "collectives." In their propaganda, the Iraqis commonly referred to
them as modern villages; in this report, they are generally described as resettlement camps. Until 1987, villagers relocated to the camps were generally paid a
nominal cash compensation but were forbidden to move back to their homes.

After 1980 and at the beginning of the eight-year Iran-Iraq War, many Iraqi
garrisons in Kurdistan were abandoned or reduced in size, and their troops were

transferred to the front. In the vacuum that was left, the Kurdish *peshmerga*—"those who face death"—once more began to thrive. The KDP, now led by one of Barzani's sons, Mas'oud, had revived its alliance with Teheran, and in 1983 KDP units aided Iranian troops in their capture of the bordertown of Haj Omran. Retribution was swift: in a lightning operation against the camps that housed the relocated Barzanis, Iraqi troops abducted between 5,000 and 8,000 males aged twelve or over. None of them has ever been seen again, and it is believed that after being held prisoner for several months, they were all killed. In many respects, the 1983 Barzani operation foreshadowed the techniques that would be used on a much larger scale during the Anfal campaign. The absence of any international outcry over this act of mass murder, despite Kurdish efforts to press the matter with the United Nations and Western governments, must have emboldened Baghdad to believe it could get away with an even larger operation without adverse reaction. In these calculations the Ba'ath Party was correct.

Even more worrisome to Baghdad was the growing closeness between the Iranians and the KDP's major Kurdish rival, Jalal Talabani's Patriotic Union of Kurdistan (PUK). The Ba'ath regime had conducted more than a year of negotiations with the PUK between 1983 and 1985, but in the end these talks failed to bear fruit, and full-scale fighting resumed. In late 1986 Talabani's party concluded a formal political and military agreement with Teheran.

By this time the Iraqi regime's authority over the North had dwindled to control of the cities, towns, camps, and main highways. Elsewhere, the peshmerga forces could rely on a deep-rooted base of local support. Seeking refuge from the army, thousands of Kurdish draft-dodgers and deserters found new homes in the countryside. Villagers learned to live with a harsh economic blockade and stringent food rationing, punctuated by artillery shelling, aerial bombardment, and punitive forays by the army and the paramilitary jahsh. In response, the rural Kurds built air-raid shelters in front of their homes and spent much of their time hiding in the caves and ravines that honeycomb the northern Iraqi countryside. For all the grimness of this existence, by 1987 the mountainous interior of Iraqi Kurdistan was effectively liberated territory, something the Ba'ath Party regarded as an intolerable situation.

With the granting of emergency powers to al-Majid in March 1987, the intermittent counterinsurgency against the Kurds became a campaign of destruction. As Raul Hilberg observes in his monumental history of the Holocaust:

A destruction process has an inherent pattern. There is only one way in which a scattered group can effectively be destroyed. Three steps are organic in the operation:

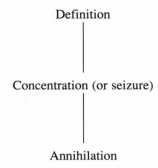

This is the invariant structure of the basic process, for no group can be killed without a concentration or seizure of the victims, and no victims can be segregated before the perpetrator knows who belongs to the group.[5]

The Kurdish genocide of 1987–89, with the Anfal campaign as its center-piece, fits Hilberg's paradigm to perfection.

In the first three months after assuming his post as secretary general of the Ba'ath Party's Northern Bureau, Ali Hassan al-Majid began the process of definition of the group that would be targeted by Anfal and vastly expanded the range of repressive activities against all rural Kurds. He decreed that "sabo-teurs" would lose their property rights, suspended the legal rights of all the residents of prohibited villages, and began ordering the execution of the first-order relatives of saboteurs and wounded civilians whose hostility to the regime had been determined by the intelligence services.

In June 1987, al-Majid issued two successive sets of standing orders that were to govern the conduct of the security forces through the Anfal campaign and beyond. These orders were based on the simple axiom on which the regime now operated: in the prohibited rural areas, all resident Kurds were coterminous with the peshmerga insurgents, and they would be dealt with accordingly.

The first al-Majid directive bans all human existence in the prohibited areas, to be applied through a shoot-to-kill policy. The second, numbered SF/4008 and dated 20 June 1987, modifies and expands these orders. It constitutes a bald incitement to mass murder, spelled out in chilling detail. In clause 4, army commanders are ordered "to carry out random bombardments, using artillery, helicopters and aircraft, at all times of the day or night, in order to kill the largest number of persons present in . . . prohibited zones." In clause 5, al-Majid orders that "all persons captured in those villages shall be detained and interrogated by the security services and those between the ages of 15 and 70 shall be executed after any useful information has been obtained from them, of which we should be duly notified."

Even as this legal and bureaucratic structure was being set in place, the Iraqi regime became the first in history to attack its own civilian population with chemical weapons. On 15 April 1987, Iraqi aircraft dropped poison gas on KDP headquarters at Zewa Shkan, close to the Turkish border in the Dohuk governorate, and on PUK headquarters in the twin villages of Sergalou (upper valley) and Bergalou (lower valley), in the governorate of Suleimaniyeh. The following afternoon they dropped chemicals on the undefended civilian villages of Sheikh Wasan and Balisan, killing well over a hundred people, most of them women and children. Scores of other victims of the attack were abducted from their hospital beds in the city of Erbil, where they had been taken for treatment of burns and blindness. They have never been seen again. These incidents were the first of at least forty documented chemical attacks on Kurdish targets over the succeeding eighteen months. They were also the first sign of the regime's new readiness to kill large numbers of Kurdish women and children indiscriminately.

Within a week of the mid-April chemical weapons attacks, al-Majid's forces were ready to embark upon what he described as a three-stage program of village clearances, or collectivization. The first ran from 21 April to 20 May, the second from 21 May to 20 June. More than seven hundred villages were burned and bulldozed, most of them along the main highways in government-controlled areas. The third phase of the operation, however, was suspended. With Iraqi forces still committed to the war front, the resources required for such a huge operation were not available. The goals of the third stage would eventually be accomplished by the Anfal.

In terms of defining the target group for destruction, no single administrative step was more important to the Iraqi regime than the national census of 17 October 1987. Now that the springtime village clearances had created a virtual buffer strip between the government and the peshmerga-controlled zones, the Ba'ath Party offered the inhabitants of the prohibited areas an ultimatum: they could either "return to the national ranks"—in other words, abandon their homes and livelihoods and accept compulsory relocation in a squalid camp under the eye of the security forces—or they could lose their Iraqi citizenship and be regarded as military deserters. The second option was tantamount to a death sentence since the census legislation made those who refused to be counted subject to an August 1987 decree of the ruling Revolutionary Command Council, imposing the death penalty on deserters.

In the period leading up to the census, al-Majid refined the target group further. He ordered his intelligence officials to prepare detailed dossiers of saboteurs' families who were still living in the government-controlled areas. When these dossiers were complete, countless women, children, and elderly people were forcibly transferred to the rural areas to share the fate of their peshmerga relatives. This case-by-case, family-by-family sifting of the population was to become a characteristic feature of the decisions made during the Anfal period about who should live and who should die.

Last, but not without significance, the census gave those who registered only two alternatives when it came to declaring their nationality. One could either be Arab or Kurdish—a stipulation that was to have the direst consequences for other minority groups, such as the Yezidis, Assyrians, and Chaldean Christians who continued to live in the Kurdish areas.[6]

The Anfal campaign began four months after the census, with a massive military assault on PUK headquarters at Sergalou-Bergalou on the night of 23 February 1988. Anfal would have eight stages in all, seven directed at areas under the control of the PUK. The KDP-controlled areas in the northwest of Iraqi Kurdistan, which the regime regarded as a lesser threat, were the target of the final Anfal operation in late August and early September 1988.

The Iraqi authorities did nothing to hide the campaign from public view. On the contrary, as each phase of the operation triumphed, its successes were trumpeted with the same propaganda fanfare that attended the victorious battles of the Iran-Iraq War. Even today, Anfal is celebrated in the official Iraqi media. The fifth anniversary in 1993 of the fall of Sergalou-Bergalou on 19 March 1988 was the subject of banner headlines.

Iraqi troops tore through rural Kurdistan with the motion of a gigantic windshield wiper, sweeping first clockwise, then counterclockwise, through one after another of the prohibited areas. The first Anfal, centered on the siege of PUK headquarters, took more than three weeks. Subsequent phases of the campaign were generally shorter, with a brief pause between each as army units moved on to the next target. The second Anfal, in the Qara Dagh region, lasted from 22 March to 1 April 1988; the third, covering the hilly plain known as Germian, took from 7 to 20 April; the fourth, in the valley of the Lesser Zab river, was the shortest of all, lasting only from 3 to 8 May.

Only in the fifth Anfal, which began on 15 May in the mountainous region northeast of Erbil, did the troops have any real difficulty in meeting their objectives. Encountering fierce resistance in difficult terrain from the last of the PUK peshmerga, the regime called a temporary halt to the offensive on 7 June. On orders from the office of the president (indicating the personal supervisory role that Saddam Hussein himself played in Anfal), the operation was renewed twice in July and August, with these actions denominated the sixth and seventh Anfals. Eventually, on 26 August, the last PUK-controlled area was declared "cleansed of saboteurs."

By this time Iran had accepted Iraq's terms for a cease-fire to end the war, freeing up large numbers of Iraqi troops to carry the Anfal operation into the Badinan area of northern Iraqi Kurdistan. The final Anfal began at first light on

25 August and was over in a matter of days. On 6 September 1988, the Iraqi regime made its de facto declaration of victory by announcing a general amnesty for all Kurds. (Ali Hassan al-Majid later told aides that he had opposed the amnesty but had gone along with it as a loyal party man.)

Each stage of the Anfal followed roughly the same pattern. It characteristically began with chemical attacks from the air on both civilian and peshmerga targets, accompanied by a military blitz against PUK or KDP military bases and fortified positions. The deadly cocktail of mustard and nerve gases was much more lethal against civilians than against the peshmerga, some of whom had acquired gas masks and other rudimentary defenses. In the village of Sayw Senan (second Anfal), more than 80 civilians died; in Goktapa (fourth Anfal), the death toll was more than 150; in Wara (fifth Anfal) it was 37. In the largest chemical attack of all, the 16 March bombing of the Kurdish city of Halabja, between 3,200 and 5,000 residents died. As a city, Halabja was not technically part of the Anfal—the raid was carried out in reprisal for its capture by peshmerga supported by Iranian Revolutionary Guards—but it was very much part of the Kurdish genocide.

After the initial assault, ground troops and jahsh enveloped the target area from all sides, destroying all human habitation in their path, looting household possessions and farm animals, and setting fire to homes before calling in demolition crews to finish the job. As the destruction proceeded, so did Hilberg's phase of the concentration, or seizure of the target group. Convoys of army trucks stood by to transport the villagers to nearby holding centers and transit camps, while the jahsh combed the hillsides to track down anyone who had escaped. (Some members of the militia, an asset of dubious reliability to the regime, also saved thousands of lives by spiriting people away to safety or helping them across army lines.) Secret police combed the towns, cities, and camps to hunt down Anfal fugitives, and in several cases lured them out of hiding with false offers of amnesty and a "return to the national ranks"—a promise that concealed a more sinister meaning.

To this point, Anfal had many of the characteristics of a counterinsurgency campaign, albeit an unusually savage one. Captured Iraqi documents suggest that during the initial combat phase, counterinsurgency goals were uppermost in the minds of the troops and their commanding officers. To be sure, Iraq, like any other sovereign nation, had legitimate interests in combating insurgency. Yet the fact that the Anfal was by the narrowest definition a counterinsurgency does nothing to diminish the fact that it was also an act of genocide. There is nothing mutually exclusive about counterinsurgency and genocide. Indeed, one may be the instrument used to consummate the other. Article 1 of the Genocide

Convention affirms that "genocide, whether committed in time of peace or in time of war, is a crime under international law." Summarily executing noncombatant or captured members of an ethnical-national group as such is not a legitimate wartime or counterinsurgency measure, regardless of the nature of the conflict.

In addition to this argument of principle, many features of Anfal far transcend the realm of counterinsurgency. These include, first, the simple facts of what happened after the military goals of the operation had been accomplished:

- The mass murder and disappearance of many tens of thousands of noncombatants—fifty thousand by the most conservative estimate and possibly twice that number.
- The use of chemical weapons against noncombatants in dozens of locations, killing thousands and terrifying many more into abandoning their homes.
- The near-total destruction of family and community assets and infrastructure, including the entire agricultural mainstay of the rural Kurdish economy.
- The literal abandonment, in punishing conditions, of thousands of women, children, and elderly people, resulting in the deaths of many hundreds. Those who survived did so largely because of the clandestine help of nearby Kurdish townspeople.

Second, there is the matter of how Anfal was organized as a bureaucratic enterprise. Viewed as a counterinsurgency, each episode of Anfal had a distinct beginning and an end, and its conduct was in the hands of the regular army and the jahsh militia. These agencies were quickly phased out of the picture, however, and captured civilians were transferred to an entirely separate bureaucracy for processing and final disposal. Separate institutions were involved—such as Amn, Istikhbarat, the Popular Army (Jaysh al-Sha'abi, a type of home guard), and the Ba'ath Party itself. The infrastructure of prison camps and death convoys was physically remote from the combat theater, lying well outside the Kurdistan Autonomous Region. Tellingly, the killings were not in any sense concurrent with the counterinsurgency: the detainees were murdered several days or even weeks after the armed forces had secured their goals.

Finally, there is the question of intent, which goes to the heart of the notion of genocide. Documentary materials captured from the Iraqi intelligence agencies demonstrate with great clarity that the mass killings, disappearances, and forced relocations associated with Anfal and the other anti-Kurdish campaigns of 1987–89 were planned in a coherent fashion. Although power over these campaigns was highly centralized, their success depended on the orchestration of the efforts of a large number of agencies and institutions at the local, regional, and national level, from the office of the president of the republic down to the lowliest jahsh unit.

The official at the center of this great bureaucratic web, of course, was Ali Hassan al-Majid, and in him the question of intent is apparent on a second, extremely important level. A number of audiotapes were made of meetings between al-Majid and his aides from 1987 to 1989. These tapes were examined by four independent experts to establish their authenticity and to confirm that the principal speaker was al-Majid. Al-Majid was known to have a distinctive, high-pitched voice and the regional accent of his Tikrit district.—both these features were recognized without hesitation by those Iraqis consulted by HRW/Middle East. As a public figure who frequently appears on radio and television in Iraq,[7] his voice is well known to many Iraqis. One Iraqi consulted on the subject pointed out that the principal speaker on the many hours of recordings in HRW/Middle East's possession spoke with authority and used obscene language. In contrast, he said, "others in those meetings were courteous and respectful with fearful tones, especially when they addressed al-Majid himself." Al-Majid, two experts noted, was often referred to by his familiar nickname, "Abu Hassan."

The tapes contain evidence of a bitter racial animus against the Kurds on the part of the man who, above any other, plotted their destruction. "Why should I let them live there like donkeys who don't know anything?" al-Majid asks at one meeting, "What did we ever get from them?" On another occasion, speaking in the same vein: "I said probably we will find some good ones among [the Kurds] . . . but we didn't, never." And elsewhere, "I will smash their heads. These kind[s] of dogs, we will crush their heads." And again, "Take good care of them? No, I will bury them with bulldozers."

Loyalty to the regime offered no protection from al-Majid's campaigns. Nor did membership in the progovernment jahsh. Al-Majid even boasted of threatening militia leaders with chemical weapons if they refused to evacuate their villages. Ethnicity and physical location were all that mattered, and these factors became coincident when the mass killings took place in 1988.

The 1987 village clearances were wholly directed at government-controlled areas and thus had nothing whatever to do with counterinsurgency. If the former residents of these areas refused to accept government-assigned housing in a mujamma'a and took refuge instead in a peshmerga-controlled area (as many did), they too were liable to be killed during Anfal. The same applied to other, smaller minorities. In the October 1987 census, many Assyrian and Chaldean Christians—an Aramaic-speaking people of ancient origin—refused the government's demands that they designate themselves as either Arabs or Kurds. Those who declined to be Arabs were automatically treated as Kurds. Furthermore, during the final Anfal in Dohuk governorate, where most Christians were concentrated, they were dealt with by the regime even more severely than their Kurdish neighbors had been. Those few Turkomans, a Turkic-speaking minority, who fought with the Kurdish peshmerga were not spared, because they too were deemed to have become Kurds.

Almost continuously over the previous two decades, the Ba'ath-led government had engaged in a campaign of Arabization of Kurdish regions. The armed resistance this inspired was Kurdish in character and composition. In 1988, the rebels and all those considered sympathizers were therefore treated as Kurds who had to be wiped out, once and for all. Whether or not they were combatants was immaterial; as far as the government was concerned they were all "bad Kurds," who had not come over to the side of the government.

To pursue Hilberg's paradigm a little further, once the concentration and seizure operation was complete, the annihilation could begin. The target group had already been defined with care. Now came the definition of the second concentric circle within the group: those who were actually to be killed.

At one level, this was a straightforward matter. Under the terms of al-Majid's June 1987 directives, death was the automatic penalty for any male of an age to bear arms who was found in an Anfal area.[8] At the same time, no one was supposed to go before an Anfal firing squad without first having his or her case individually examined. There is a great deal of documentary evidence to support this view, beginning with a presidential order of 15 October 1987—two days before the census—that "the names of persons who are to be subjected to a general or blanket judgment must not be listed collectively. Rather, refer to them or treat them in your correspondence on an individual basis." The effects of this order are reflected in the lists that the army and Amn compiled of Kurds arrested during the Anfal, which note each person's name, sex, age, place of residence, and place of capture.

The processing of the detainees took place in a network of camps and prisons. The first temporary holding centers were in operation under the control of military intelligence as early as 15 March 1988; by about the end of that month, the mass disappearances had begun in earnest, peaking in mid-April and early May. Most of the detainees went to a place called Topzawa, a Popular Army camp on the outskirts of Kirkuk, the city where al-Majid had his headquarters. Some went to the Popular Army barracks in Tikrit. Women and children were trucked from Topzawa to a separate camp in the town of Dibs; between six thousand and eight thousand elderly detainees were taken to the abandoned prison of Nugra Salman in the southern desert, where hundreds of them died of neglect, starvation, and disease. Badinan prisoners from the final Anfal went through a separate but parallel system, with most being detained in the huge army fort at Dohuk and the women and children being transferred later to a prison camp in Salamiyeh on the Tigris River close to Mosul.

The majority of the women, children, and elderly people were released from the camps after the 6 September amnesty. But none of the Anfal men was released. The presumption of HRW/Middle East, based on the testimony of survivors from the third and bloodiest Anfal, is that they went in large groups before firing squads and were interred secretly outside the Kurdish areas. During the final Anfal in Badinan, in at least two cases groups of men were executed on the spot after capture by military officers who were carrying out instructions from their commanders.

The locations of at least three mass grave sites have been pinpointed through the testimony of survivors. One is near the north bank of the Euphrates River, close to the town of Ramadi and adjacent to a camp housing Iranian Kurds forcibly displaced in the early stages of the Iran-Iraq War. Another is near the archaeological site of al-Hadhar (Hatra), south of Mosul. A third is in the desert outside the town of Samawah. At least two other mass graves are believed to exist on Hamrin Mountain, one between Kirkuk and Tikrit and the other west of Tuz Khurmatu.[9]

Although the camp system is evocative of one dimension of the Nazi genocide, the range of execution methods described by Kurdish survivors is uncannily reminiscent of another—the activities of the *Einsatzkommandos,* or mobile killing units, in the Nazi-occupied lands of Eastern Europe. Each of the standard operating techniques used by the Einsatzkommandos is documented in the Kurdish case. Some groups of prisoners were lined up, shot from the front, and dragged into predug mass graves; others were shoved roughly into trenches and machine-gunned where they stood; others were made to lie down in pairs, sardine-style, next to mounds of fresh corpses, before being killed; still others were tied together, made to stand on the lip of the pit, and shot in the back so that they would fall forward into it—a method that was presumably more efficient from the point of view of the killers. Bulldozers then pushed earth or sand loosely over the heaps of corpses. Some of the grave sites contained dozens of separate pits and obviously contained the bodies of thousands of victims. Circumstantial evidence suggests that the executioners were uniformed members of the Ba'ath Party or perhaps of Iraq's General Security Directorate (Amn).

By the most conservative estimates, fifty thousand rural Kurds died during Anfal. Although males of approximately fourteen to fifty were routinely killed en masse, a number of questions surround the selection criteria that were used to order the murder of younger children and entire families.

Many thousands of women and children perished, but their deaths were subject to extreme regional variations, with most being residents of two distinct "clusters" that were affected by the third and fourth Anfals. The personal whim of local field commanders may explain why some of the women and children were rounded up while others were allowed to slip away. Still, abuses or errors cannot adequately explain the later patterns of disappearance, since the detainees were promptly transferred alive from army custody, segregated from their husbands and fathers in processing centers elsewhere, and then killed in cold blood after a period in detention. The place of surrender, more than the place of residence, seems to have been one consideration in deciding who lived and who died. Amn documents indicate that another factor may have been whether the troops encountered armed resistance in a given area, which indeed was the case in most, but not all, the areas marked by the killing of women and children. A third criterion may have been the perceived political stance of detainees, although it is hard to see how this criterion could have been applied to children.

Whatever the precise reasons, it is clear from captured Iraqi documents that the intelligence agencies scrutinized at least some cases individually and even appealed to the highest authority if they were in doubt about the fate of a particular individual. This suggests that the annihilation process was governed, at least in principle, by rigid bureaucratic norms. Yet all the evidence suggests that the purpose of these norms was not to rule on a particular person's guilt or innocence of specific charges, but merely to establish whether an individual belonged to the target group that was to be "Anfalized," that is, Kurds in areas outside government control. At the same time, survivor testimony repeatedly indicates that the rule book was only adhered to casually in practice. The physical segregation of detainees from Anfal areas by age and sex, as well as the selection of those to be exterminated, was a crude affair, conducted without any meaningful prior process of interrogation or evaluation.

Although Anfal as a military campaign ended with the general amnesty of 6 September 1988, its logic did not. Those who were released from prisons such as Nugra Salman, Dibs, and Salamiyeh, as well as those who returned from exile under the amnesty, were relocated to camps with no compensation and no means of support. Civilians who tried to help them were hunted down by Amn. The mujamma'at that awaited the survivors of the final Anfal in Badinan were places of residence in name alone. The survivors, or *Anfalakan,* were merely dumped on the barren earth of the Erbil plain with no infrastructure other than a perimeter fence and military guard towers. Hundreds perished there from disease, exposure, hunger, or malnutrition, and the aftereffects of exposure to chemical weapons. Several hundreds more—non-Muslim Yezidis, Assyrians, and Chaldeans, including many women and children—were abducted from the camps and disappeared, collateral victims of the Kurdish genocide. Their particular crime was to have remained in the prohibited majority-Kurdish areas after community leaders declined to accept the regime's classification of them as Arabs in the 1987 census.

The regime had no intention of allowing the amnestied Kurds to exercise their full civil rights as Iraqi citizens. They were to be deprived of political rights and employment opportunities until Amn certified their loyalty to the regime. They were to sign written pledges that they would remain in the mujamma'at to which they had been assigned, on pain of death. They were to understand that the prohibited areas remained off limits; these areas were often sown with land mines to discourage resettlement. Directive SF/4008, and in particular clause 5, with its order to kill all adult males, would remain in force and would be carried out to the letter.

Arrests and executions continued, some executions involving even prisoners who were in detention at the time of the amnesty. HRW/Middle East has documented three cases of mass executions in late 1988. In one of them, 180 people were put to death. Documents from one local branch of Amn list another 87 executions in the first eight months of 1989, one of them a man accused of "teaching the Kurdish language in Latin script."

The few hundred Kurdish villages that had come through Anfal unscathed as a result of their progovernment sympathies had no guarantees of lasting survival, and dozens more were burned and bulldozed in late 1988 and 1989. Army engineers destroyed even the large Kurdish city of Qala Dizeh (population seventy thousand) and declared its environs a prohibited area, removing the last significant population center close to the Iranian border.

Killing, torture, and scorched-earth policies continued, in other words, to be a matter of daily routine in Iraqi Kurdistan, as they always had been under the rule of the Ba'ath Arab Socialist Party. Yet the Kurdish problem, in al-Majid's words, had been solved; the saboteurs had been slaughtered. Since 1975, some four thousand Kurdish villages had been destroyed; at least fifty thousand rural Kurds had died in Anfal alone, and very possibly the real figure was twice that number; half of Iraq's productive farmland had been laid waste. All told, the total number of Kurds killed over the decade since the Barzani men were taken from their homes is well into six figures.

By 23 April 1989, the Ba'ath Party felt that it had accomplished its goals, for on that date it revoked the special powers that had been granted to Ali Hassan al-Majid two years earlier. At a ceremony to greet his successor, the supreme commander of Anfal made it clear that "the exceptional situation is over."

To use the language of the Genocide Convention, the regime's aim had been to *destroy the group* (Iraqi Kurds) *in part,* and it had done so. Intent and act had been combined, resulting in the consummated crime of genocide. And with this, Ali Hassan al-Majid was free to move on to other tasks demanding his special talents—first as governor of occupied Kuwait and, then, in 1993, as Iraq's minister of defense.

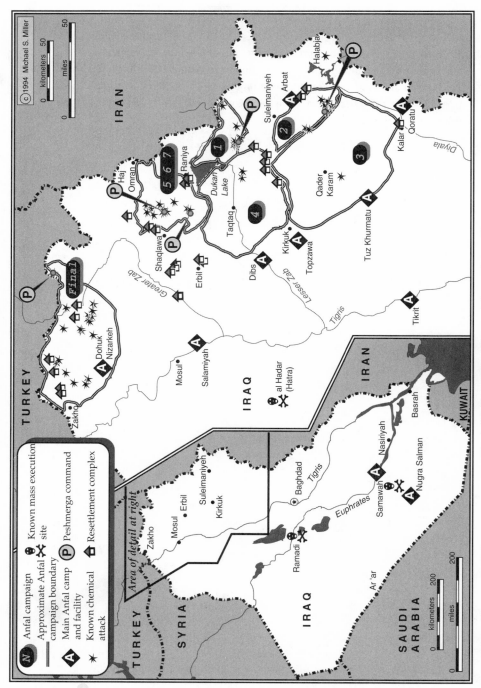

**The Anfal Campaigns: February–September 1988**

Legend:

*N* Anfal campaign

✷ Known mass execution site

—— Approximate Anfal campaign boundary

✗ Peshmerga command

**P** Main Anfal camp and facility

⬟ Resettlement complex

⬥ *A* Known chemical attack

✶

© 1994 Michael S. Miller

# 1

# BA'ATHISTS AND KURDS

Black are his colors, black pavilion,
His spear, his shield, his horse, his armor, plumes,
And jetty feathers menace death and hell—
Without respect of sex, degree or age,
He razeth all his foes with fire and sword.
        —Christopher Marlowe, *Tamburlaine the Great* (part 1, IV, i)

Each era is different. Everything changes. But Saddam Hussein is worse than Tamburlaine six hundred years ago.
                        —Abd-al-Qader Abdullah Askari of Goktapa,
                        site of chemical weapons attack, 3 May 1988

It is a land of spring flowers and waving fields of wheat, of rushing streams and sudden perilous gorges, of hidden caves and barren rock. Above all, Kurdistan is a land where the rhythm of life is defined by the relation between the people and the mountains. One range after another, the peaks stretch in all directions as far as the eye can travel, the highest of them capped year-round by snow. "Level the mountains," so the old saying goes, "and in a day the Kurds would be no more."

The Kurds have inhabited the mountains of Iraq for thousands of years. "The territories designated since the twelfth century as Kurdistan," says one scholar, "have been inhabited since the most distant antiquity and constitute one of the very first settlements of civilization. Jarmo, in the valley of Chamchamal, at present in Iraq, is the most ancient village of the Middle East. Here, four thousand years before our era, humans cultivated diverse grains (such as wheat, barley, lentils, peas), plucked fruits (olives, almonds, pistachios, and figs), and raised sheep and goats."[1]

Despite their ancient heritage, however, the Kurds have not been able to form an independent political entity of their own in modern times. From the sixteenth to the early twentieth century, their territories formed part of the Ottoman and Persian Empires. With the collapse of the Ottoman Empire after World War I, the Kurds were to be granted their independence under the 1920 Treaty of

Sèvres. But that promise evaporated as the nationalist movement of Kemal Atatürk, the father of the modern Turkish state and its first president, seized control of the Kurdish lands in eastern Turkey and the Kurds saw their mountain homeland divided once more, this time among four newly created states—Iraq, the Soviet Union, Syria, and Turkey—and one ancient land, Persia.

Each of these states has balked at assimilating its Kurdish minority, and each Kurdish group has rebelled against the authority of its new central government. In this tradition of rebellion, no state has been more persistent than Iraqi Kurdistan.[2] There are larger Kurdish populations—some 10–15 million Kurds live in Turkey and 7 million in Iran, compared to just 4 million in Iraq.[3] Yet a number of factors set the Iraqi Kurds apart from their neighbors. They were proportionately the largest ethnic minority in the region, at least until the 1980s, accounting for fully 23 percent of the total Iraqi population.[4] The proportion of Kurds in Turkey may now be fractionally higher, but this is not a consequence of normal demographic trends. The relative decline of the Iraqi Kurdish population is a political matter. Hundreds of thousands have fled into exile; tens of thousands more have been killed, most in 1988 in the course of the six-and-a-half-month-long campaign of extermination known as Anfal.

The Iraqi Kurds have also been the victims, rather than the beneficiaries, of an accident of geography, for vast oil reserves were discovered in the twentieth century on the fringes of their ancestral lands. The Kurds have repeatedly challenged the government in Baghdad for control of these areas—especially the ethnically mixed city of Kirkuk. It is this contest for natural resources and power, as much as any consideration of ideology or deep-rooted ethnic animus, that underlies the brutal treatment of the Kurds by the ruling Arab Ba'ath Socialist Party.

Since the 1920s, the Iraqi Kurds have staged one revolt after another against the central authority. Most of these rebellions had their nerve center in a remote area of northeastern Iraq called the Barzan Valley, which lies close to the Iranian and Turkish borders on the banks of the Greater Zab River. From the early 1940s to the mid-1970s, the idea of Kurdish rebellion was inseparable from the name of a charismatic tribal leader from that valley, Mullah Mustafa Barzani.

Barzani's only real success came in 1946, when Iraqi and Iranian Kurds joined forces to found the Mahabad Republic, the first quasi-independent entity the Kurds have ever had. The Mahabad experiment, however, lasted only a year before it was crushed, and Barzani fled to the Soviet Union with several thousand fighters in a celebrated "long march."[5] After the overthrow of the Iraqi monarchy in 1958, the Kurds encountered a familiar pattern under each of the regimes that followed: first a period of negotiation that invariably failed to satisfy Kurdish demands for autonomy, and then, when the talks broke down, renewed outbreaks of violence.[6] Rural villages were bombed and burned, and Kurdish fighters hunted down relentlessly. The name they adopted—peshmerga, "those who face death"—expressed accurately the condition of their existence.

In 1988, during the final six months of Iraq's eight-year war with Iran, something terrible occurred in the mountains of northern Iraq. The regime of Saddam Hussein leveled the mountains, at least metaphorically, in the sense of razing thousands of villages, destroying the traditional rural economy and infrastructure of Iraqi Kurdistan, and killing many tens of thousands of its inhabitants.

The outside world has long known of two isolated episodes of abuse of the Iraqi Kurds in 1988. In both instances, it was the proximity of the victims to international borders, and thus to the foreign media, that accounted for the news leaking out. In the first, the 16 March poison gas attack on the Kurdish city of Halabja, near the border with Iran, the Iranian authorities made it their business to show the site to the international press within a few days of the bombing. Even so, the illusion has long persisted—fostered initially by reports from the U.S. intelligence community strongly tilted toward Baghdad during the 1980–88 Iran-Iraq War—that both sides were responsible for the chemical attack on Halabja.[7] This is false. The testimony of survivors establishes beyond reasonable doubt that attack was an Iraqi action, launched in response to the brief capture of the city by Iraqi peshmerga assisted by Iranian Revolutionary Guards (*pasdaran*). The thousands who died, virtually all civilians, were victims of the Iraqi regime.[8]

The second well-publicized event was the mass exodus of at least sixty-five thousand—and perhaps as many as eighty thousand—Iraqi Kurdish refugees from the northern mountains of the Badinan area into the Turkish borderlands during the final days of August.[9] The reason for their flight was later conclusively demonstrated to have been a further series of chemical weapon attacks by the Iraqi armed forces.[10] Since World War I, the use of poison gas in warfare has been regarded as a special kind of abomination. Chemical weapons were banned by the Geneva Protocol of 1925, to which Iraq is a party, and many countries subsequently destroyed their stockpiles. Although Iraq, and to a lesser extent, Iran, had broken the battlefield taboo on many occasions since 1983, the Halabja and Badinan attacks marked a new level of inhumanity, as the first documented instances of a government employing chemical weapons against its own civilian population.

Yet Halabja and Badinan are merely two pieces of a much larger jigsaw puzzle, and they formed part of a concerted offensive against the Kurds that lasted from March 1987 to May 1989. In the judgment of Human Rights

Watch/Middle East, the Iraqi campaign against the Kurds during that period amounted to genocide, under the terms of the Genocide Convention.[11]

HRW/Middle East has reached this conclusion after more than eighteen months of research consisting of three distinct yet complementary elements. The first was an extensive series of field interviews with Kurdish survivors. Most had been directly affected by the violence; many had lost members of their immediate families. The second dimension was a series of forensic examinations of mass grave sites under the supervision of the distinguished forensic anthropologist Clyde Collins Snow. Snow's preliminary trip, to the Erbil and Suleimaniyeh areas, was in December 1991. On two subsequent visits, Snow's team exhumed graves, in particular a site containing the bodies of twenty-six men and teenage boys executed by the Iraqi army in late August 1988 on the outskirts of the village of Koreme, in the Badinan area.[12] The third and most ambitious research strand has been the study of captured Iraqi intelligence archives that describe aspects of the regime's policy toward the Kurds. For the most part, these were seized from Iraqi government buildings during the aborted Kurdish uprising of March 1991. Then, in May 1992, HRW/Middle East secured permission to examine and analyze 847 boxes of Iraqi government materials that had been captured during the intifada by the PUK. Through an arrangement between the PUK and the U.S. Senate Foreign Relations Committee, the documents became congressional records.[13] Analysis of the documents began on 22 October 1992, and in many cases it has been possible to match documentary evidence about specific villages or campaigns with testimonial material from the same locations.

As Raul Hilberg notes in his history of the Holocaust, "There are not many ways in which a modern society can, in short order, kill a large number of people living in its midst. This is an efficiency problem of the greatest dimensions."[14] The trove of captured documents demonstrates in astonishing breadth and detail how the Iraqi state bureaucracy organized the Kurdish genocide. Some of the documents were seized during the uprising by the citizens of the Kurdish city of Suleimaniyeh and later stuffed haphazardly into stout plastic flour sacks. Others, piled first into tea boxes and then wrapped in sacks stamped "PUK Shaqlawa," were taken from the offices of Iraq's General Security Directorate in Erbil and the northern resort town of Shaqlawa.[15] Often the contents of these boxes were charred in the March 1991 fighting, in which many government buildings were torched. Some are wrinkled, partly shredded, and almost illegible after prolonged exposure to moisture. The documents are crammed into bulging letter files or bound together loosely; hand-written ledgers are covered with flowered wallpaper and kept clean with sheets of transparent plastic. Sometimes their Arabic titles are lettered in ornate psychedelic script with colored felt-tip pens, by bored or whimsical clerks who had security clearance. One police binder is neatly bound in Christmas wrapping paper from Great Britain that shows a red-breasted robin singing cheerfully among sprigs of holly.

The documents show in compelling detail how the Iraqi security bureaucracy tackled the efficiency problem of eliminating thousands of Kurdish villages and murdering tens of thousands of their inhabitants. There are smoking guns here in the form of signed government decrees ordering a summary mass execution. Yet equally telling in their own way are the thousands upon thousands of pages of field intelligence notes, scribbled annotations of telephone conversations, minutes of meetings, arrest warrants, deportation orders, notes on the burning of particular villages, casualty lists from chemical attacks, lists of the family members of "saboteurs," phone surveillance logs, food ration restrictions, interrogation statements, and commendations to victorious military units. All told, these remnants are the innumerable pixels that together make up the picture of the Kurdish genocide.

For those who survived the slaughter, the experience can be summed up in a single Arabic word *al-Anfal*. The word is religious in origin; it is the name of the eighth sura, of the Qur'an. According to the Iraqi writer Kanan Makiya, whose May 1992 article in *Harper's Magazine* was the first written journalistic treatment of the Anfal campaign, the eighth sura is "the seventy-five-verse revelation that came to the Prophet Muhammad in the wake of the first great battle of the new Muslim faith at Badr (A.D. 624). It was in the village of Badr, located in what is now the Saudi province of Hejaz, that a group of Muslims numbering 319 routed nearly 1,000 Meccan unbelievers. The battle was seen by the first Muslims as vindication of their new faith; the victory, the result of a direct intervention by God."[16]

In this sura, al-Anfal means 'spoils,' as in the spoils of battle. It begins, "They will question thee concerning the spoils. Say: 'The spoils belong to God and the Messenger; so fear you God, and set things right between you, and obey you God and his Messenger, if you are believers." The sura continues with the revelation of God's will to the angels: "I am with you; so confirm the believers. I shall cast into the unbelievers' hearts terror; so smite above the necks, and smite every finger of them!" That, because they had made a breach with God and with His Messenger; and whosoever makes a breach with God and with His Messenger, surely God is terrible in His retribution. That for you; therefore taste it; and that the chastisement of the Fire is for the unbelievers."[17]

Although Saddam Hussein has often chosen in recent years to wrap his campaigns in religious language and iconography, Ba'athist Iraq is a militantly secular state. The victims of the 1988 Anfal campaign, the Kurds of northern

Iraq, are for the most part Sunni Muslims. During Anfal, every mosque in the Kurdish villages that were targeted for destruction was flattened by the Iraqi Army Corps of Engineers using bulldozers and dynamite.

## KURDISH AUTONOMY AND ARABIZATION

Yet for all its horror, it would be wrong to say that Anfal was entirely unprecedented, for terrible atrocities had been visited on the Kurds by the Ba'ath Party on many occasions in the past. Ironically, when Iraqi Kurds are asked if they can recall a period of stable peace, they speak first of the early years of the second Ba'ath Party regime, after the coup of July 1968. The radical pan-Arabist ideology on which the party was founded was hostile to the non-Arab Kurds, who are culturally and linguistically related to the Persians. Yet the new Iraqi regime made a priority of achieving a durable settlement with the Kurds.

The Ba'ath was not lacking in pragmatism. The party was weak when it came to office, and it had no desire to contend with a troublesome insurgency. Pan-Arabist rhetoric was therefore played down after 1968, in favor of a new effort to forge a single unified Iraqi identity, one whereby the Kurds would be accepted as partners—if not exactly equal ones. The modern nation-state of Iraq was an artificial creation of the League of Nations in the 1920s when the former southern *vilayet* of the Ottoman Empire were subdivided into mandate territories administered by Britain and France. Iraq's boundaries, incorporating the vilayet of Mosul, reflected British interest in achieving control over that region's oil resources.

It was oil that proved to be the Achilles' heel of the autonomy package that was offered to the Kurds by Saddam Hussein, the Revolutionary Command Council (RCC) member in charge of Kurdish affairs. On paper, the manifesto of 11 March 1970 was promising. It recognized the legitimacy of Kurdish nationalism and guaranteed Kurdish participation in government and the teaching of the Kurdish language in schools,[18] but it reserved judgment on the territorial extent of Kurdistan, pending a new census. Such a census would surely have shown a solid Kurdish majority in the city of Kirkuk and the surrounding oil fields, as well as in the secondary oil-bearing area of Khanaqin, south of the city of Suleimaniyeh. But no census was scheduled until 1977, by which time the autonomy deal was dead.[19]

As before, Kurdish ideals were hostage to larger political forces. In April 1972, the Ba'ath regime signed a fifteen-year friendship treaty with the Soviet Union; two months later it nationalized the Iraq Petroleum Company; and with the October 1973 Arab-Israeli War, Iraq's oil revenues soared tenfold.[20] In June of that year, with Ba'ath-Kurdish relations already souring, the Barzani laid formal claim to the Kirkuk oil fields. Baghdad interpreted this as a declaration of war and in March 1974 unilaterally decreed an autonomy statute.

The new statute was a far cry from the 1970 manifesto, and its definition of the Kurdish autonomous area explicitly excluded the oil-rich areas of Kirkuk, Khanaqin, and Jabal Sinjar. In tandem with the 1970–74 autonomy process, the Iraqi regime carried out a comprehensive administrative reform in which the country's sixteen provinces, or governorates, were renamed and in some cases had their boundaries altered. The old province of Kirkuk was split in two. The area around the city itself was now to be named al-Ta'mim (nationalization), and its boundaries redrawn to give an Arab majority. A new, smaller province, to be known as Salah al-Din, included the city of Tikrit and the nearby village of al-Ouja, Saddam Hussein's birthplace. Clearly, the parallel between Saddam and the legendary medieval warrior known in the West as Saladin was anything but accidental (although, ironically, Saladin was himself a Kurd and like many of his kin had initially hired himself out to Arab armies).[21] Baghdad gave the Kurds two weeks to accept its terms;[22] Barzani responded with a renewal of his dormant armed revolt.

In the belief that they have no lasting friends, Kurdish leaders have long made alliances of convenience with outsiders, and Barzani assumed that foreign support would allow his fight to prosper. Horrified by Iraq's new alignment with the Soviet Union, the Israeli government and the U.S. Central Intelligence Agency trained senior KDP leaders and kept Barzani generously supplied with intelligence and arms, including heavy weaponry. The shah of Iran, meanwhile, provided an indispensable rearguard territory as well as logistical support.

With this help, the peshmerga resisted the Iraqi assault for a year, although more than a hundred thousand refugees fled to Iran and the Kurdish towns of Zakho and Qala Dizeh were heavily damaged by aerial bombing. Barzani grossly overestimated the commitment of outsiders to his cause. In March 1975, the shah and Saddam Hussein signed the Algiers Agreement, which surprised most observers by putting an end—at least for the time being—to the longstanding quarrel between the two countries. Iraq granted Iran shared access to the disputed Shatt al-Arab waterway; as a quid pro quo, the shah abruptly withdrew his military and logistical support from the Iraqi Kurds. Within a week, Barzani's revolt had collapsed. Its leader, a broken man, was soon dead. "Covert action should not be confused with missionary work," was Henry Kissinger's famous remark on the affair.

In the eyes of the Ba'ath Party, Barzani's collaboration with Iran, the United States, and Israel marked the Kurds as Fifth Columnists. "Those who have sold themselves to the foreigner will not escape punishment," said Saddam Hussein, who at this point was deputy chair of Iraq's Revolutionary Command Council, and the official responsible for internal security matters.[23] That attitude colored Ba'ath dealings with the Kurds for the next two decades. Its culmination was the Anfal.

With the collapse of the Barzani Revolution, as the Kurds call it, the Iraqi regime shifted its anti-Kurdish activities into a higher gear. The traditional concerns of counterinsurgency planners now gave way to the more ambitious goal of physically redrawing the map of northern Iraq. This meant removing rebellious Kurds from their ancestral lands and resettling them in new areas under the strict military control of the Baghdad authorities.

In 1975 the Iraqi government embarked on a sweeping campaign to Arabize the areas that had been excluded from Kurdistan under the offer of autonomy— an effort that had first begun in 1963. Hundreds of Kurdish villages were destroyed during the mid-1970s in the northern governorates of Nineveh and Dohuk, and about 150 more in the governorate of Diyala, the southernmost spur of Iraqi Kurdistan, where there were also significant oil deposits.[24] Restrictions were imposed and maintained over the years that followed on the employment and residence of Kurds in the Kirkuk area.[25] Arab tribespeople from southern Iraq were enticed to move to the north with government benefits and offers of housing. Uprooted Kurdish farmers were sent to new homes in rudimentary government-controlled camps along the main highways.

Some were forcibly relocated to the flat and desolate landscapes of southern Iraq, including thousands of refugees from the Barzani tribal areas who returned from Iran in late 1975 under a general amnesty. Once moved, they had no hope of resuming their traditional farming activities: "The houses that the government had allocated for the Kurds in those areas were about one kilometer away from one another," recalled a returning refugee. "They told me I should stay there and become a farmer, but we could not farm there: it was all desert."[26] In November 1975, an Iraqi official acknowledged that some fifty thousand Kurds had been deported to the southern districts of Nasiriyah and Diwaniya, although the true figure was almost certainly higher.[27]

This reference to houses is misleading, for the new quarters were primitive in the extreme. The relocated Kurds were simply driven south in convoys of trucks, dumped in the middle of nowhere, and left to their own resources. "This is to prevent you from going to Mustafa [Barzani] or Iran," one villager remembers being told by a soldier.[28] Many people died of heat and starvation; the remainder survived at first in crude shelters fashioned from branches and thatch, or rugs strung on a framework of poles. In time they managed to build mud houses with the money the men earned as day laborers in the nearest towns.

In 1977–78, under the terms of the Algiers Agreement of 1975, Iraq began to clear a cordon sanitaire along its northern borders. At first, a former Iraqi military officer told HRW/Middle East, this no-man's-land extended 3 miles into Iraq; later, it was extended to 6 miles then to 9 miles, and finally to 18.5 miles. The governorate of Suleimaniyeh, which shares a long mountainous border with Iran, was the worst affected, and estimates of the number of villages destroyed during this first wave of border clearances run as high as five hundred, the great majority of them in Suleimaniyeh.[29] Again, official Iraqi statements convey some minimal sense of the numbers involved: the Ba'ath Party newspaper *Al-Thawra* admitted that 28,000 families (as many as 200,000 people) were deported from the border zone in just two months during the summer of 1978.[30] Deportees say that they were given five days to gather their possessions and leave their homes; when that deadline expired the army demolition crews moved in.

This was no haphazard operation. A new bureaucratic infrastructure was set up in August 1979 to handle the forced mass relocations in the form of the Revolutionary Command Council's Committee for Northern Affairs, headed by Saddam Hussein. (Reportedly, a Special Investigation Committee [Hay'at al-tahqiq al-khaseh] was also set up at this time, charged with identifying opponents of the regime and authorized to order the death penalty without consulting Baghdad.)[31]

Saddam Hussein's committee now began systematically to redraw the map of Iraqi Kurdistan, and the border clearances of the late 1970s marked the large-scale introduction of the mujamma'a, a network of Kurdish resettlement camps, or collectives.[32] The mujamma'at were crudely built collective villages, located near large towns or along the main highways in areas controlled by the Iraqi army. Sometimes the Kurds received nominal compensation for their confiscated lands, amounts that were usually derisory, and they were forbidden to return.

After the start of the war with Iran, which began with the Iraqi invasion of 22 September 1980, Baghdad's campaign against the Kurds faltered. Army garrisons in Iraqi Kurdistan were progressively abandoned or reduced, their troops transferred to the Iranian front. Into the vacuum moved the resurgent peshmerga. Villages in the north began to offer refuge to large numbers of Kurdish draft dodgers and army deserters. Increasing stretches of the countryside effectively became liberated territory.

In these early years of the Iran-Iraq War, it was the KDP—now commanded by Mullah Mustafa Barzani's sons, the half-brothers Mas'oud and Idris—that was the main object of Baghdad's attention.[33] Since 1975, the KDP had been based at Karaj, outside Teheran. The Iraqi regime's hostility grew only when it learned that the Kurdish group was now allying itself as readily with Iran's new clerical rulers as it had with the shah.

The villagers who had been removed from the Barzan Valley in 1975 spent nearly five years in their new quarters in the southern governorate of Diwaniya. In 1980, however, army trucks, East German–supplied IFAS, rolled up outside their desert encampment and told them they were to be relocated again. For most, the new destination was Qushtapa, a new resettlement camp a half hour's drive to the south of Erbil. Some were taken to Baharka, north of Erbil, and others to the mujamma'at of Diyana and Harir, to the northeast. There was no permanent housing in these camps, only tents, but the villagers were relieved to be breathing the air of Kurdistan once more.

However, in the last week of July 1983, the residents of Qushtapa became aware of unusual military movements. Fighter planes screamed overhead, making for the Iranian border. Troop convoys could be seen on the paved highway that bisected the camp, headed in the same direction. From Teheran radio the Barzanis learned that the strategic border garrison town of Haj Omran had fallen in an Iranian assault. What they did not know at first was that the KDP had effectively acted as scouts and guides for the Iranian forces.

Reprisals began in the early hours of 30 July. "We were all asleep when the soldiers surrounded the camp at 3:00 A.M.," said one Barzani woman living in Qushtapa at the time.[34] She went on:

> Then, before dawn, as people were getting dressed and ready to go to work, all the soldiers charged through the camp. They captured the men walking on the street and even took an old man who was mentally deranged and was usually left tied up. They took the preacher who went to the mosque to call for prayers. They were breaking down doors and entering the houses searching for our men. They looked inside the chicken coops, water tanks, refrigerators, everywhere, and took all the men over the age of thirteen. The women cried and clutched the Qur'an and begged the soldiers not to take their men away.

"I tried to hold on to my youngest son, who was small and very sick," added another of the Barzani widows, as the women are now known. "I pleaded with them, 'You took the other three, please let me have this one.' They told me only, 'If you say anything else, we'll shoot you,' and then hit me in the chest with a rifle butt. They took the boy. He was in the fifth grade."

Between five thousand and eight thousand Barzani men from Qushtapa and other camps were loaded into large buses and driven toward the south. They have never been seen again, and to this day the widows show visitors to the Qushtapa camp framed photographs of their husbands, sons, and brothers, begging for information about their fate.[35] For almost a year after the raid the Qushtapa camp was sealed. Electric power was cut off; the women were not allowed to leave, even to shop, and the townspeople of Erbil smuggled in food secretly at night. "Now that your men are gone, why don't you come and stay with us?" taunted Amn agents, recalls a woman who remained behind.

In a speech given in 1993, President Saddam Hussein left little doubt about what had happened to the Barzanis. "They betrayed the country and they betrayed the covenant," he said, "and we meted out a stern punishment to them, and they went to hell."[36] The seizure and presumed mass killing of the Barzani men was the direct precursor of what would be repeated on a much larger scale five years later during the Anfal.

## EXPLOITING KURDISH DIVISIONS

The KDP of the Barzani half-brothers, however, was not the only source of peshmerga resistance to the regime. Divisions within the Kurdish movement had deep roots, roots that were as much historical and tribal as doctrinal. The Barzan Valley's claim to leadership of the movement had long been couched in religious and mystical terms. This uncompromising attitude made the Barzanis bitter enemies with a number of neighboring tribes, such as the Surchi and Zebari.[37] Mullah Mustafa Barzani's charismatic, not to say high-handed, style of leadership had also produced a steady stream of rivals within his party. After the debacle of 1975 these conflicts erupted into the open.

The power of the Barzani half-brothers—or the "offspring of treason," as the Ba'ath regime now took to calling them—was quickly challenged by Jalal Talabani. Formerly a lieutenant of the elder Barzani and a member of the KDP politburo, Talabani had long been critical of the "feudal" style of the tribally based organization and now proposed to supplant it with a secular leftist movement rooted among urban intellectuals. In June 1975, Talabani made the break formal with the creation of the Patriotic Union of Kurdistan, and two years later open warfare broke out between the two rival groups. The bitter schism would plague them until the final two years of the Iran-Iraq War.

Other groups complicated the picture still further. In 1979 another of Mullah Mustafa's former senior aides, Mahmoud Osman, joined forces with a breakaway group of peshmerga from the PUK to form the Kurdistan Socialist Party. In the same year, the Iraqi Communist Party also took up arms against the Baghdad regime and set up headquarters to the north of the city of Suleimaniyeh, in the same valley where the PUK was.[38] A clear geographic division quickly emerged. The KDP remained the dominant force in the mountain areas of Badinan in the far north, while the PUK held sway to the east and south of the Greater Zab River. (Other, smaller groups operated locally on sufferance of the two main peshmerga organizations.) This divide was linguistic as well as cultural: to the north and west of the river, the principal Kurdish dialect is Kurmanji; to the south, it is Sorani.[39]

Hampered in its ability to solve the Kurdish problem by force, the Iraqi regime leavened its repressive policies with a strategy of divide-and-rule. This in turn had two dimensions: first, to play on the acrimonious divisions between the leading Kurdish parties, and second, to recruit as many Kurds as possible into tribally based progovernment paramilitary groups.

Baghdad's best opportunity to drive a wedge between the KDP and the PUK came with what was, on the face of it, a menacing development in the Iran-Iraq War. Talabani had bitterly opposed the Barzanis' decision to facilitate Iran's Haj Omran offensive in July 1983, and in September he grew even more alarmed when further Iranian attacks penetrated the border area around the town of Penjwin—uncomfortably close to the PUK's own strongholds in Suleimaniyeh governorate.[40] Talabani vowed that his troops would fight side by side with the Ba'ath Party to expel the invaders from Iraqi soil. Seizing the opportunity, Saddam Hussein offered the PUK leader a renewed commitment to Kurdish autonomy, hoping to win his seasoned guerrilla army permanently over to Baghdad's side. Almost a decade later, a member of the PUK team that had negotiated with the Iraqi regime recalled clearly the words of Tariq Aziz, a member of the Revolutionary Command Council and later Iraq's foreign minister. "He told us, 'If you help us, we will never forget it. But if you oppose us, we will never forget it. And after the [Iran-Iraq] war is over, we will destroy you and all your villages completely."[41] It was not an empty threat.

The negotiations dragged on inconclusively for more than a year before they finally broke down in January 1985. Although there were a number of reasons for the collapse of the talks, none was more important than Talabani's reported reiteration of Mullah Mustafa Barzani's unacceptable demand that the Kirkuk and Khanaqin regions, with their oil fields, be considered part of Kurdistan.[42] Although Saddam Hussein failed to cement a lasting alliance with Talabani, he could take satisfaction in the fact that the PUK-KDP rift was now deeper and more bitter than ever.

Tribal loyalties in much of Iraqi Kurdistan have loosened somewhat in the modern era. Where they remain strong, however, they have offered fertile soil for successive regimes to recruit militias in the drive to undermine Kurdish solidarity. Known officially under Saddam Hussein as the Command of the National Defense Battalions (Qiyadet Afwaj al-Difa' al-Watani), these paramilitary bands have long been derided by other Kurds as jahsh.[43]

The jahsh have existed in some form since at least the early 1960s, but their role has been expanded several times since. In principle, each tribal group was supposed to produce a contingent of jahsh as a demonstration of loyalty to the regime; each unit's commander enjoyed the title of mustashar. If tribal leaders did not agree to cooperate in forming jahsh units, then Amn threats would often be persuasive.[44]

The ordinary jahsh came under the operational command of military intelligence (Istikhbarat) in the final stages of the Iran-Iraq War and during the Anfal campaign. But there were also two elite forces of progovernment Kurds. The *Quwat al-Taware'* (emergency forces) carried out intelligence and counterterrorism activities in the cities under the control of the Ba'ath Party. The *Mafarez Khaseh,* meanwhile, or special units of Kurdish agents, were formed by hardcore collaborators and were an official part of either Amn or the Istikhbarat. All these groups were heavily indoctrinated by the regime against other Kurds. In an introductory seminar, a former jahsh commander recalled that military intelligence officers told the assembled mustashars that the peshmerga were neither Kurds nor Iraqis; under Islamic law, they were "infidels and shall be treated as such."[45]

The duties of the rank-and-file jahsh were broadly akin to those of similar militias in other parts of the world.[46] Poorly equipped with light weapons, they maintained roadblocks, patrolled the countryside, did advance scouting work for the regular army, searched villages for army deserters and draft dodgers, and handed over suspected peshmerga to the authorities. For obvious reasons the regime never fully trusted the jahsh's loyalties. Even though jahsh members were largely recruited from resettlement camps, towns, and villages under government control (Zakho, for instance, is said to have had as many as five thousand jahsh), their units were frequently rotated to prevent local sympathies from developing. Mustashars knew that the regime was wary of any illicit contacts they might have with nearby peshmerga commanders, and the Amn files that HRW/Middle East has examined contain extensive surveillance dossiers on jahsh leaders.

The early years of the war against Iran made it apparent that Kurdish conscripts made reluctant soldiers, and on a number of occasions groups of Kurds were released from military service and inducted into the jahsh instead. If an adult male Kurd had connections with his local mustashar, he would pull every possible string to evade military service and serve in the jahsh instead.

Many of the mustashars found their new role appealing. Some were nobodies, elevated by the government to positions of real power. Others were traditional tribal leaders who discovered that the rich opportunities for graft as a mustashar more than made up for their declining influence among the local Kurds. In addition to his fixed salary, the mustashar was entitled to a small monthly cash payment for each man nominally under his command. Yet it was a common practice for many of these men—even most, in some cases—to avoid active duty. On paper, at the peak of their numbers, the regime had 250,000 Kurdish foot soldiers at its disposal; in practice, only a small portion of that number actually bore arms. In exchange for a signed jahsh identity card that would protect them from military service, these Kurdish men were content for the mustashar to pocket their salaries as well as his own. At 85 dinars ($255) a month for each "paper" soldier, it was easy for a canny mustashar to amass a fortune. The brothers Omar and Hussein Surchi, for example, parlayed their earnings into a contracting and construction business that made them the richest men in Kurdistan.

Although the government was prepared to tolerate practices like this for the sake of a mustashar's fealty, it acted ruthlessly toward any show of independence. Several witnesses told HRW/Middle East the story of a mustashar named Ja'far Mustafa, who was executed in 1986 for insubordination. Reportedly, the man was a fervent partisan of the Ba'ath regime but would agree to head up a jahsh contingent only on condition that he be allowed to remain in his home area in the northern mountains of Badinan. In 1986 the order came for Ja'far Mustafa's transfer, and he refused to move. During the standoff his defiance of Saddam Hussein was the talk of Iraqi Kurdistan. After a week he was executed in Baghdad, and his body was then returned from the capital to his home, near the northern town of Mangesh, where it was publicly hanged for the second time. The two villages that he owned—Besifki and Dergijneek—were burned to the ground some time later.[47]

## 1985–1987: OPEN WAR

After the collapse of the Ba'ath-PUK talks in January 1985, the Iraqi regime found its control of Kurdistan eroding once more. The war with Iran, calculated to bring a swift victory, was dragging on interminably with heavy casualties on both sides. Although the government had built a chain of small forts and larger fortresses throughout the Kurdish countryside, it was simply not feasible to keep large numbers of troops pinned down there. Several dozen Kurdish settlements, mainly in PUK-controlled areas near the Iranian border, were burned in piecemeal fashion in the mid-1980s, and their inhabitants resettled in mujamma'at. The people of hundreds of other ancient villages—perhaps as many as two thousand—tried to integrate the counterinsurgency war into the rhythms of their daily lives. In the process, their communities were transformed.

The biggest threat to civilian morale came from shelling. The Iraqi army had divided up Kurdistan in a grid pattern and placed heavy artillery at regular intervals with a range of up to twenty-five miles. The guns pounded around the clock, and it was impossible to predict which targets would be hit on any given day. Routine farm work became a potentially lethal game of chance, sleep patterns were disrupted, and the constant uncertainty shredded everyone's nerves.

Helicopters regularly dropped troops and jahsh into the villages to search for draft dodgers, deserters, and suspected peshmerga. A steady stream of captured Kurds was taken away and executed. Others died in the frequent attacks by Soviet-supplied government MIGs and Sukhoi fighter-bombers.

Since the time of the first Ba'ath regime in 1963, Kurdish villagers learned to protect themselves against aerial attack by building primitive shelters outside their homes. Now the pace of shelter construction accelerated, their design becoming more elaborate. Many were virtual underground rooms, high enough to stand up in, covered with wooden planks or corrugated iron sheeting and layers of dirt, stones, and branches. The more sophisticated shelters had twisting entrance tunnels to protect the occupants against shrapnel and blast. Many whole villages moved into nearby caves and rock overhangs and came to lead a virtual nocturnal existence, emerging to tend their animals and fields only when darkness fell.

Hamlets of three or four houses and small towns of three thousand or four thousand people practiced an enforced self-sufficiency. Many villages elected their own five-person councils (in Arabic, *majlis al-sha'ab,* or *anjuman* in Kurdish). As the government withdrew its rudimentary public services from rural areas, peshmerga teachers arrived to staff the abandoned schools, and itinerant peshmerga paramedics tried to make up for the clinics that had been closed. In most cases, the villages had never had electricity or piped water, and in this sense the regime's ability to inflict additional hardship was limited. As before, the Kurds drew their water from rivers, springs, and underground streams,[48] and the more prosperous had electric power from private generators. Commerce depended on smuggling. Knowing every goat path in the surrounding hills, the villagers learned to evade government roadblocks against the transport of foodstuffs to peshmerga-controlled areas. Only women were allowed past these checkpoints. Sometimes younger boys could slip through with the help of a bribe, but it was a risky business, and some were arrested and disappeared on suspicion of aiding the peshmerga.

By now the practical distinction between peshmerga and ordinary civilians had blurred. In principle at least, active peshmerga received a salary from the organization to which they belonged and served duty rotas of fifteen to twenty days at a time, with equal spells at home to work their lands. Many of the military-age men (and even some of the women), however, were also armed and organized in each village into a so-called civil defense force (*hezi bergri milli* or *hezi peshgiri*), whose main task was to defend the village and hold off the army until peshmerga reinforcements could arrive. Light arms could be bought without much difficulty from the jahsh, and it was common for households to have more than one weapon.

The peshmerga, meanwhile, tried to keep the regime off balance with their mixture of fixed and mobile forces. Hundreds of the smallest guerrilla units, or *mafrazeh*, roamed the countryside. In mountainous areas, a mafrazeh could be as small as five men; in the villages, fifteen was the minimum number needed for successful defense. Above the mafrazeh was the *kart*, and above the kart the *teep*, which the Kurds thought of as the equivalent of an army division.[49]

By the beginning of 1987, the only parts of Iraqi Kurdistan over which Baghdad exercised effective control were the cities, larger towns, camps, and paved highways. Authority over the rural areas was roughly divided between the KDP in the north and the PUK in the south. Although the regime had long vilified the KDP as treasonous, it now saw ominous signs that the PUK, too, was acting as the military and political surrogate of a foreign power with which Iraq was at war. Talabani's group would henceforth be known officially as *'Umala' Iran*—"agents of Iran"—a term reportedly coined by Saddam Hussein himself.[50]

Insulting though it may have been, the phrase was grounded in fact, for since the latter part of 1986 Iranian-PUK collaboration was a reality. Although the KDP had long enjoyed access to Iranian sanctuaries, the PUK now felt that it had no alternative but to do likewise. In landlocked Kurdistan, the struggle could never succeed without help from a friendly neighbor. "There was no way for food and supplies to reach us, no help for our wounded, no roads out of the territory that we had liberated," claimed Nawshirwan Mustafa Amin, who was deputy commander of the PUK at the time. "Iran was our window to the world."

In October 1986, the PUK and the Iranian government concluded a sweeping accord on economic, political, and military cooperation. Both parties agreed that they would press the fight against the Iraqi regime until Saddam Hussein was toppled, and both promised to make no unilateral deals with Baghdad.[51] If either party faced a serious military threat, the other would open a second front to relieve the pressure; Iran agreed to provide the PUK with arms, financial support, and medical aid, while forswearing the right to impose an Islamic regime in Baghdad.[52] The results of the accord were apparent almost at once, on 10 October, when a group of Iranian Revolutionary Guards accompanied by Kurdish peshmerga, struck the Kirkuk oil fields, deep inside Iraqi territory. At the same time, to Baghdad's evident fury, the Iranians brokered a unity agreement between the PUK and the KDP, putting an end to their long-standing rivalry.

The Teheran accords brought a radical shift in the attitude of the Iraqi regime. Despite having the upper hand in the war against Iran, the security situation within its own borders had slipped badly. Since the resumption of the war with the PUK in 1985, Kurdish affairs had been overseen by Muhammad Hamza al-Zubeidi, head of the northern bureau of the Ba'ath Party organization. After a full-scale security review of the region, al-Zubeidi was reportedly ordered to bring the situation under control within six months; when that period elapsed, there was a six-month extension. Still, the situation continued to deteriorate, and in early 1987, Baghdad decided on harsher measures. From then on, all those still living and farming in the Kurdish mountains would be considered active enemies of the state by virtue of nothing more than their ethnicity and their physical presence in their ancestral homeland.

# 2

## THE PRELUDE TO ANFAL

I will confute those vile geographers
That make a triple region in the world,
Excluding regions which I mean to trace,
And with this pen reduce them to a map,
Calling the provinces, cities, and towns
After my name.
                   —Marlowe, *Tamburlaine the Great* (part 1, IV, iv)

All of the tendencies that had been implicit in earlier phases of Iraq's war on the Kurds reached their culmination in 1987–88 with the endgame of the Iran-Iraq War and the Anfal. In the captured Iraqi documents being studied by HRW/Middle East, the term crops up with great frequency: villages are "purified" in the course of "the heroic Anfal operation"; the reason for the flight of villagers into neighboring countries is given as the Anfal; an Anfal oil field is inaugurated and a special Anfal section of the Ba'ath Arab Socialist Party created in commemoration of the event; one of the government contractors hired to work on the drainage of Iraq's southern marshes is called the Anfal Company.[1] It is evident from the documents, and from the supporting testimony of those who survived Anfal, that the resources of the Iraqi state were deployed and coordinated on a massive level to ensure the success of the operation.

The Anfal campaign involved a concerted series of eight military offensives conducted in six distinct geographic areas between late February and early September 1988. Overall command of the operation was in the hands of the Northern Bureau of the Ba'ath Party organization, based in the city of Kirkuk and headed, after March 1987, by the "Struggling Comrade" Ali Hassan al-Majid.[2]

Al-Majid's appointment was highly significant for a number of reasons. Until 1987, military policy against the peshmerga had been set by the First and Fifth Corps of the Iraqi army, based in Kirkuk and Erbil, respectively. Now, however, the Ba'ath Party itself assumed direct charge of all aspects of policy toward the Kurds. Al-Majid's command also made the settlement of the Kurdish problem the concern of Iraq's innermost circle of power—the close network of family ties centered on the city of Tikrit and the personal patronage of President Saddam Hussein.

Saddam's father, whom he never knew, was a member of Tikrit's al-Majid family, and Ali Hassan al-Majid was the Iraqi president's cousin.[3] Al-Majid, who was born in 1941, had humble origins and first made his reputation in 1968 (as a mere sergeant) as the bodyguard of Hammad Shihab al-Tikriti, commander of the Baghdad army garrison and one of the ringleaders of the Ba'ath coup in July of that year. Al-Majid rose quickly in the Tikrit circle and in 1979 played an important role in the purge of the party leadership. During the 1983–85 negotiations between the regime and the PUK, Saddam Hussein appointed his cousin to head Amn.

Even by the standards of the Ba'ath security apparatus, al-Majid had a particular reputation for brutality. According to the (admittedly subjective) account of a former mustashar who had frequent dealings with him, "He is more of a risk taker than Saddam Hussein, and he has no respect for people. It was very difficult to work with him. He was stupid and only carrying out Saddam Hussein's orders. In the past, he used to be a police sergeant; today he is minister of defense. Saddam Hussein, by contrast, is 'a snake with deadly poison.' He pretends to be weak, but at any chance he will use his poison. . . . In tough cases, in which he needs people without a heart, he calls upon Ali Hassan al-Majid."[4]

The main military thrust of Anfal was carried by regular troops of the First and Fifth Corps, backed by units from other corps as they became available from the Iranian front.[5] The elite Republican Guards took part in the first phase of Anfal; other units that saw action included the special forces (Quwat al-Khaseh), commando forces (Maghawir), and the emergency forces—the Ba'ath Party-controlled urban counterterrorism squads. Finally, a wide range of support activities—such as preceding regular army units into populated areas, burning and looting villages, tracking down fleeing villagers, and organizing their surrender—were handled by the Kurdish paramilitary jahsh.

Yet the logic of Ali Hassan al-Majid's campaign against the Kurds went far beyond the six-month military campaign. From a human rights perspective, the machinery of genocide was set in motion by al-Majid's appointment in March 1987, and its wheels continued to turn until April 1989. Within weeks of al-Majid's arrival in Kirkuk, it was apparent that the Iraqi government had decided to settle its Kurdish problem once and for all and that the resources of the state would be coordinated to achieve that goal. A sustained pattern of decrees, directives, and actions by the security forces leaves no doubt that the intent of the Iraqi government was to destroy definitively the armed organizations of the Kurdish resistance and to eradicate all remaining human settlements in areas that were disputed or under peshmerga control—with the exception of those inhabited by the minority of tribes whose loyalty to Baghdad was indisputable. If anything stood in the way of those goals in 1987, it was logistical shortcomings—above all, the fact that a large portion of the troops and matériel required for Anfal was still tied up on the Iranian war front.

It was Iraq that launched the war in 1980 and Iraq that maintained the initiative for much of the eight years that the conflict lasted.[6] Nonetheless, the Iranians did succeed in putting Iraq on the defensive on a number of occasions. In July 1983, Iranian troops seized the important border garrison town of Haj Omran, east of the town of Rawanduz. The high point of the war from Iran's point of view, however, was its Val Fajr 8 offensive in February 1986, which included a surprise attack that seized the marshy Fao peninsula, thereby blocking Iraq's access to the Persian Gulf.

Fresh from its success in Fao, which inflicted huge losses on the Iraqi army (and reinforced the U.S. tilt toward Baghdad), Iran reopened its second front in the north, in the rugged mountains of Iraqi Kurdistan. For more than six years, the Iraqi regime had ceded de facto control over much of the rural north to the peshmerga; now foreign troops threatened to occupy more and more border territory, diverting much-needed forces from the southern front around Basra. As the October 1986 raid by Iranian pasdaran suggested to nervous Iraqi officials, the vital Kirkuk oil fields, almost a hundred miles from the border, were no longer immune.

There is debate between scholars as to the precise threat that Iraq faced from Iran at this late stage of the war. Certainly, Iran's huge Karbala 5 offensive against Basra's Fish Lake in January 1987 marked its final use of the human-wave tactic of hurling tens of thousands of troops—most of them poorly trained basij[7]—against fixed enemy targets. The resulting casualty levels were simply not sustainable, as Teheran acknowledged. On 12 February, Iranian troops returned to the Haj Omran area with a small offensive code named Fatah 4; some believe it was less a real attack than a diversionary action for propaganda purposes.[8] Three weeks later, on 4 March, a new and more alarming Iranian assault, this one code named Karbala 7, managed to penetrate eight miles into Iraqi territory east of Rawanduz with a joint military force, which this time included peshmerga of the KDP and the PUK. The Iraqi regime was infuriated by these renewed signs of collusion, particularly since they now involved both rival Kurdish parties.[9] On 13 March, in a rare interview with a foreign reporter, Iraqi cabinet minister Hashim Hassan al-'Aqrawi commented, "The Iranians are trying to use these people to carry out dirty missions, and since they know the geography of the area and its ins and outs, the Iranians use them merely as guides for the Khomeini Guards and the Iranian forces." The Kurds—or at least Talabani's PUK—even began to talk openly of dismembering the Iraqi state.[10]

On 14 or 15 March, Saddam Hussein presided over a five-hour meeting of the armed forces General Command. Ali Hassan al-Majid was also reportedly in attendance. Any outsider's account of what took place in such a secretive meeting must be highly speculative, but according to at least two accounts, the Iraqi president told his senior officers that he feared a "defeat by attrition."[11] On 18 March, the Revolutionary Command Council and the Ba'ath Party's regional command jointly decided to appoint al-Majid as secretary general of the Northern Bureau of the Ba'ath Party organization. His predecessors, Sa'adi Mahdi Saleh and Muhammad Hamza al-Zubeidi, had allowed the Kurdish problem to fester for too long; al-Majid would not repeat their mistakes.

In essence, the disagreements between scholars of the Iran-Iraq War are academic, at least as far as the Kurds are concerned. Saddam Hussein may indeed have foreseen a slow defeat as a result of Baghdad's existing policies. Or he may have seen Iran's stalled Fish Lake offensive in January as a turning point in Iraq's favor and as an opportunity to press home his advantage. Either way, it is apparent that he decided that exceptional measures were necessary to settle the Kurdish problem, that troublesome sideshow of the Iran-Iraq conflict, once and for all.

Ali Hassan al-Majid's extraordinary new powers, equivalent in the Autonomous Region to those of the president himself, came into effect with decree 160 of the Revolutionary Command Council, dated 29 March 1987. Al-Majid was to "represent the regional command of the party and the Revolutionary Command Council in the execution of their policies for the whole of the northern region, including the Kurdistan Autonomous Region, for the purpose of protecting security and order, safeguarding stability, and applying autonomous rule in the region." The decree went on to explain that "comrade al-Majid's decisions shall be mandatory for all state agencies, be they military, civilian, or security." His fiat would apply "particularly in relation to matters of the National Security Council (*Majlis al-Amn al-Qawmi*) and the Northern Affairs Committee." A second order by Saddam Hussein, issued on 20 April 1987, gave al-Majid the additional authority to set the budget of the Northern Affairs Committee.

Al-Majid's decisions and directives were to be obeyed without question by all intelligence agencies—including military intelligence (Istikhbarat)—and by all domestic security forces, by the Popular Army command (Qiyadat al-Jaysh al-Sha'abi), and by all military commands in the northern region. Decree 160 and its riders left no room for doubt: simply put, Ali Hassan al-Majid was to be the supreme commander, the overlord, of all aspects of Anfal.

Almost a year would pass before that campaign began. Yet within weeks of al-Majid's appointment, the logic of Anfal was fully apparent. Its legal framework was set in place, new standing orders were issued to the security forces, and a two-month wave of military attacks, village destruction, and forced relocations was unleashed—a rough draft, as it were, of the larger campaign ahead. "I gave myself two years to end the activity of the saboteurs," al-Majid later told his aides.[12] With the first warm days of spring and the melting of the snow in the mountains, al-Majid embarked on his brutal three-stage process of "village collectivization"—in other words, the wholesale destruction of hundreds of Kurdish farming villages and the relocation of their residents into mujamma'at.

Even his top military commanders were shocked by the brutality of what he had in mind. He later confided to aides:

When we made the decision to destroy and collectivize the villages and draw a dividing line between us and the saboteurs, the first one to express his doubts to me and before the President was [former Fifth Corps commander] Tali'a al-Durri. The first one who alarmed me was Tali'a al-Durri. To this day the impact of Tali'a is evident. He didn't destroy all the villages that I asked him to at that time. And this is the longest-standing member of the Ba'ath Party. What about the other people then? How were we to convince them to solve the Kurdish problem and slaughter the saboteurs?[13]

The timetable for the three phases of al-Majid's campaign is clearly spelled out in official documents, notably in a letter from the general staff of the jahsh to the command of the Fifth Army Corps dated 13 April 1987. This letters appears to have been in response to a verbal order from the Fifth Corps commander concerning "final obligations in winding up [illegible] procedures for the termination of sabotage in the northern region, [and] the manner and the priorities of implementing the evacuation and demolition of security-prohibited villages." The first phase of the operation would begin on 21 April and end on 20 May; the second would start immediately on 21 May and continue until 20 June.[14] Military and security maps were redlined with clear boundaries to denote areas "prohibited for security reasons." Amn set up a special "prohibited villages committee" to oversee the forbidden areas. Within the zones designated for phases 1 and 2, the order was clear and explicit: "All prohibited villages will be destroyed."[15]

A former Istikhbarat officer who later crossed over to the PUK told HRW/Middle East of a meeting in Kirkuk that spring, attended by the governors of Erbil, Kirkuk, Dohuk, and Suleimaniyeh, the commanders of the First and Fifth Army Corps, divisional military commanders, and senior Ba'ath Party officials. Al-

Majid, speaking in characteristically irascible tones, gave orders that "no house was to be left standing" in the Kurdish villages on the Erbil plain. Only Arab villages would be spared.[16] At a later meeting in Erbil, the witness heard al-Majid repeat these orders and back them up with a personal threat: "I will come and observe," he said, "and if I find any house intact, I will hold the section commander responsible." After receiving those orders, the former Istikhbarat officer said, "I got two IFAS [East German-built military trucks] full of explosives from a warehouse in Erbil. I commandeered two hundred bulldozers from civilians of Erbil—by force, with no payment. We started destroying mud villages with bulldozers and dynamiting the cement structures. We used military engineers for this." The troops went in at dawn; wells were filled in and electricity supplies torn out, leaving only the poles standing. After the engineering work was completed, Istikhbarat would inspect the affected villages by helicopter. If any structure was found to be still standing, the section commander would be ordered to return and finish the job and would risk disciplinary action. It was an extraordinarily thorough enterprise, and the evidence is visible all over Iraqi Kurdistan, with many villages not so much demolished as pulverized.

No farming of any sort was to continue in the destroyed areas. Government aircraft would conduct regular overflights to detect unauthorized farming, and local security committees would be held responsible for any violations. Stringent restrictions were imposed on all grain sales in the Kurdish areas, as well as on agricultural trade across governorate boundaries.

Al-Majid also reportedly issued specific rules of engagement at the Erbil meeting. The army was to open fire only in cases of active resistance. If resistance was encountered, the entire village population was to be killed in reprisal. There was no resistance, since the villages selected for the 1987 clearances were on or near the main roads and under government control. Only during phase 3 of the campaign would the troops venture into peshmerga-held territory.

## THE CHEMICAL THRESHOLD

Even before the first stage of the village clearances was under way, the Iraqi regime crossed a new barrier in its war against the Kurds. Throughout the early weeks of al-Majid's rule, the peshmerga—and in particular the PUK—kept up a steady rhythm of military action. In early April the PUK launched its most ambitious drive to date in the Jafati Valley, which runs southeast from Dukan Lake. The valley was home to the PUK's national headquarters, and thousands of peshmerga congregated there for the assault. In a matter of hours they had overrun dozens of small military posts and taken hundreds of prisoners.

The government's response was not long in coming. "Our leadership received information that the Iraqis were going to use chemical weapons," said a PUK peshmerga who fought in this campaign:

> They issued instructions on what to do in case of a chemical attack. We were instructed to put wet cloths on our faces, to light fires, or to go to places located above the point of impact. In the beginning, the government used chemical artillery shells. This was in the Jafati and Shahrbazar valleys [on April 15], one or two nights after our victory. We didn't realize they were chemicals. The sound was not as loud as the ordinary shelling, and we smelled rotten apples and garlic. . . . Innumerable shells fell on us, but they had little effect.[17]

This was not the case the following day, however, in the villages of Balisan and Sheikh Wasan. These two settlements lie scarcely a mile and a half apart, in a steep-sided valley south of the town of Rawanduz. The Balisan Valley was home to the PUK's third *malband,* or regional command.[18] Yet few peshmerga were present on the afternoon of 16 April, since most had been taking part in the military action in the Jafati Valley, on the far side of Dukan Lake. Instead, their families would be made to suffer the repercussions.

Balisan itself was a sizable village, which until April 1987 had about 250 households (about 1,750 people)[19] of the Khoshnaw tribe, as well as four mosques, a primary school, and an intermediate school. As the crow flies, it lay twelve miles east of the town of Shaqlawa; Sheikh Wasan, a smaller settlement of about 150 houses, lay nestled in the hills a little way to the northeast. The valley was for a long time peshmerga country; the Barzani movement had controlled it from 1961–74, and the PUK, through its third malband, since the outbreak of the war with Iran in 1980. Since about 1983 the Balisan Valley had been a "prohibited area" (*manateq al-mahdoura*), with government checkpoints attempting with only partial success to prevent the entry of foodstuffs and supplies. Food rations had been suspended, and government teachers withdrawn from the schools. Iraqi aircraft made frequent harassment attacks, to which the villagers responded by hiding away in deep, dark caves in the surrounding mountains. Still, ground troops had never managed to penetrate the valley.

In the drizzly late afternoon of 16 April, the villagers had returned home from the fields and were preparing dinner when they heard the drone of approaching aircraft. Some stayed put in their houses; others made it as far as their air-raid shelters before the planes, a dozen of them, came in sight, wheeling low over the two villages to unload their bombs. There were muffled explosions.

Until this moment no government had ever used chemical weapons against its own civilian population. The plummeting enlistment rate among Iranian volunteers over the previous year, when poison gas was widely used on the battlefield, was vivid testimony to the Iraqi government of the power of this forbidden weapon to instill terror. More gruesome yet was the decision to record the event on videotape.

The Iraqi regime had long conducted its record-keeping in meticulous fashion. (Those in neighboring countries say, only half-jokingly, that the Iraqis are the "Prussians of the Middle East.")[20] From the grandest decree to the most trivial matter, all the business of the security forces was recorded in letters and telegrams, dated, numbered, and rubber-stamped on receipt. Even when an original command carried a high-security classification, abundant numbers of handwritten or typed copies were later prepared, to be handed down the chain of command and filed, the writers apparently confident that prying eyes would never see these secrets. In the mid-1980s, the Iraqi security services developed a fascination for video technology as a valuable new form of record-keeping. The actions of the security forces were now to be routinely documented on tape: village clearances, executions of captured peshmerga, even chemical weapons attacks on civilians.

The official videotape of the Balisan Valley bombing, reportedly made by a member of the jahsh, shows towering columns and broad, drifting clouds of white, gray, and pinkish smoke. A cool evening breeze was blowing off the mountains, and it brought strange smells—pleasant ones at first, suggestive of roses and flowers, or, to others, apples and garlic. Other witnesses still say there was the less attractive odor of insecticide. But then, said one elderly woman from Balisan, "It was all dark, covered with darkness, we could not see anything, and were not able to see each other. It was like fog. And then everyone became blind." Some vomited. Faces turned black; people experienced painful swellings under the arms, and women under their breasts. Later, a yellow watery discharge would ooze from the eyes and nose. Many of those who survived suffered severe vision disturbances or total blindness, for up to a month. In Sheikh Wasan, survivors watched as a woman staggered around blindly, clutching her dead child and not realizing it was dead. Some villagers ran into the mountains and died there. Others, who had been closer to the place of impact of the bombs, died where they stood.[21] One witness, a peshmerga, told HRW/Middle East that a second attack followed an hour later, this one conducted by a fleet of helicopters.[22]

The few fighters who had been at home when the raid occurred were taken by the PUK for treatment in Iran, fearing that they would not survive a visit to an Iraqi hospital. (The presence of peshmerga in the village is, one should add, irrelevant from a legal point of view. By their very nature, chemical weapons make no distinction between civilian and military targets, and their use is outlawed under any circumstances.)[23]

The following morning, ground troops and jahsh entered Balisan, looted the villagers' deserted homes, and razed them to the ground. The same day, or perhaps a day later—having presumably left sufficient time for the gas to dissipate—army engineers dynamited and bulldozed Sheikh Wasan. The surviving inhabitants had already fled during the night of the attack. Some made their way to the city of Suleimaniyeh, and a few to Shaqlawa. But most headed southeast, to the city of Raniya, where there was a hospital. They were helped on their way by people from neighboring villages, some of which—including Barukawa, Beiro, Kaniberd, and Tutma—had also suffered from the effects of the wind-borne gas.

The people of Beiro sent tractor-drawn carts to Sheikh Wasan, and ten of these vehicles, each carrying fifty or sixty people, left for Raniya. At the Seruchawa resettlement camp, just outside the town, the tractors stopped to bury the bodies of fifty people who were already dead. The refugees who reached Raniya spent one night there. Local doctors washed their wounds and gave them eye-drops, but these did nothing to ease the effects of the gas on their vision. The refugees spent a restless night, and the hospital at Raniya was full of the sound of weeping.

The next morning, agents from Amn—and some witnesses say also from military intelligence—arrived at the hospital. They ordered everyone out of bed and into a number of waiting vans that were parked outside.[24] These would take them to the city of Erbil for medical care, the villagers were told; however, they were warned later that day that they would be given treatment only if they told the doctors that their injuries were the result of an attack by *Iranian* airplanes.[25]

At about 9:00 that morning, exhausted and bedraggled people in Kurdish dress began to stream into the emergency room of the Republic Hospital in Erbil. One witness counted four packed vans, each with twenty-one seats, and seven other vehicles—both cars and pick-up trucks. Others placed the number of arrivals at perhaps two hundred, of all ages, men, women, and children. All were unarmed civilians. Four were dead on arrival. The survivors arriving from Ranya told the doctors that they had been attacked with chemical weapons. Despite their burns, their blindness and other, more superficial injuries, those who had survived the journey from the Balisan Valley were generally still able to walk; those who were unconscious were carried by the others.

Even with the assistance of doctors who rushed from the nearby Maternity and Pediatric Hospital, the facilities were not sufficient for such a large-scale emergency. There were far from enough beds for so many victims; many of the patients were laid on the floor, and the occupants of three of the four vans were obliged to wait in the parking lot while the preliminary triage was done and the first treatment carried out. On examination, the doctors found that the victims' eyes were dried out and glued shut. Having some rudimentary notion of how to treat chemical victims, they applied eye drops, washed their burns, and administered injections of atropine, a powerful antidote for nerve agents.

The doctors had been at work on their patients for about an hour when the head of the local branch office of Amn arrived, an officer by the name of Hassan Naduri. The staff of the Erbil Republic Hospital, and especially the municipal morgue that was attached to it, had a great deal of prior and subsequent experience of Amn. The city housed not only the municipal office of the secret police agency, but also Amn's headquarters for the Erbil governorate and its operational command for the entire autonomous region of Iraqi Kurdistan. For several years the Republic Hospital morgue had received a steady flow of corpses from both Amn offices. Hospital records examined by HRW/Middle East give the details of approximately five hundred bodies received from Amn between 1968 and 1987—although there is no reason to suppose that this was more than a very incomplete record.

These deaths were recorded in the form of letters of transmittal from Amn, and the agency's bureaucracy appears to have been scrupulously efficient. Two copies of each letter of transmittal were sent to the morgue; the doctor on duty was required to sign one of these and then return it to Amn. Hospital staff also kept a second, secret ledger of their own, entitled "Record Book of Armed Dead People from Erbil." This ledger covers a three-year period beginning in June 1987; the final entry was dated 25 June 1990. The entries were cross-referenced to the number of the relevant Amn transmittal letter. In interviews with HRW/Middle East, hospital staff also estimated that they had made out three hundred death certificates, on orders from Amn, for named individuals whose bodies were never made available to them. This practice began in 1987.

There appears to have been no single standard procedure: Corpses arrived at the Erbil morgue in different ways. Sometimes the staff would receive a telephone call from Amn, often in the middle of the night, telling them that they should prepare to receive the body or bodies of "executed saboteurs" and ordering them to issue death certificates. Individual hospital porters were handpicked for the task of handling the bodies, presumably because they enjoyed the trust of the Amn agents. On some occasions the corpses arrived in pick-up trucks or station wagons, covered with blankets. At other times, hospital ambulances would be summoned to collect the bodies from the Amn headquarters in Einkawa, a Christian suburb of Erbil, or from a nearby military base. Although some showed signs of having been beaten to death, most appeared to have been executed by firing squads; they had multiple gunshot wounds, sometimes as many as thirty, and had their hands and upper arms bound behind them, as if they had been tied standing to a post.[26] The eyes were blindfolded with articles of clothing, such as a Kurdish cummerbund (*pishtend*) or head scarf (*jama-dani*). The bodies had been stripped of their wristwatches, identification papers, and other personal possessions.

However the bodies arrived, the entire operation was shrouded in secrecy, and morgue staff were ordered (under threat of death) neither to contact the relatives of the deceased nor to divulge their names to anyone else in the hospital. Doctors on duty in the morgue were not allowed to touch or examine the bodies; their duty was merely to furnish death certificates. If the cadavers arrived during daylight hours, the entire area around the morgue would be cordoned off by Amn guards, and other hospital personnel warned away from the area. Amn personnel would even take charge of the morgue's freezer facilities until municipal employees arrived to take the corpses away for secret burial in the paupers' section of the Erbil cemetery. If an especially large number of corpses was involved, a bulldozer would be commandeered from a local private contractor to dig a mass grave. The morgue staff was forbidden to wash the bodies or otherwise prepare them for burial facing Mecca, as Islamic ritual demands. "Dogs have no relation to Islam," an Amn officer told one employee.[27]

When Hassan Naduri arrived at the Republic Hospital on the morning of 17 April 1987, every doctor in the hospital was busy dealing with the emergency. The officer was accompanied by two other Amn agents; a large number of guards also remained outside in the hospital courtyard. According to some witnesses, Naduri was accompanied by Ibrahim Zangana, the governor of Erbil, and by a local Ba'ath Party official known only by his first name, Abd-al-Mon'em. The Amn officers questioned the hospital guards, demanding to know where the new patients were from and who the doctors were who were treating them. They then repeated these questions to the medical personnel and demanded to know what treatment was being given. With these questions answered, Captain Naduri telephoned Amn headquarters for instructions. After hanging up, he ordered that all treatment cease immediately. He told the doctors to remove the dressings from their patients' wounds. The doctors asked why. The captain responded that he had received orders from his superiors to transfer all the patients to the city's military hospital. At first, the hospital staff demurred, but the three Amn agents drew their pistols and ordered them to stop what they were doing at once, otherwise they would be taken off to Amn headquarters themselves.

After a second phone call, this time ostensibly to the military hospital, ambulances and trucks arrived and took the patients away, together with those who had remained, for a full hour, in the three parked vans. Later that day, the doctors telephoned the military hospital to check on the condition of their patients, but they had never arrived, and the doctors never saw any of the survivors of the Balisan Valley chemical attack again. They heard later that loaded military ambulances had been seen driving off in the direction of Makhmour, to the southwest of Erbil.

In fact, a handful of survivors told HRW/Middle East, the Balisan Valley victims were taken to a former police station that was now an Amn detention center, a stark white, cement building in the Arab quarter of the city, near the Baiz casino. There was a chaotic scene on arrival, as Amn agents attempted to sort out the detainees by age and sex, and in the confusion several people managed to escape. At least one woman fled leaving her children behind. Those who remained were thrown into locked cells, guarded by uniformed agents—some dressed all in green and others all in blue. They were held there for several days with neither food, blankets, nor medical attention.

Hamoud Sa'id Ahmad is an employee of the municipal morgue attached to Erbil's Republic Hospital, a dignified middle-aged man who has made the pilgrimage to Mecca. Over the next few days, he was summoned on several occasions to the Amn jail in the city's Teirawa quarter and ordered to pick up bodies and prepare them for burial. Over a three-day period he counted sixty-four bodies. Arriving to collect them, he saw other prisoners wandering around in the prison courtyard building. Some had a clear fluid oozing from their mouths; others had dark burn like marks on their bodies, especially on their throats and hands. He saw men, women, and children in detention, including several nursing babies in their mothers' arms. The bodies, kept in a separate locked cell, bore similar marks. None showed any signs of gunshot wounds. Most of the dead appeared to be children and elderly people. An Amn official told Ahmad that they were "saboteurs, all saboteurs we attacked with chemical weapons." An ambulance driver told Ahmad that he recognized one of the dead as a Republic Hospital employee from Sheikh Wasan.

Family members waiting outside the jail for news said that the detainees were being held as hostages, to compel their peshmerga relatives to surrender. On the last of his three visits, Ahmad saw two large buses pull up outside the prison, their windows sealed with cloths. Later in the day, a female prisoner managed to whisper to him, "Do you know what the buses were doing here? They took all the men away, to the south, like the Barzanis [in 1983]." The men were never seen alive again.[28]

After the mass disappearance of the men, the surviving women and children were taken during the night and driven away in the direction of Khalifan, three hours to the northeast of Erbil. At a place called Alana, they were left in an open plain, on the banks of a river, to fend for themselves. They were reunited there with the Balisan Valley villagers who had fled to Suleimaniyeh. These people reported that they had been detained there in a converted hospital that was guarded by Amn agents and off limits to civilians. (There is no independent account of what happened to their menfolk, some of whom also disappeared.)

At Alana, the mother who had escaped from the Amn jail in Erbil was reunited with her children. She recognized families from the villages of Kaniberd and Tutma, as well as from Sheikh Wasan and Balisan, who told her that many children had died in this place of hunger, thirst, and exposure. (With the exception of a few villages, the entire Balisan Valley had been abandoned in terror: Ironically, as we shall see, their flight may have saved thousands of lives during the following year's Anfal campaign.) Eventually, sympathetic Kurdish residents of the town of Khalifan took some of the survivors into their homes— "in their arms and on their backs"—and cared for them until they regained their health and strength. Other survivors ended up in the squalid government camp of Seruchawa, where so many of their fellow villagers had fled on the night of the chemical attack. When the elderly *mullah* of Balisan went to Ba'ath Party officials at Seruchawa to plead for an improvement in conditions in the camp, he was told contemptuously, "You're not human beings."[29]

On the basis of interviews with four survivors, and with medical and morgue personnel in Erbil, it is possible to give a rough estimate of the numbers who died as a result of the chemical bombing of Balisan, Sheikh Wasan and neighboring villages.

- 24 deaths in Balisan, as a direct result of exposure to chemical weapons. These people were buried in a mass grave in the village.
- 103 deaths in Sheikh Wasan, including about 50 buried in a mass grave in the camp of Seruchawa. The dead included 33 children under the age of four, another 28 ages five to fourteen, and 9 elderly people, aged sixty to eighty-five.[30]
- 8 or 9 deaths in the hospital at Raniya.
- 4 dead on arrival at the Erbil Emergency Hospital.
- Between 64 and 142 deaths in the Amn detention center in Erbil of untreated injuries sustained in the chemical bombing, aggravated by starvation and neglect. These included two elderly women, Selma Mustafa Hamid and Adila Shinko, and a nine-year-old girl, Howsat Abdullah Khidr.
- Two busloads of adult men and teenage boys disappeared from the Amn detention center in Erbil and are presumed by HRW/Middle East to have been executed later. Witnesses place the number at between 70 and 76: 22 men from Balisan, 50 from Sheikh Wasan, and 4 from other nearby villages. Among these were Muhammad Ibrahim Khidr,

aged eighteen, and Mohsen Ibrahim Khidr, aged twelve, the two youngest sons of the mullah of Balisan.
- "Many children" cast on the barren plain near Khalifan.

Allowing for some overlap, HRW/Middle East calculates that at least 225 and perhaps as many as 400 civilians from the Balisan Valley died as a direct or indirect result of the Iraqi air force's chemical attack on their villages on 16 April 1987.

The Sheikh Wasan and Balisan attacks are significant for several reasons. First, they are the earliest fully documented account of chemical attacks on civilians by the Iraqi regime. Second, they offer concrete evidence of the security forces' intent, on the orders of higher authority, to remove and murder large numbers of civilian noncombatants from areas of conflict in Iraqi Kurdistan. In this sense, like the mass abduction of the Barzani men in 1983, the Balisan Valley disappearances directly prefigure Anfal—although with the crucial difference that women and children were directly targeted. Similarly, the treatment of those who survived the actual bombing, in particular their separation by age and sex, their illegal confinement without food or medical care, and the abandoning of women and children in barren areas far from their homes, foreshadowed many of the techniques that were employed on a much vaster scale during the 1988 campaign. The Balisan Valley episode also illustrates the central role that would be played in the extermination campaign by the General Security Directorate. In addition, the events at Erbil's Republic Hospital constitute the gravest possible violation of medical neutrality.

The regime was far from finished with these rebellious valleys, however. Amid the thousands of pages of secret Iraqi intelligence reports on air raids and village burnings, HRW/Middle East researchers discovered one that contained an intriguing detail. It is a brief report from Amn Erbil, dated 11 June 1987, on a recent air strike on five villages in the Malakan Valley, a few miles to the east of Balisan and Sheikh Wasan. In the course of the attack, it noted, "thirty persons lost their eyesight." Two of the victims were named. Here was an unmistakable fingerprint, for there is only one kind of weapon that characteristically causes blindness, and that is poison gas.[31] During a subsequent field trip to Iraqi Kurdistan, it was possible to interview one of the two named survivors—one of many occasions on which a precise match could be made between documentary and testimonial evidence.

The man's name was Kamal, and he was living in Choman, a destroyed town on the road from Rawanduz to Iran.[32] An active peshmerga, Kamal had already experienced chemical warfare in the Jafati Valley, and his account of the 15 April attack there is included above. Hearing the news of the devastating attack on the Balisan Valley the next day, he rushed back to his family in the nearby village of Upper Bileh. He found that they had taken refuge in some caves in the mountains. It was bitterly cold, and Kamal persuaded them to return cautiously to their homes. At 6:00 A.M. on 27 May, his wife woke him to warn him that the village was under attack:

> We knew it was chemicals because the sound [of the explosions] was not loud. There were many bombs. I told my family that it wasn't a chemical attack because I didn't want to scare them, but they knew what it was. So we began burning the branches we had stored for animal feed, and they made a very strong fire. We also soaked cloths and head scarves at the spring. My aged father was there. The attack was so intense that we were unable to leave the village; that was why we lighted the fires. There was a separate spring for the women, and I told everyone, men and women, to jump into the water. The attack lasted until 10:00 A.M., and I sent my brother to the malband to get medical help. By sunset the situation was getting worse. Several people had gone blind.
>
> After sunset we crossed the stream and moved to a rocky area outside the village. Our situation was very bad. We had all been affected by the chemicals. We had trouble seeing, and we were short of breath. We had nosebleeds and fainting spells. We sent someone to the surrounding villages to fetch water, and I offered to pay them whatever they asked for. But the villagers were afraid to come, thinking that the chemicals were contagious. But people from Kandour village, who are very brave people, came to bring us milk.[33]
>
> In the meantime, my brother and a companion had reached the malband, but on the way back they collapsed because they had lost their sight. People from other villages sent mules to bring them back. They were carrying some medicine and eyedrops provided by the malband. When morning came, no one had died, but things were very bad. The third malband sent us a doctor and money to buy horses that could carry us to Iran. The women with us were in a terrible state, and we had to spoon-feed them. The small children were hardly breathing. We went to Malakan, where it was colder. We thought it would be better because of the fresh air. Then we reached the Sewaka area. There were people there who raised animals and they took pity on us. They wept a lot and gave us food. Next morning we left for Warta. We had to cover our faces because the bright light hurt us like needles stuck into our eyes.[34]

On the third night, the caravan of survivors reached the lower slopes of Qandil Mountain, a towering peak of almost 12,000 feet on the Iranian border south of Haj Omran. Once they reached Iran, they were given medical care. All of them lived through the ordeal but one—Kamal's eighteen-month-old nephew.

## THE SPRING 1987 CAMPAIGN:
## VILLAGE DESTRUCTION AND RESETTLEMENT

Five days after the Balisan Valley chemical attack, the infantry troops and bulldozers went to work on hundreds of villages in Iraqi Kurdistan. According to Resool's authoritative survey, the army obliterated at least 703 Kurdish villages from the map during the campaigns of 1987. Of these, 219 were in the Erbil area, 122 in the hilly plain known as Germian to the southeast of Kirkuk, and 320 in various districts of the governorate of Suleimaniyeh. Badinan, too, was hit, although less severely. The Kurdistan Reconstruction and Development Society (KURDS), a local relief agency, listed fifty villages that were destroyed in Dohuk governorate. Most of the villages destroyed during Ali Hassan al-Majid's "first and second phases" lay along the main roads and were under government control. Their removal had the effect of physically severing the peshmerga-controlled rural areas from the rest of the country.

For destruction on this scale, the Iraqi state had to deploy vast resources. Yet there were important differences between the village clearances of spring 1987 and the Anfal campaign of the following year. The most important concerned the treatment of the residents of the villages destroyed by the army. The 1987 campaign offered them clear, if unpalatable alternatives; Anfal did not.

The inhabitants of Narin, for example, a village in the nahya of Qara Tapa in the southern part of Germian, were relocated in 1987 to the Ramadi area, in central Iraq.[35] The villagers of nearby Zerdow were warned that it was their turn next. They left their homes and moved in with relatives in nearby towns or villages. Some were resettled in the newly opened camp of Benaslawa, six miles from Erbil on the site of an old Kurdish village. They were not punished otherwise, although Zerdow itself was razed by bulldozers a few days later. One family interviewed by HRW/Middle East lost its livestock, furniture, and food stores in the destruction of Zerdow but was paid compensation of 1,000 dinars ($3,000 at the then-official exchange rate). Later, the family was able to build a house in Benaslawa with a loan of 4,500 dinar from the state real estate bank.

This was a typical pattern. The villagers were not physically harmed; some token compensation was paid, although it might be withheld if a family refused to accept relocation in the towns or camps; there was some advance notice of the regime's intent to destroy the village (even though the advance time given was not always respected). The villagers of Qishlagh Kon, for example, in the Germian nahya of Qader Karam, were told by soldiers that they had fifteen days to evacuate; in fact, the army moved in and razed their homes well before the expiry of this deadline. According to one man from this village, army troops swept through the area populated by the Kurdish Zangana tribe in April 1987, bulldozing and dynamiting between 70 and 100 villages along the main road, spread out over three adjacent nahyas—Qader Karam, Qara Hassan, and Qara Hanjir.[36]

Many of the villagers were offered an explicit choice by the soldiers or jahsh. "Go to the saboteurs or join the government," was the message delivered to one Qader Karam village of the Jabari tribe. No neutrality was to be allowed, and a person's physical location would henceforth be taken as proof of political affiliation. Coming over to the government's side was spoken of as "returning to the national ranks," a phrase that appears in official documents with increasing frequency from early 1987 onward. Previous political loyalties were irrelevant to this new drawing of battle lines, and so was the size of the settlement. Several nahyas were cleared of their population or destroyed, or both, during the spring 1987 campaign, including Naujul, Qara Dagh, Qara Hanjir, Koks, and Sengaw. Shwan followed in September. In the northernmost governorate of Dohuk, the nahya of Kani Masi was evacuated and destroyed, apparently in retaliation for a six-day takeover by KDP forces. Some of these nahyas were towns of several thousand people.

Even a strong jahsh presence offered no protection, if the town lay within a designated area of army operations. As Ali Hassan al-Majid later told a meeting of senior Ba'ath Party officials, "I told the mustashars that the jahsh might say that they liked their villages and would not leave. I said I cannot let your villages stay because I will attack them with chemical weapons. And then you and your family will die."[37]

Notwithstanding the amount of destruction, it is apparent from one batch of official Iraqi files, found in the Amn offices in Erbil and Shaqlawa, that the regime was far from satisfied with the "first stage" of its village clearance program. A watchful, almost apprehensive tone creeps into many government documents from this period. Among the questions put to people surrendering to the authorities from peshmerga-controlled areas was one that asked, "How are the people affected economically and psychologically by the elimination of the villages and other policies?"[38]

On 20 April, Amn Erbil warns its branches that the new campaign of village destruction may provoke demonstrations to mark the fourteenth anniversary of the bombing of Qala Dizeh on the 24 April. On the same day the Erbil Security Committee, presided over by Governor Ibrahim Zangana, warns that "saboteurs" may attack government installations as a reprisal against the deportation of villagers from the prohibited areas. On 22 April, Governor Zangana predicts that the PUK may even try to bring in the International Committee of the Red

Cross to observe the clearances. Three days later, on 25 April, Amn Erbil issues an alert warning of peshmerga reprisal raids on Arab villages; it also complains that government forces destroying the village of Freez have come under attack from saboteurs and that air cover has failed to materialize as requested. By 20 May, the director of Amn Shaqlawa is complaining to Erbil that the saboteurs have been able to exploit the unpopularity of the campaign. In particular he expresses irritation that no camps have been made ready for the villagers who are to be relocated and that many of them have been obliged to remain in the open air, exposed to the elements.[39]

## EARLY USES OF AL-MAJID'S SPECIAL POWERS

In these early months of al-Majid's rule, the Ba'ath Party tightened the noose around the population of rural Kurdistan through a series of sweeping decrees and administrative orders.[40]

- On 6 April, all saboteurs lost their property rights. "By the authority vested in us by the Revolutionary Command Council's decree number 160 of 29 March 1987," writes al-Majid himself, "we have decided to authorize the chairs of the security committees [Ru'asa' al-Lijan al-Amniyeh] in the northern governorates to confiscate the real and personal property of the saboteurs, provided that their properties are liquidated within one month of the date of issuance of the confiscation decree."[41]
- On 10 April, al-Majid suspended the legal rights of the residents of villages prohibited for security reasons. "His Excellency has given instructions not to hear cases brought by the population of security-prohibited villages," writes deputy secretary Radhi Hassan Salman of the Northern Bureau Command, "and likewise those brought by the saboteurs, no matter what their character, as well as to freeze all claims submitted previously."[42]
- On 1 May, al-Majid began to order the execution of first-order relatives of saboteurs. It had long been the policy of the regime to detain and punish the families of active Kurdish peshmerga, often by destroying their homes. But al-Majid now ordered their physical elimination, at least on an occasional exemplary basis. These orders evidently remained in force throughout the Anfal campaign and for some time afterward. For example, a handwritten note dated 20 November 1989, signed "Security Chief, Interrogating Officer" and originating in Amn headquarters in the city of Suleimaniyeh, gives details

of a case in which an Iraqi citizen has petitioned the authorities for news about his missing parents and brother.

The security chief's letter informs the unnamed recipient (who is addressed only as "Your Excellency") that the missing parents, Goron Ahmad and his wife, Na'ima Abd-al-Rahman, were "liquidated" in Baghdad on 19 May 1987. Their son, Hushyar Ahmad, "a member of the group of Iranian saboteurs," was executed by hanging on 12 July 1987 by order of the Revolutionary Court (Mahkamat al-Thawrah). What is significant here is the reason for the killing of the man's parents. It was ordered, the document explains, "in compliance with the order from the Struggling Comrade Ali Hassan al-Majid, member of the regional command [of the Ba'ath Party] that was relayed to us by letter 106309 of the Security Directorate of the Autonomous Region, marked 'Secret and to be Opened Personally,' and dated 1 May 1987, regarding the liquidation of first-order relatives of criminals."

Another letter on Amn Suleimaniyeh letterhead, numbered S-T: 21308, dated 16 September 1989 and classified top secret, describes the public execution by firing squad of five "criminals" with a "connection to the internal organizations of the agents of Iran." The execution was carried out on 24 October 1987 in the presence of intelligence and Ba'ath Party officials.[43] Some time afterward, "It was decided that three families of the criminals . . . should be executed in a discreet manner." The authority for their execution was given by letter number 6806, dated 12 December 1987, from the Northern Bureau Command.

Wounded civilians could now also be executed, according to a handwritten communication (no. 3324) of 14 May from the security director of the city of Halabja, in southeastern Iraqi Kurdistan, to Amn Suleimaniyeh. This note gives details of an operation against the city's Kani Ashqan neighborhood and makes reference to a cable (no. 945) dated the previous day from the command of the Fifth Army Corps. "It was by order of the commander of the First Army Corps, on the recommendation of Comrade Ali Hassan al-Majid, to execute the wounded civilians after confirming their hostility to the authorities with the party organization, the security and police departments, and the intelligence center, and to use backhoes and bulldozers to raze the neighborhood of Kani Ashqan."[44]

## ORDERS FOR MASS KILLING

The extent of the Iraqi regime's intentions, however, are spelled out with brutal clarity in two directives issued by al-Majid's office in June 1987. Both documents lay out, in explicit detail, a prohibition on all human life in designated areas of the Kurdish countryside, covering more than a thousand villages, to be applied through a shoot-to-kill order for which no subsequent higher authorization is required.

The first is a personal directive, numbered 28/3650, signed by Ali Hassan al-Majid himself and dated 3 June 1987. Addressed to civilian and military agencies, including the commanders of the First, Second, and Fifth Army Corps, Amn of the Autonomous Region, the Istikhbarat, and *Mukhabarat,* it states the following:

1. It is totally prohibited for any foodstuffs or persons or machinery to reach the villages prohibited for security reasons that are included in the second stage of collecting the villages. Anyone who so desires is permitted to return to the national ranks. It is not allowed for relatives to contact them except with the knowledge of the security agencies.

2. The presence of people who were relocated in the first stage is completely prohibited in those areas of the villages prohibited for security reasons and also in the areas included in the second stage until 21 June 1987.[45]

3. Concerning the harvest: after the conclusion of winter, which must end before 15 July, farming will not be authorized in [the area] during the coming winter and summer seasons, starting this year.

4. It is prohibited to take cattle to pasture within these areas.

5. *Within their jurisdiction, the armed forces must kill any human being or animal present within these areas. They are totally prohibited.* (emphasis added)

6. The persons who are to be included in the relocation to the camps will be notified of this decision, and they will bear full responsibility if they violate it.

These orders were evidently relayed later to the lower echelons in the chain of command. They are repeated word for word, for example, in a letter (no. 4754), dated 8 June 1987, from Amn Erbil to all its departments and local offices.

Three days after al-Majid's directive, on 6 June, Radhi Hassan Salman, deputy secretary of the Northern Bureau Command, issued a series of general instructions to all army corps commanders, "aimed at ending the long line of traitors from the Barzani and Talabani clans and the Communist Party, who have joined ranks with the Iranian invader enemy with a view to enabling it to acquire territory belonging to the cherished homeland." Salman ordered increased combat readiness, improved intelligence, and a heightened state of alert among all units, while at the same time betraying a certain anxiety about renewed peshmerga attacks designed "to cut the chain of command."[46]

The most important document of all, however, was issued on 20 June 1987. Issued by the Northern Bureau Command over Ali Hassan al-Majid's signature, and additionally stamped with the seal of the RCC's Northern Affairs Committee, this directive, coded SF/4008, amended and expanded the 3 June instructions in very important ways—including a direct incitement to pillage, in clear violation of the rules of war, and the baldest possible statement of a policy of mass murder, ordered by the highest levels of the Iraqi regime. From the repeated references to it in official documents throughout 1988, it is apparent that directive 4008 remained in force as the standing orders for the Iraqi armed forces and security services during the Anfal campaign and beyond. For example, a letter from Amn Suleimaniyeh, dated 29 October 1988, makes reference to the directive as the basis for "the execution of nineteen accused, executed by this directorate because of their presence in the security-prohibited villages."

It is apparent that al-Majid's demand for the summary killing of people arrested in the prohibited areas caused some consternation among those who were charged with carrying out his orders. Throughout 1987 and 1988, high-level Iraqi officials issued a steady stream of ill-tempered clarifications of clause 5 of directive SF/4008—the paragraph that concerns executions. "The security agencies should *not* trouble us with queries about clause 5," complains a Northern Bureau letter of December 1987; "the wording is self-explanatory and requires no higher authority."[47] Instructions from Amn Erbil, dated 22 November 1988, insist that clause 5 must be "implemented without exception."

The full text of directive SF/4008, dated 20 June 1987, reads:
Northern Bureau Command
The Secretariat

Date [sic]:   28/4008
Ref. [sic]:   20/6/1987

[Handwritten] Sh.3 810

23/6/87

From:   Northern Bureau Command
To:     First Corps Command / Second Corps Command / Fifth Corps
        Command

[Stamp]   3
          12533
          23/6/87

Re: *Dealing with the Villages That Are Prohibited for Security Reasons*[48]

In view of the fact that the officially announced deadline for the amalgamation of these villages expires on 21 June 1987, we have decided that the following action should be taken effective 22 June 1987:

1. All the villages in which the saboteurs—the agents of Iran [the PUK], the offspring of treason [the KDP], and similar traitors to Iraq—are still to be found shall be regarded as prohibited for security reasons.

2. The presence of human beings and animals is completely prohibited in these areas, and [these] shall be regarded as operational zones in which [the troops] can open fire at will, without any restrictions, unless otherwise instructed by our headquarters.

3. Travel to and from these zones, as well as all agricultural, animal husbandry, and industrial activities, shall be prohibited and carefully monitored by all the competent agencies within their respective fields of jurisdiction.

4. The Corps commands shall carry out random bombardments using artillery, helicopters, and aircraft at all times of the day or night in order to kill the largest number of persons present in those prohibited areas, keeping us informed of the results.

5. All persons captured in those villages shall be detained because of their presence there, and they shall be interrogated by the security services, and those between the ages of 15 and 70 must be executed after any useful information has been obtained from them; keep us informed.

6. Those who surrender to the government or party authorities shall be interrogated by the competent agencies for a maximum period of three days, which may be extended to ten days if necessary, provided that we are notified of such cases. If the interrogation requires a longer period of time, approval must be obtained from us by telephone, telegraph, or through comrade Taher al-Ani.

7. Everything seized by the advisers [*mustashars*] or fighters of the National Defense Battalions [that is, the progovernment Kurdish militias] is considered theirs to keep, with the exception of heavy, mounted, and medium weapons.[49] They can keep the light weapons, notifying us only of the number of these weapons. The commands of the battalions must promptly bring this to the attention of all the advisers and company and brigade commanders and must provide us with detailed information concerning their activities in the National Defense Battalions.

cc: Head of the Legislative Council; Head of the Executive Council; [Foreign] Intelligence Agency; Chief of the Army General Staff; governors (chairs of the security committees) of Nineveh, al-Ta'mim, Diyala, Salah al-Din, Suleimaniyeh, Erbil, and Dohuk; [Ba'ath Party] branch secretaries of the above-mentioned governorates; General Directorate of Military Intelligence; General Directorate of Security [*Amn*]; Directorate of Security of the Autonomous Region; Subdirectorate of Military Intelligence, Northern Sector; Subdirectorate of Military Intelligence, Eastern Sector; security directors of the governorates of Nineveh, al-Ta'mim, Diyala, Salah al-Din, Suleimaniyeh, Erbil, and Dohuk.

For your information and action within your respective fields of jurisdiction. Keep us informed.

[Signature]
The Comrade
Ali Hassan al-Majid
Member of the Regional Command, Secretary General of the Northern Bureau

Ali Hassan al-Majid evidently insisted on a high level of personal control of even the smallest details of the campaign. For example, one order issued in the middle of the Anfal operation indicates that no town or village could be searched without his express personal approval.[50] Nonetheless, the list of institutions to whom his 20 June directive was copied gives some hint of the bureaucratic scope of the effort and the large number of civilian, party, military, and security agencies involved in its execution.

## DEFINING THE "NATIONAL RANKS": THE CENSUS OF 17 OCTOBER 1987

After 20 June the village destruction campaign temporarily abated. Although it had also targeted areas near the smaller roads that criss-cross Iraqi Kurdistan, its most striking effect was to remove a broad swathe of formerly government-controlled villages close to the highway that runs from Mosul to Erbil, Kirkuk, and Tuz Khurmatu, before turning east through Kifri, Kalar, Peibaz, and Darbandikhan. For the moment, the Iran-Iraq War deprived the regime of the military muscle that would have been required to press the campaign any further. But the political and bureaucratic logic of the spring 1987 clearances—as well as the incipient logic of Anfal—became apparent during the second half of the year. This was to effect a sharp division between the "national ranks" and the generally more mountainous peshmerga-controlled regions to the east and north. These were the prohibited areas, and their inhabitants, regardless of age or sex, would be regarded without exception as saboteurs.

They would, however, be given one last chance to change sides. As al-Majid's directive of 3 June stated, it was still possible for Kurds to "return to the national ranks"—in other words to move to the cities, towns, or mujamma'at and align themselves with the regime. To keep close track, family by family, of how the two sides lined up, the Iraqi regime had an ideal instrument at hand in the form of the national census. Iraq had carried out five censuses in the half-century since its independence. The results of the most recent, conducted in 1977, were classified as secret. Designed to be held every decade, another was due in 1987. It was scheduled for 17 October.

As the census date drew near, the authorities repeatedly insisted on improving security and intelligence measures to inhibit any contact or movement between the two sides, other than on the regime's terms. Amn Erbil ordered renewed vigilance on the camps of Benaslawa, Daratou, and Kawar Gosek, which all housed villagers relocated during the spring 1987 campaign.[51] Orders were issued to seize and destroy tractors, since these might help the saboteurs skirt the economic blockade of the prohibited areas. The tractor owners in question were to receive "the maximum exemplary punishment."[52]

On 6 September, al-Majid chaired a meeting of senior Ba'ath Party officials to discuss preparations for the census. Case by case, individual by individual, the makeup of the two sides was to be refined in the most legalistic fashion. "Subversives who repent" were to be allowed to return to the fold right up to the day of the census. No such returnees would be accepted after 17 October, however, "even if they surrender their weapons." At the same time, al-Majid regarded it as unacceptable for the families of unrepentant saboteurs to remain in government-controlled areas. These people were to be physically removed and, after stripping them of their identity papers, forced to join their saboteur kin in the prohibited areas.

This general policy had been in effect for at least two years.[53] Al-Majid now, however, demanded a full inventory of all such cases from the security committees of each of the northern governorates. This list was to reach his desk not later than 15 September. As soon as it was complete, "the families in question should be expelled to the regions where their subversive relatives are, with the sole exception of males aged between 12 and 50 inclusive, who should be detained."[54]

The local security agencies appear to have cooperated with alacrity. HRW/Middle East has examined dozens of individual expulsion orders by Amn Erbil, for example, during this precensus period. One typical case in mid-September 1987 gives the full names, addresses, dates of birth, and residence permit numbers of eighty women, children, and old men aged 51–89, taken from their homes and summarily expelled "to those regions where the saboteurs are present."[55] A single male relative born in 1949 is mentioned as having been detained "to receive the proper sentence."

Most strikingly of all, the Northern Bureau Command ordered that "mass seminars and administrative meetings shall be organized to discuss the importance of the general census, scheduled to take place on 17 October 1987. It shall be clearly emphasized that any persons who fail to participate in the census without a valid excuse shall lose their Iraqi citizenship. They shall also be regarded as army deserters and as such shall be subject to the terms of Revolutionary Command Council decree 677 of 26 August 1987."

The importance of this provision can scarcely be overstated, for RCC decree 677 stipulated that "the death sentence shall be carried out by party organizations, after due verification, on any deserters who are arrested, should the period of their flight or delinquency exceed *one year or should they have perpetrated the crime of desertion more than once*" (emphasis in original).[56] Failure to register under the census, in other words, could in itself be tantamount to the death penalty.

The results of the 1987 census were never publicly divulged. Employees of the government census office in Suleimaniyeh told HRW/Middle East that they estimated it to have been only 70 percent accurate—no doubt because large expanses of Iraqi Kurdistan, as well of the rebellious southern marshes, could not be included. Most residents of the prohibited areas opted to stay where they were; some, especially in the more remote parts of the Badinan region, said they never even learned that the census was taking place, despite a vigorous campaign conducted on government radio and television.

The instructions were quite different from those of the five previous censuses. Those who were not included in the census would no longer be considered Iraqi nationals, the official broadcasts announced; they would cease to be eligible for government services and food rations. Only two options were offered by the census: one could be either an Arab or a Kurd—nothing else. These ethnic lines were drawn with great rigidity. Official documents from 1988 and 1989 transmit orders from Saddam Hussein and Ali Hassan al-Majid to the effect that any citizen could become an Arab by means of a simple written application. In contrast, those wishing to be considered Kurds were subject to the destruction of their homes and deportation to the Autonomous Region.

People could be counted only if they made themselves accessible to the census takers. For anyone living in a prohibited area, this meant abandoning one's home. Inclusion in the census involved registering oneself as the resident of a government-controlled town or mujamma'a. (The only hope of evading this regulation was to bribe an official—a time-honored means of survival in Iraq, which continued to apply even during Anfal.) Villages that had been destroyed in earlier army operations—the Arabization drive of 1975, the border clearances of the late 1970s, and the spring 1987 campaign—no longer existed as far as the government in Baghdad was concerned. Some inhabitants of the border zone had returned illegally to their homes to rebuild, but the census would not count them. The remainder were now in camps.

As a partial indication of the scale of this exclusion, government statisticians provided HRW/Middle East with figures for Suleimaniyeh. The 1977 census had counted 1,877 villages in Suleimaniyeh; by the time of the 1987 census, this number was down to just 186. Almost 1,700 villages had thus disappeared from the official map. Of these, several hundred had been destroyed during the border clearances of the 1970s and at various stages of the war against Iran. Most of their inhabitants had been resettled in the nine camps that were also listed in the 1987 census. The remaining villages were simply not counted, because they now lay in prohibited areas of peshmerga influence.

Once the population count was complete, the consequences of not registering soon became apparent. Shelling and aerial bombing intensified. When families went to the nearest town to seek their food rations, said one man from a village near Qara Dagh, they were told that they could now forget about them. "You are Iranians," officials said, "Go to the Iranians for your food rations!"[57] The same was true of villagers seeking marriage licenses or government permits for other civil transactions.

On 18 October, the day after the census, Taher Tawfiq, secretary of the RCC's Northern Affairs Committee, issued a stern memorandum to all security committees in Kurdistan, reminding them that aerial inspection would ensure that directive 4008 of 20 June was being carried out to the letter. Any committee that failed to comply would "bear full responsibility before the comrade bureau chief"—that is to say, Ali Hassan al-Majid.[58] Several other documents from late 1987 insisted, in a tone of distinct irritation, that paragraph 5 (mandating summary execution after interrogation) did not require the authorization of a higher authority on a case-by-case basis. The Northern Bureau should no longer be troubled by these requests, since the standing orders are explicit.

The blockade of the north was now to be made even more systematic. On 29 September, al-Majid agreed to a set of harsh new proposals from an ad hoc committee chaired by Taher Tawfiq and including Khaled Muhammad Abbas, the head of the Eastern Sector Istikhbarat, Farhan Mutlaq Saleh, head of Northern Sector Istikhbarat, and Abd-al-Rahman Aziz Hussein, director of Amn for the autonomous region. The group complained that food, medicines, fuel, and other supplies were still getting through to the saboteurs. Accordingly, security would be stepped up at checkpoints; many grocery stores in the towns would be closed down; the secret police would monitor the stocks in all restaurants, bakeries and cafes; and a strict ban would be enforced on the sale of all agricultural produce from prohibited areas. Food rations would be cut back to the minimum necessary for human survival. The loyalty of all workers in the food distribution sector would be evaluated.[59]

Under this bitter regime, the inhabitants of the prohibited areas struggled to survive. During Ali Hassan al-Majid's first eight months in office, the groundwork for a final solution of Iraq's Kurdish problem had been laid. Its logic was apparent; its chain of command was set in place. But the events of 1987 were "just a preliminary step," a former Istikhbarat officer explained, "because the war was still going on. The Iraqi government was not so strong and many troops were tied up on the front. They postponed the anger and hate in their hearts," but only until the beginning of 1988, when the major winter offensive that Baghdad had feared failed to materialize and Iran's fortunes on the battlefield began rapidly to decline.

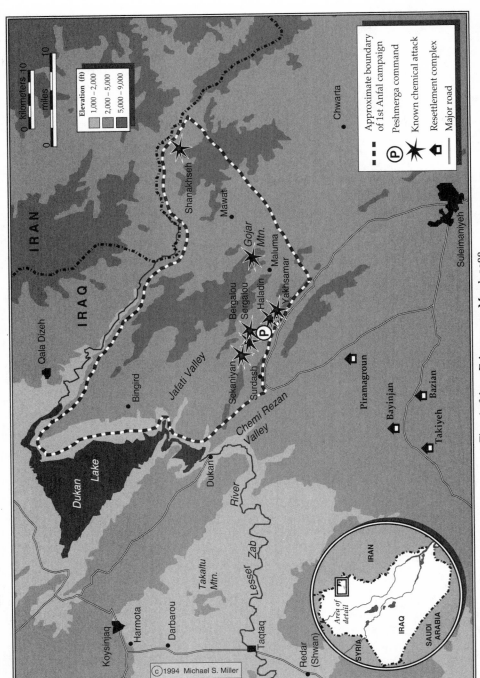

First Anfal: 23 February–19 March 1988

# 3

## THE FIRST ANFAL

### The Siege of Sergalou and Bergalou, 23 February–19 March 1988

I will, with engines never exercised,
Conquer, sack and utterly consume
Your cities and your golden palaces,
And with the flames that beat against the clouds
Incense the heavens and make the stars to melt,
As if they were the tears of Mahomet
For hot consumption of his country's pride.
                    —Marlowe, *Tamburlaine the Great* (part 2, IV, i)

It was like the Day of Judgment; you stand before God.
          —Survivor of the poison gas attack on Halabja, 16 March 1988

The nerve center of Jalal Talabani's Patriotic Union of Kurdistan lay deep in the mountains of Suleimaniyeh governorate in southeastern Iraqi Kurdistan. The organization's most important facilities were all housed there, in the long, narrow Jafati Valley, so called because its inhabitants belonged to the important Jaff tribe. The PUK's top command, its politburo, had its headquarters in the small village of Yakhsamar. Nearby Bergalou, a temporary settlement, was home to the PUK's radio station and its main field hospital. Talabani's deputy commander, Nawshirwan Mustafa Amin, had also taken up residence there, and in Talabani's absence abroad it was he who commanded the PUK during Anfal. Nearby Sergalou was home to the PUK's second malband, or regional command, responsible for peshmerga operations in the governorate of Kirkuk. Other villages, such as Maluma and Zewa, were important additional links in the chain of command.

Sergalou was a small town of some 500 households (3,500 people), half an hour by car on an gravel road from the nearby nahya of Surdash. Although the houses were of mud and stone, they boasted cement floors, and almost every home had its own water supply from nearby springs. An hour away on foot, the village of Haladin, another sizable village of about 350 households, surrounded by vineyards, housed an additional contingent of PUK fighters. "[The valley] was as important to the peshmerga as Baghdad is [sic] to the government," was how one local trader put it.[1]

Hemmed in by steep mountains, Haladin was a classic guerrilla stronghold protected by difficult terrain. It had another strategic significance, however, for it lay just a few miles east of the vital Dukan Dam and hydroelectric power station at the head of the lake of the same name, which was an important source of electricity for the cities of Suleimaniyeh and Kirkuk.[2] Seizing the Dukan Dam was a crucial element of the PUK's plan to liberate large expanses of Kurdistan on an accelerated timetable. The goal was to take the cities of Ranya, Koysinjaq, and Qala Dizeh (see map) thus encircling the lake and establishing a new frontline along the Haibat Sultan mountain range, between Koysinjaq and the western shore. That plan, which was ready to be executed in February 1988, was not to be realized.

Since 1985 and the breakdown of negotiations between the PUK and the Iraqi government, the entire Jafati Valley had been designated a prohibited area. Attacks by aircraft and artillery were frequent, with shelling occurring almost daily. The PUK headquarters was well defended, however, and all the men and some of the women in Sergalou, Yakhsamar, and Haladin were organized into an armed self-defense force. Government checkpoints on surrounding roads were largely ineffective in imposing an economic blockade.

The chemical weapons that had been used to such demoralizing effect against Iranian troops had been brought into play repeatedly against the PUK redoubt during the previous summer. For an hour on the afternoon of 8 June 1987 chemical shells from a truck-mounted multiple-rocket launcher, or *rajima,* rained down on Bergalou, Haladin, and the nearby village of Sekaniyan. The rajima was a constant presence in the villagers' lives for many months after this, although the casualties appear to have been limited. One farmer told HRW/Middle East that this was thanks in part to the high mountains, dense tree cover, and natural shelters of the area and in part to the notorious inaccuracy of the Iraqi gunners. The worst casualties were in Haladin, where one shell hit a house and killed a man named Yasin Abd-al-Rahman and six members of his family. Otherwise, the main effects of the gas shelling were shortness of breath and tearing; later chemical attacks produced additional symptoms, including blistering and burns. Those who died did so in fits of shivering within an hour of exposure to the chemicals; others acted deranged and stumbled around laughing hysterically.[3]

The Iraqi air force also attacked the valley repeatedly. In the past, only helicopters had been used in aerial harassment operations, but the Iranians now supplied the PUK with antiaircraft missiles that kept the Iraqi helicopters at bay, and airplanes were pressed into service. Sometimes, the attacks were carried out by small Swiss-manufactured Pilatus planes, more commonly used as trainers or for crop spraying. At other times, supersonic Soviet-made Sukhoi fighter bombers took part, with as many as fifteen or twenty aircraft joining in the attacks. At first the raids employed only conventional weapons, but on 15 April and again in July, the war planes also dropped chemical bombs. Dispersed on the breeze, the main effect of the gas was temporary blindness, lasting about two weeks. But it also killed people, most of them civilians. By the summer of 1987, the peshmerga had supplies of gas masks, donated by the Iranians, and each division, or teep, had an officer who was expert in defense against chemicals. Ordinary villagers had to defend themselves against the wind-borne gas as best they could, fleeing to higher ground, covering their faces with wet cloths as the Iranian-trained peshmerga doctors had instructed them, or setting fires in the caves and underground shelters where they sought refuge.[4]

Throughout late January and February 1988, a flurry of intelligence reports from Amn Suleimaniyeh and the Iraqi Army's First Corps warned that new joint actions were being planned by the 'Umala' Iran and the Teheran regime. According to Amn, mercenaries from the Iranian Revolutionary Guards, operating out of PUK base camps, were "carrying out surveillance missions in the direction of al-Ta'mim governorate"—in other words, westward, toward the Kirkuk oil-fields. The PUK's first malband, based in Qara Dagh, was "facilitating the entry of Khomeini's guards from the Darbandikhan sector." On 1 February, the Ba'ath Party branch in Qara Dagh informed Amn that "the Iranian enemy plans to help the saboteurs" in attacking targets—including the sizable Kurdish town of Halabja. On 8 February a report from a secret informant briefed Amn on the enemy's state of preparedness. It noted that Jalal Talabani himself was out of the country. "The number of saboteurs in Sergalou-Bergalou," it continued, "is between six hundred and eight hundred."[5]

Despite its long history of living under attack, the PUK seems to have been unprepared for the ferocity of the attack that came later that month. Perhaps the peshmerga had overestimated how much the Iraqi regime was now psychologically tied down by the war against Iran. They did quickly understand its thinking in laying siege to the Jafati Valley. Success there would not only decapitate the PUK; it would also prove, to devastating psychological effect, that the regime could prevail over the peshmerga wherever it chose, on any terrain.

At about 1:30 or 2:00 A.M. on 23 February, the people of Yakhsamar, Sergalou, and Bergalou awoke in the dark and rain to the thunderous sound of shelling from rajima. Although there is no definitive evidence that the Iraqi army was yet using the word *Anfal* to describe its operations, these artillery shells may be considered for all intents and purposes the first shots fired in the Anfal campaign.[6]

It is evident that the regime attached a special significance to the new campaign from the beginning. An Iraqi Defense Ministry order, for example, signed on 23 February circulates a Revolutionary Command Council decree that those who fall in the coming fight against the "saboteurs" and the attendant campaign of village "purification" are to be venerated as "Martyrs of the Glorious Battle of Saddam's *Qadissiyah*"—that is to say, the war against Iran.[7]

At daybreak on 23 February, government ground forces attacked from all directions. "The army that laid siege to the headquarters was so big that it looked like a fence that was separating the area from the rest of Kurdistan," recalled one peshmerga who was in Sergalou that day.[8] The frontline stretched for a full forty miles, from Bingird on the eastern side of the lake to Dukan, and thence to Suleimaniyeh and the towns of Mawat and Chwarta. The PUK held out for more than three weeks, even though the assault involved the army, air force, and the elite Republican Guards, who were apparently employed only during the initial stages of Anfal.[9] The armed forces' target was not just the PUK headquarters, but all the villages in the valley, some twenty-five to thirty in all.[10] According to other PUK sources, between 200 and 250 people were killed in the course of the siege, most of them active peshmerga. As long as the peshmerga resisted, most of the villagers hid in nearby caves. But in the early days of March, the villages began to fall one by one as tanks and armored vehicles smashed through the PUK's defensive lines. The inhabitants fled, most in the direction of Iran. After they had departed, crews of army engineers moved in with bulldozers and razed their villages.

Enveloping the Jafati Valley on three sides, the army was unable to close one escape route—to the east and the Iranian frontier, about twelve miles from Sergalou across the mountains. According to official intelligence reports, by 25 February, with Iranian assistance, the PUK had opened at least two rough roads to the border.[11] Most of the armed peshmerga managed to withdraw in relatively good order, with ideas of redeploying their forces farther to the south, in the broad hilly plain known as Germian. But they found their way blocked by government troops and were forced instead to circle northward to the security of Qandil Mountain, on the Iran-Iraq border near Haj Omran. Others fled to the grasslands on the shores of Dukan Lake, where they defended themselves until they ran out of ammunition. The bedraggled survivors eventually ended up in Iran. Still others set up a temporary base camp in the village of Shanakhseh, until that too was hit by chemical weapons on about 22 March.

That morning, Iraqi war planes flew over and dropped balloons. Six aircraft returned at about 2:00 P.M. and dropped bombs. "The area was full of peshmerga and fleeing families," said a PUK fighter who was there. "There were thousands of people, many living in tents. I myself was injured, my face became black and my skin was painful. I had trouble breathing. But these were mild symptoms; others who were closer to the point of impact had severe blisters. Some men suffered from swollen testicles." A PUK local commander believed that as many as twenty-eight people were killed and three hundred injured, mostly peshmerga families. (Other sources believe the figure may be somewhat lower.) Some of the dead were civilians who were already exhausted from their attempt to cross the mountains into Iran.[12]

Given the intensity of this new campaign, which they would soon come to know by the name of Anfal, the peshmerga had realized that they could do little to protect the civilians, and they told them as much, advising the villagers that they would have to take their chances alone. At this point, with the PUK leadership still relatively intact and with frequent warnings being broadcast over the clandestine peshmerga radio station, civilians seem to have been given fair notice of the dangers they faced. This no doubt saved countless lives. Yet by the time Anfal spread to other areas, it was much harder to warn civilians. After the siege of the PUK headquarters, the peshmerga began to grasp the direction that the campaign would take. They could do little or nothing about it.

Most of the villagers from the Jafati Valley survived. Although some fled to the city of Suleimaniyeh, the majority headed for Iran, through the heavily mined no-man's-land along the border, in the first large-scale refugee exodus since the crushing of the Barzani-led revolt thirteen years earlier. It was March, and the harsh Kurdish winter was not over.

"We left behind all the properties accumulated over fifty years," added a middle-aged villager from Sergalou. "The people moved like a panicked herd of cattle through the mountains in the direction of Iran. It was raining. There were war planes overhead. . . . Six people from Sergalou froze to death along the way, and another thirty from other villages in the same valley."[13]

"The people were running, and lost their shoes," said a fifty-seven-year-old woman from the village of Qara Chatan. "There was much snow. We were shivering from the cold."[14] People with children suffered especially from the cold since they could not move quickly. The single most tragic incident involved a group of people who made it as far as Kanitou, a ruined village north of Sergalou that had been evacuated during the 1978 border clearances. Peshmerga from several parties were present in Kanitou, but they fell to bickering between themselves. In the chaos, a large band of fleeing villagers tried to cross the high snow peaks into Iran. They left too late in the day, and darkness overtook them when they were still several hours from safety. At least eighty died of cold and exposure; by one estimate, the number may have been as high as 160.[15]

Although the siege of the Jafati Valley was not accompanied by mass disappearances, some villagers from the first Anfal theater vanished during late April, several weeks after Sergalou and Bergalou had fallen. A farmer from Haladin told HRW/Middle East that after three days on the run, his family found refuge on the border in tents supplied by sympathetic Iranian Kurds. "They stayed there for a month," he remembered, "then the army came to the border and arrested all these people, including my entire family. This was on 20 April. The army dropped troops from helicopters. There was a bad snow, and people were exhausted." The young man lost nine of his relatives that day. They included his mother, three sisters—two of them pregnant—and three nieces under the age of six. The witness escaped to Iran; only his father, a man in his late fifties, was ever seen alive again.[16]

Others who fled the siege of the PUK headquarters disappeared in a different manner. Three brothers from Sergalou recrossed the border into Iraq after two weeks in Iran, having heard false rumors of an amnesty for those who turned themselves in.[17] They surrendered to the mustashar at a camp called Sengasar, outside the town of Qala Dizeh. But the man turned them over to the government, and they were never seen again. Similarly, a group of fifteen army deserters who had been hiding in the mountains for several weeks gave themselves up to the mustashar in the village of Chermaga. The mustashar had given one of the families his word of honor that no one would be harmed. These young men, too, disappeared into the custody of Amn in Suleimaniyeh. Trick amnesties and broken promises would be repeated again and again in the subsequent stages of the Anfal campaign.

## THE 16 MARCH CHEMICAL ATTACK ON HALABJA

For years, the hostility between Iran and Iraq appeared to the Kurdish parties as a geopolitical loophole that they could exploit to their advantage. After withstanding the siege of Sergalou-Bergalou for two weeks, the PUK took the desperate decision to open a second front with Iranian military support. As their target, the peshmerga chose Halabja, a town on the plain just a few miles from the border, in a feint that was designed to draw some of the Iraqi troops away from the siege of Sergalou and Bergalou. The plan turned out to be a tragic miscalculation, as the once beneficial alliance with Iran turned into a crippling liability. For the Halabja diversion only cemented the view of the Iraqi regime that the war against Iran and the war against the Kurds was one and the same thing.

At the end of February, Iraq stepped up its missile attacks on Teheran as part of the "War of the Cities";[18] the escalation was designed to push the weakened Iranians to the negotiating table on terms favorable to Baghdad. A confident senior official even admitted to Patrick Tyler of the *Washington Post* that Iraq was trying to lure its adversary into a trap by overextending its forces. "For the first time in our history, we want the Iranians to attack," the official said.[19] At Halabja, the Iranians obliged.

Halabja was a bustling Kurdish town with a busy commercial section and government offices. Villagers displaced from their homes by the war had swollen its population of forty thousand to sixty thousand or more. The peshmerga had been strong there for almost thirty years, with several clandestine parties active—Socialists, Communists, and others—in addition to Jalal Talabani's PUK. A group with particular local strength was the pro-Iranian Islamic Movement Party (Bizutnaway Islami Eraqi). As a reprisal against local support for the peshmerga, Iraqi troops had already bulldozed two entire quarters of the town, Kani Ashqan and Mordana, in May 1987.[20] Since about 1983, Iranian troops had been making secret reconnaissance visits to Halabja under cover of darkness. The town lay on the very edge of the war zone, and dozens of small villages between Halabja and the Iranian border had been razed in the late 1970s, their inhabitants resettled in camps on the edge of the city. The greater strategic importance of Halabja, however, was its location just seven miles east of Darbandikhan Lake, whose dam controls a significant part of the water supply to Baghdad.

During the first two weeks of March, a stream of Iraqi intelligence reports noted the buildup of Revolutionary Guards and peshmerga to the west of Halabja and the shelling of the nearby town of Sayed Sadeq to the north by Iranian forces.[21] On 13 March the Iranians officially announced that they had launched a new offensive, Zafar 7, in the Halabja area. According to Teheran radio, the offensive, which was conducted by a joint force of PUK peshmerga and pasdaran, was in retaliation for the Iraqi regime's recent chemical attacks on the Kurds.[22] A second attack, apparently coordinated, followed the next day. This one was called Bait al-Maqdis 4, and the Iranians claimed that it had taken their forces within twelve miles of Suleimaniyeh. On 16 March, Teheran announced yet another offensive, code named Val-Fajr 10.[23] Iran boasted that its forces had now advanced to the eastern shore of Darbandikhan Lake, controlling over three hundred square kilometers of Iraqi territory and 102 (presumably destroyed) villages. But the main thrust of Val-Fajr 10, Teheran declared, was the "liberation" of the town of Halabja.

Halabja had been subjected to three days of heavy Iranian shelling from the surrounding hills, beginning on 13 March. One by one, the small Iraqi military posts between Halabja and the border were routed, and their occupants pulled back to the safety of the town. Some stripped off their uniforms and took refuge in the mosques, while some took up temporary defensive positions in local army bases. Others fled altogether. Yet the Baghdad regime resisted the temptation to reinforce Halabja with large numbers of ground troops, for it had an entirely different strategy in mind.

Some Iranian pasdaran had reportedly begun to slip into town as early as 13 March. By the night of 15 March, they were openly parading through the streets, accompanied by Iraqi Kurds, greeting the townspeople and chanting "God is Great! Khomeini is our leader!" They billeted themselves with local Kurdish families and ordered them to prepare dinner. Some rode around Halabja on motorcycles; others were very young, barely teenagers, and carried only sticks and knives. Many carried gas masks. They asked bewildered people in the streets how far it was to the holy cities of Karbala and Najaf.[24] Militants of the Iraqi Islamic Movement did a victory dance outside the headquarters of Amn and the Istikhbarat building, which they took over for themselves. Yet among the townspeople as a whole there was grave apprehension, especially when public employees were ordered on 15 March to evacuate their posts.[25] Swift Iraqi reprisals were widely expected; one Amn cable the next day spoke with notable understatement of the need for "a firm strengthening of military power."[26]

The Iraqi counterattack began midmorning on 16 March with conventional air strikes and artillery shelling from the town of Sayed Sadeq. Most families in Halabja had built primitive air-raid shelters near their homes. Some crowded into these, others into the government shelters, following the standard air-raid drills they had been taught since the beginning of the Iran-Iraq War. The first wave of air strikes appears to have included the use of napalm or phosphorus. "It was different from the other bombs," according to one witness. "There was a huge sound, a huge flame, and it had very destructive ability. If you touched one part of your body that had been burned, your hand burned also. It caused things to catch fire." The raids continued unabated for several hours. "It was not just one raid, so you could stop and breathe before another raid started. It was just continuous planes, coming and coming. Six planes would finish and another six would come."[27]

Those outside in the streets could see clearly that these were Iraqi, not Iranian aircraft, since they flew low enough for their markings to be legible. In the afternoon, at about 3:00, those who remained in the shelters became aware of an unusual smell. Like the villagers in the Balisan Valley the previous spring, they compared it most often to sweet apples, or to perfume, or cucumbers, although one man says that it smelled "very bad, like snake poison." No one needed to be told what the smell was.

The attack appeared to be concentrated in the northern sector of the city, well away from its military bases, although by now these had been abandoned. In the shelters there was immediate panic and claustrophobia. Some tried to plug the cracks around the entrance with damp towels, or pressed wet cloths to their faces, or set fires. In the end they had no alternative but to emerge into the streets. It was growing dark, and there were no streetlights; the power had been knocked out the day before by artillery fire. In the dim light, the people of Halabja saw nightmarish scenes. Dead bodies—human and animal—littered the streets, huddled in doorways, slumped over the steering wheels of their cars. Survivors stumbled around, laughing hysterically, before collapsing. Iranian soldiers flitted through the darkened streets, dressed in protective clothing, their faces concealed by gas masks. Those who fled could barely see and felt a sensation "like needles in the eyes." Their urine was streaked with blood.[28]

Those who had the strength fled toward the Iranian border. A freezing rain had turned the ground to mud, and many of the refugees went barefoot. Those who had been directly exposed to the gas found that their symptoms worsened as the night wore on. Many children died along the way and were abandoned where they fell. At first light the next morning Iraqi war planes appeared in the sky, apparently monitoring the flight of the survivors. Many kept away from the main roads and scattered into the mountains, despite the ever-present menace of land mines. According to one account, some six thousand people from Halabja congregated at the ruined villages of Lima and Pega. Another thousand or so gathered among the rubble of Daratfeh, the last village on the Iraqi side of the border.[29]

The Iranians were ready for the influx of refugees. Iranian helicopters arrived at Lima and Pega in the late afternoon, and military doctors administered atropine injections to the survivors before they were ferried across the border. In Iran, all agreed that they were well cared for, although some had injuries that were untreatable, and they died on Iranian soil. The sickest were transferred to hospitals in the Iranian cities of Teheran and Kermanshah and to the smaller town of Paveh. The remainder spent two weeks in a converted schoolhouse in the town of Hersin, where they received medical attention. From there, they were taken to two refugee camps—one at Sanghour, on the Persian Gulf near Bandar Abbas, the other at Kamiaran in Kermanshah province, close to the Iraqi border. There they waited until the Anfal was over and felt it was safe to return home.

There would, however, be no homes to return to, for virtually every structure in Halabja was leveled with dynamite and bulldozers after Iraqi forces finally retook the city. So, too, were Zamaqi and Anab, two camps that had been built on the outskirts of Halabja in the late 1970s to rehouse villagers from the destroyed border areas. So, too, was nearby Sayed Sadeq, a town of twenty thousand. In both Halabja and Sayed Sadeq, the electric substations were also dynamited.[30] Even after the razing of Halabja, many bodies remained in the streets to rot where they had fallen four months earlier.[31]

"The loss of Halabja is a regrettable thing," remarked Foreign Minister and Revolutionary Command Council member Tariq Aziz, adding, "Members of Jalal al-Talabani's group are in the area, and these traitors collaborate with the Iranian enemy."[32] As the news of Halabja spread throughout Iraq, those who asked were told by Ba'athist officials that Iran had been responsible. A Kurdish student of English at Mosul University recalled his shock and disbelief at the news; he and his fellow Kurds were convinced that Iraqi government forces had carried out the attack but dared not protest for fear of arrest.[33]

Not until July did the Iraqi regime move to recover Halabja, which was left under de facto Iranian control. In the days following the mass gassing, the Iranian government, well aware of the implications, ferried in journalists from Teheran, including foreigners. Their photographs, mainly of women, children, and elderly people huddled inertly in the streets or lying on their backs with mouths agape, circulated widely, demonstrating eloquently that the great mass of the dead had been Kurdish civilian noncombatants. Yet the numbers have remained elusive, with most reports continuing to cite Kurdish or Iranian estimates of at least 4,000 and as many as 7,000.[34] The true figure was certainly in excess of 3,200, which was the total number of individual names collected in the course of systematic interviews with survivors.[35]

## THE FALL OF PUK HEADQUARTERS

Halabja was a symbolic show of Iraqi force in a war that Iran could never win. The mass gassing also served a more important purpose by delivering a crushing psychological blow to the Kurdish peshmerga and their civilian sympathizers. Halabja was exemplary collective punishment of the most brutal kind, carried out in bald defiance of all international prohibitions on the use of chemical weapons. The PUK fighters had been exposed to poison gas several times during the preceding weeks; now the will of the civilian population was to be broken.

The Halabja chemical attack was a harbinger of later Anfal policies. During each of the eight phases of the military campaign, these forbidden weapons would be used against Kurdish villages, dozens in all—enough to terrify their residents with a reminder of what had befallen Halabja. Yet Halabja, although remaining the single greatest atrocity of the war against the Kurds, was *not* part of Anfal. In that sense, it was the clearest possible illustration of the bureaucratic logic of the Anfal campaign. On 15 March, the very eve of the Halabja attack, the Northern Bureau Command ordered that "the families of subversives who take refuge with our units should be detained in special guarded camps set up for that purpose under the supervision of intelligence officers from the First and Fifth Army Corps."[36] These camps were the first step in establishing the weblike bureaucracy of mass killing that operated during Anfal. Yet the fleeing survivors of Halabja were not detained and taken to the camps, because the Iraqi regime did not consider Halabja to be a part of Anfal. The reason was quite simple: Halabja was a city, and Anfal was intended to deal with the rural Kurdish population.[37]

After Halabja, PUK headquarters did not resist for long. At 10:10 on the night of 18 March, army units stormed into Sergalou, causing heavy losses among its final defenders. Bergalou fell the following afternoon. Saddam Hussein had fulfilled his promise to cut off "the head of the snake." By the end of the day, the General Command of the Iraqi armed forces had prepared its official victory declaration, and a jubilant announcer on Iraqi radio informed his listeners that "thousands of the sons of our Kurdish people took to the streets of Erbil, expressing their joy and chanting in support of President Saddam Hussein."[38] The army communiqué contains the first official reference that HRW/Middle East has been able to find to the operation known as Anfal. The successful conclusion of each subsequent phase of the campaign would be announced in the Iraqi press with similar fanfare. The 19 March communiqué reads:

In the name of God, the merciful, the compassionate. Like all covetous invaders, the Zionist Khomeinyite forces relied on some of those who betrayed the homeland and people in the northern area of Iraq—those who our good Kurdish people expelled from their ranks. Those elements performed shameful services for foreigners. Among their shameful acts was facilitating the missions of the invading forces in entering in the Halabja border villages in the Suleimaniyeh governorate.

As an expression of the will of the great Iraqi people, the brave armed forces, and the good honorable nationalists from our Kurdish people, and in response to the treason of this stray clique, the brave Badr forces, the brave al-Qa'qa' forces, the brave al-Mu'tasem forces, and the forces affiliated with them from our armed forces and the National Defense battalions, carried out the Anfal operation under the supervision of Staff Lt. Gen. Sultan Hashem, who is temporarily assigned to this mission in addition to his regular duties.[39] Our forces attacked the headquarters of the rebellion led by traitor Jalal Talabani, the agent to the Iranian regime, the enemy of the Arabs and Kurds, in the Sergalou, Bergalou, and Zewa areas and in the rough mountainous areas in Suleimaniyeh. At 1:00 P.M. today, after a brave and avenging battle with the traitors, the headquarters of the rebellion was occupied. The commander of the force guarding the rebellion headquarters, traitors, and misguided elements were captured with God's help and with the determination of the zealous men of Iraq—Arabs and Kurds. Many were killed and others escaped in shame.

This is unique bravery and faithfulness. This is a struggle admired by the entire world, the struggle of leader Saddam Hussein's people, Arabs and Kurds, who placed themselves in the service of the homeland and gave their love and faithfulness to their great leader, the symbol of their victory and title of their prosperity. Our people have rejected from their ranks all traitors who sold themselves cheaply to the covetous foreign enemy.
Praise be to God for His victory. Shame to the ignominious.
[signed] The Armed Forces General Command, 19 March 1988[40]

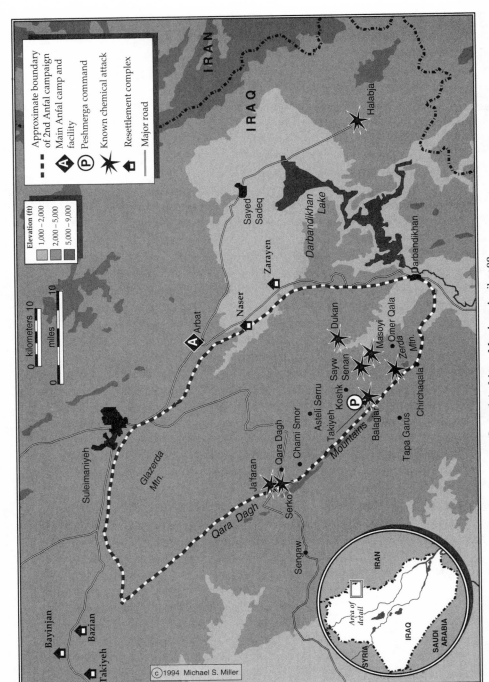

**Second Anfal: 22 March–1 April 1988**

# 4

## THE SECOND ANFAL

### Qara Dagh, 22 March–1 April 1988

Bring your families. Nothing will happen to them.
—Army officer to villagers fleeing from southern Qara Dagh

Although the siege of Sergalou-Bergalou consumed enormous resources, the Iraqi armed forces were not so rash as to neglect other targets. To block any attempt by the PUK to reinforce its beleaguered national headquarters, the regime maintained a steady rhythm of attacks against other regional commands, such as the first malband, which was based on Qopi Mountain in Qara Dagh and charged with all operations in the governorate of Suleimaniyeh. At each stage of Anfal, as the main assault changed its geographic focus, this pattern of secondary pressure was maintained.

Few parts of Iraqi Kurdistan are as lovely as Qara Dagh. Its chain of jagged, serrated peaks runs southeast for seventy miles as straight as a razor's edge. The features of its beauty, however, were also those that made Qara Dagh vulnerable. To crush resistance in the Jafati Valley, which is hemmed in by steep mountains, took three weeks for twenty-seven army divisions together with Kurdish jahsh. Qara Dagh was the opposite: a thin line of mountains flanked by almost indefensible lowlands. To the west lies the hilly plain of Germian, the "warm country." To the east, until 1988, dozens of small farming villages nestled in green valleys of astonishing fertility. Fields of winter wheat, barley, tobacco, and rice flourished next to rich plots of okra, peas, green beans, tomatoes, melons, and grapes. At the southernmost tip of the Qara Dagh chain lay the six-thousand-foot sentinel of Zerda Mountain, a peshmerga stronghold. Beyond this, to the east, a narrow corridor carried the highway from Suleimaniyeh past the town of Darbandikhan and the lake of the same name, with its strategic dam. Even as the first Anfal raged to the north, Iraqi intelligence kept a watchful eye on the lake, ever fearful of a waterborne attack by Iranian forces on the dam and its power station.

The government had relinquished control of rural Qara Dagh in the early days of the Iran-Iraq War. In 1987 the district center, or nahya, itself was emptied, and its population relocated to the nearby camps of Naser and Zarayen. Troops and jahsh took over the deserted town, but they were quickly routed from their positions by the peshmerga. Retaliatory air raids soon destroyed what was left of Qara Dagh, although PUK forces continued to control the territory. Like the civilian population of the surrounding villages, the people of Qara Dagh learned to live with constant artillery shelling from a half dozen government fire bases between Suleimaniyeh and Darbandikhan.

Since 1983 the twin hubs of peshmerga activity in Qara Dagh had been the villages of Takiyeh and Balagjar, which housed armed contingents of the Iraqi Communist Party as well as the PUK. A dirt path linked these two villages, which lay less than two miles apart. The center of Qara Dagh was three hours distant on foot; three miles to the east was the large village of Sayw Senan, where the peshmerga installed a field hospital that serviced much of the surrounding population.

During the early months of 1988 Iraqi intelligence cables were filled with references to Iranian pasdaran moving freely in and out of the Qara Dagh peshmerga camps. A force of Revolutionary Guards, two hundred strong, was reported to be in Balagjar on 25 January; by 6 March their number had risen to four hundred.[1] Eighty members of "the impostor Khomeini's guard" were said to be in Sayw Senan on 9 March, and they were heavily armed.

Sometime in February (the date is unclear) eight Iraqi aircraft carried out a chemical attack on Takiyeh and Balagjar. "Many bombs were dropped," said Omar, a Takiyeh man who witnessed the raid. "I don't know how many, maybe eight or nine. When they fell, there was a loud explosion, a little smoke, and it was like salt spread on the ground. People who touched it ended up with blisters on their skin. Animals that ate the infected grass died instantly." But there were no human fatalities; all the Takiyeh villagers had fled to temporary shelters in the fields because of the daily attacks. "In Balagjar, however, many of the pasdaran and PUK peshmerga, and many other people too, lost their sight for three days; the pasdaran moved out of Balagjar three or four days before the Qara Dagh Anfal began."[2]

The continual chemical attacks during the first Anfal, and now on Qara Dagh, seem to have had the effect that the Iraqi government intended. An Amn intelligence report dated 16 March, the day of the Halabja massacre, noted that a dozen teep (divisions) of the PUK had dispersed from their bases throughout southern Iraqi Kurdistan during the previous few days in fear of further chemical attacks. The next day another cable reported, "We have learned from our reliable secret sources that a few days ago the treacherous al-Hasek group [the Kurdistan Socialist Party] took possession of an estimated 1500 protective gas masks. They received these from the Zionist-Iranian regime."[3]

These precautions, however, were of little help, for Anfal came to Qara Dagh to the village of Sayw Senan on 22 March with one of the most lethal chemical attacks of the entire campaign. It was the day after Nowroz, the Kurdish New Year and the first day of spring, which the peshmerga celebrated by lighting bonfires and discharging their guns into the air.[4] Despite the news of the attacks on Sergalou-Bergalou and Halabja and despite the recently reported presence of Iranian pasdaran in their village, the people of Sayw Senan seemed to have a curious and ill-founded sense of immunity. "People were saying, 'It will be the same as in the past. They will attack us and we will defeat them," recalled one villager.[5] Although Sayw Senan was home to a PUK division, there were few peshmerga in the village at the time; most had been summoned to the defense of Sergalou-Bergalou. At the dinner hour on 22 March villagers heard the whistling sound of shells fired from a rajima and smelled the odor of apples. One shell landed in the courtyard of a house, instantly killing thirteen of the fourteen people in the family of a man called Mahdi Hadi Zorab. Only one son, a peshmerga, survived, by fleeing to the mountains. Six separate estimates given to HRW/Middle East by local villagers and PUK officials place the total number of dead in the chemical attack on Sayw Senan at between seventy-eight and eighty-seven.

"When we received the news of the attack from people fleeing, many men from our village went to Sayw Senan to help," said Omar, the farmer from Takiyeh. "We saw the bodies of those who had died inside the village. I helped bury sixty-seven with my own hands in Koshk village after we took them there on tractors. We laid them all in one big grave in the Haji Raqa graveyard, with their clothes on. Another fourteen bodies were buried in Asteli Serru village. They had died instantly. They were bleeding from the nose; it was as if their brains had exploded."

The following day, 23 March, the chemical rajima hit Dukan, another PUK base in a village of seventy houses.[6] On the night of 24 March, it targeted Ja'faran, a farming village of two hundred houses that had no PUK presence but housed the small headquarters that controlled KDP operations in the governorate of Kirkuk. According to two villagers, this was not the first time that Ja'faran had been attacked with gas. In May 1987, MIG fighter planes had dropped chemicals on the outskirts of the village; one man counted fourteen bombs, which produced red, green, and white smoke. Ja'faran was lucky, for neither of the chemical attacks killed anyone, even though hundreds of farm animals perished. The May 1987 bombing took place when most people were outside the village, and peshmerga paramedics from a nearby base provided emergency medical care.[7] The first attack scared people enough so that they rarely returned to their homes and even slept in temporary shelters in the fields. The rajima attack of March 1988 found the village deserted.

## THE EXODUS FROM QARA DAGH

By now the hillsides were alive with people fleeing Anfal, for the army's ground assault had begun on the afternoon of 23 March. Troops from the army's 43d Division, backed by jahsh and Amn emergency forces, converged from four directions on the area between Qara Dagh and Darbandikhan, driving the villagers from their homes like beaters flushing out game birds.[8] The general sense of panic was enhanced by the news, carried by word of mouth and over the peshmerga field radios, of the devastating poison gas attack on Sayw Senan.

The mass exodus was mainly to the north, where people hoped to find sanctuary in Suleimaniyeh or in one of the camps along the main highway. One group of villagers from Chami Smor smelled the nauseating odor of rotten apples carried on the wind that blew from the direction of Ja'faran. Another family, from the village of Masoyi, took refuge in a cave a few minutes walk from their home. They made the mistake of leaving a lantern burning when they fell asleep. In the night they were awakened by the throb of helicopters, which had evidently been attracted by the light, and the sound of explosions. Suddenly the cave was filled with the suffocating smell of sweet melons. The family stumbled outside and fled, carrying two children who had been overcome by the fumes. By good fortune they survived and hid on the slopes of Zerda Mountain. Three days later they watched as the army burned the village of Masoyi.[9]

What the regime intended to do with civilians caught in the second Anfal remains murky. By this time Istikhbarat had received orders from the Northern Bureau to set up special temporary camps to house those who were displaced. The roundups during the last week of March, however, were much less systematic than those in the later phases of the Anfal operation. Between Qara Dagh and Suleimaniyeh a physical obstacle loomed before the fleeing villagers—the 4,300-foot Glazerda Mountain. They found its slopes swarming with troops, jahsh, commandos in camouflage uniforms, and members of the emergency forces. Everywhere there were ragged people, tractor-drawn carts, and farm animals. Helicopters hovered overhead. There was tank and artillery fire from every side: "It was like a boiling pot," said a man from Ja'faran who survived.

Yet the army's attitude was ambiguous. In the first few days of the second Anfal, some villagers were told to make their own way to the city and the camps (although Amn later carried out house-to-house searches of Naser, Zarayen, and Suleimaniyeh to track these people down.) Others fled by back trails into the mountains as soon as they saw the soldiers and eluded the dragnet that way.

Word of the Qara Dagh exodus reached Suleimaniyeh, and the city relatives of some families made their way to Glazerda Mountain to fetch them.

In spite of the massive military presence, the survivors of the Sayw Senan attack heard rumors of a temporary amnesty and remained on the mountainside unmolested for several days in the rain. On the fifth day soldiers at the checkpoint on the Qara Dagh–Suleimaniyeh road began to arrest them. Some, especially the elderly and the infirm, were helped to escape by the jahsh in an early hint of the contradictory role that the Kurdish militia would play throughout Anfal. Between twenty-five and thirty people from Sayw Senan remained and were taken away at this point and never seen again.

The attitude of the troops seems to have changed with an incident that was witnessed by Omar, the farmer from Takiyeh:

When we arrived, the army had not yet started arresting people. The officers were asking us only if there were saboteurs in our area, and we told them that there were. Then something happened. A tractor cart laden with old wheat grain was blocking the road because it had a flat tire. The owner had abandoned it there. So a tank came and tried to move the cart out of the way. Instead, it overturned it completely and a lot of Kalashnikov rifles came tumbling out from underneath the grain, enough to arm a whole squad. Then the army put out a radio call to units in different areas to set up roadblocks, and they started to arrest people—men, women, children— even the people who had come from Suleimaniyeh.

I was twenty meters from the tank, behind the army lines. There were five hundred of us. We fled into the mountains; it was the jahsh who told us to run if we were able to. . . . My brother Khaled was still behind the tractor cart when the incident occurred. We were close to one another, close enough to call out to each other. He was arrested and taken to Suleimaniyeh.[10]

Khaled was never seen again; nor were three other young men from Takiyeh who were arrested with him. Omar escaped to the city and survived.

Those who were arrested at the checkpoint were loaded into military IFA trucks and driven to the emergency forces base in the Chwar Bagh (Four Orchards) quarter of Suleimaniyeh. There were thousands of prisoners there from the Qara Dagh region, and every day hundreds more arrived. The soldiers recorded their names and confiscated whatever valuables and identity documents they were carrying. One man from the village of Dolani Khwaru described being held at first on a nearby military base supervised by Istikhbarat officers before being transferred to the emergency forces headquarters.[11]

There the prisoners remained for as long as three or four weeks. Some groups of young men were blindfolded and separated from the rest, while others were taken out for a couple of days but later returned to their cells. The detainees were given almost nothing to eat, although it was possible to buy food from the guards. Although it was the army that had detained them, the villagers who passed through the Quwat al-Taware' base said that the daily interrogation sessions were conducted by Amn agents. "Are your sons peshmerga?" they were asked; "What peshmerga activity is there in your village?" The interrogators appeared to regard even children of grade-school age as potential "saboteurs." After an average of two or three weeks, buses and vans arrived to take the detainees away. They drove off west, in the direction of Kirkuk.

HRW/Middle East interviewed survivors from ten Qara Dagh villages affected by the second Anfal. In every case, they could name the young men of draft age who had disappeared after detention in the Suleimaniyeh emergency forces base. From Serko, nine never came back; four were lost from Takiyeh, and another four from nearby Balagjar; two from Berday, three from Koshk, two from Dolani Khwaru, three from Deiwana, nine from Mitsa Chweir, five from Chami Smor. Repeated across the whole nahya of Qara Dagh, with its eighty villages, one may reasonably assume that several hundred young men disappeared during the second Anfal.

The story, however, is more complex, as the experience of villages like Chami Smor suggests. The five young men of Chami Smor who vanished from Suleimaniyeh were army deserters who gave themselves up to the authorities as part of the general exodus. The village's location at the very edge of the high Qara Dagh Mountains, however, tempted others into what proved to be a terrible mistake. Although the majority fled north, two families struck out across the forbidding peaks toward the Germian plain, hoping to be safe in the town of Kalar, which would not be touched by Anfal. There were seventeen people in the group altogether, including men, women, and children. None of them ever reached their destination. Nor did hundreds of others who fled south with the same idea. It must be presumed that they were all seized by the Iraqi authorities.[12]

## FLIGHT TO SOUTHERN GERMIAN

There are striking regional differences in the pattern of mass disappearances during the Anfal campaign. After the first Anfal, adult men and teenage boys who were captured by the army disappeared, a pattern that was repeated in all areas. In several places, however, notably southern Germian, huge numbers of women and children were also taken away and never seen again. The criteria for this selection seem to have included not only one's place of birth but also the area in which one was captured. In many cases, but not all, the pattern of disappearances appears to have reflected the level of resistance that the troops encountered. If the peshmerga fought back strongly, women and children captured in the vicinity were more likely to disappear along with their husbands and fathers. This may be what is implied in an Amn letter, dated 2 August 1988, that requests information on whether those who had been given into its custody had surrendered in an area where combat had taken place.[13]

Women and children who fled north from Qara Dagh toward Suleimaniyeh and the camps were not harmed. Those who crossed into southern Germian vanished. Two men, three women and six children disappeared from the village of Aliawa. Forty-seven villagers from Masoyi, including many children and nursing infants, were captured near Kalar and never seen again.[14]

The population of Omer Qala, a village of twenty houses at the southern tip of Zerda Mountain, had fled en masse on hearing of the gas attack on nearby Sayw Senan. Taking with them only such essentials as money and blankets, together with their animal herds, they skirted the mountain and headed southwest in the direction of Germian. Although they were not peshmerga, all the men carried weapons, as is common practice among Iraqi Kurdish males; all but three of them were either army deserters or draft dodgers. The twenty families walked for several days, sleeping in caves or in the open air. They hoped to return to their homes when the government was driven out of their area, as had always happened in the past. This time was different. Reaching the village of Bakr Bayef on the eastern edge of Germian, they learned that the whole Qara Dagh area had fallen to government forces. All their villages had been razed; there were no homes to return to. Behind them, the army's chemical shells rained down on Zerda Mountain, and in the early morning of 1 April, the army captured the crucial peshmerga villages of Takiyeh and Balagjar.[15]

Far from outrunning the army, the people of Omer Qala had run straight into the jaws of the enemy. Germian was the next target of the Anfal, the villagers of Bakr Bayef told them, and its inhabitants had been given seventy-two hours to surrender. The twenty families gathered that night to decide on their next move. They concluded that there was no alternative but to surrender. After all, the more optimistic among them reasoned, walking toward government lines had offered protection in previous rounds of fighting between the army and the peshmerga. In the morning they headed in the direction of the government forces as far as the village of Boysana. Less than a mile farther on lay a place called Sheikh Tawil, which was to become perhaps the single most stubbornly defended target in the entire Anfal campaign.

In the course of the last week of March, the people of Sheikh Tawil, who belonged to the Tarkhani tribe, offered refuge to hundreds of fellow Kurds fleeing from Qara Dagh. Although they were from different tribes, said one man, "We sheltered them. We became one."[16] In the wake of the arrival of the panicked civilians came a fresh contingent of peshmerga, fleeing their rout on

Zerda Mountain. The triangle between the mountain, Sheikh Tawil, and Darbandikhan was by now a raging cauldron. There was constant shelling from all directions, some of it Iraqi and some from the Iranian side. No one could any longer tell the difference. Confusion reigned. From 3 to 5 April, the army and the peshmerga fought their first, inconclusive battle for control of Sheikh Tawil. In the general chaos that preceded the fighting, most of the civilians of Sheikh Tawil evacuated their homes and made for the highway that runs southwest from Darbandikhan Lake to Kalar. Seventy-nine would be captured and disappear. But this was not yet the third Anfal, the Germian Anfal. The horror of that was still to come.

The Omer Qala families watched as four old men of Boysana went forward to meet the troops, carrying white flags. "Bring your families," they were told. "Nothing will happen to them." Trusting the officer's promise, men, women, and children turned themselves in. They were promptly arrested. Those who remained behind later learned that the others had been taken to the army brigade headquarters in Kalar. That was the last that was ever heard of them.

The remaining Omer Qala villagers fled once more, walking until they reached the village of La'likhan on the main road. They found a huge crowd of people from many different villages milling around and a large fleet of trucks that the army had brought to collect them. Again the villagers conferred. Despite their terror, they again agreed that surrender was their only hope. Akram, an eighteen-year-old from Omer Qala, was still suspicious, however. Fearing punishment as a draft dodger, he hid himself in an empty barrel to observe the mass surrender. Five hundred gave themselves up. Only twenty, including Akram, stayed behind. Akram survived; he had no knowledge of where the others went. The five hundred disappeared.[17]

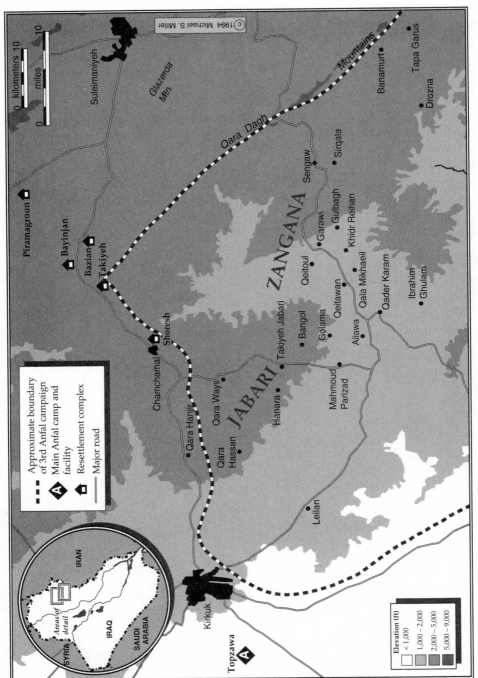

Third Anfal (North): 7–20 April 1988

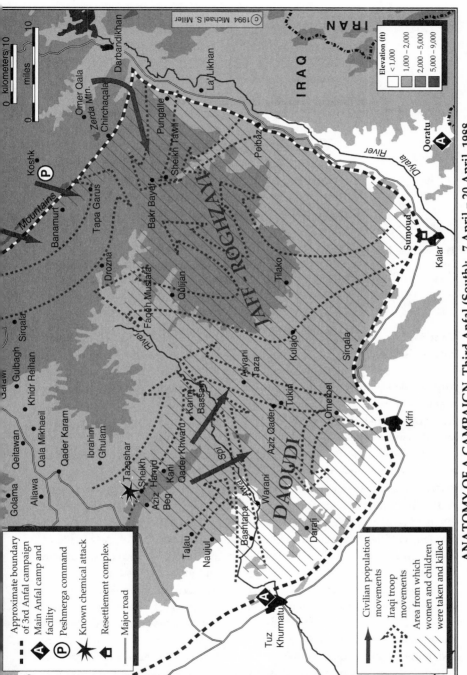

ANATOMY OF A CAMPAIGN  Third Anfal (South):  7 April – 20 April  1988

© 1994 Michael S. Miller

# 5

## THE THIRD ANFAL

### Germian, 7–20 April 1988

This was the first time people were taken away to be finished off.
—Farmer of Golama village, Qader Karam

Germian is in Sorani-speaking Iraqi Kurdistan bordering on Iraq's Arab heartland. It is bounded to the west by the highway between the oil-rich city of Kirkuk and the town of Tuz Khurmatu, to the north by the Kirkuk-Chamchamal road, to the east by the Qara Dagh Mountains, and to the south by a shallow triangle of towns—Kalar, Kifri, and Peibaz.[1] Almost exactly in the geographic center of Germian lies the nahya of Qader Karam, once a busy market center of ten thousand people.

By the end of the first week in April, the straggling remnants of defeated peshmerga from the Sergalou-Bergalou area had worked their way southward to take refuge in the PUK's strongholds in Germian. Villagers fleeing the second Anfal also headed south and west as well. Some fighters from the second malband took up fresh defensive positions in Sheikh Tawil, which had been flooded with the refugees from Qara Dagh. Others headed for the village of Bashtapa on the Aqa Su River, which bisects the Germian plain.[2] (Local people call it the Awa Spi, or "white river," for the milky color of its flow.)

Compared to the Jafati Valley and even to Qara Dagh, the terrain of Germian was much less favorable to guerrilla warfare. This was, however, the political center of the PUK revolt, and the sons of its farming villages made up the bulk of the organization's fighting forces. The villages were also filled with deserters and draft dodgers, and the peshmerga enjoyed an extensive and well-organized network of local support. "They used to come at night and get food from the villagers and give political lectures to the villagers as to why they should fight the government and why they should not join the jahsh," said a woman from the village of Sheikh Hamid, which lay close to the important PUK stronghold at Tazashar.[3] "The peshmerga had ordered each family to buy a weapon," added a man from the nearby settlement of Kani Qader Khwaru. "It was like a law, and the people agreed with this because they saw it was necessary. The armed civilians would join the peshmerga in the defense of their villages. They were referred to as the 'backing force.' All the villages had this type of civil defense unit."[4]

Yet there was little the peshmerga could do to withstand the ferocious assault of the Iraqi army. This was a more conventional war, though of a grossly one-sided kind. For more than a week the area was enveloped in wave after wave of assaults by infantry, armored divisions, artillery, air force, and jahsh. The people of Germian were persuaded to surrender by the near impossibility of escape; never before had they seen such overwhelming concentrations of troops and militia. The army did not leave the area until all living things had been captured, and they pursued any fleeing villagers by helicopter and on foot into the mountains and into the towns and cities.[5]

The Iraqi army mercilessly exploited the PUK's weaknesses in Germian. There were no strongly fortified bases there—no Bergalou, no Yakhsamar, no heavy weaponry. The few peshmerga villages with a fixed troop detachment, or teep, were easily cut off from their supply lines. Deprived of reinforcements, the isolated fighters could either flee or fight until they ran out of ammunition. Peshmerga arriving from the areas of the first and second Anfals were exhausted, and there was a general collapse of morale in the wake of the chemical attacks on the Jafati Valley, Qara Dagh, and Halabja. The Iraqi regime seemed to have found poison gas much less necessary during the Germian campaign, although it did come into play against at least one troublesome target.[6] Some beleaguered peshmerga strongholds held out for as long as five days, but in most places the resistance crumbled quickly.

It is possible to reconstruct the battle plan of the Iraqi army in Germian in some detail, thanks to a sequence of thirty-three "secret and urgent" military intelligence cables that give an hour-by-hour update of conditions on the battlefield.[7] These documents depict a series of enormous pincer movements, with troop columns converging from at least eight points on the perimeter of Germian, encircling peshmerga targets, and channeling the fleeing civilian population toward designated collection points by blocking off all other avenues of escape (see map). The cables describe 120 villages "stormed and demolished" or "burned and destroyed." Almost none of these villages is described as a military target. In only a handful of cases is there any report of resistance; in the rare cases where a village was searched, the soldiers found nothing more incriminating than "pictures of saboteurs and the charlatan Khomeini."[8]

The intent of the operation could not be more clear—to wipe out all vestiges of human settlement; several of the Istikhbarat field reports make this explicit. "Since most of the villages were not marked on the map, all the villages that the convoy passed through must have been destroyed and burned," reports the Kalar column on 13 April. The Pungalle column returned to base on 20 April, "after completing the demolition of all the villages within its sector."[9] No matter how thorough, a single pass was not enough; in mid-August the troops returned to "burn and remove all remaining signs of life."[10] In one case after another, the names of the villages eliminated correspond to the site of mass disappearances described to HRW/Middle East by survivors.

## THE PLAN OF CAMPAIGN: (1) TUZ KHURMATU

Early on the morning of 7 April the first troops and jahsh battalions moved out from their base in Tuz Khurmatu at the southwestern corner of Germian. Over the next two days, other units left Kirkuk, Leilan, Chamchamal, and Sengaw, all converging from different directions on the town of Qader Karam. The Tuz Khurmatu column quickly divided into three task forces. One headed southeast from the town of Naujul toward the Awa Spi River. A second, larger task force moved east along the sandy river valley. Preceded by airstrikes, it dealt quickly with the resistance from the second malband survivors at Bashtapa and quickly reported having wiped out seventeen villages at the cost of just eleven dead, eight of them jahsh.[11]

Two of these villages were Upper and Lower Warani, a new fallback position for the peshmerga in Bashtapa. The Waranis had suffered grievously in the past, having been burned down three times since 1963. The twin villages also provided a bitter illustration of the effects of Ali Hassan al-Majid's demand for aerial and artillery bombardment designed to "kill the largest number of persons present in . . . prohibited zones."[12]

In the months preceding Anfal, there were three fatal attacks by government helicopters. One killed an old man resting in his fields at harvest time; another, a fifteen-year-old girl and her mother who were fetching water from the river; another, two young shepherd boys, brothers, aged eight and eleven.

But Anfal was different. The troops arrived at breakfast time, set fire to the houses, killed all the farm animals, and rounded up many of the villagers. Some villagers managed to flee into the hills, where they remained for several days. They realized that they were encircled on three sides and had no alternative but to head south toward the highway, where they surrendered to a jahsh unit commanded by a mustashar named Adnan Jabari. It was the first day of Ramadan, the Muslim month of fasting, one elderly man remembered, 17 April. Trucks were waiting to take them away, and many were never seen again. The surviving villagers later made a list of 102 people from Warani who had disappeared.[13] As with all the villages in the Daoudi tribal area, those who vanished included large numbers of women and children.

Meanwhile, the third Tuz Khurmatu task force launched a ferocious attack on the PUK base in Tazashar, some twelve miles due north of the Awa Spi River. Tazashar was a perfect example of the dilemma that the PUK faced in Germian. A small village of only about twenty households, it had assumed a certain strategic importance because of its location on an all-weather road close to the main Tuz Khurmatu–Qader Karam highway. A small contingent of twenty to twenty-five peshmerga dug in to fight the army forces that were advancing southward from the main road. The army brought in heavy weapons and tanks; airplanes and helicopters lent aerial support. The outnumbered and outgunned peshmerga put up a spirited defense from 8 A.M. until the early afternoon of 9 April. Yet in a valley surrounded by low hills, they were at a huge disadvantage; meeting resistance, it was a simple matter for the army to withdraw temporarily and send troops around behind Tazashar to encircle it. The soldiers seized control of the surrounding hilltops and destroyed three other villages that lay in their path—Upper and Lower Kani Qader and Sheikh Hamid.

Several witnesses from neighboring villages say that the army resorted to chemical weapons in Tazashar. One man in Kani Qader Khwaru, four miles away, told HRW/Middle East that he intercepted radio communications from the officer in command saying that gas was the only way to dislodge the resistance.[14] This witness then saw British-supplied Hawker Hunter aircraft bombing Tazashar, sending up billowing clouds of white smoke. An hour later the army entered the village. All its defenders died.

Aisha, a pregnant twenty-year-old woman from Sheikh Hamid, watched the attack from her family's hilltop wheat field. She did not realize at first that chemicals were involved, since the Iraqi air force had bombed the area so often in the past. When she came down from the hillside that evening, she saw the bodies of twenty-five peshmerga. "It was then that I found out they had used chemical weapons because I also saw a lot of dead goats and cows and birds." On the night of 10 April, Istikhbarat in Tuz Khurmatu cabled Eastern Region headquarters that it had removed "the bodies of fifteen subversives who were buried near the Tuz Military Sector Command; before burial they were photographed, and the film will be sent in a further dispatch."[15] Having dealt with Tazashar, the column proceeded south, eliminating another half dozen villages before finally wiping out the last peshmerga resistance at Karim Bassam and so reaching the north bank of the Awa Spi River.

Like everyone else from Sheikh Hamid, Aisha fled. As she was leaving the area, she encountered a mustashar, a man by the name of Sheikh Ahmad Barzinji, who had come in search of his own relatives. She asked him what had happened. "I don't know," the mustashar replied. "You should just surrender to the army. This is the best thing you can do. I cannot do anything; even my relatives have been killed."

Aisha took her children and made for the hills. She could not find her husband. With the mustashar's words in mind, she first struck out northward in the direction of Qader Karam to surrender. The army had in any case closed off all other avenues of escape. On the way, however, she changed her mind and decided instead to hide out in a cave with a group of fellow villagers. The mountainsides south of Qader Karam were covered with clusters of refugees. They hid in the cave for three days. On the second, Aisha gave birth to her baby. She was hungry and too weak to nurse and had no covering to protect her child against the cold night air. On the third day, she ventured out in search of food, leaving her day-old baby in the cave.

As soon as she left the safety of her cave, however, Aisha was spotted by a jahsh patrol tracking down survivors. She was surprised at how kind they seemed; they promised they would take her to the mustashar, who would arrange for her to be amnestied. They found their commander on the outskirts of Qader Karam. It turned out to be Sheikh Ahmad Barzinji, the same man she had encountered three days earlier in the rubble of her village.

> He took me and promised me that he would help me, and he put me in a nearby school. I felt safe in the school, and he gave me some food. But after a few hours they brought a lot of people into the school. A lot of villagers were coming in to surrender; they were encouraged to do so by Sheikh Ahmad's jahsh. The army separated the men from the women, handcuffed all the men and put them in a separate room. When the army took charge, they pushed the jahsh aside. Sheikh Ahmad disappeared, and I did not see him again. Then the soldiers took all the men and put them into military buses. Soon after that, they began to do the same thing to the women and children.[16]

Aisha's story remains one of the strangest of the Anfal campaign; in an apparently arbitrary act of clemency, an army officer eventually allowed her to leave the Qader Karam school and go to Suleimaniyeh. Aisha not only survived Anfal, but she was even reunited in the end with the baby she had left behind in the cave. Most people from her area were less fortunate—if that is the word to use—since Aisha herself lost her husband, three brothers, and twelve other members of her family. They were among a group of at least eighty men from Sheikh Hamid who surrendered to the mustashar and were never seen again. From nearby Karim Bassam, at least twenty-five people disappeared; from Aziz Beg, a village between Tazashar and Talau, the list ran to ninety-two, many of them women and children.

## THE PLAN OF CAMPAIGN:
## (2) QADER KARAM AND NORTHERN GERMIAN

Meanwhile, other army units were pursuing a similar campaign of terror north of Qader Karam under the direction of Special Forces Brig. Gen. (in Arabic, *'Amid*) Bareq Abdullah al-Haj Hunta, who appears to have been the overall commander of the third Anfal operation in Germian.[17] Columns moving in from the west reported an uneventful advance—hardly surprising, since they were following the main Kirkuk-Chamchamal highway through an area that had largely been destroyed and depopulated during the spring 1987 campaign. They reached Qader Karam rapidly, by the late afternoon of 10 April. The following morning a column of jahsh under Sayed Jabari set out from the nahya to take care of the single isolated village of Ibrahim Ghulam in the rocky hills south of Qader Karam.[18] The population had already fled after hearing of the fighting nearby, but they straggled down from their hiding places after a few days to surrender. HRW/Middle East was given a list of the names of fifty-one men from Ibrahim Ghulam who were never seen again.[19]

Ibrahim Ghulam was a village belonging to the Zangana tribe, and the Zangana and the neighboring Jabari were the victims of some of the worst ravages of the third Anfal.[20] In April 1988, the Zangana inhabited dozens of villages to the east of Qader Karam; the villages of the Jabari dotted the low mountains to the north. Columns of troops operating out of bases in Sengaw and Chamchamal wiped out all of them. Some of the Jabari villages did manage to escape northward through a temporary breach that the peshmerga had opened on the Kirkuk-Chamchamal road. Others tried but failed to outrun the oncoming army troops. At the time of the third Anfal the inhabitants of Taeberz, a tiny Jabari hamlet on the paved road a half hour west of Qader Karam, were trying to rebuild the homes that the army had burned down the previous summer. Hearing that waves of troops were moving toward them in a huge pincer movement from Kirkuk and Chamchamal, they fled at dawn but were only two hours from the village when the army and jahsh tracked them down. A convoy of army IFA trucks was waiting for them on the paved road. It took them to Leilan, a nahya a little to the south of Kirkuk.

Other Jabari hamlets were deserted by the time the troops arrived. Such was the case of Mahmoud Parizad, another small settlement close to the main road and only a half hour's drive from both Qader Karam and Kirkuk. In many ways Mahmoud Parizad was typical of the whole Jabari area: twenty-five houses of mud or cement blocks, each with its own bomb shelter; neither electricity nor running water; a small mosque, as well as a schoolhouse that had been closed down and its government teacher withdrawn when the area fell under peshmerga control in the mid-1980s.

When Anfal reached Mahmoud Parizad on 11 April, the army met modest resistance from the peshmerga in two neighboring villages, and the people of Mahmoud Parizad fled to the mountains to escape the incoming artillery fire. They were joined there by a steady stream of refugees from other Jabari villages, perhaps a thousand in all. Word had spread rapidly of the previous day's chemical attack on Tazashar, and the women and children decided to surrender to the army; their menfolk, most of them active peshmerga, remained in hiding for another two days.

At noon the women and children returned to their village as a helicopter hovered overhead and shellfire sounded all around. The army had already taken Mahmoud Parizad and with them was a small contingent of jahsh. The first houses were already in flames. The soldiers stripped the villagers of whatever possessions they had taken with them to the hills. Before torching the houses, the troops also looted whatever they could lay their hands on, even down to small domestic animals like rabbits and pigeons. Then they bundled the villagers into a line of waiting IFAS and drove off north in the direction of Chamchamal, away from the flames that now engulfed Mahmoud Parizad.

A few Jabari villagers did manage to escape the advancing troops, sometimes with the help of advance warning from their fellow Kurds in the jahsh. This happened, for example, in Hanara, which lay farther north toward Chamchamal, and was linked by a rough mountain path to the local PUK headquarters at Takiyeh Jabari. There had been fighting in the vicinity for years, and some villagers had died in bombing raids. Whenever the injured were taken to the hospital, said one who survived, the doctors told them, "You deserve to be treated like this because you are traitors and work with the Iranians." The people of Hanara had grown accustomed to a routine of spending their days in the hills with their flocks, hiding when necessary in their air-raid shelters and returning to their homes only at night to bake bread.

When Anfal came to Hanara—with helicopters and fighter planes in the morning and ground troops in the evening—only a few peshmerga combatants were present. The other villagers took the risk of making contact with the jahsh units that they spotted nearby and pleaded with them not to destroy Hanara. These jahsh did not take them into custody but instead urged everyone to flee. That night, the villagers came down from the hills to find nothing but smoldering rubble. Everything had been bulldozed, including the mosque. Under cover of darkness, the villagers set out on foot and on tractors for the town of Leilan. "I turned off my tractor's lights," one man from Hanara remembered. "While I was driving to Leilan, it was all dark, but I could see my village burning. I cried; I knew it was the end of everything."[21]

In Leilan, the fleeing residents of Hanara met up with refugees from two other villages. Townspeople of Leilan, at great personal risk, sheltered all of them until morning. From there, relatives succeeded in spiriting away many of the villagers, taking them to Kirkuk, where they hoped to find anonymity among the crowds. Some also managed to vanish into the crowds of displaced Kurds in the large new resettlement camp of Shoresh, outside the town of Chamchamal, which at this point was little more than an open field. There they survived. As a result, Hanara suffered proportionately less than many Jabari villages from the Anfal. According to survivors, twenty-seven people from a single family disappeared from Golama; nearby Bangol lost forty-one.[22] Hanara's disappeared numbered only seventeen—comprising the *Imam* of the local mosque and sixteen teenage boys who surrendered to an especially notorious mustashar named Tahsin Shaweis, whose empty promise of amnesty was repeated on a wide scale in the Qader Karam area. One survivor told HRW/Middle East:

> [The mustashar] told the villagers that there was a general amnesty, and he gave his word of honor that the youths would be protected. He would help them reach a safe place if one could be found. Otherwise, they should surrender and they would be protected by the amnesty. A man brought the sixteen young men, all relatives of his, to the jahsh leader. None was a peshmerga. After two or three months, the father went back to Tahsin to ask what had happened to the boys. Tahsin told him that Ali Hassan al-Majid had talked to all the mustashars and told them that no one should ask about the fate of those who had disappeared.[23]

The Zangana tribal villages to the east fared even worse. A large army task force, including scores of tanks, set out from the nahya of Sengaw and moved west with the goal of subduing an important PUK base in the Gulbagh Valley, less than ten miles east of Qader Karam. It took the army a whole day to crush the resistance in this area, although it was clear that the peshmerga were fighting against impossible odds. Three of them died in Qeitoul; another seven fell in Garawi. The PUK's 59th teep, together with survivors from the 55th teep in Qara Dagh, entrenched themselves in Upper and Lower Gulbagh on 10 April and held off the troops until nightfall. Two more peshmerga were martyred there, and by 8:00 P.M. the survivors realized that their position was hopeless and withdrew to the south.[24]

The people of Qeitawan, a village of a hundred mud houses on the Baserra River, were alerted to the arrival of Anfal by the sound of government aircraft bombing the nearby village of Garawi. Hoisting the small children onto their shoulders, with only the clothes they wore, they fled. The army dragnet caught up with them before nightfall. "We were rich," said an old woman who survived. "We had fruit, gardens, all was looted. They took our tractors, water pipes, even the lantern we used to light the rooms when it was dark."[25] Deciding that they had no alternative, her four sons, aged thirty-five to forty-one, made their way to Aliawa, an old destroyed village on the outskirts of Qader Karam, where they gave themselves up to a mustashar by the name of Sheikh Mu'tassem Ramadan, of the Barzinji tribe.[26] "But Mu'tassem handed them all over to the government," and she never saw them again.

The people of nearby Qeitoul, by contrast, had taken to the hills a full two weeks before Anfal reached them, as soon as they heard news of the fall of the Sergalou-Bergalou PUK headquarters on 19 March. There were no peshmerga nearby at the time, and they felt unprotected. From their hiding places above the village they saw the soldiers entering Qeitoul, preceded by jahsh units and helicopters providing air support. After a brief debate they decided to make for the town of Chamchamal, several hours walk to the north. They were captured in the mountains by troops under the command of Brigadier General Bareq. The army registered their names and sent them off in two groups of trucks. One headed east toward Suleimaniyeh; the other west, in the direction of Kirkuk. Many never returned.

Other villagers nearby were caught unawares in their homes by the army's lightning attack. This happened, for instance, in Qirtsa, a remote village of one hundred houses on a dirt road beyond Qeitoul. Qirtsa was a peaceful place— "We were living naturally, no peshmerga, no government," remembered one resident—and the attack, early in the morning, found the villagers still in bed. Only a handful managed to reach the safety of the mountains. Bareq himself was in personal command of the troops that came that morning, rounding up all the village men on the spot and handcuffing their hands behind their backs. The men were trucked away first. Then another army IFA departed loaded with the villagers' livestock. Finally the women, children, and elderly were driven off, but only after the soldiers had looted their homes. As they waited for the IFAS and vans that would take them away, the women watched the village set afire and then leveled with bulldozers. Sixty people disappeared from Qirtsa, including every male under the age of forty and many of the women. Another sixty vanished from neighboring Qeitoul. "I am not sorry for myself but for the young women," a female survivor of Qirtsa told HRW/Middle East. "We do not know what happened to them. They were so beautiful. If they were guilty, of what? Why? What had they done wrong?"[27]

They had done nothing wrong, of course. They were simply Kurds living in the wrong place at the wrong time. But their fate may shed important light on one of the great enigmas of the Anfal campaign. Throughout Iraqi Kurdistan, although women and children vanished in certain clearly defined areas,[28] adult males who were captured disappeared en masse—as the standing orders of June 1987 demanded. In some cases, such as the Gulbagh Valley, these mass disappearances occurred in areas where the troops had encountered significant peshmerga resistance.

## THE PLAN OF CAMPAIGN: (3) SENGAW AND SOUTHERN GERMIAN

Some peshmerga had managed to escape to the north, hiding out in the hills above the Kirkuk-Chamchamal road. Others were driven in the opposite direction, however, as army units swept methodically southward from the nahya of Sengaw to the village of Drozna, near the source of the Awa Spi River. According to witnesses, close to twenty villages were overrun and destroyed in this one small area: the PUK bases at Darawar and Banamurt (from which large numbers of people reportedly disappeared); a nearby cluster of villages including Upper and Lower Hassan Kanosh, Tapa Arab, Kareza, Dobirya, and three adjacent hamlets, each called Penj Angusht[29]; and a little farther to the east, Hanjira, Segumatan, Kelabarza, Darzila, Kalaga, and Darbarou.[30] The hundreds of villagers captured in this sector were taken to Chamchamal; the nahya of Sengaw would have been closer, but it had been destroyed during the campaigns of 1987. The surviving peshmerga were now driven hard up against the southern edge of the Qara Dagh Mountains, where the second Anfal had been fought to such devastating effect. This confined area, where the peshmerga now also had to contend with other troop units coming from the south, was one of the bloodiest cockpits of the Anfal campaign.

At the southernmost extreme of Germian, where it borders on the Arabized area of Diyala, the first column of troops had set out from the town of Kifri at 6:30 A.M. on 9 April. Later that same morning, other columns departed from their bases at Kalar, Peibaz, and Pungalle. Their basic strategy was the same as in northern Germian: to launch a huge enveloping movement from several directions at once; to carry out mass arrests of all the civilians they encountered; to destroy their villages; to funnel escaping villagers toward the main road or to prearranged collection points; and to channel the surviving peshmerga into confined areas from which there was no escape. The first step, however, was to annihilate known PUK strongholds.

The initial target of the Kifri column, under the command of a Brigadier General Sami of the First Corps, was the large village of Omerbel, home to the tribe of the same name.[31] There had been a PUK base on the outskirts of Omerbel for several years, and a hundred fighters were on hand when the army attack began. This was a battle-hardened peshmerga force, one that had managed to repel a major army offensive the previous April. Although the assault force had included tanks and armored personnel carriers, it had been forced to retreat after taking heavy casualties, and its failure was emblematic of the regime's inability to achieve its goals during the spring 1987 campaign.

Sami's force reached Omerbel by midmorning and immediately encountered fierce resistance from peshmerga using the heavy weapons that they had captured a year earlier. According to the PUK commander who directed the battle, the siege lasted for two whole days, as borne out by the terse battlefield reports from Istikhbarat.[32] The army responded, however, as it had in Tazashar, by sending advance units on a flanking mission to destroy the villages that lay immediately beyond the target. "1015 hrs: village of Chwar Sheikh stormed and demolished," a cable of 10 April reported. (Chwar Sheikh was three miles to the north.) Omerbel was now under siege on all sides, and by nightfall the peshmerga, realizing that further resistance was useless, had withdrawn. The civilian population had already fled, but they were quickly surrounded by troops in the mountains, arrested, and trucked away.

The main column continued northward, mopping up a smaller PUK base at Tukin and then recording a steady sequence of another twenty villages "destroyed and burned" over the course of the next week, as far north as the Awa Spi River. One of these was Aliyani Taza (New Aliyan), a small village of twenty homes, where a retreating band of PUK fighters had taken up defensive positions.[33] "Muhammad," a thirty-two-year-old member of the peshmerga backing force, was at home when the troops arrived on the morning of 13 April. "The government was advancing from all directions, so it was impossible for us to stay. We headed for Mil Qasem village. We took our wives and children and put them in tractor carts, and we took the animals, and we put all our belongings on the carts. We thought that the army was going to put us in tents at the division base [firqa] on the other side of the [Diyala] river. That is what we heard as we were leaving. The peshmerga didn't stay; they dispersed and went to the mountains."[34]

It took Muhammad and his family three days to reach Mil Qasem, normally a journey of less than two hours. From there the soldiers led them to the main road and ordered them to drive under armed guard to the fort at Qoratu, headquarters of the army's 21st Infantry Division. The fort would be the first stop in Muhammad's journey through the bureaucracy of Anfal.

Meanwhile, on 11 April, a secondary task force under the command of Capt. Abed Awad of the 417th Infantry Regiment had split off temporarily to take care of Daraji, an outlying village a few miles to the west of Omerbel. "The inhabitants who surrendered to the column were evacuated to a specially prepared camp close to the 21st Infantry Division," that evening's intelligence report noted—a rare official comment on the removal and mass detention of civilians and an explicit reference to the fort at Qoratu.[35]

After pitching camp at Daraji that night, Captain Awad's task force retraced its steps the next morning to rejoin the main column. On the way, it paused to burn Belaga al-Kubra and Belaga al-Sughra, which like Daraji were villages of the Daoudi tribe. Affection for the peshmerga ran deep there, according to Rashad, a farmer in his early sixties: "They were all our sons and daughters, all our brothers, all our people. We loved them." Rashad was at home when the bombing and shelling began at lunchtime. With the rest of the village, he and his wife, Fekri, fled to the hills, but the aircraft pursued them; Fekri was hit by gunfire and killed. Those who survived the air attack were soon hunted down by a contingent of jahsh headed by two mustashars from Kifri, Sheikh Karim and Sa'id Jaff, and trucked away—presumably also to the specially prepared camp at Qoratu, the first step in a journey that would end in their deaths. Among the villagers who disappeared from Belaga al-Kubra that day were Rashad's son Akbar, three nephews, two nieces, and their six young children, all aged one to seven.[36] Such a heavy proportion of women and children among the disappeared was characteristic of Anfal in the Daoudi tribal area.

The first targets of the army units that left Kalar on the morning of 9 April, commanded by Major Munther Ibrahim Yasin, were the twin villages of Upper and Lower Tilako, where part of the shattered first malband of the PUK had installed itself after the rout in Qara Dagh.[37] The troops' advance seems to have been relatively painless, and by the early morning of 11 April, both Tilakos were destroyed after a short fire fight that left just four soldiers wounded. This area, inhabited by the Roghzayi branch of the Jaff tribe, was poorly mapped, and helicopters were needed to airlift troops into zones that were inaccessible by road. Major Yasin's forces passed through several villages whose existence was not even officially recorded. They destroyed them all, regardless.

Few, if any, Kurdish tribal groups were worse hit by Anfal than the Jaff-Roghzayi. One of a half dozen subdivisions of the Jaff, the Roghzayi used to inhabit more than one hundred villages in this area. All of them were wiped out during Anfal. The head of the Roghzayi, an elderly man named Mahmoud Tawfiq Muhammad (b. 1927), lived in Barawa, a village tucked away in a narrow plain at the southeastern tip of Germian, close to the Qara Dagh Mountains and ringed by important PUK bases. Although Barawa fell within the third Anfal theater, its inhabitants were terrified into flight by the chemical attacks that took place at the end of March during the second Anfal.

Mahmoud was a prosperous man, and twenty-four members of his immediate family lived in a large, sprawling house surrounded by vineyards and rich gardens where they grew apples, figs, and pomegranates. Artillery fire and aerial bombing had become part of daily life, and it took chemical weapons to destroy their morale. After the attacks on Sayw Senan and other targets in Qara Dagh at the end of March, the people of Barawa held an urgent meeting. Even though the PUK was present in the village, Mahmoud remembered, "We decided to surrender to the government, the father of the people, since we were only poor farmers with no relations to any political party. Instead, they did what they did." His son added, "When we went to them, the government captured us, looted everything, and Anfalized us. Nothing remained."[38]

The people of Barawa abandoned their homes and their property and headed for another Roghzayi settlement called Kulajo, a place of forty or fifty households that lay several days' walk away, over the mountains to the southwest. Although the third Anfal had not yet officially begun, the hills were already full of soldiers. At each checkpoint, the villagers explained that they were making for the government lines in order to surrender. The troops allowed them to pass unhindered and eventually they reached Kulajo, where they spent two nights safely. On the third day they saw that the village where they had sought refuge was surrounded.

According to army intelligence reports, the Kalar task force arrived at Kulajo at 11:15 on the morning of 13 April. Just before the troops got there, they encountered a brief flurry of resistance on their right flank, from a place called Tapa Sawz. A cable recounts: "This village was crushed and destroyed, and four rifles were confiscated."[39] Taymour Abdullah Ahmad, a boy of twelve at the time of Anfal, had lived in Kulajo since he was three.[40] His father, a wheat farmer, owned a little land there and like all the men was a member of the village's "backing force." Taymour was the eldest of four siblings. Since the family's move from nearby Hawara Berza, three daughters were born. Unlike their kinfolk fleeing from other villages in the area, Taymour told HRW/Middle East, the people of Kulajo had stayed in their homes until the last moment. Then, seeing the tanks and heavy artillery advancing from Tilako, an hour's walk across the plain, each family ran up a white flag from its roof and took flight. The men, including Taymour's father, concealed their weapons in village wells and other hiding places. Taymour helped his parents to cram a few household possessions on their rickety tractor-drawn cart. Assuming that they would return to their homes before too long, they planned to take temporary refuge in the large new camp of Sumoud, outside Kalar, where some relatives had been relocated as a result of the village clearance campaign of the previous spring. The people of Kulajo and the fugitives from Barawa, however, found that the army had left only a single exit route open, a "funnel," as it were, that directed them south toward the village of Melistura, close to the main Kifri-Kalar highway.[41] The journey to Melistura took two hours by tractor; they moved slowly because the vehicle was so heavily laden.

Having destroyed Kulajo, the troops pressed on to the north, followed by a line of bulldozers and empty IFA trucks. They soon reached Hawara Berza,

Taymour's birthplace, and it, too, is recorded on the daily intelligence report as having been "burned and demolished."[42] The next tiny hamlet, Kona Kotr, was abandoned by the time the army arrived. All six of its families had already fled, but they ran into an army patrol in the mountains, and they also were ordered to proceed to Melistura. An officer promised that no one would be harmed and that they would all be rehoused in a new camp soon to be built. As it turned out, however, thirty-four people were to disappear from Kona Kotr's six households, a pattern that was repeated across the Jaff-Roghzayi area. Mahmoud Tawfiq Muhammad of Barawa, the elderly tribal head, lost thirty-seven members of his extended family from Barawa village, including his two wives and ten children, aged two to fifteen, as well as his son and daughter-in-law and their six small children. Another twenty-five relatives disappeared from neighboring Tapa Garus village, a peshmerga base. More than half of them were children.[43]

On 15 April, in heavy rain, the troops of the Kalar column reached the northernmost limit of their operations, storming and burning Qulijan, a village close to the Awa Spi River. One family fleeing Qulijan ran into a contingent of jahsh in the hills, headed by a local mustashar named Fatah Karim Beg. "Your time is over," he told them. "This is the time of the government."[44] They, too, were left with no option but to head south toward the main highway.

The displaced villagers spent two days in Melistura, unable to go any farther, sleeping in the open fields. The crowds swelled until it was impossible to count them. "It was like the Day of Judgment," recalled one man from Kona Kotr who reached Melistura safely with his family and his farm animals. On the third day the soldiers instructed everyone to move on. Army trucks were brought in from the military base at Kalar, and those who had their own means of transport were ordered to follow. This rough caravan crossed the Diyala River into a stony, arid area that had been forcibly Arabized in 1975 and then laid waste in the border clearances of the late 1970s and the first years of the Iran-Iraq War. Its destination was the fort at Qoratu, headquarters of the Iraqi army's 21st Infantry Division and the specially prepared camp that had been set up under Istikhbarat control in accordance with the 15 March order of the Ba'ath Party's Northern Bureau Command.[45]

By about 18 or 19 April, ten days into the third Anfal, the Kifri and Kalar columns had completed their missions. All resistance between the Kalar-Kifri highway and the Awa Spi River had been crushed. Not a stone of any village remained standing. A little way to the east, the Peibaz and Pungalle forces were able to report similar success. The Peibaz task force, commanded by Lt. Col. Muhammad Nazem Hassan, took a couple of days to subdue PUK forces in the villages of Sofi Rahim and Ali Wasman, and there were complaints that an unnamed mustashar in charge of the 75th National Defense Battalion had fled the field. Once these problems were surmounted, however, the rest of the expedition proved uneventful, and after razing another fourteen villages the task force returned to base.

More serious obstacles lay in the path of the troops operating out of Pungalle, a village eight miles south of the important Darbandikhan dam. On its first day, the task force ran into stiff resistance from a peshmerga unit defending the village of Sheikh Tawil, already the scene of a fierce battle a few days earlier. The army commander, Lt. Col. Salman Abd-al-Hassan of the 1st Commando Regiment of the 17th Division, was wounded in an early exchange of fire, and without him the chain of command fell apart. One of the supporting jahsh battalions, the 131st, retreated in disarray; part of the army force, including another officer, was cut off and pinned down by peshmerga fire. The remainder pulled back two miles and called in reinforcements from the 21st Division at Qoratu.

Even with the help of air strikes, tanks, missile-firing helicopters, and heavy artillery, it took the army five full days to subdue the fifty peshmerga in Sheikh Tawil. Yet on the night of 13 April the village's defenders received the order to withdraw.[46] At 2:30 the next afternoon, the new commanding officer of the army task force, a Major Salem, reported to headquarters that Sheikh Tawil and the neighboring village of Bustana had both been "occupied and destroyed." Fifty-three families were duly reported to have "returned to the national ranks."[47]

With this, the troops were free to drive deeper into an area that had been partly abandoned two weeks earlier by the large group of villagers headed by Mahmoud Tawfiq Muhammad, tribal chief of the Jaff-Roghzayi. The PUK, along with smaller contingents of peshmerga from the Iraqi Communist Party and the Islamic Movement, were pinned back into their last redoubts in Germian—the string of bases along the western flank of the 5,900-foot Zerda Mountain. This area had already been pounded from the east during the second Anfal. Now it was under siege by troops advancing from the west and by helicopter-borne Special Forces. It was impossible for the peshmerga to resist any longer. The last PUK defensive base at Zerda Likaw fell quickly. Thousands of villagers flocked to the village of Faqeh Mustafa, where they were rounded up by troops and jahsh and trucked away. Others made the arduous trek north along the spine of the Qara Dagh Mountains, accompanied by the last of the peshmerga survivors. On the morning of 20 April the Pungalle task force returned to base, reporting that all its objectives had been accomplished.[48]

## THE COLLECTION POINTS

These people are heading toward death. They cannot take money or gold with them.
                            —Iraqi army officer during the looting of a village

Villages and small towns like Melistura, Faqeh Mustafa, and Maidan in the south of Germian, and Aliawa and Leilan in the north, were the first collection centers through which fleeing civilians were funneled. In some cases their places of origin were noted at this stage, and their identity documents given a cursory examination. After their initial capture, the vast bureaucratic machinery of specialized party, police, and intelligence agencies would be brought to bear on the problem of the Kurdish "saboteurs." At this early stage of the operation, almost all those in evidence on the government side were either regular army troops or members of the jahsh militia. It would be inaccurate to describe the initial collection points as improvised, since the Kurds were clearly directed toward them in a coherent fashion. At the same time, collection centers like Aliawa and Melistura showed real signs of weakness—the only point at which the efficiency of the Anfal campaign seemed to break down. In part this was undoubtedly because even the Iraqi army's considerable resources had been stretched in dealing with such huge numbers of prisoners. It also reflected the deeply ambiguous role that would be played in the roundups by the jahsh. (For a description of the jahsh, see chapter 1.)

For the villagers swept up in the northern Germian campaign, there were at least four principal collection centers: Leilan, Aliawa, Qader Karam, and Chamchamal. Many captives were processed through two and sometimes three of these centers in succession.

Leilan, a small nahya to the southeast of Kirkuk, appears to have lacked any sophisticated infrastructure for handling the large numbers of Kurdish prisoners who passed through. People fleeing the Jabari tribal villages arrived in Leilan in various ways. Some made the trip on their own initiative, perhaps hoping that a town (even one of this modest size) would offer more protection than the exposed countryside did, as well as food and water. They were, however, given a hostile reception. As they approached Leilan on foot, said one woman from the village of Qara Hassan, soldiers fired into the air above their heads. Others, men, were taken to Leilan from Qader Karam, where they had gone to surrender in the custody of the jahsh. They were blindfolded and handcuffed.

On arrival at Leilan, the army noted basic details on each newcomer. The women wept and begged for mercy, but they were repeatedly told that they had nothing to fear, that they would be granted land by the government in a new camp and allowed to lead a normal life. Nonetheless, the women grew fearful when they were forcibly separated from their husbands, sons, and fathers, who were crammed into an animal pen in the open air behind barbed wire. There was "a huge number of people" there, said one witness; "more than two thousand men, women, and children," according to another. There were army and jahsh guards everywhere, although security was less vigilant for the women and children, and several managed to slip away in the initial confusion before their names could be registered. At least one woman was allowed to leave by army officers after being interrogated. Those who remained slept in the open air for eight or nine days, in the rain and hailstorms of early April, before the men were driven away in army IFA trucks to an unknown destination.

Although Qader Karam itself served as the main processing point for all the villages in its jurisdiction, Aliawa, a destroyed village a little to the west, was the primary collection center for many people. During the third Anfal it was the headquarters of the notorious mustashar Sheikh Mu'tassem Ramadan Barzinji, brother of the governor of Suleimaniyeh. Mu'tassem's name came up repeatedly in interviews with Anfal survivors, along with those of five other local jahsh commanders—Adnan Jabari, Sayed Jabari, Raf'at Gilli, Qasem Agha, and Tahsin Shaweis—as one of the principal agents of the roundup and mass surrender of villagers from central Germian.

Many factors drove the fleeing villagers—naive expectations that this campaign was no different from its predecessors, slender hopes of escape, fear of being captured in a prohibited area, terror of the troops who were burning their villages wholesale. A further inducement was now added: the promise of amnesty for those who gave themselves up. Using loudspeakers attached to the mosques of Qader Karam, the authorities repeatedly broadcast a message that all villagers had three days to turn themselves in—from Sunday, 10 April, to Tuesday, 12 April. During that time, they would even be permitted to return to their hiding places in the hills and recover their possessions. All the males who gave themselves up would be obliged only to serve a tour of duty in the jahsh. News of the offer spread quickly among the refugees, as townspeople told their relatives that they had nothing to fear. Jahsh units under Sheikh Mu'tassem and the other commanders also dispersed into the hills. "They said that the government would not harm the men who surrendered and that they would be given jahsh papers. They told them to bring their families and surrender," reported one survivor.[49]

Mu'tassem's jahsh units detained a large group of male prisoners for two days in Aliawa, where army personnel registered their names. "There were thousands of men there," according to one who passed through the transit facility: "peshmerga, deserters, draft dodgers, and ordinary civilians from peshmerga-controlled villages." Here, the mustashars' message was repeated. The men would be taken to jahsh headquarters in Chamchamal, an hour's drive to the north. There they would be issued jahsh identity papers before being returned to Qader Karam. At that point they were to go find their families and livestock before relocation in a government-controlled mujamma'a.

On the second or third day of the roundup, Aliawa received a personal visit from Bareq. In his presence, the prisoners were filmed. According to another witness, a similar scene unfolded, probably on the same day, at the police station in the center of Qader Karam, where several hundred prisoners were also being held.[50] This time a helicopter touched down on the adjoining landing pad, and three men stepped out—Bareq, First Army Corps Lt. Gen. Sultan Hashem, and Ali Hassan al-Majid himself. Again, there was a videotaping session, and the footage was later broadcast on national television as a film of "captured Iranian saboteurs." The news clip was broadcast repeatedly over the following weeks, until the National Security Council began to complain that its use was becoming counterproductive: people were beginning to see that these were ordinary villagers, not peshmerga fighters.[51]

Hundreds of other prisoners—as many as two thousand according to one estimate—were briefly detained in the deserted camp of Qalkhanlou, just outside Qader Karam, which had been built originally to house relocated villagers from the spring 1987 campaign. Hundreds more were held at an elementary school in Qader Karam, where the sexes were separated. "I was put in a room with many other older women," one woman remembered. "I was the only young woman there. I was very scared, so I covered my face with my scarf. I did not want to see anybody. We were held there for two days. Through the window I could see the soldiers blindfolding and beating the men."[52] After two days, a military bus came and took the older women to Chamchamal, where they were abandoned in the streets, far from their homes and with no means of sustenance. This was an exceptional case, however, and the reasons for it remain obscure.[53] According to one of the very few young male survivors from the Qader Karam area, "The people who surrendered to the government all disappeared. Saved were those who managed to stay in the hills, those who went into hiding with relatives in the towns or were saved by relatives in the jahsh, or those who paid a bribe to the local mustashar."[54]

Qader Karam itself did not survive Anfal. Once the town had served its purpose as a holding center, soldiers and Ba'ath Party members came from house to house to register the names of the inhabitants. At the same time, Amn warned the population by loudspeakers that no one should shelter Anfal fugitives, as had happened in some towns. The people of Qader Karam were given fifteen days to evacuate their homes and move to new housing in the Shoresh camp, outside Chamchamal, and in early May the town was bulldozed. In a telling illustration of the logic of Anfal, however, these people were not otherwise harmed. They were even paid compensation of 1,500 dinars ($4,500 at the time) each for the destruction of their homes. The population of Qader Karam, after all, had been recorded in the October 1987 census. Despite its location in the middle of the war zone, the town was still, in bureaucratic terms, within "the national ranks."[55]

Chamchamal was the last of the smaller-scale detention places for the captured villagers of northern Germian. A large town and qadha, it is one of the few population centers that remains intact in this part of Iraqi Kurdistan. For those who were trucked to Chamchamal from another preliminary assembly point, such as Leilan or Qader Karam, the destination was either the headquarters of the local army brigade (*liwa'*) or the headquarters of the jahsh.

Some male detainees were brought there by bus, and soldiers came aboard to take additional statements from them. Again, the prisoners were reassured that an amnesty had been declared and that they had nothing to fear. Yet the mood was ominous, and through the bus windows the detainees could see thousands of hungry, ragged men, women, and children on the army base.

Other men were roughly transported to Chamchamal in open-backed army IFA trucks. "We suffered much at the hands of the guards," said one. "We were blindfolded and had our hands tied, and we were made to get on and off the trucks several times. The trucks had a door and a step, but because we could not see or use our hands, many fell. It was chaotic."[56] "At the brigade headquarters," another man added, "we were literally thrown out of the trucks, and they took our names and addresses."[57] After the stop at army brigade headquarters, it became apparent that other government authorities were becoming involved for the first time. Winding through the streets of Chamchamal, the prisoners soon found themselves outside the offices of Amn, the feared secret police agency.

At this point, an almost unprecedented act of mercy and solidarity occurred. During Anfal there were many quiet acts of individual courage, both by members of the jahsh and by Kurdish townspeople, and these acts saved many lives. Nothing compares, however, to the response of the townspeople of Chamchamal as they saw their fellow Kurds being trucked through their streets. At enormous risk to their own lives (and in some cases at the cost of their lives), the townspeople staged a spontaneous unarmed revolt to liberate the detainees.[58]

The jahsh undoubtedly had a hand in the Chamchamal protest, and chance also played its part. The trucks that were being used to ferry prisoners from Chamchamal brigade headquarters were not military IFAs but commandeered civilian vehicles with civilian drivers. Surreptitiously, the jahsh guards persuaded several of these drivers to free their women prisoners. The drivers seized the opportunity to do so in the uproar that ensued when townspeople stoned the trucks and smashed their windows. "Even young children put stones in their clothes, threatening to break the windows," said Perjin, a twenty-year-old woman from Qirtsa village who was able to break free.[59] The soldiers opened fire on the demonstrators and even called in MIG fighter planes and helicopter gunships to rocket the crowd. "My clothing was full of bullets from the Bareq soldiers," Perjin said. According to one account, five people died and twelve were injured.

The uprising seemed at first to have been a partial success. Several dozen people escaped, and the residents of Chamchamal offered them refuge "for the sake of humanity." Yet this was not the end of the story. Those fugitives who were later hunted down by Amn agents were publicly executed, and in a macabre detail that recurs in many testimonies from Iraq, the surviving family members were even required to pay for the cost of the bullets.[60]

On her second day in hiding in Chamchamal, Perjin watched a report about Anfal on an Iraqi television news program. This was almost certainly the film shot while Ali Hassan al-Majid and his military commanders were visiting the police station at Qader Karam on 10 April. It showed a group of "captured Iranian agents who belonged to [Jalal] Talabani." Perjin thought she recognized her husband, Fareq, despite his blindfold, and other men from her village. It was the last time she saw her husband alive.

In the southern part of Germian, there were two principal counterparts to the holding centers. Those Kurds captured from the Daoudi tribal area, as well as other villagers who fled into this sector in the wake of the chemical attack on the PUK base at Tazashar, were taken first to an empty youth center in Tuz Khurmatu. Some had already been separated by sex at their point of capture; those who had been trucked in together were now placed in two separate buildings at the youth center and held there for periods that ranged from three days to about a week. The building that housed women and children contained about four thousand people, according to one survivor who was able to recognize people from at least a dozen Daoudi villages.

As at Leilan, a few managed to escape with the help of the jahsh, who were placed on guard duty. A sympathetic mustashar reportedly even smashed one of the school's windows, allowing many women and children to escape at night. His action almost certainly saved their lives. The regular soldiers, most of whom were Arabs, behaved much more harshly, stripping the women of any money and valuables they were carrying and telling them that "they deserved all they got because they had supported the peshmerga." Those who disappeared forever from Tuz Khurmatu after the trucks came to collect them included hundreds of women and children. An elderly woman from a Daoudi village never again saw her brother, husband, father, and cousin—or her two daughters-in-law and the elder one's six small children. Her younger daughter-in-law, "a very pretty girl called Leila, newly married," was dragged away by soldiers. She clung to her mother-in-law's dress, while the older women pleaded with the soldiers not to take her. They shoved the old woman aside, and Leila was never seen again.[61]

For the rest of southern Germian, including the villages of the Jaff-Roghzayi, the main processing center was the 21st Infantry Division base at Qoratu, a large, ugly Soviet-designed fort typical of those erected throughout Iraqi Kurdistan during the 1980s. After the Kurdish uprising in Suleimaniyeh in September 1991, Qoratu was dynamited by Iraqi troops as they retreated to a new frontline farther south. Two months later, the Iraqi writer Kanan Makiya visited the fort. On the side facing the Iranian border, he saw "forty, maybe fifty wagons of the sort Kurdish farmers hook up to the back of their tractors when carting feed or livestock." It was in just such a high-sided wooden cart that Taymour, the twelve-year-old from the village of Kulajo, had arrived with his parents and three small sisters. Makiya went on, "Piles of faded dresses and *sharwal,* the traditional Kurdish trousers, were tumbling now from these wagons, or lay rotting amid the dirt and clumped yellow grass. Everywhere were plastic soles, all that remained of so many pairs of shoes."[62]

"There were at least ten thousand people in the fort," one villager recounted to HRW/Middle East. "They were all tired, hungry, and frightened. Nobody knew what was going on, but I knew something horrible was in the making. No one could talk to each other. We were all silent and waiting to see what would happen."[63]

Some of the prisoners stayed in Qoratu for just a single night, during which they received neither food nor water. Others said they were held there on a starvation diet for longer periods: "We stayed in tents at the division headquarters for three days. We received one piece of bread per person per day, and water. There were countless people there. The army registered all their names and asked them questions: the name of their tribe, whether they were with the peshmerga or the government. Everybody was afraid to say that they belonged to the peshmerga. They all said that they were farmers or shepherds."[64]

Taymour himself, recalled the scene at Qoratu clearly four years later. "All the people from the Kalar area villages were there," he said. "All the halls were filled. There were perhaps fifty halls, and each hall held from 100 to 150 people. We had very little food: soup, bread, and water. Families were allowed to stay together. The guards all seemed to be army, all dressed in khaki. They didn't speak to the detainees. We were afraid that we were going to be killed, and everyone was talking to each other about this because we knew this government campaign was different from the previous ones. The jahsh had lied to us."[65]

## THE AMBIGUOUS ROLE OF THE JAHSH

The mustashars had indeed lied, or at least made promises that they were in no position to keep. A final word must be said here about the contradictory role of the jahsh forces during Anfal. As accomplices of the army, they undoubtedly helped to send thousands of Kurds to their deaths. Jahsh units performed a wide range of appointed tasks. They protected army convoys and went into the villages ahead of the troops as advance scouting parties, or as cannon fodder. They combed the hillsides for those who fled the army's advance and brought them into custody, often flagrantly breaking their promises of safe conduct. They lied to the refugees, promising them the benefits of an amnesty that never existed, promising them in effect that this was to be just another in the government's unending series of resettlement campaigns, as a result of which they would enjoy the blessings of "modern life" in a government-controlled mujamma'a. On occasion, the jahsh also reportedly made false claims to army officers that villagers in their custody had been "captured in combat," either to curry favor or perhaps in the hope of a monetary or material reward.

And material reward there was: it was the jahsh who benefited most directly from the application of Anfal in the literal, Qur'anic sense of the word, as the "spoils of the infidel." As the standing orders for the Anfal campaign had stipulated, "Every item captured by advisers [mustashars] of the National Defense regiments or their fighters shall be given to them free, with the exception of heavy, supportive, and medium weapons."[66] "Give the men to us, and you can have the property," was how a Ba'ath Party "comrade" translated this to one jahsh leader.[67] "The peshmerga are infidels, and they shall be treated as such," a former mustashar was told in a seminar run by army intelligence officers. "You shall take any peshmerga's property that you may seize while fighting them. Their wives are lawfully yours [hallal], as are their sheep and cattle."[68] Indeed the jahsh looted the abandoned villages mercilessly before they were burned and bulldozed to the ground. The account given by one villager was typical of many:

My husband and I were captured by jahsh in a cave where we were hiding. They did not say anything, tell us anything or give us any reason. They just asked for my husband's identification, took it, and did not return it. The jahsh took everything from my house while I was standing there, everything, including all the furnishings. I did not have any money, but they took my jewelry and the animals and the tractor and loaded everything into a truck. They cleaned out all the houses in the village in the same way. Then I saw them burning the things they found inside the house that were not useful to the soldiers and jahsh, like people's clothes. They used kerosene to set fire to the houses. I saw them.[69]

Although many jahsh assiduously performed the duties assigned to them, it is also true that the Iraqi regime's old doubts about the political reliability of the Kurdish militia were well founded and that individual jahsh members were responsible for spiriting many people away to safety in towns and camps during the initial sweeps. It was only because of the jahsh, in fact, that this villager, having seen her home looted and burned, was able to survive at all. "Other jahsh guarded the Zils," she related.[70] "They told the army at checkpoints that the covered Zils contained sheep. The jahsh saved most of the women and children from this village in that way."

It seems likely that some of the jahsh's acts of clemency were inspired by bribery, a simple appeal to the same venal motives that led to their looting sprees. One young man from the Zangana village of Qeitawan in the nahya of Qader Karam recalled how at great personal risk he persuaded the jahsh to help: "I was able to save many family members, women and children, taking them in groups to Kirkuk, Qader Karam, and so forth. At the checkpoints I bribed the jahsh with yogurt and food and everything else I had."[71]

Other testimonies, however, suggest that the most plausible reason for the jahsh's occasional flashes of generosity was that they sincerely believed the lies they told the villagers, having been told the same lies themselves. HRW/Middle East located a former mustashar whose unit, or *fawj,* had been informed by the army that it was "going to arrest and kill or bring in men from the villages." This was isolated testimony, however, and it came from a village in the northern governorate of Dohuk, the scene of the eighth and final stage of Anfal, during which the army's standing orders appear to have been modified in several important respects. A much more widespread sentiment, certainly representative of the third Anfal in Germian, was that the mustashars and the men under their command remained ignorant of the regime's intentions until the roundups had reached an advanced stage.

"I was never told by the army where the captured villagers were being sent," said a mustashar from the Jaff-Roghzayi tribe, whose unit served in villages in southern Germian, including Kulajo, the home of Taymour Abdullah Ahmad. "I always thought they were being taken to the south.[72] I never thought they might be slaughtered. All the jahsh did was to assist the army in finding the best ways to get to the villages and to capture escaping villagers and deliver them to the army." One day he asked an officer what was to happen to the captives. "We are taking them to modern villages," the man replied. This mustashar became suspicious later, however, when he had occasion to visit an army camp (presumably Qoratu) and saw large crowds of detainees there. Again he asked an officer what was going on. This man answered, "It is none of your business." When the mustashar's suspicions turned to conviction, he says he was filled with remorse: "We spit on ourselves for taking part in this operation; it was a crime."[73]

For some members of the jahsh, the moment of realization appears to have come at the processing center in Tuz Khurmatu. Their change of heart was visible to the prisoners. "When the mustashars saw that the men and women were separated from each other," said one former detainee, "they knew what was going to happen, and they were upset. The mustashars tried to take the women away secretly."[74]

Another of the Warani villagers had been captured by jahsh who took her to Tuz Khurmatu and handed her over to the army. Soon, however, "the men were separated from the women and packed into trucks that took them to Tikrit. When we asked what was happening, the officers said that Tikrit would be more comfortable for them." At this the jahsh became suspicious. "Some of them came to rescue the same people they had previously captured and handed over to the army. One jahsh freed ten women in this way. Then they took us to their homes and hid us."[75]

The real question about the role of the jahsh is what power they actually enjoyed. In the operational hierarchy of Anfal, the Kurdish militia was at the bottom of the pyramid, lower than the most ordinary foot soldier of the regular army. Until the appointment of Ali Hassan al-Majid, membership in the jahsh had conferred some measure of protection. Amn documents on village destructions carried out during 1986 explicitly spare those whose menfolk were jahsh.[76] Then the rules had changed, and some pro-regime villages were burned and bulldozed along with those of other Kurds.

The promises that the jahsh made to the captured villagers, even if sincerely meant, were empty. A prosperous farmer from the Jaff-Roghzayi village of Qulijan in southern Germian, fleeing his burning village, sought out the forces of Fatah Karim Beg, the most powerful mustashar in the district, for help. He was told to have no fear. "He issued me a paper saying that I was with him, the mustashar, and that I had seven families with me. He told me that if I carried this letter, the army would leave me alone."[77] Comforted by this encounter, the farmer made his way down to the main road to Sarqala, where a group of soldiers ordered him to halt. With confidence, he handed them the mustashar's letter of safe conduct. "Who is this Fatah Beg?" a soldier asked, and using an expression that is grossly insulting in Arabic, he sneered, "He is my shoe." The letter was worthless, and the farmer was taken with all the other detainees to the 21st Division fort at Qoratu.

Several former mustashars have given HRW/Middle East accounts of meetings in Erbil and Kirkuk with Ali Hassan al-Majid and the commanders of the army's First and Fifth Corps. At one of these meetings, in August 1988, al-

Majid told the mustashars that the Anfal campaign was now to be taken into Badinan, the mountainous northern stronghold of Mas'oud Barzani's KDP. On the personal orders of Saddam Hussein, however, the Badinan Kurds were to be given one final chance to "return to the national ranks." Clemency would be shown to any saboteurs who surrendered from that area, presumably until military operations began in the north.[78]

Al-Majid asked for questions, and several men rose to speak. Among them was Sheikh Mu'tassem Ramadan Barzinji, the powerful and widely feared mustashar from Qader Karam who had handed over thousands of civilians to the army. According to another mustashar who was present that day in Erbil's Hall of the Cultural Masses, Sheikh Mu'tassem appeared skeptical. Would the promise be honored, he asked, given what had happened in the earlier stages of Anfal?[79] Even the qualms of such an influential Kurdish collaborator, a man who had done all that the regime had demanded of him, were contemptuously flicked aside. Al-Majid told Mu'tassem that he was "a black spot on a white mirror." If he did not sit down, al-Majid would have him taken away and executed, "even if Allah intercedes." Before the secretary general of the Ba'ath Party's Northern Bureau, even God Himself had limited powers.

Fourth Anfal: 3–8 May 1988

© 1994 Michael S. Miller

**Elevation (ft)**
- < 1,000
- 1,000 – 2,000
- 2,000 – 5,000
- 5,000 – 9,000

Area from which women and children were taken and killed

Approximate boundary of 4th Anfal campaign
Main Anfal camp and facility
Peshmerga command
Known chemical attack
Resettlement complex
Major road

Area of detail

SYRIA
IRAQ
IRAN
SAUDI ARABIA

0 kilometers 10
0 miles 10

Erbil
Benaslawa
Daratou
Koysinjaq
Harmota
Darbarou
Qamisha
Dukan
Surdash
Chemi Rezan Valley
Piramagroun
Takaltu Mtn.
Gird
Khabar Gomashin
Qaranaw Galnaghaj
Jelamort
Kanibi
Kani
Hanjir
Mamlesi
Kleisa
Goktapa
Haydar Beg
Askar
Aghjalar
Bayinjan
Bazian
Takiyeh
Shoresh
Chamchamal
Qara Hanjir
B Z E I N I
Redar (Shwan)
Taqtaq
Palkana
Turki
Serbir S H E I K H
Khurkhur
Lesser Zab River
Altun Kupri
Dibs
Kirkuk
A
P

# 6

## THE FOURTH ANFAL

### The Valley of the Lesser Zab, 3–8 May 1988

Some were blind; some could not reach our village. The spirit left them on the way;
they were all black.
—Na'ima Hassan Qader of Galnaghaj, describing the exodus of villagers
from the chemical attack on the neighboring village of Goktapa, 3 May 1988

After the initial blitzkrieg in Germian—there is no other word for what took
place there—the remaining peshmerga forces headed north. Although the army
prepared to confront them there, the intelligence apparatus spared no effort to
track down those who had slipped to safety in the towns or mujamma'at. On 4
May, the General Security Directorate issued orders for anyone who had surrendered in combat areas of the first three Anfal operations to be rounded up by the
army and given into its custody for case-by-case evaluations.[1]

In the northern part of Germian, many villagers escaped this dragnet and
survived by melting into the anonymous crowds of Kirkuk and the smaller
Kurdish towns. Those in the south, however, were less fortunate. Hemmed in on
all sides by troops, mountains, well-guarded main roads, and an Arabized desert
area, they had little chance to elude their captors. Only a few lucky ones made it
as far as Tuz Khurmatu or the new camp of Sumoud (meaning steadfastness in
Arabic), outside the town of Kalar. Those who were caught accounted for the
heaviest single concentration of disappearances during the Anfal campaign.
Although males aged fifteen to fifty routinely vanished from all parts of Germian, only in the south did the disappeared include significant numbers of
women and children. Most were from the Daoudi and Jaff-Roghzayi tribes. Yet
their tribal affiliation was unlikely to be the cause; there seems to be no reason
why the Iraqi regime should have harbored a special hatred for these two
groups. Furthermore, people from other tribes who fled or strayed south of the

Awa Spi River were subject to the same treatment. Nor can the explanation lie with brutal or overzealous local army commanders, since the detainees were transferred within a matter of days, still alive, to centralized processing camps. It was there that the intelligence services singled them out, referring to the highest authorities where necessary for a ruling on what to do in the cases of individual detainees.[2]

No single theory can adequately explain the mass disappearances of women and children from southern Germian, although they may in part reflect a mentality of reprisals for the stiff resistance the army faced in such PUK-controlled villages as Tazashar, Omerbel, and Sheikh Tawil. It was the inhabitants of these places and scores of others like them who suffered so grievously. In some cases, entire village populations appear to have been wiped out, with the exception of some of the elderly. In the absence of a comprehensive statistical survey, it would be careless to speculate about the total numbers who perished during Anfal. Yet a most conservative estimate would be that at least ten thousand Kurds disappeared from this one small area alone.[3] In only one other area was a similar pattern repeated—in a cluster of villages along the Lesser Zab River during the fourth Anfal, in the first week of May 1988.

Beyond the town of Chamchamal, the land falls away sharply. Immediately to the north is the broad valley of the Nahr al-Zab-al-Saghir, the Lesser Zab River, which forms the borderline between the governorates of Erbil and al-Ta'mim (or Kirkuk, as al-Ta'mim governorate is referred to by the Kurds). (The Kurds call the river Awi Dukan, the waters of Dukan, because it flows from the dam on the lake of that name.) It was this area that offered temporary sanctuary to PUK forces fleeing from the third Anfal.

By about 13 April, the peshmerga in Germian realized that further resistance was futile. The military leadership met secretly that day in Tilako—two days after the village had been burned by the army—and decided to organize an orderly retreat. They pulled back first to the village of Masoyi Bergach (Sengaw nahya), and then on 15 April split up into three columns, with each taking responsibility for the safety of large contingents of women and children. Two groups headed for the Redar (Shwan) area, northwest of Chamchamal.[4] The other column, led by the surviving nucleus of the first malband, made for the town of Askar, a few miles south of the Lesser Zab.[5]

In 1988, the river valley was studded with little Kurdish towns: nahyas like Aghjalar, Taqtaq, and Redar, as well as other population centers of local importance, such as Askar and Goktapa. Farther north spread the Koysinjaq plain with its untapped oil reserves; to the northwest lay the city of Erbil and the handful of villages on the Erbil plain that had escaped the army's spring 1987 assault. These were now targeted as part of the fourth Anfal. To the north and east, the operation extended as far as the western shore of Dukan Lake and the last outcroppings of the Qara Dagh Mountains.

As the fourth Anfal began, the morale of the Iraqi troops could hardly have been higher. On 17–18 April, in a devastating counterattack that cost ten thousand enemy lives, Iraq had retaken the Fao peninsula at the head of the Persian Gulf, reversing the most humiliating loss of the eight-year war and paving the way for Iran's final defeat.[6]

## THE CHEMICAL ATTACKS ON GOKTAPA AND ASKAR

Goktapa means "green hill" in Turkish, a language whose influence is often apparent still in this former part of the Ottoman Empire's Mosul vilayet. Although the village had been built on the slopes of the hill, during the first Ba'ath regime some families resettled on flat farmland on the south bank of the Lesser Zab when Goktapa burned down in 1963 after the first of many fierce battles between government forces and peshmerga. In truth, Goktapa was more a small town than a village, with at least three hundred (some say as many as five hundred) households, as well as a school, clinic, and two Sunni mosques. The surrounding fields produced rich harvests of cotton, wheat, tobacco, sunflowers, potatoes, eggplant, sweet pepper, beans, okra, grapes, apricots, figs, and watermelon. Goktapa even had electricity, but water was still brought from the river on donkeys.

Goktapa had endured the repression familiar to most villages in the prohibited areas. From a checkpoint outside Aghjalar, half an hour away by car on a paved road, the army tried with mixed success to impose a blockade on all foodstuffs reaching the villages on the south side of the Lesser Zab. In 1982 or 1983, after a pitched battle between government forces and peshmerga, Goktapa was savagely attacked by helicopters, aircraft, tanks, and ground troops. Among those killed was a forty-five-year-old woman named Miriam Hussein, who was shot from a helicopter. There had been peshmerga in Goktapa since the far-off days of Mullah Mustafa Barzani, and after 1984 the village housed an important PUK command post. As a result it was bombed frequently. "We spent most of our lives in shelters," said one woman. When asked to describe the attitude of the civilian population toward the peshmerga, Fawzia, a woman of sixty, smiled. "The peshmerga were loved by the people," she said. "No one hates his own people." The peshmerga protected them from the army and jahsh." She added: "Naturally, if there were no peshmerga, they would kill us with knives, cut out our tongues."[7]

The third of May 1988 was a lovely spring day. The river valley was carpeted in green and dotted with roses and other flowers. Although it was still Ramadan and the people were fasting, the women of Goktapa were baking bread, and the children were splashing in the waters of Dukan. Throughout April, Goktapa had seen many peshmerga coming and going, stopping briefly in the village to eat, bringing news of the rout in Germian and Qara Dagh, spending the night and then moving on. Still, there had been no fighting in Goktapa itself, and ten days had passed since the last Kurdish fighters had been sighted.

An hour or so before dusk the late afternoon stillness was broken by the sound of jet engines. Abd-al-Qader Abdullah Askari, a man in his late sixties, was a little distance from his home when he heard the aircraft. Everyone in this part of Iraqi Kurdistan knew of Abd-al-Qader and his famous family. His late father, Abdullah, had been the head of the Qala Saywka tribe, which owned thirty-six villages in the hills around Aghjalar. By the time he died, the old man's property had dwindled to seven villages, which he divided among his sons. Abd-al-Qader was given Goktapa, although "I always worked with my hands; I never liked to exploit anyone."[8] His brother Ali received the nearby village of Askar—hence the name "Askari." In time Ali became a senior PUK commander and a close confidant of Jalal Talabani.

Askar, an hour and a half on foot from Goktapa, seems to have been the aircraft's first target on 3 May, no doubt because the PUK's first malband, in retreat from Germian, had tried to set up its new base there. A formation of MIGs swooped low over the village, which was now full of peshmerga. There were eight dull explosions, followed by a column of white smoke that smelled pleasantly of mint. Borne on a southeasterly wind, it drifted as far as Haydar Beg, a couple of miles away. When it cleared, nine villagers of Askar lay dead. Members of the PUK rushed around administering atropine injections to those who had been exposed to the gas.[9]

Askar was not visible from Goktapa, and Abd-al-Qader was not especially alarmed when he looked up and saw the aircraft approaching. "I did not pay attention because we suffered from many bombardments. I thought it would be the same as in the past. We did not go into the shelters in front of our houses. No one paid any attention to the planes; we were accustomed to them. But when the bombing started, the sound was different from previous times. It was not as loud as in the past. I saw smoke rising, first white, then turning to gray. I ran away." The wind from the southeast carried the smoke toward him. "I ran fifty meters then fell down. The smoke smelled like a match stick when you burn it. I passed out."

The bombs fell at exactly 5:45 P.M., according to Abd-al-Qader's daughter-in-law Nasrin, the forty-year-old wife of his son Latif, a former schoolteacher. Nasrin remembered the time with precision because her family had a rare luxury: a clock mounted on the wall. She recalled counting four aircraft, although some villagers said there were six and some added that a second flight of six dropped their bombs later. The smoke, said Nasrin, was red and then turned to blue. It smelled of garlic.

There was general panic and confusion; villagers were screaming, running in all directions, and collapsing from the fumes. Nasrin remembered the general advice that the peshmerga had given: in the event of a chemical attack, head for the river and cover your faces with wet cloths. She grabbed a bunch of towels and ran to the riverbank with seven of her eight children. Her eldest daughter, who ran off in another direction, was later arrested and disappeared. The advice about wet towels may well have saved the lives of Nasrin and her family, since the wind blew the gas straight across the Lesser Zab River where she had fled, and one bomb even fell in the water. Dead fish floated to the surface.[10]

Today, a simple monument on top of the green hill memorializes those who died in the chemical attack on Goktapa. Survivors say that they buried as many as 300, although a list compiled later by the PUK gives the names of 154.[11] Some died in the fields as they tended their crops. Other bodies were found in the river. With the help of a borrowed bulldozer, some of the villagers dug a deep trench in front of the mosque that had been destroyed by the army in an earlier raid and buried many bodies that same night. Menawwar Yasin, a woman in her early sixties, helped with the burial. "Some of their faces were black," she said, "covered with smoke. Others were ordinary but stiff. I saw one mother, nursing her infant, stiffened in that position." Other corpses were covered over by the army with a rough layer of dirt when the ground troops destroyed Goktapa several days later. There was no time to do it any other way, an officer explained to a visiting member of the Askari family. It was hot and the bodies were beginning to smell; if they were left uncovered they might cause health problems for his men.[12] Whatever the exact number of those who died, it was the heaviest toll from any confirmed chemical attack other than Halabja six weeks earlier.

In the wake of the Goktapa attack, villagers remembered, the waters of the Lesser Zab rose quickly. It was a trick they had seen the regime use in earlier campaigns, opening the sluices at the Dukan Dam to block any attempt at flight across the river. The survivors from Goktapa, Askar, and Haydar Beg scattered in all directions. Some fled south in the direction of Chamchamal hoping to find sanctuary in the camps of Takiyeh and Bayinjan on the main road to Suleimaniyeh. Others headed west by back ways and goat tracks, traveling parallel to the river into the area inhabited by the Sheikh Bzeini tribe. More than fifty families from Askar were arrested on the morning of 4 May by troops approaching along the main highway and were taken east in trucks to the camp of Suseh.

After passing out from the effects of the chemicals, Abd-al-Qader knew nothing more until he awoke the next morning in a strange room. A voice told him that he had reached the village of Mamlesi, five miles west of Goktapa. He had been brought there unconscious by his son Latif, the former teacher. There was a smell of burning, and looking out they saw that most of the houses in Mamlesi were on fire. Abd-al-Qader and Latif crept into an air-raid shelter and waited there for three days and two nights until they were forced out by a sudden burst of gunfire at the entrance. Outside were four armored personal carriers, a contingent of troops under the command of an army major, and an IFA truck. The old man and his son surrendered and were driven away.

Meanwhile, Abd-al-Qader's daughter-in-law Nasrin and her seven crying children had found refuge in a cave. With her were thirty refugees from Goktapa and another twenty from Mamlesi. At first light on 4 May at 5:00 A.M., they went outside and saw helicopters hovering over the valley below. Some of the men had field glasses, and they watched in silence as the troops entered Goktapa later that morning. This account is borne out by army documents from the fourth Anfal campaign, which note that troops reached Askar at 5:30 A.M. on 4 May and were advancing north toward Goktapa.[13] Seeing the troops approach, Nasrin and her children fled into the hills, where they survived for ten days by extraordinary good fortune before finally reaching safety in the camp of Takiyeh. Another daughter-in-law, Fahima, was not so lucky; she was captured by troops in the village of Jelamort and disappeared. (Yet another member of this ravaged family, a three-month-old child named Avan, was involved in an incident that is reminiscent of the baby-snatching practiced by the Argentine military during the "dirty war" of the 1970s. Avan survived the chemical attack, although her mother, brothers, and sisters all died. A member of the jahsh, however, abducted the infant from her crib and took her to his childless wife in Koysinjaq. The child was eventually retrieved by an uncle.)

## THE ANFAL DRAGNET: EAST OF TAQTAQ

As in Germian, it appears that the army pursued a strategy of envelopment, attacking the fourth Anfal area with at least a dozen separate task forces from several directions at once. Fragmentary handwritten field reports of the fourth Anfal from the commander of the First Army Corps, Lt. Gen. Sultan Hashem, show that troop columns hit the Lesser Zab Valley at first light on 4 May, twelve hours after the chemical bombing of Askar and Goktapa. Some, operating out of Koysinjaq, attacked the villages along the north bank of the river; others converged on the south bank from Suseh and Chamchamal; two convoys moved out of Taqtaq, one headed north toward Koysinjaq, and the other crossing the river and cutting through the area inhabited by the Sheikh Bzeini tribe.

Most of the task forces reported only token resistance, but in a couple of places the peshmerga fought back hard and even pinned the troops down under sustained artillery and rocket fire. On the morning of 4 May, Hashem reported "fierce opposition" on Takaltu Mountain, a few miles to the northeast of Taqtaq. By the end of the day, however, the mountain had been "cleansed after killing nine of them, whose bodies were left on the site." In the rugged Chemi Rezan Valley, to the east of Goktapa, the task force operating out of Suseh ran into difficulties in one village after another: "7:40 A.M.: task force reached Surqawshan village, confronted saboteurs numbering twenty to twenty-five. . . . 9:00 A.M.: task force was able to burn Awdalan and Kalabash after removing resistance. . . . 9:45 A.M.: Talan village burned after destroying resistance, consisting of four groups of ten saboteurs." Hashem even found it necessary to call in reinforcements, more than seven hundred helicopter-borne Amn troops from Suleimaniyeh.[14]

By the late afternoon of 4 May, however, the Chemi Rezan Valley was quiet.[15] The next day was punctuated only by brief firefights in Goktapa and across the river in Gomashin. By 6 May the entire area was under army control. Over the next two days, military units moved north along the shore of Dukan Lake, burning everything in their path. By 8 May the fourth Anfal was over.

Along both sides of the Lesser Zab River, the consequences for the civilian population were devastating. Those to the north, with few escape routes, were the worst hit, and 1,680 people are listed as having disappeared from the six large villages of Kleisa, Bogird, Kanibi, Qizlou, Kani Hanjir, and Gomashin. Many people from the south bank villages, such as Nasrin and her children, reached the safety of camps. Even so, the losses were catastrophic. As many as 500 are estimated to have disappeared from Goktapa alone, and hundreds more disappeared from villages such as Galnaghaj, Gird Khaber, Jelamort, Qasrok, and Qamisha.[16] A daily field report from the army's First Corps for 6 May gives a notion of how many of these people were women and children. In addition to 37 saboteurs, the report notes the surrender close to Taqtaq that day of 60 men, 129 women, and 396 children.[17]

Those who lived north of the river had no way of learning about the chemical attack on Goktapa, since the army had disabled the cable ferry that the villagers used to pull their rafts across the river. The panicked flight of the survivors, many of them blind or dying, alerted people in the villages on the south bank to the fact that Anfal had now reached them. Some fled as soon as they heard the news from Goktapa; others stayed where they were. At midnight on the day of the gas attack, the survivors arrived "smelling of apples" at the village of Darbarou, an hour and a half to the west on foot. Despite this, the people of Darbarou did not seem to feel that they were at immediate risk and stayed in their own beds that night. At 10:00 the next morning, they found themselves surrounded by jahsh and regular army troops arriving from Taqtaq. Aircraft flew overhead, bombing, and helicopters hovered over the village with their loudspeakers announcing, "Come out. There is a pardon for you." The villagers were rounded up and trucked away in IFAS as their homes went up in flames.[18]

Goktapa survivors also turned up toward midnight at Gird Khaber, a village of the Sheikh Bzeini tribe. People there already sensed that trouble was brewing, and some of the men had taken the precaution of sending their wives and children away to the safety of the towns, taking refuge themselves in caves in the surrounding hills. As in Germian, there were false promises of an amnesty for those who surrendered, issued in this case by Qasem Agha, a one-eyed mustashar from Koysinjaq, whom people called Qasma Kour (Qasem the blind one). With the aid of this trick, Qasem Agha's forces captured two hundred men fleeing from the Gird Khaber area.

Others in Gird Khaber were still at home when the Goktapa survivors arrived. They met early the next morning in the predawn darkness to decide what to do. Some of the young men decided to take their chances in the mountains with the peshmerga, and it seems that some survived in this way. But most felt there was no alternative but to surrender. Accordingly, they made their way that morning to the village of Qamisha, where they knew the army was located, fearing that otherwise they too would be attacked with chemicals. It took them two hours to reach Qamisha, traveling packed into nine tractor-drawn trailers.

Army tacticians appear to have assigned Qamisha a role similar to that of Germian villages like Melistura and Aliawa—that of an initial assembly point toward which fleeing villagers could be funneled. The refugees from Gird Khaber found Qamisha occupied by a jahsh unit commanded by a mustashar named Borhan Shwani. Regular army troops were also in attendance, as well as a camouflage-clad contingent of commandos (Maghawir). "The army was firing into the air over people's heads, scaring them," one elderly resident of Gird Khaber said. "They were merciless with the old people."[19] A man from Gird Khaber recognized faces from a half dozen villages. An army officer with the two stars of a first lieutenant was carrying out body searches and confiscating "money, gold earrings, everything." Identity documents were taken away and never returned.

A somewhat different procedure appears to have been followed during the army attack on Jelamort, another Sheikh Bzeini tribal village a few miles south of Gird Khaber. The troops did not reach Jelamort until 6 May, but the inhabitants had already heard of the Goktapa bombing from fleeing peshmerga. They took to the mountains, where they joined hundreds, perhaps thousands, of other refugees hiding in caves or under trees. They were quickly surrounded by the army. The troops opened fire, killing two men, and everyone else came out quickly with their hands held high. Men and women were separated on the spot, and those from Jelamort were marched back to their village. Again, as in Qamisha, the troops stripped everyone of their money, valuables, and documents while other soldiers and jahsh completed the business of looting their homes. Some of the houses were already burning, and the bulldozers were at work on the cement structures. Three empty army trucks waited nearby. The sight of the looting was apparently too much for one jahsh member, who protested loudly. He was confronted by an angry military officer who told him, "These people are heading toward death, they cannot take money or gold with them. The law of the state says they are going to die." The commander of the jahsh unit came over at this point and disarmed his rebellious underling, telling him, "It is the law of our state. You cannot do anything."[20]

In Jelamort, then, the sexes were separated at the point of capture rather than later at one of the regime's processing centers. This was also the procedure in Galnaghaj (although married women from this village were eventually trucked away with their husbands), and in Qaranaw, just outside the town of Taqtaq, where all the women were spared for reasons that remain obscure. "The army officers took all the men," an elderly woman from Qaranaw told HRW/Middle East. "Then they held us in the village for two days. We could not eat or do anything. We just sat in one big line. While we were waiting in the village, the jahsh and the soldiers burned all the houses."[21] After two days, the women of Qaranaw were driven to Chamchamal in army buses and dumped in the street. "I asked one of the soldiers why they were leaving us like this in the city where we didn't know anybody. They replied, 'You are lucky that you have ended up here. Your men have gone to hell.'"

To the north of the Lesser Zab, it was much the same story, as one village after another was captured and demolished by the task forces operating out of Koysinjaq. The villages of Gomashin and Kleisa, for example, lay on the north bank of the river, almost directly across from Goktapa. Anfal reached Kleisa on 4 May, the day after the chemical attack. Most of the villagers had moved out of Kleisa two years before Anfal to build new homes along the Lesser Zab, which narrows to a gorge at this point. They called the place Qolti Karez, "the pit of the underground stream." It was there that Anfal surprised them, and after a brief attempt to hide out in caves in the mountains, they were all arrested and disappeared.

In October 1986, Gomashin and neighboring Qizlou provoked the wrath of the regime when a group of Iranian pasdaran passed through the two villages, making an unusual sortie so far from the border. Aircraft had rocketed Gomashin a short time afterward, and the villagers assumed that the raid was in reprisal. One projectile hit a woman named Aisha as she carried water from the spring, killing her instantly. Another pierced the wall of a house, wounding a woman named Hajer and her eighteen-month-old child. Since there were no cars to take them to a hospital to have their wounds treated, both died within hours.

Peshmerga fleeing the rout in the south had converged upon Gomashin in the days before the fourth Anfal. One teenager from Gomashin, a boy of thirteen at the time, estimated that 200–300 peshmerga were in the vicinity at the beginning of May. The day after the chemical attack on Goktapa, they decided to try to make their way to Iran, appropriating the village's tractors for transport. The people of Gomashin pleaded with them not to deprive the villagers of their only means of escape, but the peshmerga brushed aside their objections. At dawn, however, the empty tractors came back with their drivers, and the villagers now used the vehicles to flee in the direction of Koysinjaq.[22] The following day Iraqi aircraft and ground forces attacked Gomashin. Many of the villagers were captured in flight and disappeared. One witness said that 115 people from Gomashin were Anfalized; another put the number at 130.[23] On 6 May, the First Corps reported that Gomashin had been razed to the ground, together with Gird Khaber and a string of other villages.[24]

## THE SHWAN AREA

While the region east of Taqtaq was being devastated in this way, other army units turned their attention to the nahya of Shwan (the town of Redar), a short way to the west. Once again they were assisted by jahsh contingents under the command of the stout mustashar Qasem Agha of Koysinjaq. The small town of Shwan itself had been destroyed in September 1987, and several of the seventy villages in its jurisdiction were razed during the clearances that spring and their inhabitants relocated to the newly built camps of Daratou and Benaslawa on the southern outskirts of the city of Erbil.

As one moves west, the landscape becomes flatter and less dramatic. The Lesser Zab Valley begins to broaden into the plain between Erbil and Kirkuk, although it is still broken up by craggy hills and horizontal rock outcroppings. On the face of it, the terrain is far from ideal for guerrilla warfare. Yet from the evidence of a dozen interviews that HRW/Middle East conducted with Shwan villagers, it is apparent that small peshmerga units (both PUK and a few KDP) hung on there for several weeks, fighting occasional skirmishes before retreating. A considerable number of civilians also managed to escape to safety through the army lines.

Many of the Shwan villages, being in relatively low-lying land closer to the highway and the cities, had never been "liberated territory" in the same sense as the more mountainous interior was. More than one survivor spoke of government forces and peshmerga taking turns at controlling these villages. During

periods of greater peshmerga influence, there was brutal, if intermittent, government harassment in all the forms familiar in the rest of Iraqi Kurdistan—
punitive jahsh incursions, burning and looting, shelling from artillery, and
rocketing and occasional bombing from the air. After the spring 1987 campaign
of village destruction, many army deserters rebuilt crude homes in sheltered
areas, and most of the remaining villages harbored large numbers of draft
dodgers. In the Shwan village of Dellu, for example, a village of eighty mud and
stone houses, fully half the men considered themselves active peshmerga, and
the population was swelled by fifty or sixty fugitives from military service.

Dellu had been destroyed and rebuilt twice before, once in 1963 and then
again in 1976. The fourth Anfal reached the village on the morning of 5 May
with rocket attacks from helicopters and fixed-wing aircraft softening up the
area for advancing ground troops from the 77th Special Forces. Some villagers
died in their homes. According to one witness, three or four elderly women and
four or five children died in the initial attack, either burned to death or killed by
artillery fire.[25] Twenty-eight villagers were arrested in the army roundup and
disappeared; they included three women and one small child. The remainder
fled to the hills, and many managed to hide, eluding Amn's house-to-house
searches, in Kirkuk, Chamchamal, and in the Benaslawa camp.

Many people were also lucky enough to escape from Khala Kutia, a fifteen-
minute walk from Dellu, and from Zigila, where the army managed to capture
only six elderly people, including the mullah, from a village of thirty households. All the others had been forewarned and fled. From a hideout on a nearby
mountainside fifty villagers from Darmanaw, in the Sheikh Bzeini area,
watched as the army and jahsh looted and burned their village. They survived
for twelve days in caves, eating nothing but wild grasses. Hunger eventually
drove them down to the town of Taqtaq, where "we threw ourselves on the
mercy of the people, kissing their hands." With the help of the townspeople and
a local mustashar, hundreds of fugitive villagers from the Sheikh Bzeini area
hid out for several days in a poultry farm, huddled together in the chicken sheds.
Remarkably, the army never found them.[26]

Even some draft-age males escaped the Anfal sweep in the Shwan area. This
happened, for example, in the village of Palkana after it was attacked by regular
troops and commando units backed up with artillery fire, aerial bombardment,
and tear gas. The villagers took flight on the morning Anfal reached them,
crossing the Lesser Zab River on wooden rafts to outrun the approaching troops.
Even without food supplies, this group managed to remain in the mountains for
two months, after which young draft dodgers and army deserters slipped into
the Benaslawa camp, which appears to have been carelessly monitored by the
security forces.

More remarkable still in some ways was the escape of a group of sixty young draft dodgers from the village of Ilenjagh, a little to the east of Palkana and a few miles to the south of Taqtaq. Although Ilenjagh lay in the Shiwasur Valley, a peshmerga stronghold, the village was vulnerable since it was situated close to an army base and a paved road. It was destroyed in 1987 during a fierce battle, but the villagers defiantly returned to rebuild their homes in a secluded location a little farther from the army base. Almost the entire population survived Anfal. First, the women and children went into hiding in Taqtaq. Then the sixty young men fled with their weapons to hiding places in the hills. Only two were captured. Moving from place to place, the rest held out until the public amnesty of 6 September 1988.[27]

## ZBEIDA'S STORY

The drama of the Shwan villagers' flight from Anfal with the help of the peshmerga is well captured in the testimony of Zbeida, a young woman who was nineteen at the time. Zbeida was a native of Serbir village, a sizable place on the plain, toward the main Erbil-Kirkuk highway. Although Serbir was not a peshmerga village, it was destroyed in the spring 1987 campaign that leveled scores of government-controlled villages on the Erbil plain. At first the villagers were given two months to evacuate. Officially, they were told their homes were being razed to "protect them from harassment" by the peshmerga. A week later, their period of notice was shortened to just twenty-four hours, and they were ordered to move into the Benaslawa and Daratou camps, which at this time were merely open fields with neither shelter nor infrastructure.

Zbeida and her parents moved into the city of Erbil—not into one of the camps as the soldiers had ordered. Her two brothers, however, who were both active peshmerga, made for the PUK stronghold in the Sheikh Bzeini area. After being harassed by Amn in Erbil for three months because of their sons' affiliation, however, the parents and Zbeida moved to the prohibited area in September 1987. Their new village was under constant government attack, and during an air raid in February 1988, the family smelled a powerful aroma of apples from their shelter. When they emerged two hours later, they found that although some peshmerga had suffered chemical burns, none had died.[28]

Anfal reached them on the morning of 4 May, a year to the day after the destruction of Serbir. A helicopter had been seen circling overhead on the previous day, so the attack was not entirely unexpected. At 4:00 A.M., the shelling began, and villagers immediately sought refuge in caves. From this vantage point they could see the army entering villages along the north bank of the Lesser Zab, rounding up the population and burning their houses. They witnessed the destruction of the villages of Qashqa and Khurkhur on the far shore.

What they did not realize was that the soldiers were not only in the valley below but also in the mountains above their hideout.

Zbeida's family decided to flee in the opposite direction, to the east. They were fortunate, for the army soon descended on the caves and captured and their occupants, who subsequently disappeared. Zbeida's family, which was accompanied by Rahman, one of the two peshmerga brothers, returned home and paused there for a few minutes. They could see the army approaching with tanks and armored personnel carriers, and they ran again. Looking back, they could see the soldiers tossing barrels of kerosene over the houses and setting them aflame. They ran on, with the troops in hot pursuit. Shells fell around them, but after crossing a series of small streams, they seemed to have thrown off their pursuers, and they stopped to rest in the village of Turki, another peshmerga stronghold.

Turki itself soon came under shellfire, and the refugees ran toward the Lesser Zab, hoping to cross to the other side. They tried to wade but gave up when the water reached their necks. Behind them, the peshmerga were putting up a determined defense with rocket-propelled grenades and mortars. Eventually, Zbeida's brother Rahman managed to fashion three crude rafts from planks and inner tubes, and Zbeida, her parents, and sister managed to get across. Rahman, who remained on the bank, yelled at them to make for the safety of the peshmerga-controlled Qala Saywka area.[29]

On the north bank of the river, they found themselves in another abandoned village; this was Shaytan. In one of the empty houses, they found bread and dry clothes. Behind them, they could still hear Rahman shouting, "Go! Go! Run to Qala Saywka and follow the peshmerga!" They walked all that night and early morning of 4 and 5 May along a narrow path, resting for a few hours at dawn until they reached the mountains and a safe-looking cave. Setting out from their shelter in midmorning, they could see the army continuing to burn villages in the flood plain below. In the late afternoon, by an extraordinary coincidence, they chanced upon Omer, the second peshmerga brother. He wept to hear that Rahman had been left behind and insisted on going back to join him, to try to help civilians cross the river and get away from the advancing army. But first he led his parents and sisters north, away from the river to another village, Nerajin, where they managed to pay for places in a grossly overcrowded tractor-drawn cart. Finally, at about 4:00 A.M. on 6 May, the exhausted family reached the relative safety of the Benaslawa camp.

Omer came to Benaslawa just once, in the middle of May. He stayed for two weeks, then left again in search of his brother. In August, the family received news that the two brothers had found each other and fought together in a battle with the army near Turki village in June. In this part of Iraqi Kurdistan, in other words, some peshmerga units held out for at least a month after the initial assault of the fourth Anfal. The peshmerga who brought news of the reunion of Omer and Rahman also brought news of their capture. Through binoculars, their comrades had seen them being arrested by the jahsh and driven away in army IFAS. Their parents and their sister never saw the two again.

## THE FOURTH ANFAL COLLECTION POINTS

The villagers who were driven from their homes by the fourth Anfal were subsequently taken to at least three temporary holding centers in the Lesser Zab Valley. Harmota, an army camp outside the town of Koysinjaq, held detainees from Gomashin and other villages for three days after their capture. Takiyeh, a camp built in 1987 on the main road leading east from Chamchamal, was the initial destination for the trucks that carried away survivors from the chemical attack on Goktapa and its environs. One Goktapa woman learned that her daughter, son-in-law, and five children were seen in an army truck at Takiyeh; another held her brother-in-law and his family of twelve. "The elder girl was seen crying to people to save them. She caught sight of a relative and yelled at him to try to save them, but he could do nothing."[30] Many refugees also made their way to Takiyeh in the wake of the fourth Anfal, hoping to find refuge there, even though the residents of the mujamma'at had been warned that anyone offering shelter to an Anfal escapee would have their home demolished.[31]

It was the town of Taqtaq, an important regional center of ten thousand people on the north side of the Lesser Zab, that acted as the principal collection point for villagers rounded up during the fourth Anfal. As in Qader Karam to the south, the numbers of detainees were such that more than a single holding center was pressed into service. Some prisoners described being taken to the *ameriya* —the town's military garrison, housed in one of the innumerable forts that dotted Iraqi Kurdistan, built to a standard design during the 1970s. An elderly man from the village of Darbarou told of being brought there in a convoy of IFAS, some carrying fellow villagers and the remainder loaded down with their chickens, sheep, goats, and cows.[32] Along the way a pregnant woman in his truck gave birth. At the garrison he recognized people from more than a dozen villages in the valley, from both sides of the river, packed into inner rooms, with men and women held separately. The villagers spent a single night there before being trucked off to a new, unknown destination.

The second location has variously been referred to by survivors as a corral, a fenced-in area used for animals, a livestock pen near the bridge, and some sheds used for cows and horses. Once again, there were hundreds of people there from villages along the Lesser Zab Valley. Some witnesses said that families remained together there; others disagreed, saying that young and old were segregated. Guards stood watch, but at this point there was no interrogation. These were extremely primitive facilities, and they were used for only a few hours. The soldiers also had less than total control of the crowds, and as in Germian, members of the jahsh aided in several escapes. As one convoy of trucks pulled into the detention area, a young woman jumped off, clutching her baby, and managed to run away even though the military guards opened fire on her fleeing form with machine guns. In the confusion of arrival, two siblings from the village of Qasrok—an eleven-year-old boy named Osman and his elder sister— were approached by a jahsh guard, a stranger, who whispered to them, "Take a chance, there are no soldiers here, run away. If anyone asks you where you are from, tell them Taqtaq." Being a resident of a town or a camp would of course offer immunity, given Anfal's rigid bureaucratic logic. The pair ducked into a jahsh car that was bringing food to the corral and managed to slip out through the army lines. It was the last time that Osman saw his parents, two brothers, or remaining three sisters, the youngest just three years old.

After their brief sojourn in the cattle pen, the family was hustled once more into the waiting trucks, which lumbered across the bridge over the Lesser Zab and headed south, like so many of their predecessors, in the direction of the oil city of Kirkuk, home of the Ba'ath Party's Northern Bureau. Army documents from the fourth Anfal provide revealing evidence, from the government side, of what happened to the detainees. Buried in the scrawl of his handwritten field reports, Hashem notes briefly that two groups of captured civilians from the Shwan area—fourteen men, twelve women, and twenty children in all—were "sent on to the Amn administration of al-Ta'mim [Kirkuk] governorate." This is the clearest possible proof of the destination of those heavily laden convoys of IFA trucks.[33]

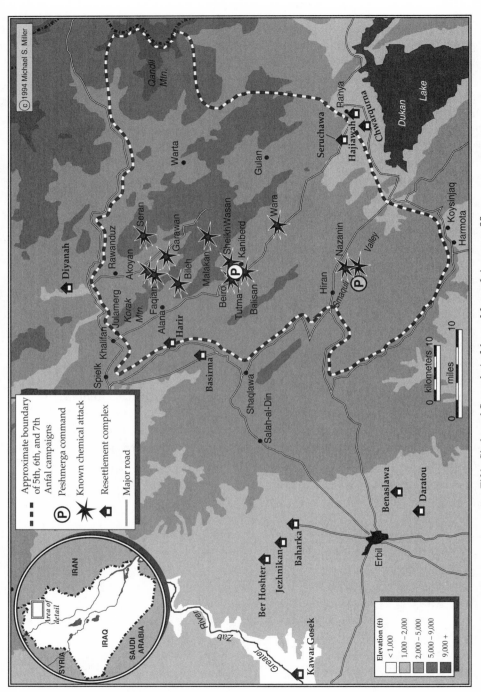

Fifth, Sixth, and Seventh Anfals: 15 May–26 August 1988

# 7

# THE FIFTH, SIXTH, AND SEVENTH ANFALS

## The Mountain Valleys of Shaqlawa and Rawanduz, 15 May–26 August 1988

The forces of the "agent of Iran," Jalal Talabani, were driven from their principal headquarters in the Jafati Valley, from their mountain strongholds in Qara Dagh, from the broad plains of Germian, and from the valleys and flatlands that stretch west to Erbil. Here and there, in caves and isolated outposts, pockets of resistance lingered. Several dozen peshmerga even remained behind in the desolation of Germian throughout Anfal and beyond, but most of the remnants of the PUK made their way to the remote strongholds to the north of Dukan Lake for their final stand, to the steep mountains and narrow valleys that lie south of the town of Rawanduz and west of the Iranian border.

To the west of the lake, battered units of peshmerga had learned of—and in some cases witnessed—the rout of the villages around Goktapa in the first week of May. Along the lakeshore, in the final engagements of the fourth Anfal, the survivors of the battles at Takaltu Mountain and the Chemi Rezan Valley tried vainly to resist the army's onslaught. They hid as best they could for three or four days, some of them hunkered down in the grasslands by the water's edge, and resisted until their ammunition ran out. At night, according to one peshmerga, when the government helicopters could no longer spot them, they pulled back, leaving the last civilians behind. At last, by the second week of May, they had reached Korak Mountain and their familiar sanctuaries in the Balisan Valley.

It was to Balisan and the neighboring thinly populated valleys that Anfal came in the middle of May 1988. This was the climax of the regime's drive to destroy the PUK once and for all as a fighting force, to punish those civilians who continued to sustain it, and to expel the last Iranian troops from the northern front of the Iran-Iraq War.[1] The mass relocation—and mass killing—of civilians would not be a pressing issue for the army in this phase of Anfal. The borderlands of Erbil governorate were now empty, their Kurdish population having been removed in two great sweeps, the first in 1977–78 and the second in 1983–84. The valleys to the south and southeast of Rawanduz had been largely evacuated by civilians after the chemical attacks of April 1987.

From a strictly military point of view, the Anfal campaign continued to follow the logic of the great sweep that had begun three months earlier with the siege of Sergalou-Bergalou. The movement of the troops somewhat resembled the motion of a car's windshield wiper, first clockwise and then counterclockwise, driving the diminishing forces of the peshmerga before it at every stage and "purifying" the countryside of the last of the Kurdish villages to remain intact under PUK control. Yet the fifth Anfal, unlike the earlier stages of the operation, gave the Iraqi army a great deal of trouble. A second and a third assault on these recalcitrant valleys would be required, and the Iraqi army would designate these new campaigns Anfal 6 and 7.

The Balisan Valley was the headquarters of the PUK's third malband, controlling operations in Erbil governorate from the villages of Beiro and Tutma. Other parties were also present in this rugged and beautiful area, where bears and other wild animals still roamed the steep mountainsides. The Socialist Party of Kurdistan had been present there since its foundation in 1979, and there were also armed units from the Iraqi Communist Party and from Mas'oud Barzani's KDP, whose main strongholds lay farther to the northwest, near the Iraqi-Turkish border.

The leadership of the third malband knew full well that Anfal was on its way north. As the fourth Anfal ended, the peshmerga began to gather food and ammunition, carrying supplies through the high mountain passes on muleback to hide them in inaccessible caves, stockpiling enough to withstand a prolonged siege.[2] Hundreds of fighters congregated around the twin villages of Upper and Lower Garawan, seven or eight miles to the southeast of Rawanduz, while others took up positions in nearby Malakan, Akoyan, and Warta.[3]

At least this time the peshmerga did not have to worry about how to protect the civilian population. Almost all the residents of these valleys had fled from their homes after the murderous poison gas attacks of the previous spring. There were only a few exceptions, such as Lower Bileh and Wara, where for very different reasons the villagers felt secure. Lower Bileh, tucked into folds of the mountains far from the road, had been a peshmerga base since before the start of the Iran-Iraq War. Despite the chemical attack on the upper village on 27 May 1987,[4] the people of Lower Bileh felt that they were protected by the remoteness of the place and had chosen to stay where they were. Bileh was newly vulnerable, however, since it was a transit point for peshmerga defending the frontline on nearby Chilchil and Jajouk mountains.

Wara was a different matter. There were no peshmerga in the vicinity, and the village was planted squarely on the paved road from Khalifan to the run-down town of Ranya, close to Dukan Lake. Its location made it useless as a base for the peshmerga, and experience had taught the residents of Wara that their closeness to the government lines conferred a measure of safety. Although some had moved a few miles to Hartal, higher on the mountainside, most stayed put.

At dusk on 15 May the people of Wara were preparing for the 'Id al-Fitr, the festival that breaks the fast of Ramadan. Some of the former residents of the village, now living in Hartal, saw two airplanes fly low overhead, but they paid little attention to them, never thinking that Wara might be their objective. The nearest peshmerga units immediately realized what was happening, however, when they saw the jahsh lighting fires on the darkening mountain peaks—a sure sign that chemicals were being used. The people in Hartal were stunned when the first survivors came running to them, two hours later, to report that Wara had been hit with gas. "As soon as we arrived," said one man from Hartal, "we saw four or five people in the orchard on the hillside. They were obviously dying. Then we walked on a little farther and found three people dead in the graveyard. When we reached the center of the village, we saw that the place was a mess. Food was still on the stoves. There were animals lying all around, dead or dying, and we could hear their screams."

A young woman named Amina was outside her house when aircraft made a bombing run over Wara. "The sound I heard was like when a car races at very high speed and then you step on the brake. Then there were four explosions, and smoke covered the village." Amina's two-year-old daughter, Najiba, was one of thirty-seven villagers who lost their lives that night.[5] The survivors buried thirty-three bodies in a mass grave outside the village. Three were interred in the nearby village of Khateh, where they had been taken by tractor cart to the PUK field hospital, and one in the camp of Seruchawa, which already held the graves of fifty of the victims of the previous year's gassing of Sheikh Wasan.

Morning brought an unnatural calm, which lasted for more than a week. Then, in the early afternoon of 23 May, waves of aircraft dropped chemicals in Balisan, Hiran, and other neighboring valleys. The attacks became so frequent at this point that the peshmerga lost count of them. An old woman from Upper Garawan, hiding in a cave, saw two war planes swoop down over nearby Malakan and release bombs that produced a blue smoke that "covered the place and made everything dark." The gas, which smelled pleasant at first, quickly made the cave's occupants dizzy. Several of them fell to the ground, vomiting and teary-eyed, their skin turning black. A mother and her son in the cave died.[6]

While the entire valley suffered the effects of gas attacks against the peshmerga on Chilchil Mountain, witnesses said that the largely abandoned villages of Sheikh Wasan and Balisan were hit directly for the second time. Soviet-built Sukhoi fighter-bomber aircraft carried out a twenty-minute raid on Sheikh Wasan with both cluster bombs and chemical weapons. Although some of the peshmerga had German-made gas masks, there were not enough for their families, and everyone fled, combatants and noncombatants alike. In Bileh, the chemicals killed at least three children, including two siblings, Suran and Haydar Saleh Majid, aged two and three.[7] Two people also reportedly died in the village of Nazanin, gas and cluster bombs fell over Seran village, chemical shells from a rajima rained on the mountain of Rashki Baneshan, and the heavy vapor drifted down into Akoyan village. Late on the night of 23 May or early the next morning, the ground troops made their simultaneous advance from three directions.

Most of the remaining civilians had fled to the hills as soon as this latest round of attacks began. "There was a nasty smell in the places that had been bombed," recalled one woman who fled, and the corpses of horses and sheep overcome by gas still littered the fields. Like many others, the people of the village of Akoyan scattered in three directions. Some set out on foot or on horseback for the Iranian frontier, thirty-five miles away. Others sought sanctuary in the camp of Hajiawa, which had been built in 1987 at the northern edge of Dukan Lake, a three or four days' walk distant. Others tried to hide in the mountains.

After an arduous journey across rough, steep terrain, hundreds of refugees, including many of those from Akoyan and Garawan, converged on the uninhabited village of Gulan, almost halfway to Ranya. They spent up to a month there, sleeping in the open air and surviving on the charity of local people. They found themselves in the fiefdom of a powerful local leader called Swara Agha, of the Ako tribe. "He was the government in Gulan," said a fleeing villager who arrived there. "He had his own soldiers and jahsh. He owned everything except Saddam's airplanes."[8]

Yet tribal loyalties are relatively loose in this part of Iraqi Kurdistan, and even though they were not his people, Swara Agha made a deal with the newcomers that seems to have been unique in the story of Anfal. Those who wished to could stay in his village, he told them; he would not let the military touch them. "He told the government we were all jahsh," according to a man from Garawan. Indeed those who made it as far as Gulan seem to have been spared. Some chose to remain there, while others, especially those who had family members in the peshmerga and were not in the mood to take any chances, opted for the sanctuary of Iranian refugee camps. Swara Agha guaranteed them safe passage as far as the border—a trek that took all day and all night, with frequent detours to avoid Iraqi troop patrols.

Others who reached Gulan decided to surrender to the army and be relocated to the Hajiawa camp, outside the town of Ranya. It appears that they were allowed to do so freely, although conditions in the mujamma'a were abysmal. For the remainder of the summer it was hot and insanitary, and there was no regular water supply. The camp was monitored by a police post, and its agents warned the inmates not to go too far: only to shop in Ranya or the larger camp of Seruchawa. After September, the searing heat gave way to bitter cold, and Zara, a woman from Garawan, lost two of her seven children that winter—Shilan, aged three, and Isma'il, aged two.[9]

The experience of the third group of fugitives from Akoyan, those who tried to survive in the mountains, is summed up in the experience of Amina, a woman in her early thirties. Amina had left home one day at 7:00 A.M., before the soldiers reached her village. By noon she had found a hiding place, where she met up with other refugees from Bileh and Garawan. They were fifty households in all in the group, and they hid for several days until word came that the troops were closing in on them. After wandering around in the mountains for hours, they reached another hiding place overlooking the village of Faqian. Here, too, they remained for four days, until the artillery fire came too close for comfort. They walked on again, losing all track of time, heading northwest over the high peaks, venturing out only after nightfall, until they reached the government-controlled village of Julamerg, exhausted and out of food.[10]

These were the unlucky ones, even though the first signs were encouraging. Jahsh manning the checkpoints at Julamerg declined to arrest them, telling them that "this is not the appropriate time to come to the butcher's hand."[11] Despite this, they were quickly rounded up by army troops. Their names were recorded, their photographs taken, and they were taken to the nearby military post at Spielk, outside the town of Khalifan, where they were housed for several days under canvas, eight or nine families to each tent, in an area enclosed by barbed wire. The women and children who had surrendered after the attack on Lower Bileh were also here; their menfolk, who fled to the mountains briefly before turning themselves in, were brought to Spielk later.

According to survivors, Lower Bileh was the only village in the area to suffer large-scale civilian disappearances during Anfal. The events in Lower Bileh are also referred to in official Iraqi documents. One handwritten Amn field report notes that "on the night of 2–3 June, thirty families from the village of Lower Bileh were received by the military command of FQ 45. They were counted and surveyed by us. We will presently send you lists of their names, addresses, and birth dates."[12] Here is further official confirmation of what survivors reported with numbing frequency—that a specific civilian group was in government custody at the moment it vanished. The Amn note indicates again that there was nothing indiscriminate about these disappearances; no one was to be Anfalized until his or her personal data had been recorded and analyzed on a case-by-case basis.

Some of those affected by the fifth Anfal disappeared from Spielk. Others were glimpsed through a window in a prison in Rawanduz. Still others vanished into the custody of Amn in Erbil. As in the previous four phases of Anfal, the same detail recurs in one account after another: from these interim places of detention, the prisoners were bundled into army IFA trucks, which always departed south in the direction of Kirkuk.

## THE PUK'S LAST STAND

The battles raged on and off for more than three months. During periods of fighting, says a peshmerga who saw action in the Balisan region, "The heaven was never empty" of government aircraft.[13] Although government forces quickly occupied twenty villages in these valleys, the peshmerga felt that the difficult landscape frustrated the regime's goal of cutting off their main escape routes to Iran. The villagers who remained in the mountains also saw that their homes were being left intact for the time being. With the terrain limiting the movement of ground forces, the campaign of village demolition waited until special helicopter-borne engineering units were flown in toward the end of the year.

Upper and Lower Garawan seem to have been a particularly tough nut for the army to crack. The twin villages were the subject of contradictory field reports exchanged between local and regional branches of Amn during June 1988. Telegram 1132 from Amn Sadiq to Amn Shaqlawa, dated 3 June, refers to the "purification and burning of Lower Garawan." Telegram 1136 from Sadiq to Erbil, dated 6 June, however, refers to a continuing "siege of Upper and Lower Garawan," indicating that peshmerga forces there were still putting up resistance. Telegram 1137, dated the next day, announces the "fall of Upper and Lower Garawan." Another telegram, no. 1179, dated 14 June, again from Amn Sadiq, informs regional headquarters in Erbil that several villages had been burned, including Garawan.[14]

After hiding in the mountains for weeks, several people from Garawan crept back into their village in search of food. Some homes were destroyed by shelling, but most were still standing at this point, and official records suggest that the destruction was carried out sporadically over the next several months.[15]But leveled they were. When the inhabitants were at last able to return to Garawan in 1991, after the postwar uprising, they found that "everything had been destroyed, exploded by dynamite. Even the pipes were taken that brought the water from the spring." All signs of life had vanished, even the beehives. The poplar trees used for roofing material had been cut down. Yet this was not enough it seems. "They also destroyed a martyrs' cemetery [for peshmerga who had fallen] that had been built in the area of Zenia," said a fighter from Garawan, who was hiding nearby and had relatives interred there. The man watched from the mountainside through binoculars as a group of jahsh and soldiers dynamited and desecrated the graves.[16]

From the regime's point of view, the fifth Anfal had been a messy and inconclusive operation, the only phase of the operation so far that had lacked a clear beginning and end. The government's intention had been to wipe out the PUK and then move on to the Badinan area, running to the Turkish border, which was controlled by the KDP. This goal had to be postponed for several months, however, because the resistance of the third malband's forces was more tenacious than the Iraqi army had anticipated.

The atmosphere of frustration and repeated delays can be gleaned from the telegrams that flew back and forth between local Amn offices: 4 June, "Met strong resistance while advancing on Korak Mountain"; 8 June, "Special Anfal Operations: Attack by Saboteurs"; 27 June and again 8 July, "Purification of Gelli Resh, Badawara, Gilga"; 15 August, "Request complete picture of purification of the region within twenty-four hours."[17]

The sense that the fifth Anfal was not a great success also emerges clearly from an unusually detailed military document entitled "Analysis: Final Anfal Operation" (Khatimat al-Anfal). This is a report to the army General Command from Brig. Gen. Yunis Muhammad al-Zareb, deputy commander of the Fifth Army Corps, classified Strictly Confidential and Personal. In essence, the report is a glowing review of the brief, triumphant campaign against the KDP-held areas of the north between 28 August and 3 September 1988. In reviewing the background to the final Anfal, however, it speaks of innumerable delays in "purifying" the Rawanduz-Shaqlawa sector. It also provides a revealing picture of the chain of command that ordered the successive stages of the Anfal operation.

"After the completion of Operation Anfal V on 7 June 1988, preparations and plans were embarked upon for Operation Anfal VI," General Zareb writes. "A cleansing operation was planned to crush the saboteurs in the Alana and Balisan valleys (Anfal VI). This plan was sent to the army chief of staff on 30 May 1988 in my strictly confidential and personal communication 1049." This first plan did not materialize, for "the army chief of staff, in his confidential and urgent communication 1475 of 7 June 1988, ordered the postponement of the operation until a more suitable time. The chief of staff, in his strictly confidential and personal communication 519 of 7 June 1988, ordered a plan to be devised to crush the saboteurs in the Balisan and Smaquli regions."

The main reason for the decision to suspend the campaign temporarily seems to have been the obstinate resistance of the PUK around Korak Mountain, a seven-thousand-foot peak at the head of the Alana Valley. The temporary cease-fire, however, which held until well into July, may also have been connected to the June visit to Washington, D.C., by PUK leader Jalal Talabani. Although the peshmerga were excited by this trip, which was seen as a diplomatic breakthrough, it can scarcely be considered a success. Senior U.S. officials declined to meet with Talabani, and midlevel State Department personnel who did see him commented only that, "Because of his Iranian alliance, his group has enjoyed a certain degree of military success at the expense of the Kurdish population as a whole."[18] This remark essentially reflected the line of the Iraqi government toward the PUK. Since Talabani is known to have informed U.S. officials about the Anfal operation and the recent chemical attacks against the Kurds, his visit also raises the question of how much Washington may have known about the Kurdish genocide as it was happening.[19]

"The plan for the destruction of the saboteurs' headquarters in the Smaquli area," Zareb continues, "was provided in our communication 1572, dated 15 August 1988 [sic]."[20] "In a confidential and personal communication 2544/K of 23 June 1988, sent to us by the army chief of staff in communication 641 of 24 June, the Office of the President of the Republic (the secretary) gave its agreement to launch the operation and destroy the headquarters of the saboteurs in the Balisan basin and the Smaquli region." President Saddam Hussein himself, then, evidently saw fit to involve himself in operational decisions about Anfal, at least when the campaign was running into difficulties. Zareb went on:

"In a confidential and personal communication 14671 of 16 July 1988 from the Office of the President of the Republic, relayed to us by the army chief of staff in confidential and personal communication 861 of 20 July, we were informed that the Anfal operations should be completed with a high momentum after the religious feast [of the 'Id al-Adha], if God so desires."[21]

God did not appear to be smiling on the enterprise, and several days after the 'Id al-Adha the offensive remained stalled. "In a meeting held at the headquarters of the First Army Corps in Kirkuk on the morning of 29 July 1988, attended by the assistant chief of staff for operations and the director of military movements, and pursuant to confidential communication 943 of 29 July, the sixth and seventh Anfal operations were postponed until operational requirements were completed."

Although the Iraqi regime grappled with the delays to the sixth and seventh Anfals, events elsewhere were giving the peshmerga fresh cause for alarm. On 17 July, then Iranian president Ali Khamenei notified U.N. Secretary Gen. Javier Pérez de Cuellar that his country was willing to accept U.N. Security Council Resolution 598.[22] As far as the PUK was concerned, Iran's decision to end the fighting was a breach of the terms of their October 1986 Teheran agreement, which had stipulated that neither party would make a unilateral deal with Baghdad. They were, however, powerless to do anything about it, as powerless as Mullah Mustafa Barzani had been when the Shah cut off his supply lines to the KDP in 1975.

On 26 July, the day after the 'Id al-Adha, the commanders of the third malband held an emergency meeting and decided that a partial withdrawal was its only option. Anyone who was unable to fight should take their families to safety in Iran; the able-bodied peshmerga would stay behind to harass the troops and protect the retreat. Even as the evacuation began, the Iraqi air force launched another fierce chemical attack. Again it struck all the main valleys: Balisan, Malakan, Warta, Hiran, and Smaquli. Thirteen people died in different locations, said a peshmerga who fought in this theater; fifteen, according to another account. The clouds of gas drove the peshmerga to seek safety on the upper mountain slopes, but early the next morning a second attack with cluster bombs drove them down again. Many of those who remained scattered in confusion, and the last of the civilians were mopped up quickly.

A contingent of jahsh arrived in the Smaquli Valley one August morning to find the population fleeing from artillery fire. By loudspeaker, the mustashar urged them to surrender, and after five days a considerable number of people turned themselves in. They were divided into three groups by age and sex, and their names were registered. The men were told that they would be pardoned, but only if they surrendered with their weapons. Since many of them were unarmed civilians, this was difficult, and they were reduced to digging up caches of peshmerga arms in order to hand over guns. Some were even allowed to buy guns from the jahsh so they might qualify for a pardon. The men were then ordered to sign a confession that they were indeed peshmerga. Once this grim charade was over, the mustashar recalled, "All these people disappeared by way of Topzawa," the Popular Army camp outside Kirkuk that served as the main processing center for the victims of Anfal.[23]

During the weeks that followed, hardly a day passed without further chemical attacks, even after the Iranians accepted Saddam Hussein's terms for the cease-fire on 8 August. Although the peshmerga were now in full flight, the Iraqi army never did manage to cut off the two main avenues of escape to Iran. Sympathetic jahsh commanders like Swar Agha helped the last families to reach the border, and on 26 or 27 August the remaining peshmerga contingents in the Balisan Valley dynamited their headquarters and fled. By the 28th, ground and airborne forces occupied the entire area. The PUK was finished as a fighting force, and the whole territory where it had once held sway was under the control of the Iraqi government.

With this, the regime turned its attention farther north, to the region of Badinan, the principal stronghold of the KDP. This time, the campaign would not be given a number; it would simply be designated the final Anfal. As Zareb's report indicates, the plans had been in the works for several weeks, concurrently with preparations for the seventh Anfal. Zareb writes: "In a highly confidential and personal communication 941 of 28 July 1988, sent to us by the general commander of the Armed Forces, instructions were given to deal the saboteurs a crushing blow in the Badinan sector."

"A meeting was held on 7 August at the headquarters of the First Army Corps in Kirkuk," the general continues, "chaired by Comrade Ali Hassan al-Majid, member of the regional command and secretary general of the Northern Bureau. This meeting was also attended by the deputy chief of staff and the directors of military movements and the air force." There is a laconic hint of what must have been al-Majid's fierce mood: "Instructions were given to put an end to all acts of saboteurs in the northern region."

After additional meetings to fine tune the details, the army's responsibilities were assigned. "It was decided that the First Army Corps should operate in the Balisan-Smaquli sector and that the Fifth Corps should operate in the two areas of Sheikhan and Zakho in the Badinan strip. This was in accordance with the highly confidential and personal communication 1076 of 16 August 1988 from the army chief of staff."

It remained only to fix dates. There were two. The preparatory, or softening, stage of the final Anfal would commence on 25 August, and as in almost every preceding phase of Anfal, this meant attacks from the air with chemical weapons. On 28 August the ground troops would go in "with the first rays of the dawn."[24]

# THE CAMPS

Away with them I say and show them death.
　　　　　—Marlowe, *Tamburlaine the Great* (part I, V, i)

For the young, the final stage was Topzawa.
　　　　　—Rahman, an elderly man from Darbarou village, Taqtaq

## THE POPULAR ARMY CAMP AT TOPZAWA

Topzawa is one of the commonest place names in northern Iraq; the map of Kurdistan is dotted with Topzawas. Most were tiny anonymous hamlets of the sort that were destroyed by the hundreds during Anfal. Like many place names, it is incongruous. Goktapa, the site of the chemical attack of 3 May, means "green hill"; Buchenwald, the name of the Nazi concentration camp, means "beech forest." *Top,* in Kurdish, means "artillery," and *zawa* "betrothed." Combined, the words evoke sniggers among schoolchildren, for they refer, somewhat brutally, to the act a male performs on his wedding night.

Just as no Kurd will ever again think of Anfal as a sura of the Qur'an, so no one will ever again hear the secondary meaning of Topzawa as a smutty joke. They will remember a sprawling army base on a highway leading southwest out of the oil-rich city of Kirkuk. Covering about two square miles, Topzawa is bounded by two underground oil pipelines, a railroad repair yard, and a military air field. For the villagers who were trucked away from their burning villages by the army during Anfal, all roads seemed to lead to Kirkuk and to Topzawa. At Topzawa, the notion that Anfal was simply a counterinsurgency campaign evaporates.

No official documents have so far come to light from the Kirkuk headquarters of the various agencies that were involved in Anfal. A letter from Amn Suleimaniyeh, however, to the unnamed director of security of the Autonomous Region, dated 29 October 1988, alludes to the Topzawa operation and gives a hint of its scale. Almost two months had then passed since the completion of Anfal, and the regional security director in Kirkuk evidently telephoned to ask for a progress report from the Suleimaniyeh governorate. The reply is classified as "secret and personal, to be opened by addressee only."

It begins, "In the name of Allah, the Beneficent, the Merciful: Distinguished Director of the Autonomous Region, with reference to our telephone conversation, the statistics requested are as follows." There is a brief recitation of actions taken: 9 criminal subversives executed, along with 18 members of their families, as ordered by Ali Hassan al-Majid's office; another 19 people executed for being found in prohibited areas, in violation of directive 4008 of 20 June 1987; another 47 subversives sentenced to death by the Revolutionary Court; and finally this: "2,532 individuals and 1,869 families totaling 9,030 persons, who were among those arrested during the heroic 'Anfal' operations, were sent to the Popular Army camp in the governorate of al-Ta'mim (Kirkuk)."[1] In other words, to Topzawa.

From the collection points at Qader Karam, Qoratu, and Leilan they came, from Chamchamal, Aliawa, and Taqtaq, crammed into the swaying IFA trucks like farm beasts. "From Taqtaq we were taken the next day [about 7 May] in a military truck with a cow," remembered Abd-al-Qader Abdullah Askari, the dignified old village leader of Goktapa, with a rueful laugh. "This was insulting. You know what cows do, they shit. At the turnoff on the road from Redar to Erbil, they dropped off the cow. I said to the cow, 'We're both going to be slaughtered, pardon me if I have done something wrong to you in the past'"— this being a traditional Muslim way of bidding final farewell.[2]

The truck lumbered on to Kirkuk, where it stopped for an hour or so outside the Ba'ath Party building. (Many witnesses recalled making a brief halt either here or at the Kirkuk headquarters of Amn.) Abd-al-Qader counted fourteen young men being hustled onto the truck by soldiers. Before long the vehicle drew up outside the gates of Topzawa. Only the few villagers who were literate could read the name on a sign at the entrance. "It was very late at night when we arrived at Topzawa," said Yawar, a seventy-year-old man who believed he was Anfal's only survivor from his home village of Karim Bassam (nahya Qader Karam).

> We were all hungry and exhausted. We were almost dead. We had not eaten for several days. We had even lost our sense of time. We did not know what they wanted to do with us. When we reached the base they announced over the loudspeakers that we should not get out of the trucks until they told us to do so. There were eight or nine trucks that arrived together. Their backs were covered; we could not see anything inside. We stayed in the truck for about an hour before the soldiers opened up the back and said, "The men,

just the men will get off first." I was so hungry and exhausted that I could not move, so I was the last to get off. The young ones got off first. As soon as they did, they were handcuffed.[3]

With only minor variations, this was the standard pattern for sorting new arrivals. Men and women were segregated on the spot as soon as the trucks had rolled to a halt in the base's large central courtyard or parade ground. The process was brutal, and it did not spare the elderly. A man of seventy from the nahya of Shwan was dragged out of line for no apparent reason, beaten by an officer wearing the three stars of a captain on his shoulder, and robbed of 3,000 dinars ($9,000 at the official 1988 exchange rate). Abd-al-Qader of Goktapa recalled that a colonel (*aqid*) was in charge of processing the new arrivals, assisted by a captain (*naqib*).[4]

A little later, the men were further divided by age, small children were kept with their mothers, and the elderly and infirm were shunted off to separate quarters. Men and teenage boys considered to be of an age to use a weapon were herded together. Roughly speaking, this meant males of between fifteen and fifty, but there was no rigorous check of identity documents, and strict chronological age seems to have been less of a criterion than size and appearance. A strapping twelve-year-old might fail to make the cut; an undersized sixteen-year-old might be told to remain with his female relatives. A prematurely gray or grizzled-looking peasant could be spared, even though he might be in his forties.

"We joined thousands of other Kurds who had been brought there before our group," said one such man, Jalal, a forty-five-year-old farmer from southern Germian who was transported to Topzawa in mid-April from the 21st Division fort at Qoratu. "We just did not know what would happen. We could not speak. Fear would not let us speak, everyone was mute. The only sound that we heard was when the military officers called out names. 'Accused Ali Rahman, son of so and so. . . . Accused Mustafa Taher, son of so and so.' They were announcing the names of the youths over the loudspeakers. They did not call the old men."[5]

It was then time to process the younger males. They were split into smaller groups. In lines of eight, one said; seated in a smaller courtyard, said another. No one told the prisoners why they had been brought there or what was to happen to them. After separation into groups, they were body-searched by soldiers or Istikhbarat agents. Some had their identification papers removed at this point, but not all—perhaps, as one survivor suggested, because the guards were simply overwhelmed by the magnitude of their task. Combs, razor blades, mirrors, knives, belts, worry beads—everything was taken from the prisoners but the clothes they stood in. "I saw a pile of watches, belts, and money taken from the villagers and heaped on the floor," one woman remembered. "You could weep."[6]

Some of the detainees were interrogated immediately; others were hauled from their cells at night. In any event, for most of the newcomers the interrogation was perfunctory. It was no more, really, than the taking of a brief statement and a few simple questions: name, mother's name, number of siblings, marital status, year of marriage, number of children.[7] "How long have you been a saboteur?" the men were asked. "What actions did you take part in?" Many feared to give truthful answers. "I have never been a saboteur," one young man answered typically. The interrogator, who was wearing the uniform of the army Special Forces wrote down "saboteur" anyway.[8]

Once duly registered, the prisoners were hustled into large rooms, or halls, each filled with the residents of a single area. One witness counted twenty-eight of these halls, and estimates of the numbers of prisoners held in each varied from one to two hundred. Using these figures as a rough guide, the total population of the Topzawa base at any given time may have been four thousand to five thousand. The inmates shifted constantly, with most remaining there for as little as a single night or as long as four days before being taken to their next destination.

Although the conditions at Topzawa were appalling for everyone, the most grossly overcrowded quarters seem to have been those where the male detainees were held. "We could not leave our hall," said one boy from near Qader Karam who was held with others who were considered under the age for military service but too old to stay with their mothers. "It was made of cement, heavily built, and very strong, with bars on the windows and doors but no glass. The hall measured about six meters by thirty and was very crowded. There was no room to lie down."[9] Other men described being forced to squat on their haunches all night and being beaten if they attempted to stand up. Many of their companions fainted from exhaustion.

Sanitation was nonexistent. The prisoners used cans in the room for their bowel movements and urinated out the door or simply on the floor where they stood. If they were fortunate, they might be taken to the toilet twice a day, at gunpoint and in groups of five or ten, by guards who sometimes beat them on the way with a strip of electric cable. Most were suffering from diarrhea by this time, especially if they ate the prison food. "It was something that it is better not to describe," said one of the few young men who survived Topzawa. "If you were not hungry you would not eat it. It was a type of soup with leftover bones and a lot of oil floating in it. Everybody got sick." For many inmates of Topzawa, there was not even this, but merely two small pieces of stale pita bread (*samoun*) each day and a little water. Some received no food at all. Again, women and children fared a little less harshly, and some of them told of occasionally being given meager rations of rice, tea, and cheese and even, in one case, a little meat.

Nonetheless, the women and children suffered grievously in other ways. After a short time in which they remained together, baton-wielding guards dragged the older women violently from their daughters and grandchildren and bundled them off to yet another unknown destination. In at least two reported cases, soldiers and guards burst into the women's quarters during their first night at Topzawa and removed their small children, including infants at the breast. All night long the women could hear the cries and screams of their children in another room. In one instance, the children were returned to their mothers the next morning without a word of explanation, after a six- or seven-hour separation. In another case, the families were not reunited until the next stage of their ordeal, when they were herded once more into army IFAS and transferred from Topzawa to a prison for women and children at Dibs, on the road that leads northwest from Kirkuk to Erbil and Mosul. Taymour Abdullah Ahmad, the twelve-year-old boy who was captured by the army on 13 April in the village of Kulajo, said he was held at Topzawa with his mother and three sisters for a month, an exceptionally long stay.[10] During that time, he witnessed the deaths of four children, aged five to nine, apparently from starvation. Soldiers removed their bodies, and Taymour learned later that they were thrown into a pit outside.[11]

Above all the women and children of Topzawa endured the torment of seeing their husbands, brothers, and fathers suffer and, in the end, disappear. Through the barred windows of their halls, they could see their menfolk in another part of the prison. Every two or three days, said Taymour, the inmates of his cell were let out for air and allowed to mingle in the central courtyard. The children would take advantage of the moment to slip across to the men's quarters and throw bread in at the windows.

For the men, beatings were routine. Even old Abd-al-Qader Abdullah Askari of Goktapa was beaten, a man in his late sixties still weak and disoriented from the chemical bombing of his village several days earlier. On the night of his arrival, a guard ordered him to stand up. He replied that he could not, because of the poison gas he had suffered. The guard rushed at him in a fury and beat him, screaming that it was forbidden for anyone to speak of poison gas attacks.[12]

A young army deserter from the Qader Karam area, known to his friends as Ozer, was held captive for four days in Topzawa. During that time, one of his cellmates was a bearded man from the village of Khalo Baziani, in the nahya of Qara Hassan. The man told Ozer that he had been tortured. They had to talk discreetly because of the ever-present guards, but Ozer was able to learn that the man had been beaten with a cable, hanged from a ceiling fan, and scorched with a piece of hot steel. Guards had stomped on his back with their boots while he lay face down on the floor. The man was in great pain. He said he had been singled out for harsh treatment because of his beard, which was presumably taken as a sign of Islamic fundamentalism and pro-Iranian sympathies.[13] An officer had told him that he would be executed if the beard were not gone by the following day. That evening, Ozer cut off the beard of this man and five others with a small pair of nail scissors that one of the prisoners had managed to keep hidden.

On the fourth day of Ozer's confinement, at 1:30 A.M., an army captain came in and ordered the prisoners to stand. He told them that he would read a list of names; anyone who failed to answer when they were called would be executed on the spot in front of the others. One after the other the prisoners were summoned to the officer's table. Ozer saw that each man was assigned a serial number; his was 375. As their names were called, the prisoners were led from the room in groups of eight. After four days on a starvation diet, they were weakened and disoriented. Ozer found himself in a second, empty hall. After the stuffy heat of his previous, overcrowded quarters, he was chilled by the cold of the mid-April night. The floor was stained with diesel oil, and there were three patches of fresh blood. A bloodstained Kurdish head scarf lay in a corner, along with a coat and a pair of baggy Kurdish pants. At about 4:00 A.M. the prisoners heard the sound of engines outside. They tried to peer through the keyhole, but it was impossible to make out anything in the darkness. For another four hours they waited, numb with cold, hunger, and fear.

These early morning movements of male prisoners were observed by women and older people in other sections of Topzawa. "We saw them taking off the men's shirts and beating them," said one elderly man. "They were handcuffed to each other in pairs, and they took away their shoes. This was going on from 8:00 A.M. until noon."[14] Sometimes the men were blindfolded as well as handcuffed. According to some accounts, they were stripped to their shorts. At last they were packed into sinister-looking vehicles, painted white or green and windowless, which were variously described as resembling buses, ambulances, or closed trucks.

This was the last that was seen of the men who were held at Topzawa. As the windowless vehicles left in one direction, buses drove off in another, filled with other detainees. For many of the women and children—but by no means all of them, as we shall see—the next destination was the prison of Dibs. For the elderly, the road led south, through the river valleys of central Iraq, before turning southwest into the desert. "The Kurds are traitors, and we know where to send you," a military officer told one old man from Naujul. "We will send you to a hell that is built especially for the Kurds."[15] Its name was Nugra Salman.

## THE POPULAR ARMY CAMP AT TIKRIT

Many tens of thousands of Kurdish villagers swept up in the third and fourth stages of Anfal passed through the Popular Army base of Topzawa in this way. So did smaller numbers of Kurds from the second, fifth, sixth, and seventh Anfals. The Popular Army barracks in the town of Tikrit, which lies southwest of Kirkuk on the banks of the Tigris River, close to the birthplace of President Saddam Hussein is also important. Tikrit appears to have performed a broadly similar function as Topzawa, but on a smaller scale and for a much shorter period. Indeed, all the witnesses who spent time in Tikrit belonged to a single large batch of prisoners from the Daoudi tribal area along the Awa Spi River in southern Germian. All of them were captured in the initial stages of the third Anfal by army units operating out of Tuz Khurmatu, and all of them were brought to Tikrit after first being detained at the Tuz Khurmatu Youth Hall (see chapter 5).

Tikrit, then, was probably pressed into service as a temporary overflow center for a few days in mid-April when the third Anfal was in full swing in Germian and Topzawa was filled to capacity. As at Topzawa, the guards were identified as regular army troops, with Amn and Istikhbarat agents also in attendance. One man, however, said that he also recognized members of the Popular Army.

Conditions at Tikrit were extremely brutal. According to the account of Muhammad, a man from the village of Talau who was sixty-three at the time of Anfal:

On the first morning, they separated the men into small groups and beat them. Four soldiers would beat one captive. The other prisoners could see this. About fifteen or twenty men were in each group that was taken a little way off to be kicked and beaten with sticks and [electric] cables. They were taken away in the early morning and returned in the afternoon. The soldiers did not gather the men by name, but just pointed, "You, and you," and so on. They were Amn from Tikrit and Kirkuk—butchers, we know them.[16] When one group of beaten men returned, they took another and beat them. That night, I was in a group of ten or twelve men that was taken out and blindfolded with our hands tied behind us. They took us in three or four cars to somewhere in Tikrit. We drove around all night, barely stopping. They asked me no questions. The captured men could not talk to one another. Everyone was thinking of his own destiny. Of the ten or twelve they took out that night, only five returned. The next night, when I was back in the hall, Amn came and asked for men to volunteer for the war against Iran. Eighty men volunteered. But it was a lie; they disappeared. A committee was set up by Amn to process the prisoners, who were ordered to squat while the Amn agents took all their money and put it in a big sack. They also took all our documents. The Amn agents were shouting at us to scare us. "Bring weapons to kill them," said one. "They are poor, don't shoot them," said another. And another: "I wish we had killed all of them." Later that night the Amn came back and took all the young men away. Only the elderly remained. The young men were taken away in Nissan buses, ten or more of them, each with a capacity of forty-five people. Their documents had already been taken. They left with nothing but the clothes on their backs.

Among the young men who disappeared that night were Muhammad's son Salah, his brother's son, and several other relatives. "I never heard from them again," he concluded. "There were no messages, nothing. No one ever saw them again. Only Saddam Hussein knows."[17]

## THE PRISONERS FROM BILEH AND HALABJA

The treatment of those captured in other phases of the Anfal campaign appears to have been slightly different. During April and early May 1988, Topzawa was processing Anfal victims on what can only be described as an industrial scale. By the end of May, when Anfal reached the areas north of Dukan Lake, the rules had changed somewhat.

HRW/Middle East interviewed three dozen former inmates of Topzawa. Of these, five were from the areas affected by the fifth, sixth, and seventh Anfals. Four were from Upper and Lower Bileh; the other was a young woman named Amina, from the nearby village of Akoyan.[18] These witnesses reported being held apart from the other prisoners. Almost the entire group was from Bileh, although they also recognized a handful of people from nearby Kandour, the village whose residents had shown such kindness to the victims of the May 1987 chemical attack on the Malakan Valley. All of them had been brought there after a few days in the army fort at Spielk, near Khalifan. One man told of an additional night in an underground cell at the Amn headquarters in Kirkuk; several others reported an overnight stay in Erbil.

The Bileh group was apparently held at Topzawa for eight to ten days, considerably longer than most of the detainees from earlier periods. Their conditions seem to have been marginally less harsh, and the women were able to take water and cigarettes to their husbands, who were detained in a separate large cell. After a week or so the women and children were transferred, like their predecessors, to another army base at Dibs. Most of the elderly were driven south to the prison at Nugra Salman, although one old man was taken directly from Topzawa to Arbat, a town to the south of the city of Suleimaniyeh. This was in mid-June. From Arbat, he made his own way to Basirma, a government-controlled camp that had been set up after the chemical attacks on the Balisan Valley in April 1987.

An even more notable exception to the earlier pattern of detentions was the case of Faraj, a thirty-nine-year-old teacher from Halabja. His testimony shows again how survivors from that town were treated differently from those who were swept up in Anfal. It also demonstrates that Topzawa remained in operation until the very end of the campaign. Faraj had fled to Iran with his wife and two of his six children immediately after the chemical attack of 16 March. After two and a half months in Iranian hospitals and refugee camps, the family crossed back into Iraq, but they were soon picked up by soldiers at a checkpoint in Ranya. After a period of interrogation by Amn agents in Suleimaniyeh, Faraj and his family were transferred to Topzawa in a bus that contained twenty-five people from Halabja and the Kalar area.[19]

The conditions that Faraj observed in Topzawa were broadly similar to what earlier prisoners had described. The sexes were still being segregated on arrival; 150 people or so were crowded into a single large cell; and they existed on starvation rations. A Kurdish army doctor was now in attendance, a man named Najib, who hailed from Khanaqin. Faraj became aware that all his fellow prisoners were from Halabja and that many of them had not fled to Iran as he did but had been captured inside Iraqi Kurdistan after the bombing of the city.

At night, he heard the sound of weeping from other parts of the building and asked a guard what was going on. "Those are the Anfal prisoners," the guard replied, "and they are leaving the prison." Halabja, in other words, was not part of the Anfal operation. "Where are the Anfal prisoners being taken?" Faraj asked another guard the next morning. "That is none of your concern," the man answered. "If you ask that question again, you will be sent off with them too, to be lost forever."

From eavesdropping on their conversations, Faraj, who could speak Arabic, learned that the Topzawa guards had all been posted here from Baghdad. One even gave the prisoner his telephone number and suggested that he call if he was ever in the capital to see whether "we may have a job for you." Later, the same guard aroused the teacher's suspicions further when he gave him a letter that he said was from a Kurdish girl in another section of the prison, telling her relatives in the men's cells about her failing health and her fears of death. Faraj refused to get involved. Some time later his suspicions about the guard were confirmed when the man told him point-blank that Amn was interested in having him spy on his fellow Kurds.

Amn's clumsy attempts to recruit Faraj may partially explain the leniency shown to him, although it is clear from his testimony that Halabja survivors were treated more indulgently than were the Anfal prisoners. For the first two weeks, Faraj was even allowed brief visits to his wife, although those privileges were withdrawn when another prisoner was caught trying to escape through a hole in the ceiling. To discourage any other thoughts of flight, guards beat the man to death in front of his fellow inmates. The Halabja teacher remained in Topzawa for fifty-two days altogether, a much longer period of confinement than any other surviving witness has described. He was eventually released shortly after the end of the Iran-Iraq War and resettled in the Bayinjan camp, between Suleimaniyeh and Chamchamal.[20]

## THE WOMEN'S PRISON AT DIBS

Karim, a twenty-year-old technology student from Dibs, had been aware for some time of unusual troop movements on the outskirts of town close to the junction with the Kirkuk-Mosul highway.[21] Residents of Dibs had seen civilian buses and vans approaching from the direction of Kirkuk and converging on the Dibs army base—a so-called fighting school, where Iraqi commando forces (Maghawir) were trained. They had also seen sealed green police buses leaving the base accompanied by armed men in olive-green fatigues. Local shopkeepers grew accustomed to visits from groups of six or seven female prisoners accompanied by guards and soon learned that they came from the Dibs base.

These women and their children were being transported from Topzawa to Dibs in large numbers from mid-April onward as part of the three-way segregation process that took their elderly relatives off to the prison of Nugra Salman and their menfolk, stripped to their shorts, handcuffed, and blindfolded, to an unknown destination. One of the Dibs guards told a newcomer that the camp (two buildings within a single compound) held seven thousand Kurdish prisoners. On arrival, some of the women found themselves reunited with the children who had been plucked from their arms by the guards at Topzawa. They would remain at Dibs for four to five months, until the Iraqi regime declared its final victory over the peshmerga and announced a general amnesty for the Kurds.

The women were tormented by not knowing what had become of their husbands, brothers, and fathers. Yet after the abysmal conditions at Topzawa, Dibs offered significant relief. There was room to stretch out and sleep on the filthy concrete floor, and there were no restrictions on the use of the bathrooms. Water was readily available from a faucet. The food was bad, but it was at least more regular: lentil soup and hard pita bread or rice twice or three times a day. After a few weeks, there was even a little added variety to the diet. By the time that Amina, the young woman from Akoyan, arrived in June, the rations at Dibs included two eggs a week, yogurt, and tea, and at the end even a little watermelon. The guards sold soap, tea, and sugar to those women who still had money, and the authorities provided one blanket for every seven prisoners. The women were allowed to do their washing in the prison courtyard, sit under trees in the shade, and even sleep outdoors if the heat inside was oppressive. At least some were allowed into town under guard to shop. One woman who was pregnant when she arrived at Dibs was taken (albeit under military guard) to a hospital in the town, where her delivery was attended by a Kurdish woman doctor. Another said that doctors visited the base twice a week, dispensing shots and tablets, although other witnesses disputed this.

Yet for all these comparative advantages, Dibs was also a regime of unremitting horror. Ironically, the inmates found that the base was run by a fellow Kurd, a man from the Erbil area named Haji Ahmad Fatah who had made the pilgrimage to Mecca. Children who were old enough to do manual labor were forced by the guards to sweep out the halls and clean the bathrooms. "We were guarded by Amn, Istikhbarat, and Ba'ath Party people," recalled a fourteen-year-old boy who spent five months at the Dibs base. "They were always coming and beating the prisoners without any reason. They tied up my hands and beat me several times. Three Amn agents beat me with a stick on my back and legs. Twice they kept me tied up without food for a whole day for no reason inside the hall where I slept, from morning until night. I could not ask why. It was impossible for anyone to intervene in Ba'ath rules."[22]

This child at least survived. Many, perhaps hundreds, did not. There were few fatalities at first, but the rate increased as spring gave way to the heat of summer. Amina, the woman from Akoyan, gave birth to a baby daughter in Dibs, but within two months the child sickened and died. Four or five children died from Bileh. Nabat, a twenty-eight-year-old mother from Qader Karam, lost two of her infant children within a month of each other. Her three-year-old daughter, Sharo, died first; a month later, it was the turn of her two-year-old son, Diar. "They died of fear," Nabat said. "They were scared, got sick, and died. They had diarrhea and were vomiting."[23] Sherzad, a boy of fourteen, counted seven infant deaths at Dibs in a single night. Muhammad, a boy of nine, estimated that there were fifty deaths in his family's large cell during the five months of their captivity. Most were small children, but some older women also died. Habiba, who was eight at the time of Anfal, recalled being forced to sleep among dead bodies before guards came to remove them.[24]

The emaciated bodies of Nabat's two children were taken away by two guards from the Popular Army, who washed the bodies and interred them in the town's Gumbat Cemetery as Nabat watched. Other infant corpses were simply dumped at the town's Old Mosque, according to Karim, the twenty-year-old student who had watched the Dibs commando base fill up with prisoners earlier that spring. Townspeople would come to the mosque to wash the bodies, and young men from the locality, including Karim himself, would dig the burial plots in an old, abandoned children's cemetery about a mile away. Karim himself helped to bury four infants and with his friends buried at least fifty, all less than a year old. The people of Dibs marked off a special plot for the new arrivals, and each of the tiny graves was marked.[25]

At regular intervals, sealed buses would drive up to the Dibs base and carry off large numbers of prisoners. On at least two occasions, these groups were made up of people from the Kalar area of southern Germian—five hundred women and children in all, according to one estimate; these were transported to the prison at Nugra Salman for reasons that remain obscure (see chapter 11).[26] Thousands of others, perhaps half the total population of Dibs, were driven off to unknown destinations and vanished into the darkness of Anfal. Sherin, for example, a twenty-three-year-old woman from the village of Qeitoul Rasha (nahya of Qader Karam), lost two of her young nieces this way: Perjin Ja'far Hassan, aged twelve, and her younger sister, Nabat. Given that the survivors of Anfal were eventually resettled in camps that corresponded to their places of origin and that five years have now passed without a word of news, the strong presumption must be that these two girls, and the thousands who vanished from Dibs with them, were murdered by the Iraqi authorities.[27]

## A PRISON CAMP FOR THE ELDERLY

If you know about hell, this is hell. We have seen it.
    —Muhammad Hussein Muhammad (b. 1912), a survivor of Nugra Salman

While the trucks and buses drove north to Dibs, others headed south from Topzawa and Tikrit, through Iraq's Arab heartland and then farther south still, into the vast deserts that stretch toward the Saudi border, until at last they reached the abandoned fortress prison of Nugra Salman, the "Pit of Salman." The prisoners came in four main batches, and the total population of Nugra Salman during Anfal appears to have been somewhere between six thousand and eight thousand.[28] The first to arrive were thousands of captured villagers from Qara Dagh and Germian (the locations of the second and third Anfals, respectively), aged from about fifty to ninety, who came in huge caravans of sealed buses in mid-April 1988. Next, in early May, a somewhat smaller number of elderly people arrived from the Lesser Zab Valley (the site of the fourth Anfal). Third, over the course of the summer, several busloads of women and children from southern Germian were transferred from the prison at Dibs to be housed in separate quarters at Nugra Salman. Finally, in late August, just a few days before the military declared a formal end to its Anfal campaign, several hundred returning refugees from the gas attack on Halabja were brought to Nugra Salman, having surrendered to the Iraqi army as they crossed the border from Iran. According to some reports, the Halabja contingent was of all ages and may even have included young men.[29]

One of the Halabja survivors was a thirty-three-year-old woman named Urfiya. One of her five children had died on the road to Iran after the bombing. With the other four, Urfiya crossed the border and spent five months in the Iranian camps. On 23 August, she recalled, the Iranians bussed two thousand Halabja families back to the border. The Iraqi army was waiting for them and took them in military trucks to Suleimaniyeh, where the Emergency Forces held them on a bread-and-water diet for five days. The place where they were confined, said Urfiya, was "full of people from Qara Dagh." At the end of this time, the young men were separated from their families and driven off in vehicles that resembled ambulances, painted white or green and with a single tiny window in the rear. They were never seen again. The women and children and the elderly were crammed into civilian buses and driven by way of Kirkuk, Tikrit, Baghdad, and Samawah to Nugra Salman, arriving there on 29 August.[30]

The journey from the outskirts of Kirkuk to Nugra Salman took between twelve and fifteen hours, with fifty or sixty prisoners crammed into windowless buses designed to hold half that number. At the head and tail of each convoy, Amn and Istikhbarat agents rode in cars with walkie-talkie radios. Some convoys moved off early in the morning and arrived at Nugra Salman late the same evening. Others left in darkness and drove all night. By guessing at the time and direction or by peering out the rear door when it was left open a crack for air, the prisoners could tell when they passed through a city—first Tikrit, several hours later Baghdad, and then finally Samawah. They could hear sirens wailing and glimpse curious Arab crowds lining the streets to watch the sealed vehicles go past with their human cargo. There were no stops; the detainees were given no food or water, and the presence of guards with Kalashnikovs silenced any complaint.

At Samawah, the elderly prisoners sometimes became aware that the convoys were dividing into two. While their vehicles continued to head south, others peeled off in a different direction. These were the buses that carried the younger Kurdish prisoners from Topzawa, and they were never seen again. After Samawah, there was nothing but barren desert, dotted with the rubble of destroyed settlements—"like our villages, flattened by bulldozers," said one woman.[31] Three hours to the southwest of Samawah, the tableland dropped away sharply, and there in the depression below, visible only at the last moment, lay the town of al-Salman. A mile and a quarter away in the desert, surrounded by a barbed-wire perimeter fence and guarded by watch towers at each corner, was the prison of Nugra Salman itself.

The buses entered through one of the two large gates and came to a rest in a huge central courtyard "three times as long as the soccer field at Suleimaniyeh."[32] The first arrivals from Topzawa in mid-April found Nugra Salman dark and empty. It was an old building, dating back to the days of the Iraqi monarchy and perhaps earlier.[33] It had been abandoned for years, used by Arab nomads to shelter their herds. The bare walls were scrawled with the diaries of political prisoners. On the door of one cell, a guard had daubed "Khomeini eats shit." Over the main gate, someone else had written "Welcome to Hell." Over the rear entrance, another sign read: "It is rare for anyone to survive three months in this place."

Whatever interrogation the Iraqi authorities deemed necessary for these elderly and infirm victims of Anfal had already been carried out at Topzawa. Here, at Nugra Salman, there was only a quick registration of name, occupation, and place of residence, accompanied by jeers and threats from the guards. "You are here to die," said one, "on the orders of Saddam Hussein and Ali Hassan al-Majid." With this, the new arrivals were shoved into the cells, or halls, that filled both stories of the prison. The bare rooms varied greatly in size; some of them held only fifty or sixty prisoners, others several hundreds.[34] The doors were locked from 10:00 P.M. to 7:00 A.M. At other times the inmates could circulate freely.

The arrival of the first detainees coincided more or less with the beginning of Ramadan on 17 April, and during the holy month the food was better than it had been at Topzawa.[35] There was rice, vegetable soup, potatoes, and tomatoes and even meat and fruit on occasion. Water came from a well, through a standpipe in the yard, though it was hot, salty, and bitter, "like snake poison," said one man. Many inmates believed that the first health crisis at Nugra Salman was connected to drinking this water. The first deaths occurred early in May, soon after the arrival of the second wave of prisoners, those from the Lesser Zab Valley.

One of those who arrived in this batch was Abd-al-Qader Abdullah Askari, the sixty-eight-year-old village head from Goktapa who had lost sixteen members of his family in the chemical weapons attack on 3 May. During his four months in Nugra Salman, Abd-al-Qader—one of the few literate prisoners and also an Arabic speaker—emerged as a natural leader of the inmates, and his testimony is worth quoting at length. After the first night at Topzawa:

At 8:30 A.M. a military man came in and announced, "Prepare yourselves." We had nothing, we were ready, we had nothing to pack. They told us to leave the room. We noticed 150 or 200 vehicles waiting in two groups, like ambulances, but green.[36] These could take only ten people, but they put twenty-seven in ours. There were two doors: a small narrow one that only the guard could enter and a second door through which they pushed us. It was very hot, but they closed the door and locked it. In our car there were only elderly people.

After an hour or an hour and a half, we called for water. I told them in Arabic, "We are thirsty; give us water." [They answered,] "Water is forbidden for you, it is not allowed." After a while, a friend wanted to get out to relieve himself. I informed the soldier. "It is not allowed for you," he said. After ten minutes the man could not hold himself any longer and we smelled a bad smell in the car. Five fainted from the smell and the heat. We wished for death. Nothing was allowed to us. All the men took their clothes off because of the heat, wearing only their shorts. The car went on moving and we did not know where it was going.

One and a half hours before nightfall we arrived at a fort and got out. It was deserted. They took us into a long yard, with soldiers and police all around. More cars were arriving and emptying out men and women. The number reached four hundred. They brought water in buckets without any glasses. We were like cows, putting our heads down to get the water at once, three at a time drinking from the bucket. The water was hot, the temperature to wash with, and it was salty.

[After registration] a guard asked for newcomers and told them to go with him. It was fifteen minutes before dark. We went to the second floor, and they put sixty-four of us into one room, about eight meters by six. I objected: "We are not animals to be crowded all in one room. How can we sleep and eat." The man in charge answered, "Shut up. This is what we prepared for you." After three minutes he left, and another came to the door with a sack on his shoulder. It was a prisoner. He said, "Brothers, we know you were not given anything because you are newcomers. We brought our shares for you tonight. Take this bread since they will not give you any food until the morning."

In the morning a prisoner from another hall came and recruited four of us to go with him to get the bread rations for the cell. After twenty minutes the four men came back with three sacks of bread. Each prisoner got three samoun for the entire day, breakfast, lunch, and dinner.[37] The bread was not made from wheat but from *zorat* [corn, normally used as animal feed].

## DEATHS AT NUGRA SALMAN

The Ramadan rations were now a thing of the past, and on the new starvation diet of bread and contaminated water, the conditions at Nugra Salman deteriorated sharply. The prisoners were fatigued and infested by lice. By late May there was a steady stream of deaths, some days three, some six or seven, and sometimes as many as a dozen. Abd-al-Qader tried his best to keep a count of the deaths. By early September, when he was finally released, he had tallied 517, all victims of the inhuman conditions at Nugra Salman and the depraved indifference of the Iraqi authorities. Later, after his release, he heard that another forty-five had died over two successive nights in September.

Abd-al-Qader's figures, which suggest an average of four or five deaths a day during the period of his imprisonment from starvation, disease, and physical abuse, are extremely credible. Certainly, they bear out the more impressionistic estimates given by many other witnesses. The additional forty-five deaths may have been connected with an epidemic that some survivors say broke out after the arrival of the returned refugees from Halabja at the end of August 1988. This outbreak prompted the arrival of a dozen "white-coated doctors" from Samawah who advised the prisoners to stop drinking the water.

The authorities at Nugra Salman appear to have responded to the steady stream of fatalities in two ways. The first was to arrange for a daily delivery of water by tanker truck from Samawah; the second was for the guards to initiate a petty extortion racket, selling food at grossly inflated prices to those prisoners who had managed to make it through Topzawa with cash still in their pockets.

The tanker usually came from Samawah twice a day, although sometimes it missed a day altogether. When the water arrived, there was pandemonium as the prisoners rushed the truck. They were allowed only a few minutes to fill their pitchers, struggling for access to the plastic hosepipe as the guards taunted them, allowing the precious fluid to splash on to the ground and lashing out at people randomly with sticks and strips of electric cable. Sensing easy money, the truck driver took to selling the prisoners buckets of water for 4 dinars ($12) each. Later, he also offered to bring canned milk and meat, lentils, tomato paste, and soap.

The driver's example was quickly taken up by the guards, who were from Amn, according to some witnesses, or from Istikhbarat, according to others. A cup of rice was 1 dinar, cigarettes were 3 dinars ($9) a pack, and tomato juice in cans (past their expiry date) cost 12 ($36). According to Abd-al-Qader:

> We told the prisoners in charge of the food to speak to the guards to find a way to get rid of the bad food and get sugar and tea, even if we had to buy them, because the deaths were very bad. They managed to get sugar, tea, and oil with our money. The food came secretly at night. They sold us tomato paste for 4 dinars [$12], in cans that were priced for sale by the government at six dirhems [about 90 cents]. We paid 80 dinars [$240] for a sack of sugar and 70 dinars [$210] for a sack of rice—official price, 11 dinars [$33].

The first thing we got was the tomato paste. We managed to borrow a pot from a cell whose prisoners had been there longer than us, and we cooked food in it. We put our bread into the tomato paste soup and absorbed all the liquid. This was really like a feast to us.[38]

The effects of this black market were short-lived, however, other than for the lucky few who had managed to keep money after Topzawa. The prisoners grew weaker, scarcely able to take advantage of the brief afternoon exercise period, when they were allowed to mingle in the central courtyard. The deaths continued, and among the dead were some of the children who had been newly transferred to Nugra Salman from Dibs.

The dead were not permitted the dignity of a decent burial. Indeed, they were often not even moved from the spot where they died, but left there for as long as three days to rot in the summer heat. This was evidently a matter of deliberate policy. "After a few weeks," one woman recalled, "my husband died in my arms. He had gotten extremely weak and thin, and he had been badly beaten by the prison guards. My husband's body lay in the prison hall for one day. The guards did not let me bury him, and I had to beg them. The guard said the body had to remain in the prison until it rotted."[39]

Eventually Amn agents would register the names of the dead, strip them of any remaining money and valuables, and order the corpses to be stuffed into sacks and loaded onto handcarts of the sort normally used for garbage disposal. The theft of money in particular infuriated Abd-al-Qader:

One man died with 400 dinars [$1,200 at the time] on him. An Amn man came, took the money, kissed it, and said this was for the government. I insulted the prisoners about this, telling them, "You are not animals! Anything that the dead relatives leave is yours. Do not leave it for others. Use it, you need it." They answered, "What else could we do? We are afraid." I told them, "Inside this building, nothing can be sent to you from the outside. You cannot live without that money. You may be afraid of God, but God will not punish you, I assure you. I will answer for you on the Day of Judgment." They followed my advice. From then on, they left only a dinar or a half dinar in the pockets of the dead for the guards. The guards came two or three times, but when they found such small amounts they abandoned the search.

The prisoners tried as best they could to wash the bodies and prepare them for burial according to Islamic doctrine. At first, if there was money, the tanker driver from Samawah might be persuaded to bring a shroud. But when the money ran out, the only shroud available was the dead person's Kurdish head scarf or one of the scarce prison blankets. Groups of prisoners—at least two, sometimes four or six men, weakened and fatigued by hunger—would be assembled to carry the corpse away, while prison guards kicked and punched them to hurry the process along, shouting epithets all the while. "You are saboteurs, and you deserve to die like dogs," one guard shouted.

A ten-minute trudge through the stony desert brought them to the grave site, which lay a few hundred yards east of the prison. It comprised a series of long trenches, no more than three feet deep, dug by bulldozers. There were no markers, although the mourners tried when they could to mark the spot with stones. The bodies were laid roughly inside and dirt was tossed over them. The guards allowed no time for prayers for the dead. When thirty or forty corpses filled a trench, the bulldozer would smooth it over to remove all traces and proceed to dig another.[40]

When the burial party returned the next day, broken limbs and bloody rags would be strewn around, for during the night the freshly turned grave site attracted packs of wild desert dogs. The guards were terrified by these animals, believing that they became rabid after eating human flesh, and shot at any they could see. Few of the remains of those who died at Nugra Salman were allowed to rest in peace. "Go bury the bodies for the dogs," the guards would taunt the survivors.

The man who presided over this cruel regime was named Hajjaj, an Amn lieutenant by most accounts.[41] Hajjaj was a feared and detested figure, described by one witness as a "bald, husky young man" from Amn headquarters in Baghdad who drove a red Volkswagen Passat manufactured in Brazil. His deputy was a man called Shamkhi. An uncle of Lieutenant Hajjaj, one Khalaf, was one of the guards.

Hajjaj and his associates were notorious for beating prisoners on the slightest pretext, or none at all. One man in his sixties was beaten for requesting a light bulb. "Go to [PUK leader Jalal] Talabani for bulbs," a guard told him mockingly.[42] Another inmate, weakened by hunger, fell asleep one day when Hajjaj was in his cell. "He slapped me right away," the man recalled, "and said, 'You shall never sleep in my presence.' Then he made me go and sit in the place where the garbage was kept."[43] Age and gender offered no protection. "Is this child a peshmerga?" the same man asked a guard one day. "Is this woman?" The guard answered, "Yes, they are. They are all peshmerga, and they are criminals." On another occasion, Abd-al-Qader Abdullah Askari saw Hajjaj kicking and hitting with a length of plastic tubing a group of young women who had recently arrived from Dibs.[44]

Hajjaj also punished prisoners by forcing them to crawl on their bellies. If the result was not to his liking, a guard would stomp on the small of the prisoner's back to force him lower. The punishment most favored by Hajjaj, according to many accounts, was to expose prisoners to the blazing midday sun. Men, women, and children alike were subjected to this treatment, even if they were too weak to walk and had to be dragged to the spot. The prisoners would be forced to squat with their heads lowered, normally for two hours. Any movement would be punished with a beating. A variant on this routine was to tie the prisoner to a metal post in the sun. There were nine of these posts sunk in concrete in the central courtyard at Nugra Salman, each taller than a person and thicker than an electricity pole.[45] Some prisoners were reportedly suspended upside down from the posts and tied at the feet by their Kurdish cummerbund, their unbound hands barely clearing the ground.

The inmates of Nugra Salman had to endure Hajjaj's brutal custody until 6 September, when the general amnesty allowed them to go free, but not home.

# THE FIRING SQUADS

Hell and Elysium swarm with ghosts of men
That I have sent from sundry foughten fields
To spread my fame through hell and up to heaven.
> —Marlowe, *Tamburlaine the Great* (part I, V, i)

It was God's wish.
> —Mustafa, who escaped a mass execution during Anfal

## MUHAMMAD'S STORY

At least six people—the youngest a boy of twelve, the eldest a man of thirty-eight with nine children—have survived to tell the truth about what happened to the tens of thousands of Iraqi Kurds who were driven in convoys of sealed vehicles from the Popular Army camp at Topzawa. All six were from the Germian area, the scene of the third Anfal.

Muhammad, the thirty-two-year-old member of the peshmerga backing force from the village of Aliyani Taza in southern Germian, arrived with his family at the army fort at Qoratu on about 16 April (see chapter 5). They spent three days there before being moved to Topzawa, where Muhammad was separated from his two wives and seven children. None of his family ever returned alive, with the exception of his parents, who survived Nugra Salman.[1]

Muhammad spent two days in Topzawa. He was not questioned. He was given nothing to eat. On the third day the guards came to his "hall," which held about five hundred prisoners. They handcuffed the men in pairs and took them to a line of vehicles painted in camouflage colors. Muhammad counted the seats; each vehicle held twenty-eight prisoners. It was the middle of the afternoon when the convoy moved off. They drove for perhaps six hours, but Muhammad quickly lost all sense of direction and had no idea where they were going. All he could tell was that most of the journey was on paved highway; the final hour was on a bumpy dirt road.

When the convoy eventually stopped, the driver kept the motor running. Over the throb of the engine, Muhammad could hear the sound of gunfire outside. The prisoners were hustled out into the darkness and searched for any identity cards and money that might have been missed earlier. Muhammad lost his last 700 dinars. When the search was completed, the guards removed the handcuffs that bound Muhammad to his neighbor, a man from the village of Babakr, close to Aliyani Taza. In place of the handcuffs, the guards used a length of string to tie the twenty-eight prisoners in a single line by their left hands. The men were ordered to stand facing the edge of a freshly dug trench, just long enough to accommodate the twenty-eight bodies as they fell.

The knot binding Muhammad's left hand had been carelessly tied, and he managed to tug it free from his wrist. He broke away a moment before the soldiers opened fire. Beyond the trench was an open field, and the spring grass had grown tall enough to conceal Muhammad from the truck headlights that were now trained in his direction. To his astonishment, the guards did not give chase. Behind him, the clatter of gunfire continued.

Muhammad ran and walked for four days without food, drinking rain water from puddles along the way. Trying to chart his route by the sun, he set out in what he thought was the direction of Germian, across an endless flat plain planted with wheat and barley. From the clothes of the shepherds he spotted at intervals, he could tell that he was in an Arab area. After four days, so exhausted that he could not walk another step, he stumbled into an Arab village. The people gathered around to stare. "Look," they said, "it is a Kurd who has fallen out of an airplane."

The remainder of Muhammad's odyssey is too long to recount in detail here. He was imprisoned and beaten by the Arab villagers, handed over to the police, interrogated, taken to Mosul, jailed again, transferred to the Kirkuk police and then to Suleimaniyeh, to Kalar and back once more to Suleimaniyeh, amnestied, and finally inducted into the army. Miraculously, the police believed his story, which he never varied, that he was a member of the jahsh of Fatah Beg, the mustashar from Kalar. The ordinary Iraqi police, who almost certainly were not privy to the truth about the Anfal mass executions, never realized that they were dealing with an Anfalakan. Amn, which would certainly have pressed the matter further, was never brought in to elucidate Muhammad's case. The man was truly blessed with a talent for survival.

## OZER, OMAR, AND IBRAHIM

Remarkably, four of the other five survivors of the Anfal firing squads traveled together to their execution site as part of a single convoy. Three were even in the same vehicle, although one of the three did not know the others and has not met them since. It is possible, then, to reconstruct their composite story in considerable detail.

Ozer, the young man who had spent his last night at Topzawa shivering with cold as he listened to revving bus engines and contemplated the pools of diesel oil and fresh blood on a cement floor, was perhaps the most articulate of these witnesses. Ozer was twenty-five at the time of Anfal, an unmarried construction worker who had seen action in the war against Iran and had deserted several times from the Iraqi army. He was born not ten miles from Topzawa, in the village of Tarjil, on the main road between Kirkuk and the nahya of Leilan. He had moved around a lot before settling in nearby Jafan, a tiny hamlet of just seventeen houses. There he stayed until April 1987, when the army attacked and burned the village. This time Ozer moved to Khidr Reihan, a peaceful village two and a half hours on foot from the nahya of Qader Karam that was home to several other deserters and draft dodgers.

Like so many others, Ozer took to the hills when the third Anfal approached his home on about 10 April. Hearing the rumor of a temporary amnesty in Qader Karam, he was one of the thousands who surrendered to the jahsh forces commanded by Qasem Agha, the one-eyed mustashar from Koysinjaq. Over the next few days, Ozer passed through the Qader Karam police station and the army brigade headquarters in Chamchamal. The truck that took him from there to the local office of Amn was part of the convoy that was caught up in the attempted revolt of the townspeople of Chamchamal. Ozer was not one of those they succeeded in rescuing, and finally, on 14 April, he arrived at Topzawa.

At this stage, Ozer met up with an acquaintance whom we shall call Omar, a twenty-two-year-old draft dodger who had also fled from Jafan the previous year and resettled in Khidr Reihan. Omar fled to the hills when Anfal began and surrendered to Qasem Agha's men two days after Ozer did. From Chamchamal, they were trucked together to Topzawa, where most of their cell mates were strangers. Two of these men, however, were destined to share with Ozer and Omar what was intended to be their final journey.

Both were draft dodgers from peshmerga-controlled villages in the nahya of Qader Karam. The elder of the two was "Mustafa," a thirty-eight-year-old resident of Top Khana; the other, "Ibrahim," was a twenty-three-year-old father of four from Kani Qader Khwaru. Neither man was an active fighter, but Ibrahim had carried an Iranian-made Kalashnikov rifle as a member of the civilian defense force and was a friend or blood relative of most of the peshmerga who died in the army's bloody assault on the PUK base at Tazashar at the opening of the third Anfal campaign. Like Ozer and Omar, both Mustafa and Ibrahim were fooled by the phony offer of a three-day amnesty in Qader Karam. Mustafa had turned himself in to the jahsh led by Sheikh Mu'tassem; Ibrahim had surrendered to the forces of the mustashar Raf'at Gilli. Both men had passed through the first-stage collection facility at Aliawa.

Although the testimonies of these four men contain minor discrepancies over dates, at some point between 15 and 17 April (the first day of the holy month of Ramadan), at about 8:00 in the morning, they were hustled, together with hundreds of others, into the prison yard at Topzawa. A caravan of sealed vehicles waited under military guard with their engines running. They were of two kinds. Some (eighteen, by one count) were windowless police buses, painted either green or white, and Ozer, Ibrahim, and Omar were shoved into one. Ozer had time to notice that it had a Mosul registration; its license plate read "Nineveh Police," and the number was 5036 or 5037. Mustafa traveled in the second type of vehicle, which resembled a large ambulance or covered truck. The smaller police buses held thirty-four or thirty-five people each, in forward-facing rows two abreast, divided by a central aisle. Mustafa's truck held between fifty and sixty prisoners, squashed together on four benches that ran lengthwise along the vehicle.

To the last, it appears that the prisoners were grouped according to place of origin. Ozer recognized faces from towns in the Leilan–Qader Karam area— Khidr Beg, Qashqa, and Qarachiwar—as well as two from his own home village of Khidr Reihan. Everyone in the bus was young, aged from twenty to forty, Ibrahim recalled. Ozer thought that some of the men were much older, "with white beards."

The inside of the bus was hellish. The vehicle in which Ozer, Ibrahim, and Mustafa rode was thick with old urine and human feces. Its previous occupants had scrawled brief messages in Kurdish on the seat backs: "To the Saudi border. . . . To the Kuwaiti border. . . . To Ar'ar."[2] In these smaller buses, the prisoners were separated from the driver's compartment by a padlocked sliding door. The driver entered by a separate door on the right of the bus. A military guard rode alongside him, armed with a Kalashnikov rifle with a folding stock and wearing the distinctive uniform of the army's Special Forces—camouflage fatigues of yellow drab with irregular green splotches and a red beret with the golden insignia of a bird of prey with outstretched wings.

Set into the sliding door that separated the two compartments was a small wire-mesh opening, perhaps six inches square, through which the prisoners closest to the front could see the road ahead and the driver's rear-view mirror. Ozer estimated that his was the thirty-fifth vehicle in the convoy.[3] To the front and rear of each bus, he could glimpse pick-up trucks of the sort used by Amn, with mounted machine guns.

Seated toward the front of the bus was a man named Anwar Tayyar. A dark, stout man, Tayyar was a former peshmerga; he had worked as a driver and knew the roads intimately. For this reason, his fellow prisoners asked him to figure out where they were heading. Sneaking glances through the wire grille, Tayyar at first reported that they were following the road to Mosul. There was a gasp of fear, because, as Ibrahim recalled, "most of the government's killers are in Mosul."[4] The passengers were convinced they were going to die.

Soon, however, the bus swung off the Mosul road and turned to the southwest. "We have been saved," said Anwar Tayyar with a sigh of relief. Perhaps, the men speculated, they were merely being transferred to another prison. But the buses drove on, stopping occasionally for a few minutes. At intervals, the men begged the Special Forces guard for water. "Just a minute," the man answered, but the water never arrived. In the airless heat and stench of Mustafa's bus, the prisoners were reduced to drinking their own urine from their shoes.

As the afternoon wore on, Anwar Tayyar began to lose his bearings. "Samawah!" he exclaimed at one point, but then someone else recognized Falluja, a sizable town on the Euphrates. Just outside Falluja, Ozer noticed that the convoy was splitting into two parts. The majority of the vehicles continued in a different direction; five, including Ozer's bus and the larger green truck carrying Mustafa, drove due west into the rapidly approaching sunset. Before long, they passed the larger city of Ramadi to their left. After leaving Ramadi behind them, they continued for at least another fifteen minutes, perhaps as much as half an hour, on the paved highway, turning right once at a junction to cross a heavily guarded bridge over a river, presumably the Euphrates.

At the far end of the bridge, the five vehicles halted. It was now about 6:30 P.M., and ten hours had passed since their departure from Topzawa. Through the wire-mesh screen, the prisoners could see that they had stopped outside a police station, under a clump of date palms. They could hear a conversation between one of their army guards and an officer at the police station. Although the man was addressed as "sir," his uniform bore no insignia of rank. It was clear that the guard was transferring the prisoners into this officer's custody. He handed over a list of their names and told the officer that the vehicles were to remain with the police "until the mission is completed," at which time they should be returned.

The drivers and Special Forces guards climbed down from the vehicles at this point. Their replacements were dressed all in green with black berets, a uniform characteristic of both Amn and the Ba'ath Party as well as the regular Iraqi police. The officer and several other men jumped into two Toyota Landcruisers. There were also two bulldozers.

With the bulldozers in the lead, the new nine-vehicle caravan drove west along a bumpy paved road that ran parallel to the Euphrates. In the fading light, the silhouettes of date palms fringed the road to the right. One of the prisoners in Ozer's bus was weak and faint, and a prisoner who spoke a little Arabic begged the new driver for water. This was not allowed, the driver answered. "Let the man die," he said. "You are all men of Jalal Talabani."

After half an hour, the convoy turned right onto a dirt road. Ahead the prisoners saw only desert and darkness. Some began to pray, muttering the *Shehadeh:* "There is no God but Allah, and Muhammad is his Prophet." Remembered images of his family flashed through Ibrahim's mind. By now all the men were weeping, asking what they had done to deserve such a fate, kissing each other's beards, and exchanging words of forgiveness, as is the Muslim custom among those who know they are about to die.

It was almost dark, and the meaning of time had begun to dissolve. Ozer thought that the sealed buses traveled along this rutted desert track for about ten minutes; Omar estimated that the journey took from fifteen to thirty minutes; Ibrahim said that it felt more like an hour. Suddenly, the bus lurched to a stop, bogged down in the deep sand. The vehicle behind, the last one in the convoy, swerved to the right to avoid it and got stuck as well. Through the wire-mesh screen in the sliding door, Ozer could see that the three remaining buses, as well as the two Landcruisers and one of the two bulldozers, had driven on. In the half-light he could just make out the tops of the vehicles bobbing as they crested a rise and dipped into a shallow depression in the desert a quarter of a mile or so ahead. The driver turned off the engine.

Since the final turn onto the dirt road, there was no longer any room for denial or wishful thinking. The men knew exactly what lay in store for them, and they began to plan feverishly, speaking in Kurdish in the knowledge that neither the guard nor the driver could understand them. When the guards arrived to kill them, they would put up a struggle. "Even if only one of the thirty-five survived, it was worth the try," said Ibrahim.

In the sudden quiet, the prisoners could hear the steady chatter of gunfire from automatic weapons and the churning, whining sound of bulldozer engines. After perhaps twenty minutes, the guns fell silent. Out of the darkness, a bulldozer lumbered toward them and took up position behind the bus. Gears screaming, it tried several times to push the vehicle out of the sand, but the front wheels only dug in deeper. Next it tried to lift the bus out by its rear end, and Ozer thought the driver meant to tip them headlong into a trench, bus and all. At last, the bulldozer managed to drag the stalled vehicle out frontward. The driver climbed down from his cab, exhausted by the effort, and took out his hip flask. The prisoners begged for water, banging on the windowless steel walls. The driver drank deeply and jeeringly held up his flask as the rest of the liquid trickled away into the sand.

It was now 7:30 P.M. and quite dark. The men were just able to tell the time by squinting at a watch that a prisoner from the village of Khidr Beg had somehow managed to keep at Topzawa. Twice more there were volleys of gunfire and the sound of screams. After about half an hour, the two Landcruisers returned with the officer who had joined the convoy at the bridge over the Euphrates. The driver of Ozer's bus climbed down from his seat, walked around to the back of the vehicle, and turned off the overhead light in the rear compartment. Having done this, he went back to his cab and turned his headlights on full beam. As Ozer and his companions whimpered in panic, the three dozen occupants of the second stalled bus were dragged into the pool of light, and a uniformed firing squad opened up on them with Kalashnikov rifles and pistols. When the firing stopped, the men were dragged into a freshly dug pit. Ozer noticed that some of the bodies were still moving. Only one busload of prisoners remained.

The men's plan was this: when the first guard entered the bus to take the prisoners away, the strongest of them would overpower him, grab his weapon, and try to wedge the door open. Most of the men were too weak to assist, but Ozer, Omar, and a handful of others were willing to try. They watched the sliding partition door. Ibrahim waited fearfully at the back, ready to bolt if he could. Through the grille, Ozer could see that two guards with pistols had taken positions on either side of the door. Another, who carried a Kalashnikov rifle, stood by the driver's seat, while a fourth man, also armed with a Kalashnikov, guarded the outer door with one foot planted on the step and the other on the ground.

After a few moments one of the uniformed guards, a burly man with a thick neck, removed the padlock and slid back the connecting door to the driver's compartment. As soon as he did so, a prisoner named Salam lunged forward to strike him. But a second guard in the driver's cab opened fire with his pistol, killing Salam instantly, and slammed the door shut again. Ozer heard the first guard, apparently an officer, declare that he would execute the prisoners one by one.

Seizing command of the situation, Ozer issued his instructions. When the guards took the first prisoner out, Omar would throw his weight against the rail of the sliding door to prevent it from being closed. The other men would hurl themselves into the breach. And that is essentially what happened. The burly guard returned, pulled one prisoner into the open doorway and tied a white cloth around his eyes as a blindfold. As he turned to drag the man away, half a dozen prisoners rushed forward. Several of them laid hold of the shoulder strap of the guard's rifle while he kept a firm grip of the stock and the barrel. Ozer yelled at another prisoner to punch the officer in the face. Although the man, like everyone, was weakened by several days without food, he succeeded in landing a blow in the officer's eye. Ozer wrenched the rifle free, but the officer managed to break loose, unclip the magazine, and hurl it out of the bus behind him, rendering the weapon useless.

Pouring through the open door, the prisoners cut off the escape of the guard who had been standing by the driver's seat. Gunfire erupted, and two men fell dead on top of Ozer. Another prisoner tried to leap from the bus and was also cut down. As Ozer struggled to free himself, he saw the second of the four guards, the one who had killed Salam, stagger toward him, bleeding profusely from the shoulder. The man was screaming, "Abu Saleh, come and help me!" It appeared that he had been shot by another guard—his own partner. Ozer reached for the man's pistol but could not find it. Instead, he wrestled him to the ground by grabbing the guard's injured arm, and the guard lay still, apparently unconscious. Meanwhile, whoever was outside, soldiers or police, continued to rake the bus with gunfire, and the men in the passenger compartment cowered under the bus seats. Bodies piled up inside the bus, and Ibrahim took a painful flesh wound in the right buttock. He was also dimly aware that he could no longer see through his right eye. In the confusion, Omar managed to wriggle under the vehicle as bullets ricocheted from it on all sides. Ozer felt his leg grazed by a flying piece of shrapnel. As he lay there, he heard a strange sound between the bursts of firing. At first he could not place it, then he realized that it was the sound of blood dripping from the bus. Almost all of his fellow prisoners were dead.

## MUSTAFA'S STORY

The remaining three vehicles that accompanied the convoy from Kirkuk had come to a halt a few hundred yards ahead in the shallow depression that Ozer had glimpsed through the driver's window. Here, the executions had proceeded in a more orderly and efficient fashion. It was *maghreb,* sunset, when the guards flung open the rear door of the truck in which Mustafa, the thirty-eight-year-old father of nine from the village of Top Khana, had traveled from Topzawa. The men were dragged out in pairs. In his fear, Mustafa left his shoes behind; he had taken them off in the bus because of the heat. He, too, was aware of the constant rat-a-tat of gunfire, which seemed not to come from a single site but from many directions at once. Yet he could see nothing, only darkness and desert.

The guards carried out a hasty body search, stripping Mustafa of his military identification papers but somehow failing to find the 200 dinars that he had hidden in his clothing at Topzawa. He felt his hands being roughly bound behind him with his Kurdish cummerbund. His eyes were blindfolded with his head scarf, as were his companion's. The two men were ordered to walk. Mustafa, knowing that he was to die, began to recite under his breath the *Ayat al-Kursi* from the Qur'an: "God, There is no god but He, the Living, the Everlasting."[5] He moved forward about twenty yards and then felt himself stumbling down a slight incline. From a distance, the voice of a guard ordered the two men to lie down on their backs. As he obeyed the command, Mustafa felt himself sandwiched between his companion and another, inert body. His ears picked up the sound of a bulldozer's engine revving.

The next thing Mustafa heard was automatic weapons firing. To his side he felt a jolt and heard a groan. The clatter of gunfire ceased, and Mustafa heard the guards walk away. He realized that the bullets had missed him. Praying that he was unobserved, he tried to wriggle sideways, feeling more dead bodies as he moved, and struggled to loosen the cummerbund that bound his hands. Minutes later, he heard the guards return with another two prisoners, who lay down in the trench and were riddled with gunfire; then another pair and another round of firing, this time a little farther away. Mustafa was still unharmed. "It was God's wish," he thought.

This time when the guards departed, Mustafa managed to work his blindfold loose. He saw that he was lying in a long shallow trench, perhaps twenty feet wide and eighteen inches deep. The end of the trench, where the bulldozer had exited, was close by: this was the shallow incline into which he and his fellow prisoner had stumbled. In the other direction, the trench stretched as far as Mustafa could see. It was filled with hundreds of corpses.

This macabre scene was illuminated by the headlights of the bulldozer, which now stood at the shallow entrance to the mass grave, its engine running. The driver appeared to be waiting for orders to cover the bodies with dirt when the trench was full, as it then almost was. Over the lip of the trench, Mustafa could still make out the dark shape of the vehicle that had brought him there. For fifteen minutes he lay where he was, listening to staccato gunfire and screams. After a while he realized that the sound was not in fact coming from all sides. The area behind him was silent, and Mustafa began cautiously to clamber over the bloody piles of dead bodies, away from the noise of the firing squads. Peering out, he saw that his was the last of many trenches. Behind him there was only desert. Mustafa ran.

He ran until morning, stopping only occasionally to catch his breath. Wild dogs chased him, smelling blood, and he kept them at bay by throwing stones at them. He saw lights in the darkness but was afraid to go toward them. When the sun rose, he stumbled onto a dirt road. In the distance, he could see a city. Yet before he could reach it, he realized that the nearest building was a military base; two soldiers caught sight of him and waved him away onto another dirt road but did not come close enough to see the bloodstains on his clothes. The road that the soldiers indicated brought Mustafa to a river. When he had washed the bloodstains from his clothes, he set off once more in the direction of the city. Before long, he ran into a shepherd and asked the old man where he was. "Ramadi," the shepherd answered.

The old man explained that he was an Iranian Kurd who had been resettled in a nearby mujamma'a.[6] He was curious about why Mustafa was barefoot. Thinking quickly, Mustafa replied that he was a government public works employee and had been in a car crash. Since he had left all his papers in the wreck, he was anxious to avoid military checkpoints. The old man gave Mustafa an address in the camp and told him how he could sneak in without being observed by the guards.

Reaching the house, Mustafa smelled the aroma of fresh bread. He found a woman baking. What was this place, he asked. She told him it was a camp that had been built for Iranian Kurds, although she herself was an Iraqi Kurd from Khanaqin.[7] Her husband was at market, she explained, but would return before long. When the man arrived, Mustafa repeated his story and asked for advice on how he could get back to Baghdad. A bus would soon be leaving the camp for Ramadi, the man said. He gave Mustafa instructions on how to evade the checkpoints and pressed on him some food and a pair of slippers. When Mustafa got to the entrance to the camp, the bus was just pulling away, but he flagged it down, and the driver stopped. As Mustafa boarded the bus, he recognized one of the other passengers. It was someone he knew from the Jafan area. It was Ozer.

After the massacre in the bus, Ozer had managed to slip away into the darkness. He ran for a while, confused and angry, before tripping headlong into a trench. He fell on top of a body. It was bleeding from the nose, but the man was still breathing. This trench was very different from the one in which Mustafa had lain for execution. It was ten or twelve feet deep, Ozer remembered, and only about six feet wide. He estimated that it contained four hundred bodies. Scrambling out, he fled into the desert. Fearful of being recognized as a Kurd, he stripped off his clothes and rolled them into a bundle, which he carried on his shoulder. Like Mustafa, he had left his shoes behind. He walked or ran for hours. "I passed only trenches filled with bodies. I could tell what they were by the smell," he recalled. "I also saw many mounds made by bulldozers. The whole area was full of trenches with corpses."

At one point he crossed a paved road and came to a body of water, perhaps a lake. On the other side he could see the tall shapes of date palms. He knelt down to drink but stopped short when he saw the headlights of a vehicle approaching. Afraid that it was one of the Landcruisers from the execution squad, he plunged into the water and started to wade toward the far shore. When he was waist-deep, he noticed with relief that the car had turned in another direction. Now, Ozer also saw the lights of distant buildings, and he headed toward them. It was perhaps 4:00 A.M.

It turned out to be the same camp that Mustafa had reached. Ozer learned later that it housed thousands of people from the Qaser Shirin border area who had been kept here as virtual hostages since the early days of the Iran-Iraq War. The camp was encircled with barbed wire, and its residents were barred from leaving other than with eight-hour passes that allowed them to shop at the market in Ramadi. Ozer peered through the doorway at the first building he passed. He saw two people asleep in an inner courtyard and knocked. A man's voice called out in Kurdish, "Who's there?" Ozer answered, "A poor man in need of bread and water."

Neighbors, aroused by the noise, came out from the building next door to see what was happening. When they saw Ozer, they promptly slammed their door shut again. In answer to repeated knocking, it was opened once more, and Ozer saw an old man and his two sons brandishing sticks at him. When he blurted out his story to the men, they agreed to give him some food: bean soup and bread. But they were too afraid to shelter a ragged Kurdish fugitive in their home. In the early dawn, Ozer went begging from door to door, until a man named Ahmad agreed to take him to the terminal, where he could catch a minibus to Ramadi. On the bus, he met Mustafa. The two men traveled together as far as the Baghdad bus terminal, where Mustafa thought he recognized an Istikhbarat officer he had seen in Topzawa and fled into the crowd. Ozer eventually reached the Kurdish quarter of Kirkuk. That night, watching television, Ozer saw himself in a news report that showed the Iraqi army watching over captured "Iranian agents." It was the film shot at the Qader Karam police station on 10 April.[8]

## TAYMOUR'S STORY

Through a series of chance occurrences in the desert, five men—Ibrahim, Muhammad, Mustafa, Omar, and Ozer—survived the culmination of the Iraqi regime's Anfal campaign. From the testimony of these five survivors, it is apparent that a principal purpose of Anfal was to exterminate all adult males of military service age captured in rural Iraqi Kurdistan. Firing squads murdered these Kurds by the tens of thousands with no semblance of due process, by virtue of nothing more than their age, their ethnicity, and their presence in prohibited areas, supposedly influenced by the parties of the Kurdish peshmerga. As Ali Hassan al-Majid insisted on many occasions, paragraph five of Northern Bureau Command directive SF/4008 was being carried out to the letter.[9]

The bodies of many of the victims of Anfal lie in mass graves outside the Iraqi town of Ramadi, ploughed in by bulldozers in a desert area that, for the moment, remains inaccessible to outside observers. It is apparent, however, that the Ramadi site was not the only mass execution site used during Anfal. On this score, the testimonies of Ibrahim, Mustafa, Omar, and Ozer leave several enigmas still unanswered. Their accounts indicate that thousands lie buried outside Ramadi; yet they also say that only five buses from an original convoy of more than thirty took the road to Ramadi that night. The remainder broke off outside Falluja and drove off in another direction. The inference must be that these prisoners were taken to be executed elsewhere.

HRW/Middle East has received detailed reports, based on hearsay, of at least three other mass execution sites. One was near the archaeological site of al-Hadhar (Hatra), sixty miles south of the city of Mosul. (There is ample material here for connoisseurs of historical irony, since Saddam Hussein had spent lavish resources on excavating al-Hadhar as part of his search for the ancient origins of the Iraqi Arab nation, only to dig it up again as a burial place for his non-Arab enemies.)[10]

Another reported execution site was near Hamrin Mountain, to the south of Tuz Khurmatu. One account, which cites an eyewitness, speaks of forty bus-loads of Kurds in the custody of Republican Guards being machine-gunned on a dirt road leading to the Otheim River. A third report speaks of mass executions at another part of Hamrin Mountain, between Tikrit and Kirkuk, involving an estimated two thousand women and children.

The lists of those who disappeared during Anfal, which are routinely pressed on all visitors to Iraqi Kurdistan, are by no means restricted to the names of young and middle-aged men. Indeed, from the fragmentary lists given to HRW/Middle East, it is apparent that more than half of those who disappeared from southern Germian and the Lesser Zab valley were women and children. Some of those who disappeared were no doubt infant refugees who perished on the freezing roads to Iran or Turkey. Many other small children were allowed to die of starvation and disease in the prison at Dibs. Hundreds of children (whose fates are known and thus do not figure in these lists of the disappeared) were among the victims of the chemical gas attacks on Halabja, Goktapa, and other sites. Many children also went before the firing squads.

One of these children of Anfal was Taymour Abdullah Ahmad, the twelve-year-old from Kulajo in the nahya of Tilako in southern Germian, just six or seven miles from Muhammad's home village of Aliyani Taza. Taymour was the first—and only, until recent HRW/Middle East interviews—known survivor of a mass execution during Anfal. He remains the only eyewitness to the mass killing of women and children. His story has been well documented elsewhere, but it bears repeating here in its proper context.[11]

Taymour had lived in Kulajo from the age of three. His father, Abdullah, was a wheat farmer, and the family—Taymour, his parents, and his three younger sisters—lived in a humble four-room mud house. The siblings were close in age. In 1988, Taymour was twelve. His eldest sister, Jelas, was a year younger, Laulau was ten, and Sunur nine. Kulajo was swept up in the massive three-day army sweep through southern Germian in the second week of April. Fleeing before the advancing troops, Taymour and his family were funneled through the first collection point at Melistura. They hoped to make their way to the camp of

Sumoud, where relatives had been relocated in 1986 and 1987, but this was impossible. From Melistura they were taken by tractor-hauled cart to the fort at Qoratu, and thence, after ten days, to the Popular Army camp at Topzawa.

By now Taymour knew that this campaign was different from any in the past, and even in Qoratu he began to fear that he and his family were to be executed. At Topzawa, his father was taken away, and Taymour never saw him again. Through the window of his hall, he watched as male prisoners were handcuffed together, stripped to their undershorts, and hustled away. The rest of Taymour's family remained at Topzawa for a month and were fed bread and water and a little cheese. During this time Taymour saw several younger children weaken and die.

One day in late May, at about six in the morning, the guards led Taymour, his mother, and sisters into the courtyard and checked their names off on a list. A convoy of vehicles awaited, apparently the same kind in which Mustafa had been driven to Ramadi about a month earlier. They were painted either green or white, and Taymour thought that the absence of windows made them look like oversized ambulances. He counted fifty or sixty women and children seated along the four benches that stretched the length of each bus. To enter the passenger section, the prisoners had to pass through two small guards' compartments, connected by an interior door. Other guards rode in front with the driver. The only ventilation came from a small wire-mesh opening at the rear. Taymour could not see outside.

They drove until sunset along a paved highway, halting only once. Taymour craned to look out through the wire-mesh screen, but all he saw of their stopping place was a large water tank painted in camouflage colors. The heat was oppressive, the doors remained locked, and there was nothing to drink. As the bus drove on, three children collapsed and died, all of them younger than Taymour. Still they did not stop. No one spoke. "They were too afraid," Taymour remembered, "too exhausted, too hungry and thirsty, too desperate."

It was nightfall when the caravan stopped and the guards took the prisoners outside. In the darkness, Taymour could see nothing but endless desert. He could see that there were about thirty vehicles in the convoy. Dozens of soldiers milled around; they appeared to have accompanied the buses in Toyota Land-cruisers.[12] They gave the prisoners a little water to drink from their canteens and then blindfolded each one with a strip of white cloth. Since there were hundreds of people, the process took a long time—about an hour, Taymour thought. When it was over, the prisoners reboarded the buses, and Taymour promptly removed his blindfold. The jolting of the bus told him that they had left the highway and were driving along a dirt road into the desert.

After half an hour the bus stopped again, and the guards threw open the rear doors. Taymour saw that each vehicle was neatly positioned next to its own burial pit, fifteen feet square and less than a yard deep. A fresh mound of dirt rose up behind each pit. The guards shoved the prisoners roughly over the edge, and in the panic and confusion Taymour was separated from his mother and sisters. Almost at once an officer and a soldier opened fire with their Kalashnikov rifles. Taymour was hit in the left shoulder. Despite the pain, he began to stagger toward the soldier who had shot him. He remembered noticing that the man had tears in his eyes. But as Taymour tried to grab hold of him and climb out of the pit, the officer barked out an order in Arabic, and the soldier fired again. This second bullet caught Taymour on the right side of his back, just above the waist. This time he lay still.

Apparently satisfied, the soldiers walked away. Taymour could no longer see the men, but he could hear their voices in the darkness some distance away. He also became aware of movement next to him. He could see that it was a young girl, and she appeared to be unhurt. "Let's run," Taymour whispered to her. "I can't," the girl answered. "I'm too afraid of the soldiers." Without stopping to argue, Taymour clambered onto the hard-packed mound of dirt behind the grave. He later heard a rumor that a young Kurdish girl had been found alive in the desert at about this time and surmised that it was the companion he had left behind. As for his mother and three sisters, they did not survive the execution squads that night.[13]

Like the girl, Taymour was at first too scared to run since the Landcruisers were still driving around the execution site, their headlights sweeping in circles through the darkness. Taymour scooped out a shallow hole in the top of the mound and lay down flat. Each time the headlights moved away, Taymour dragged himself to the next trench. His had been the last one filled with bodies. In the direction he was now heading, the pits were still empty. As he reached each one, he stopped and flattened himself against the earth mound, hoping that he would be invisible from below.

The next thing he knew, it was much later. He had passed out on top of the fifth or sixth mound. The blood was still flowing freely from his wounds. The whole area was quiet now. The sealed buses and Landcruisers had gone, and although Taymour never saw or heard any bulldozers, the pits that contained the bodies of that night's execution victims had been filled with dirt and smoothed flat. No fresh bodies were visible, and Taymour passed another twenty empty trenches as he fled into the darkness. He remembered thinking just one thing as he dragged his injured body away from the killing grounds: "If I get out of this alive, I will give five dinars to the poor."

There was no moon. Once he saw car headlights in the distance behind him. He came to the intersection of two dirt roads and struck out blindly along one of them. After a couple of hours, he discerned the shadowy outline of a bedouin encampment. Dogs barked, and the noise woke the owner of the nearest tent, who emerged with a flashlight. Seeing a boy in Kurdish dress, covered in blood, he yanked Taymour inside. They could not communicate; the bedouin spoke no Kurdish, and Taymour knew not a word of Arabic. Neither could the man do anything to treat Taymour's wounds, although these proved not to be life-threatening. The man kept Taymour safe in the tent for three days and then drove him in his truck to the nearest town, which was Samawah, the city south of Baghdad that had been the final stop for the convoys of sick and elderly people who were taken to Nugra Salman. Taymour stayed there, sheltered by a friendly Arab family, for more than two years. Eventually, the family managed to smuggle a message through intermediaries to a surviving uncle of Taymour's in Kalar, letting him know that the boy was alive and well. In October 1990, Taymour and his uncle were reunited. The following year, after the failed Kurdish uprising, Taymour's story began to filter out, giving the outside world its first real glimpse of the horror that was Anfal.

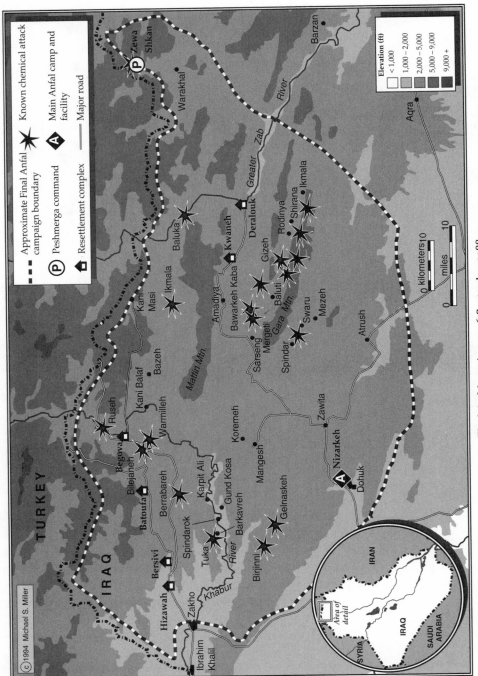

Final Anfal: 25 August–6 September 1988

# 10

## THE FINAL ANFAL

### Badinan, 25 August–6 September 1988

There was medicine from the airplane.
—Victim of the chemical attack of 25 August on the village of Gizeh, Amadiya

With only the last remnants of the PUK continuing to resist, Baghdad's plans for wiping out Mas'oud Barzani's Kurdistan Democratic Party began to advance rapidly. On 7 August 1988, as we have seen, Ali Hassan al-Majid personally stepped in to urge the Iraqi army to hasten the completion of the Anfal operation. The following day, the army high command issued its "communiqué of communiqués," to announce that a cease-fire had come into effect on Iraq's terms, putting an end to the eight-year Iran-Iraq War that had cost as many as a million lives.[1]

The cease-fire gave the Iraqi army the critical boost it required to bring Anfal to a close. The First Corps, which had handled the earlier phases of Anfal from its base in Kirkuk, would now mop up the lingering resistance in the Shaqlawa-Rawanduz valleys. The Fifth Army Corps, based in Erbil, would take charge of operations in Dohuk governorate, along the Iraqi-Turkish border. Other divisions, reportedly including elements of the Third, Sixth, and Seventh Armies, were now redeployed to Iraqi Kurdistan from the southern war front around Fao and Basra.

In his review of the final Anfal campaign, Fifth Corps commander Zareb wrote, "The high morale was clear on the faces of the fighters from the beginning and especially after the collapse of the Iranian enemy in the victorious campaigns, starting from the eternal battle of Fao through the battle of Muhammad the Prophet of God.[2] The formations that took part in [Anfal] also took part in those battles."[3] This massive concentration of firepower was necessary, the general felt, because of the difficult logistic problems that his troops had to face in classic guerrilla warfare country:

> The land is generally mountainous, with rugged terrain in its northern and eastern parts, which lie parallel to the Iraqi-Turkish border. There are abundant orchards, forests, and natural trees. The land in the highlands consists of rocky soil and a sedimentary surface. The lowlands are a combination of rocky land and a mixed soil of sand and clay that gradually descends westward and southward toward the Sleivani and Agra plains. This area has many valleys and streams that run from the north and east toward the south and west, forming rivers. The movement of armed forces and equipment is greatly hindered by mountain chains, high peaks, valleys and gorges.[4]

It was a military planner's inelegant description of Badinan, the traditional mountainous heartland of Mullah Mustafa Barzani and his sons, the "offspring of treason."

Although the terrain complicated the logistic needs of a regular army, the campaign against the KDP was in other respects more straightforward than the drive to destroy the PUK. The KDP peshmerga were largely concentrated in a single geographic area, Badinan, where its operations were run from a head-quarters at Zewa Shkan, an abandoned village hard against the Turkish border.[5]

Although the Ba'ath Party had devoted five months to purifying the areas under the control of the PUK, it never abandoned its particular hatred for the KDP. Once allied with the Shah, the KDP rekindled a close relation with the clerical regime in Teheran and on several occasions acted as scouts for the Iranian army on the northern front. The strength of this alliance was curious, for religious fervor had never been a part of the KDP's identity. Instead, the party was deeply imbued with the traditional values of the steep, narrow valleys of Badinan, a four-thousand-square-mile chunk of the Zagros Mountains bounded on the east by the Greater Zab River and on the north by Turkey. There are no major cities in this inhospitable terrain. Badinan has none of the cosmopolitan sophistication of a Suleimaniyeh, none of the thriving industry of Erbil or Kirkuk. Tribal structures and loyalties remained powerful, and the KDP had long made common cause with conservative local aghas and sheikhs who were still touched by a certain nostalgia for the days of the Ottoman Empire, when tribal fiefdoms in Kurdistan were granted a large measure of autonomy.[6]

Although the KDP inspired a devoted partisan following historically centered on the Barzan Valley, it also made powerful enemies among other tribal leaders. These schisms in turn meant that the final stage of Anfal had characteristics that set it apart from the rest of the operation. Some of the tribal groups who had made a separate peace with Baghdad managed to avoid the worst of Anfal. A considerable number of villages survived in Badinan and on its fringes, at least for a time, especially those of the Surchi, the Zebari, and the Dolamari. Kurdish villagers who might otherwise have died were spared if the local mustashar could convince Baghdad that they were not contaminated by peshmerga sympathies.

It was never easy for outsiders to guess the numbers of active peshmerga in the KDP. According to an estimate of 1985, the party had 6,000 fighters, compared to 5,000 for the PUK.[7] A later estimate put the strength of each group at 10,000 in 1988.[8] In fact, these figures, cited by sympathetic writers, may have been inflated. Military and civilian intelligence reports told Fifth Corps commander Zareb that the total strength of the saboteurs in Badinan was no more than 2,600.[9]

Against this puny force and against the civilian population of Badinan, Ali Hassan al-Majid's Northern Bureau sent as many as 200,000 troops. According to several former Iraqi military sources interviewed by HRW/Middle East, between fourteen and sixteen regular army divisions of 12,000 men each took part in the final Anfal campaign, in addition to a chemical weapons battalion, units of the Iraqi air force, and the National Defense battalions, or jahsh. The regime's strategy, wrote Zareb, was "based on the guidelines issued by the Northern Bureau and those of the chief of staff in the 7 August Kirkuk conference." The underlying doctrine was the simple one that had worked so well in the earlier phases of Anfal—the application of overwhelming force "to operate by moving from the outside toward the inside in order to encircle the saboteurs," with "different forces act[ing] simultaneously to guarantee the encirclement."[10]

Larger geopolitical considerations also seem to have played a part in this thinking. "The area of operations was adjacent to the international Iraqi-Turkish border," Zareb observed, "and this caused perplexity. . . . Accordingly, all forces were ordered to tackle the matter in the best possible way and to ensure the secrecy of the operation by not transgressing the frontier."[11]

The general's final headache was a logistic one. "The magnitude of the engineering work needed for the destruction and removal of the remnants of the saboteurs and their dwellings in the areas covered by the operation . . . was so great that it put an extra burden on the shoulders of the command of the unit."[12] The removal of the remnants of the "saboteurs and their dwellings": in other words, the destruction of three hundred to four hundred Kurdish villages in Badinan.

## BADINAN ON THE EVE OF THE FINAL ANFAL

In the days that preceded the final Anfal, there were ample signs of what was to come. The massive buildup of ground troops was visible along the main highways of Dohuk governorate, and the area was prepared by intense shelling and aerial bombing, sometimes with cluster bombs. In the village of Spindar, for example, on the southern slopes of Gara Mountain, aircraft dropped cluster bombs on 24 August, killing two small boys, cousins aged four and five, as they tended their family's goats in the fields.[13]

Even as these preliminary attacks began, some families began to flee, especially if their villages lay within walking distance of the Turkish border. Others stayed where they were, waiting for the violence to pass. After all, they reasoned, villages like Spindar had been attacked many times since the mid-1960s. Although Spindar itself had been burned down more than once, the government had never prevented the inhabitants from returning to rebuild.

The regime's control of Dohuk governorate had dwindled to a handful of towns and camps along the main roads. From these strongholds, army troops brutally maintained thorough checkpoints since the mid-1980s. "No food was allowed through," one villager recalled, "not even small cans of infant formula, and produce was not permitted to be taken to market."[14] Another villager added, "For three or four years before Anfal only women were able to pass through the checkpoints. People resorted to smuggling—flour, rice, salt, oil, kerosene, soap, detergent, and sesame paste—but everything cost much more this way. At the checkpoint [in the town of Sarseng] the soldiers confiscated anything they found and set fire to it. Sometimes women were able to hide things underneath their dresses."[15] Several witnesses told stories of boys and men being arrested, and disappearing, if they were found concealing food, which was presumed to be destined for the peshmerga.

In Badinan, as in the Sorani-speaking areas to the south, the Kurds had long grown accustomed to the harsh routines of wartime. Aircraft bombed, strafed, and rocketed them whenever the armed forces received intelligence reports of peshmerga movements. When the planes approached, villagers fled to caves and makeshift shelters, or "shades." Occasionally, helicopters would drop infantry troops into a village for house-to-house searches for draft dodgers and deserters. Artillery emplacements in the nearest large town or military base rained down poorly directed shellfire, which would sometimes kill some luckless farmer working his fields. As if these Iraqi attacks were not enough, the inhabitants of some border areas also had to contend with raids from Turkish aircraft on search-and-destroy missions against contingents of guerrillas from Turkey's Kurdistan Workers' Party (PKK), which maintained bases inside northern Iraq.[16]

In the spring of 1987, in accordance with the first decrees issued by the newly appointed Ali Hassan al-Majid, virtually the whole of Dohuk governorate—an area a little smaller than the state of Connecticut—was redlined. As in the

Sorani-speaking areas, there was a fresh flurry of village burning that April and May, with forty-nine villages being destroyed in various parts of Badinan.[17] The redlining was announced on the official radio, said a man from a village near the town of Mangesh. Those who came over to the government side would be considered "our people," the broadcast declared. Those who did not would be regarded as Iranians. To drive home this message, the government blocked off the dirt roads leading to prohibited villages with mounds of earth.[18] When the October census came, it had only a limited effect in rural Badinan; many villages, HRW/Middle East was told, did not even know of its existence.

Despite the grim news about Anfal that had filtered through to Badinan through KDP radio broadcasts from Iran, villagers appear not to have believed that the government campaign of 1988 would be any different from its predecessors. Inexplicably, this absence of any unusual alarm afflicted not merely the civilian population but the KDP itself, whose central committee was meeting inside Iran as the final Anfal approached and seemed not to be anticipating anything out of the ordinary. Although local peshmerga alerted villagers to the possibility that chemical weapons might be used, the KDP leadership seems not to have broadcast an emergency alert. "After Halabja, we thought the international community would stop Saddam Hussein," one regional commander said—an astonishingly sanguine attitude in view of the dozens of chemical attacks that had followed that spring and summer.[19]

Even in its own highly classified internal documents, the Iraqi military was evasive, almost to the point of silence, on the matter of chemical weapons during the final Anfal.[20] Zareb's report noted only that a battalion specialized in their use had played "a unique role" in the campaign, "just like all the other groups." The unit was kept in a state of readiness and supervised the use of flamethrowers by infantry troops. Otherwise, Zareb wrote, "It did not have another role during the battle because the battle was within the national geographic boundaries." This was a curious scruple on the general's part, given how widely chemical artillery had been used on Iraqi soil in the earlier stages of the Anfal campaign.

Zareb's assertion may appear contradictory, given that the use of chemical weapons in the Badinan campaign was given wide publicity by the international press. The explanation, however, is simple: chemical bombing operations during the final Anfal were the exclusive responsibility of the Iraqi air force, and the army's chemical artillery pieces that were reportedly deployed in a half dozen locations remained silent.[21]

Through the testimonies of traumatized Kurdish refugees in Turkey, the world learned quickly of the use of mustard gas and nerve agents in Badinan.[22] Listing forty-nine villages that were "exposed" to gas, Galbraith and Van Hollen concluded that Iraq had "used chemical weapons on a broad scale against its Kurdish population beginning 25 August 1988," and that the attacks had "been accompanied by large loss of civilian life."[23]

## "APPLES AND SOMETHING SWEET": THE CHEMICAL ATTACKS OF 25 AUGUST

The first gas fell on the KDP headquarters at Zewa Shkan, close to the Turkish border, late in the evening of 24 August. Reportedly, ten peshmerga died. The next morning, 25 August, between about 6:30 and 8:30 A.M., Iraqi war planes launched separate and almost simultaneous attacks, perhaps a dozen in all. Many were probably carried out by the same flight of aircraft since they were concentrated within a strip measuring approximately sixty miles wide and twenty deep. Some of the aircraft targeted a single village or peshmerga base, but in at least two cases the planes hit a whole string of villages in rapid succession (see map). Perhaps twenty civilians died on the spot, and about the same number of peshmerga. Hundreds more, especially children, succumbed in the weeks that followed.

The precise cause of their deaths remains unknowable; it may have been the lethal aftereffects of a combination of mustard gas and Sarin nerve gas; the consequences of exposure, cold, and hunger in the mountains where they fled; the malnutrition and disease they endured in the camps after they were captured; or a combination of all three. The question is, in a sense, academic. Whatever the precise cause may have been, it was the Iraqi government that was responsible for their deaths.

In one interview after another, those who lived through the chemical attacks of the final Anfal told very similar stories.

The village of Birjinni, in the nahya of Zawita, had the misfortune to lie almost midway between two of the KDP's most important bases—one, the party's regional headquarters, located due north in the village of Tuka, just across the Khabour River, and the other a little way to the east, in the village of Gelnaski. All three places were hit by chemical weapons at breakfast time on 25 August. The people of Birjinni had been watching the sky since dawn. For several days they had been aware of unusual numbers of aircraft overhead, and they were fearful of a conventional bombing attack. As eight airplanes came into view, many of the villagers fled in fear to the shelters they had built nearby. Three of the planes made a low pass over the village, from east to west, and dropped four bombs each. Surviving villagers told of clouds of smoke billowing upward, "white, black, and then yellow, rising about fifty or sixty yards into the air in a column. Then the column began to break up and drift. It drifted down into the valley and then passed through the village. Then we smelled the gas."

It was a pleasant smell at first. "It smelled of apples and something sweet." Others said it reminded them of "pesticides in our fields." Soon, however, "it became bitter. It affected our eyes and our mouths and our skin. All of a sudden it was hard to breathe."[24] The villagers later found that four people from a single Birjinni family had died, including a fifty-eight-year-old man and his five-year-old grandson. The aircraft continued to circle overhead for perhaps a half hour, apparently observing the results of the raid. Others came later that day, dropping conventional weapons that set the tinder-dry late summer fields ablaze. From the mountain saddle on which Birjinni was built, the villagers could see that the surrounding area was filled with refugees, all fleeing northward in the direction of the Turkish border.[25]

A few miles to the north of Birjinni, close to the Khabour River, the planes hit Tilakru, a large village that was home to many army deserters. A woman named Halima was preparing breakfast for her children when the bombs fell. She heard muffled explosions and looked out to see clouds of white smoke turning yellow. Her husband, a peshmerga on active duty, had told her how to recognize the signs. Having served in the Iran-Iraq War, he knew very well what a chemical attack looked like.

Halima's children were asleep on the roof, so she pulled them down as quickly as she could, one by one, and bundled them into the family's air-raid shelter, a hole in the ground covered with wood, leaves, and dirt. Looking round in horror, she realized that her one-year-old baby, Zozan, was missing. Halima found her crawling around in the courtyard. By the time she reached her, the child's face had turned yellow, and she was gasping for breath and trying to vomit. Halima rushed her into the shelter and flung wet blankets over the walls. But her infant daughter could not be saved, and she died several days later in a prison camp, as did several other children from Tilakru.[26]

From a vantage point in the village of Spindarok, on the far bank of the Khabour, a farmer named Suleiman watched through binoculars as two aircraft attacked the KDP base at Tuka and the hamlet of Barkavreh, a few hundred yards away. With his radio tuned to an air force frequency, Suleiman even overheard snatches of the two pilots' cockpit conversation: [First pilot,] "They are firing at us." [Second pilot,] "Drop the bombs on the high places." [First pilot] "Don't fire while you are behind me. Hold your fire until you are next to me."

Suleiman concluded that the pilots were responding to ground fire. A friend, Obeid, said that in this area at least there were specific warnings of reprisals:

"The government told people that if a single bullet were fired from a village, a chemical bomb would be dropped. People came from government-controlled areas bringing this information." In the course of 350 HRW/Middle East field interviews, this was virtually the only example cited of the government issuing any prior warning of its intentions.

Suleiman counted thirteen bombs in all. Although most of them fell outside the village, he learned later that two bombs had landed close to the peshmerga headquarters on the western outskirts of Tuka. According to three separate accounts, fourteen peshmerga and one civilian died there. Since the wind was blowing from the east, all the farm animals on the western side of the village died, although no one inside the perimeter of the village was harmed.[27]

The village of Warmilleh lay a little nearer to Turkey, between the Khabour and the western edge of Mattin Mountain, a peshmerga stronghold. The nearest guerrilla camp was in Bazeh, a three-and-a-half-hours' walk across the mountains to the east. The people of Warmilleh, like those of Birjinni, were expecting an attack on the morning of 25 August. Again, it came at about 8:00 A.M. This time, they counted six aircraft, but only two of them took part in the attack, each dropping six bombs. "We were lucky," a villager remembered, "for the wind was in the opposite direction to where the people were sheltering under the trees, half a kilometer away."[28] Five people were affected by the drifting gas. They vomited; their skin turned black and peeled off. A peshmerga doctor arrived later that afternoon, administered injections, and the five injured villagers joined their families' northward flight to the Turkish border.

Directly across the river, the planes also hit the village of Bilejaneh. The chemicals drifted on the wind to a hamlet called Bani. "I got sick and had to vomit," said a man who lived there. "We left Bani that afternoon and went to Bilejaneh and Girka. After that we had to cross the main road [from Begova to Kani Masi]. The army was not there yet. The first troops arrived at 2:00 A.M. on 26 August and cut off the escape route to Turkey. Those who crossed the main road before this were lucky. We got there at about 1:00 A.M., just before the soldiers."[29]

North of the main road, a direct route to Turkey led through the villages of Ruseh and Nazdureh. "When the military came and began camping out on the road to Nazdureh, people expected an attack and fled," according to a KDP peshmerga from Ruseh, who had sent his family on ahead to Turkey.

The army attacked the next morning. The Iraqis were trying to seal the border area. People who were close to the border managed to cross, but those who failed were arrested and disappeared. I was near the border when the chemical attack happened. I saw yellow smoke. I was on top of the mountain, but people in the valley below were affected. My brother, who was two or three hundred meters away from me on the mountainside, was also affected by the chemicals. He began frothing at the mouth and choking, and his skin became dark. Then he died. His name was Salim, and he was forty-five years old. We buried him there on the spot.[30]

The most concentrated attacks, however, came along Gara Mountain, the great ridge that begins near the town of Sarseng and stretches east for twenty miles or more. Here, the air force targeted at least fifteen and perhaps as many as thirty villages.[31] On the southern slopes, the neighboring villages of Avok, Swareh, Sidara, and Spindar (nahya of Sarseng) were all hit at about 8:00 A.M. on the same morning, 25 August. There was a peshmerga base in the mountains nearby, and the people of Swareh had moved to the ravines and caves of Avok a year or so earlier in response to the government's continuous bombing and shelling.

A young women named Khadija was in one of these caves with her nine children when the bombs fell. Her elder sister, Aisha, had just gone outside to wash the dirty plates from breakfast. Khadija heard a series of powerful explosions, as if the bombs had fallen right overhead, and the mouth of the cave was quickly obscured by white smoke. The smoke smelled like "the same medicine that is sprayed on apples," and everyone inside the cave grew dizzy and found it hard to breathe. Their eyes burned and teared. Two teenage boys who had been hiding among the bushes outside tried to sprint to safety. But the planes cut them down with machine-gun fire, and both youngsters died.

After about an hour, when the smoke had cleared, the family ventured out fearfully to look for Aisha. They found her lying on the ground outside the cave. She was sighing and moving her lips as if she wanted to speak, but no words came. She had vomited, and her skin was black. A few yards away the grass was burned, and dead farm animals lay all around. Aisha lived only another two or three hours. When the family washed her body that night for burial in the village cemetery, her dry and blackened skin came off in their hands.[32] Another young woman, Amina, also died in the attack. Others died later as they tried to hide in the mountains, but many families managed to escape by walking through the narrow Ashawa Valley, close to the extravagant mountaintop palace that President Saddam Hussein had recently built.

On the north side of Gara Mountain, the villages of Bawarkeh Kavri and Mergeti (Meadow of the Mulberry Tree) lay next to each other in a small valley, separated only by a ten-minute walk. The army had burned Bawarkeh Kavri four times before Anfal, but the village had always been rebuilt. The valley had been redlined by the government in 1987, and both villages housed peshmerga bases.

Again, the bombing began at about 8:00 A.M. on 25 August. Five or six bombs fell in Bawarkeh Kavri, and nine or ten in Mergeti, witnesses said, but they struck some distance from the KDP base. There was white smoke, and all the chickens, birds, and goats died. Yet no villager died in the attack, even though those who were downwind of the gas suffered the usual symptoms of vomiting, tearing, and dizziness. They ascribed their good fortune to the peshmerga, who had warned them a few days before that an attack might be imminent and showed them how to protect themselves by closing all the doors and windows and shrouding their heads in wet towels and blankets. That same evening, the villagers saw the ground forces approaching and fled to the mountains.

It was a similar story in Sarkeh and Gizeh, neighboring villages deep in the folds of Gara Mountain, about ten miles south of the town of Amadiya. There were no guerrilla bases here, although fighters did pass through frequently. As the villagers sat down to breakfast, Mushir, a peshmerga in his early twenties, saw six aircraft discharge bombs over Sarkeh before flying on to attack Shirana, the next village to the east. Mushir ran west toward Gizeh, the village of his birth. It was deserted; the war planes had already paid their visit.

"There was medicine from the airplane," said Khadija Sa'id, an old, partially sighted woman from Gizeh. "We noticed smoke, felt dizzy, and fell down. My sister went blind. The smoke smelled like old alcohol, but the smell did not stay." Her sister, Fahima, added, "I felt dizzy, about to faint. Tears were coming from my eyes, and I fell down. I tried to wash my face. I vomited. Those who vomited survived. Others died at the beginning. Now I am like this. I can see only a little bit." The villagers of Gizeh fled to caves in the mountains, as they had in the past. On the evening of the same day, they watched ground troops enter the village and burn it to the ground.[33]

In psychological terms, these attacks were every bit as devastating as the regime presumably intended them to be. The raids terrified peshmerga and civilians across Badinan. With no village farther than twenty miles from the chemicals, word of them spread rapidly. The suddenness and intensity of the attack on so many fronts at once threw the KDP into disarray, and many peshmerga simply abandoned their posts to try to rescue their families and reach the border. Said one fighter, "I could not find any of my fellow peshmerga. They had all gone to help their relatives, and the chemical weapons created a lot of fear among the people. We did not know how to fight them. We knew how to fight tanks, how to chase a military caravan until we ambushed it, and how to escape aerial bombardments. But we did not know how to fight chemicals."[34]

Immediately after the bombs fell word reached the villages that resistance was useless. According to a young man who was a peshmerga in Spindar, the next village to the west of Swareh,

Even before the army entered our village we received a message from Mas'oud Barzani not to resist. The [KDP] leadership command told us, "Everything has ended. The revolution is over. We cannot fight chemical weapons with our bare hands. We just cannot fight chemical weapons." The KDP's First Branch told us, "You have a choice: if you want to surrender, do so in order to save the civilians because the party does not have the ability to care for so many civilian casualties." We could not take so many elderly people and children to the border.[35]

Such scattered fighting as did take place after the first wave of chemical attacks cannot properly be called resistance. The best that the KDP could manage was a string of isolated rearguard actions in which splintered groups of peshmerga tried to slow the army's advance. Their efforts were useless, however, for the places where the peshmerga tried to make a stand, such as the narrow defile known as Darava Shinyeh (or Shinyeh Passage), were also acutely vulnerable to renewed attacks from the air. According to a KDP veteran, these battles were "all very short ones, like pinpricks," and military helicopters continued to harass the fleeing peshmerga throughout the next day, 26 August.[36]

Perhaps the most cowardly of all the chemical attacks was the bombing of the bridge at Baluka, one of the main crossing points on the fast-flowing Greater Zab River. The village of Baluka itself had been emptied in the border clearances of 1976, although a few families had straggled back, accompanied by the peshmerga. Now, with the sanctuary of Turkey barely four miles away across the mountains, villagers began to converge on the Baluka bridge from all directions, in flight from the army. At about 1:00 P.M. on 25 August, the war planes appeared over Baluka. They released two bombs on the village and several more over the river. The bridge was quickly covered in a greenish cloud, and the corpses of farm animals piled up on the bridge, making it impassable.

By nightfall on 26 August, the combat was effectively over. "The zealousness of the [army] fighters was boosted by the collapse of the saboteurs and their complete inability to resist," Zareb noted with satisfaction in his written report on the final Anfal.[37]

In many cases, the ground troops and jahsh—or *chatta* (bandits), as they are known in the Kurmanji-speaking areas—moved into the abandoned villages on the same day as the chemical attacks. In others, they waited a day or two. But the occupation of Badinan was effectively complete by dawn on 28 August, exactly according to Zareb's original schedule. Tens of thousands of refugees headed for Turkey; others were captured in their homes or surrendered after a brief, vain attempt at flight. Others hid in the mountains until the 6 September amnesty.

In coordination with the first wave of attacks, the Iraqi army occupied the highway that runs east from the small border city of Zakho until it meets the Greater Zab River at Baluka. The idea was evidently to seal off the Turkish border and stem the flood of refugees. In this, however, the army was strikingly unsuccessful. Although many died along the way, some were caught, and others were chased and strafed by fighter aircraft, between sixty-five thousand and eighty thousand Kurds did manage to make the crossing. In the impromptu camps that a reluctant Turkish government found itself obliged to open along the border, the refugees told their stories and displayed their injuries to the few members of the foreign press who managed to gain access. Those who lived in villages south of the highway found it more difficult to escape, and a lower proportion of these reached safe havens in Turkey.[38]

Many of those who could not break through the blockade line along the Zakho-Baluka road still managed to evade capture by hiding in the mountains. They watched helplessly as bulldozers crawled back and forth across the valleys below, crushing everything in their path. Along the great east-west spine of Gara Mountain, south of Amadiya, the scattered peshmerga fighters took charge of a sprawling caravan of thousands of refugees. On foot and on horseback, they traveled east for three days but found it impossible to get across the Greater Zab because all the bridges were controlled by the army. Retracing their steps to the west again, the refugees heard on the radio that the peshmerga carried that thousands of their fellow Kurds had found sanctuary in Turkey. As news of the recent chemical attacks spread, the peshmerga tried to keep up the morale of the civilians by telling them that foreign pressure on the Iraqi regime would soon force Saddam Hussein to declare a halt to the fighting.

Although they had no bread or other supplies, meat was abundant in the form of abandoned farm animals. The most pressing problem, however, was the lack of drinking water: all the rivers and springs lay in the valleys below, and these were in the hands of the army and jahsh, who were shooting at anything that moved. The fugitives went for three days without water, and according to at least one account, many young children died on Gara Mountain as a result of diarrhea and dehydration.[39] A surprising number did survive the ordeal, and on their twelfth day in hiding, just after the radio broadcast noon prayers, news came that the Revolutionary Command Council had decreed a general amnesty.

Many thousands of others were less fortunate. The villagers of Gizeh, for example, which had been attacked with chemical weapons on 25 August, held out in the mountains for ten days, not quite long enough to benefit from the amnesty. Starving and exhausted, they were eventually hunted down by soldiers, who made them walk for four hours to Amadiya. There they were hustled into trucks that drove off to the west, in the direction of Dohuk. Gizeh was one of the worst hit villages in the whole of Badinan. According to Mushir, the young peshmerga from Sarkeh, ninety-three of its men were captured by the army and were never heard from again. Only Mushir and two others survived.

Some were captured in their homes on the first day of the assault. Part of the population of Mergeti, on the north side of Gara Mountain, fled immediately after the 25 August chemical attack, but almost a hundred other people, including many of the older residents, were seized as soldiers and Kurdish chatta forces reached the village that evening. The troops warned them that if there was any resistance from peshmerga in the vicinity, they would all be executed on the spot.

In Warakhal, some way to the east in the nahya of Nerwa Reikan, a local mustashar told the village elders that their people should turn themselves in to the army; since they were not peshmerga, they had nothing to fear. The villagers obeyed and were rounded up and packed into trucks. Their first destination was the camp of Deralouk, built where the main east-west highway crosses the Greater Zab. They remained there for three hours, crowded into animal pens, before being separated by age and sex. The women counted as eighty-three men from Warakhal were loaded into IFAS and driven off. They asked the jahsh what was to become of them but were ordered to shut up. There is evidence that the militiamen knew the answer only too well, for some of the women heard them muttering among themselves that it would be "a great loss for these people to disappear."[40]

From this point, the story of the final Anfal closely parallels what happened in earlier stages of the campaign. The captured villagers were detained, for a few hours or a few days, in temporary holding centers on or near the main east-west highway. Sometimes there was a rudimentary interrogation. Several of these processing points were camps like Deralouk, built to house displaced Kurds during earlier periods of the Iran-Iraq War. Captives from the area around Gara Mountain were kept briefly in the camps of Sori Jeri and Kwaneh and in a school in Sarseng. In the town of Amadiya itself, the police station, the army base, and the headquarters of the teachers union were all used. The temporary facilities were badly stretched, and the transportation of so many prisoners proved to be a problem, with many of the army IFAS breaking down. One civilian truck driver told HRW/Middle East that his vehicle was commandeered, along with two civilian buses, to transport fifty or sixty prisoners—men, women, and children—from the army brigade headquarters in Amadiya to Sarseng and thence to Dohuk.[41]

Closer to Zakho, the camps of Bersivi and Hizawah served the same purpose. Many people also told of being taken to the army fort in Mangesh or to a primary or intermediate school in that town, sometimes lured there by false promises of amnesty. They remained in Mangesh for up to three days. Some were given meager rations of Kurdish flat bread and sun-warmed water; others received nothing at all, although sympathetic townspeople reportedly threw food in through the windows.[42] After three days, the IFAs were set to move again, this time to the south, toward Dohuk.

## ON-THE-SPOT MASS EXECUTIONS

In the Sorani-speaking areas of Iraqi Kurdistan, faced with orders to exterminate prisoners on an industrial scale, the executioners were sometimes sloppy about their work. From the third Anfal alone, the Germian campaign, at least six survivors have surfaced to tell their stories. This is not the case for Badinan, where after more than a year of intensive research HRW/Middle East has been unable to find a single male who emerged alive from the camps and the firing squads.

Between April and September 1992 and again in April 1993 HRW/Middle East staff traveled extensively in Badinan, conducting dozens of interviews with survivors of the final Anfal. In each former village group, surviving witnesses were asked to construct a list of those who had died or disappeared. In many cases, they were able to do so, giving complete names where possible and identifying anyone who had been an active peshmerga, a draft dodger, or an army deserter. The lists provided by villagers from Badinan invariably included only adult and teenage males, with the signal exception of Assyrian and Chaldean Christians and Yezidi Kurds, whose fate is detailed below.

The numbers reported to HRW/Middle East from thirty-six villages give a hint of the probable death toll from the Badinan campaign. Some places went unscathed, with everyone making it across the border into Turkey. Some lost a single man, many a dozen or 20, and a few suffered brutally, losing almost their entire adult male population: 74 from the village of Ikmala in the nahya of al-Doski, for example; either 83 or 87 (according to two separate accounts) from the village of Warakhal in the nahya of Nerwa Reikhan; and 93 from Gizeh. In all, these thirty-six villages lost 632 of their menfolk to Anfal, including a few boys as young as twelve or thirteen.[43]

All these men and boys were last seen alive in Iraqi army custody, either crammed into IFA trucks, handcuffed by the roadside at their place of capture, or (predominantly) in the fort at Dohuk, which functioned as did Topzawa in the north.[44] None of them has been seen alive since their disappearance almost five years ago, and the only possible conclusion is that they were all killed by firing squads, just as their predecessors were in the earlier stages of Anfal.

Hundreds of women and young children perished, too, as a result of the final Anfal campaign. The causes of their deaths were different—gassing, starvation, exposure, and willful neglect—rather than bullets fired from a Kalashnikov. In the first seven Anfal operations, the mass disappearance of women and children frequently mirrored the pattern of peshmerga resistance. In the final Anfal, there was no resistance to speak of. The KDP was simply routed, and this may help explain why the women and children of Badinan were spared. As for their menfolk, the standing orders could not have been clearer.

"We received orders to kill all peshmerga, even those who surrendered," HRW/Middle East was told by a former lieutenant colonel in the Iraqi army. "Even civilian farmers were regarded as peshmerga if they were working within a prohibited area. All men in the prohibited areas ages 15–70 [sic: the actual range was 15–60] were to be considered saboteurs and killed. The prohibited areas were shown in red on the army maps, and they covered everything except the paved highways." These orders, the officer explained, were conveyed in writing to the divisional level (tahriri) and then passed on orally to the lower-ranking officers. The reference is clearly to Northern Bureau directives 3650 and 4008 of June 1987, which contained the standing orders for the two-year period including Anfal. The lieutenant colonel went on to explain that women and children in his own local area of operations were to be rounded up, trucked to the army's divisional headquarters at Begova where he was stationed, and then later resettled in a government camp.[45]

"Ali Hassan al-Majid's orders were clear," agreed another former officer who had served in the Istikhbarat. "They were to kill all men aged fifteen to sixty. He did not want to see them again, they must be killed off." However, "people were killed according to the mood of the officer in charge. Some were good-hearted and let people go, while others killed them."

The good-hearted behavior of some officers is borne out by the testimony of witnesses. A Yezidi Kurd from the village of Mezeh (nahya of Sarseng) was among the thousands who hid in the mountains after fleeing before the army's attack at the end of August. "Some forty to fifty women could no longer bear the hardship," he recalled, "and surrendered to an army unit in Shkafkeh village. The commander, who was friendly, gave them food and water but told them he was under orders to kill everyone. So he sent them back into the mountains, saying that he was incapable of killing women and children, and told them to wait for an amnesty."[46] Chatta units in this area also crossed peshmerga lines to warn everyone to stay where they were, since there was a general order to kill anyone who surrendered.

At least one large group of villagers was spared as the result of a private deal with the army. This startling case involved a group of 160 families from the village of Spindarok, that tried to flee toward Turkey on the first day of the final Anfal. They had made it only as far as the main road when they encountered an important tribal leader, the father of one of the mustashars. They assured the man that there were no peshmerga in their ranks, and he in turn approached military intelligence on their behalf. The following afternoon they surrendered to the army, which trucked them to the Zakho headquarters of Istikhbarat. There they handed over their weapons and gave statements. After this they were allowed to go free, moving in with relatives in Zakho. (Their own village of Spindarok was burned and bulldozed.)[47]

Some of the captured men and boys of Badinan were lined up and murdered at their point of capture, executed by firing squads on the authority of a local army officer. The most notorious case is that of Koreme, a village of 150 households just two and a half miles north of the town of Mangesh.[48] Koreme was known locally as a progovernment village, and many of its men served as agents of Amn. By the time of Anfal, however, Koreme was already a village-in-hiding. Since the previous year its population of about a thousand had taken refuge beneath damp rock overhangs in the ravines nearby. In the aftermath of the 25 August chemical attacks, the people of Koreme, like those in innumerable other villages, fiercely debated what to do. By the 27th, several hundred people had decided to risk fleeing to Turkey. Later that same day, however, other terrified villagers they encountered in the mountains warned them that they had delayed too long; all routes to the border were now blocked by soldiers.

The Koreme refugees turned back, accompanied by people from the village of Chalkey who had joined them in the ravines. They walked all night, in constant fear of attack. By the afternoon of 28 August, they had reached the outskirts of Koreme once more. The soldiers and the jahsh, however, had got there first. As soon as they saw the troops, the men raised their hands high in the air to signal surrender.

The officers in charge, two young lieutenants in their twenties, had the villagers separated on the spot by age and sex. This done, they appeared unsure of what they should do next, but after a pause one of the lieutenants ordered a group of thirty-three men and teenage boys to stand apart from the others.[49] Their ages ranged from thirteen to forty-three. As the other villagers were led away behind a hill, out of sight, the men were made to squat on their heels. The soldiers continued to tell them that no harm would come to them and even offered them cigarettes and water. While they waited, one of the officers called his superiors in nearby Mangesh on his walkie-talkie. He reported that he had captured a group of "armed subversives" and asked for instructions. As soon as he put the radio down, the lieutenant shouted the order to his men to open fire. Twenty-seven of the thirty-three prisoners were killed—eighteen from Koreme and nine from Chalkey. Remarkably, however, six survived, even though the soldiers later went down the line to administer the coup de grace.[50] The bodies were left to lie where they had fallen and to rot in the hot summer sun for more than a week before soldiers returned to bury them in two shallow pits.

To this day there is considerable speculation as to why Koreme should have been singled out in this way. Of all the theories that have been floated, the most plausible may be that their former role in Amn holds the key to the mystery. As a loyalist village, Koreme would have been expected to abide by the redlining of 1987 and to register its inhabitants under the October census. Instead, the village went into hiding. The regime would therefore have regarded its former Amn agents as especially traitorous; captured official documents make it clear that this kind of desertion was punishable by summary execution.[51]

Koreme was not the only case of a mass execution in the field. Something similar took place on a smaller scale in Mergeti, the village on the northern slopes of Gara Mountain that had been attacked by chemical weapons on 25 August. Most of the men were peshmerga, and they escaped to the mountain. As we have seen, however, as many as a hundred villagers were captured in their homes by soldiers that same night. They were held for an hour or so alongside the spring that was Mergeti's only source of water. As they waited there, the soldiers set fire to their homes.

An Istikhbarat officer then reportedly called his superiors by walkie-talkie and told them that some saboteurs had been arrested. A member of the jahsh who was standing nearby and spoke some Arabic quietly told the villagers what the man had been ordered to do: "Separate the men and women and kill all the men older than fifteen." Twelve men were made to stand aside, and at nightfall the women were taken away on foot to the nearby town of Sarseng. In the confusion and darkness, an apparently tender-hearted infantry officer managed to conceal four of the men in the larger group of women in an attempt to save them.[52] The other eight were taken by their captors to the nearby village of Bawarkeh Ka'ba, away from the mountains.

The soldiers' commanding officer was furious. "Why did you bring them here?" he shouted. "I ordered you to kill them. Why did you not implement my orders?" The man repeated his command: the men were to be taken back to their place of capture and shot. At a spot about three hundred yards outside Mergeti, the prisoners were bound together hand and feet, blindfolded, and handcuffed, and shot with Kalashnikov rifles.[53]

Thanks to Zareb's meticulous account of troop movements during the final Anfal, it is possible to say with some precision who was responsible for the Mergeti and Koreme murders.[54] Although Mergeti is not mentioned by name in Zareb's report, the village clearly fell within the area of operations of the Iraqi army's 41st Infantry Division. The 41st controlled a detachment of commandos from the Sixth Army Corps, as well as three infantry brigades, numbers 103, 114, and 706. The commander of one of these three brigades—it is not specified which—was in charge of the division's first joint task force, which was deployed against Gara Mountain from its base in Sarseng and would have moved eastward through Mergeti in the first hours of the campaign.[55]

Within the plan of attack devised by the Fifth Army Corps, Koreme was part of the Khabour Basin area of operations (see map). Stretching from Zakho and Batufa in the north to Mangesh in the south, this theater was in the hands of the 29th Infantry Division. Three infantry brigades were also assigned to the operation—numbers 84, 238, and 435—together with a tank battalion, an assortment of mechanized forces, field engineers, artillery units, waterborne troops, and sixteen National Defense battalions, or jahsh.

The campaign was further subdivided into eight joint task forces, two of which—the sixth and seventh—were based in Mangesh.[56] While the seventh task force was instructed to drive eastward and take the villages of Majalmukht and Alkushki, the sixth was to move north, as far as the twin villages of Upper and Lower Baroshki, on the south bank of the Khabour River. A secondary detachment was to head northeast and take Koreme. It was this unit that carried out the executions. From the testimonies of witnesses, the assumption must be that the order came from the sixth task force commander of the 29th Infantry Division, based in Mangesh.

Zareb was well pleased by the performance of his officers. By 29 August, he was able to report that the 29th and 41st Infantry Divisions had "occupied all [their] target places" and "completed all the duties assigned to [them]."[57] Over the course of the next week, other units and task forces continued mopping-up operations and drove the last of the peshmerga into Turkey and Iran. By 6 September, the last strategic border hilltop had been occupied, and from a military point of view the final Anfal was complete. Zareb applauded the "military and civilian security authorities" for laying the groundwork for the successful campaign and paid tribute to the comrades of the Ba'ath Party for "raising the level of enthusiasm and zealousness of the fighters."[58]

The general detected the same sterling fighting qualities in the jahsh. "The combatants of the National Defense battalions zealously and enthusiastically fought to achieve the target of destroying the saboteurs in their positions," he wrote. "In all the convoys, they marched ahead of the troops because they knew the area and also because of their good physical fitness, especially for mountain climbing. They . . . played an active role in the destruction of villages and the collection of plunder."[59] There was a meticulous inventory of the plunder: cattle and goats; rugs, mattresses, and blankets; watches, cash, and pieces of gold; picture albums, eating utensils, packets of powdered milk, and toothpaste.[60]

His forces had met "almost no resistance," the general reported, and this was reflected in the army's casualty figures. Only thirty-one men died in the final Anfal; eighteen of those were jahsh who had dutifully played the role of cannon fodder assigned to them by the army and the Ba'ath Party. As for the "saboteurs" taken into army custody during the Badinan campaign, they were listed as follows:

| | |
|---|---|
| Saboteurs Surrendered | 803 |
| Saboteurs Captured | 771 |
| Men | 1,489 |
| Women | 3,368 |
| Children | 6,964 |
| Total | 13,395 |

Others, of course, had died in the field. These, however, were not tallied accurately, with the exception of forty-eight peshmerga reported killed in clashes with the 29th Division. Instead, Zareb contented himself with a terse notation: "Too many bloodstains were seen in all the places cleaned by our forces."

## THE FORT AT DOHUK AND THE WOMEN'S PRISON AT SALAMIYEH

The Dohuk Fort squats by the roadside at Nizarkeh on the eastern outskirts of the capital of the governorate. It is a huge concrete structure built of Soviet design in the 1970s and protected by a battery of four anti-aircraft guns on the roof. Of the 13,395 saboteurs captured in Badinan, most were taken to the fort, trucked there in army IFAs from their place of capture. Some male prisoners from the southern part of Badinan were reportedly also taken to the city of Mosul, but apparently no one has returned alive to tell the story of what happened there.

Most of the inmates were held on the second floor of the fort, which was so crowded that the prisoners spilled over into the corridors. They stayed in Dohuk for between two and five days, although some old people were kept there longer, for periods of as much as a couple of weeks. Some women spent the whole of the first night in the courtyard of the fort, confined to the same trucks that had brought them. As in Topzawa, the newcomers were segregated on arrival: men and boys of military service age to one side, and women, children, and the elderly to the other. Soldiers took brief statements from the men and confiscated their identification papers, but no one else was questioned. With their customary fondness for keeping documentary records, the security agents made videotapes of these brief interrogation sessions.

As their wives and sisters stood by, powerless to help, the men were beaten with wooden batons and lengths of plastic tubing, kicked, punched, and slapped. Army guards amused themselves by putting lighted matches to the prisoners' beards and mustaches. Children screamed and tried to run to their fathers but were driven back with kicks and blows. Iram, a young woman from Gizeh watched as soldiers beat her brother-in-law bloody. She begged them "by God and by the Prophet" to let her cross the courtyard to wash his wounds. The soldiers refused. "You have no God and no Prophet," they sneered.[61]

When the registration process was completed, the prisoners were dispersed to filthy communal cells that were strewn with human waste. "It was like living in a toilet," one elderly woman recalled in disgust. There were thousands in the fort, men packed into the ground-level cells, and women, children, and the elderly on the floor above. Hundreds more arrived each day. They were from all the major tribes of the Badinan area: Doski, Sindi, Reikan, Barwari, Sleivani, and others. Several hundred of the prisoners were from Yezidi and Assyrian Christian villages, and these people were segregated from the Muslim detainees by a partition wall.

In many respects the conditions at Nizarkeh were even more squalid than at Topzawa. Most striking was that there was no attempt to feed the inmates. Although there were faucets in the courtyard, guards barred the prisoners from using them. Small amounts of unsanitary, sun-warmed water were available from barrels in the yard, but there was no effort to distribute this systematically. There was not even bread. "You Kurds have been sent here to die," was the comment that many prisoners reported hearing from their guards.

Small gestures of sympathy from local townspeople helped to ward off starvation, something that happened at several other detention facilities for Kurds during Anfal. Once, a Kurdish guard dumped two sacks of bread in the courtyard, and the fitter children scrambled for these. Other children and some of the older adults succumbed to hunger and disease. As many as twenty died in one two-day period in early September, according to one account.[62] Over time, the longer term elderly inmates were able to buy food from their jailers in the same way as their fellow Kurds in Nugra Salman. When only the elderly remained, security also became more lax, and some relatives managed to slip inside the fort for brief visits. At night, the prisoners would slip out to the barbed wire perimeter fence to collect large plastic sacks of food that the people of Dohuk left there.[63]

For the younger inmates, the guards' brutality continued as a matter of daily routine. New arrivals saw recent bloodstains on the floors and walls. Any woman attempting to visit her husband on the lower level of the fort was beaten back. Men were savagely beaten with pruning hooks of the sort that Kurds customarily use in their fields. One overweight young man was pummeled senseless, stuffed into the trunk of a Volkswagen Passat, and driven out of the fort. He was not seen again. Others were pounded on the head and upper body with concrete blocks, sometimes when they were tied to posts in the courtyard. "I saw it myself when officers killed one young man with such a block," said an old man from the Amadiya area. "I cried and prayed to God to save us all."[64]

On another occasion, a prisoner saw soldiers and Istikhbarat officers taking turns to beat a group of twelve young men in peshmerga dress. The army men were yelling and cursing them: "Are you not ashamed of being saboteurs, donkeys, sons of dogs!" Later, the witness saw the bloodied bodies of the twelve young men being dragged away by soldiers. He was told by a guard that they were peshmerga who had surrendered or had been captured by helicopter on Mattin Mountain.[65]

Another young man who was a carpenter in Dohuk learned that a friend's father was among the detainees in the fort and rushed there immediately with sacks of bread and grapes. At the gate of the fort he asked an Amn agent for permission to enter. "How could you go in?" the man asked. "You'll get beaten. Let me show you what happened to some of the people in there." The Amn man took the carpenter to a patch of lower ground outside the fort and pointed to bloodstains, as well as what appeared to be the remains of human brains. The guard explained that these belonged to people from the villages of Spindar and Swareh, on the slopes of Gara Mountain. Eighteen of them had been killed there, summarily executed.[66]

After a few days in this hellish atmosphere, the first groups of women and children were told to assemble in the huge central courtyard, where vehicles were waiting to take them away to a new destination. Sometimes these were closed buses with two small windows in the rear, sometimes minibuses or vans, and sometimes ordinary army IFAs. Armed guards, identified as Amn and Istikhbarat, waited to accompany the convoys. The final images that the women took with them from Nizarkeh were of the continued sufferings of their menfolk. As one group waited to depart, they saw cursing soldiers beating men in the courtyard with cement blocks and sticks. The men were blindfolded and handcuffed. As the buses pulled away, one woman cried, "Let our children die too, now that their fathers are dead."[67] In the days that followed, the older inmates of the Dohuk Fort saw more buses come—some of them khaki-colored, others blue—to take away the younger men.[68] With hardly an exception, they were never seen again.

The vehicles carrying the women and children headed south toward Mosul, before turning on to the Baghdad road. In one truck, a pregnant woman from the Amadiya area began to go into labor. The other women yelled at the driver to stop, but he refused, and a belligerent soldier aimed a kick at the pregnant woman. As the crowded truck continued to bump along the highway, she gave birth to her baby. The child survived, and they called it Hawar, or "scream."

About five hours after leaving Dohuk, the convoys pulled up outside a prison, or military base, in the small town of Salamiyeh, on the east bank of the Tigris a few miles south of Mosul. On arrival, there was a brief registration process and Istikhbarat, which had overseen the Dohuk Fort, handed the women and children over into the custody of new guards, whom witnesses identified as belonging to the Iraqi police and Popular Army. The prisoners found themselves in a huge single-story building, divided into perhaps two dozen large, overcrowded halls, each fifty yards long. Every hall held people from a particular region, but all the inmates were from Badinan; not a word of Sorani was heard. Here the women were to stay for between ten days and two weeks.

The prison regime at Salamiyeh was a distinct improvement over the Nizarkeh fort, and none of the women reported being specifically harassed or abused. Recollections of Salamiyeh varied from case to case. Perhaps memory is dimmed by time and trauma; yet, it may well be that the prison conditions changed over time. Some women recalled a diet of nothing but "hard, rough bread" and water from tanks in the yard; others said that they received three meals a day, including bread, rice, soup, and jam, and that water was readily available from faucets. There were even ice blocks to counter the summer heat and a small prison shop that sold a few basic staples. Although there was no soap, the women could wash their clothes each day in the courtyard.

Even so, conditions at Salamiyeh were grim. The prisoners were detained there with no semblance of legal process. No charges were ever brought against them, and they were never given any reason for their confinement. Women and children slept on the bare concrete floor without blankets and used filthy, overflowing toilets. The inmates of different halls were forbidden to communicate with one another. There was no medical attention, and at least two deaths were reported during the two weeks that the Salamiyeh prison was in service. One of the dead was a child from Gizeh village, who was crushed under a water tank. Soldiers removed the body and refused to tell the child's mother where they were taking it.

Above all, the women suffered the constant mental torment of not knowing what had become of their husbands and brothers. At least two witnesses said that some of the Badinan men *were* taken for a time to Salamiyeh, although they were held in separate quarters. One woman from the nahya of Guli learned from the guards that her husband and three brothers were alive in the prison. Another, who was held in hall 7 with other prisoners from the Sarseng area, found one day that the steel door of her cell had been locked. It remained that way for six days. On the sixth morning, it was left open for two hours. From her vantage point close to the door, the woman had a partial view of the courtyard outside. "I saw men, blindfolded with their hands cuffed behind them," she told HRW/Middle East. "They were wearing Kurdish cummerbunds and head scarves." It was the first time she had been aware of male prisoners at Salamiyeh. "I saw those men being put into military vehicles, closed vehicles with only a small hole at the back." As each pair of vehicles was loaded, they drove away. Another two took their place, then another two, and another. She saw many men moved out of Salamiyeh in this way. She surmised that this had been going on during the six days that the door of hall 7 had remained locked: "It had to be for a purpose. Otherwise the doors were always left open."[69]

Shortly after the removal of these blindfolded male prisoners, there was a sudden burst of gunfire. it turned out to be nothing more ominous than joyful guards letting off their weapons into the air. President Saddam Hussein had declared a general amnesty, they told the women. Now their husbands would be safe. There was to be music, a big party. They even expected the Kurdish women to dance with them.

# 11

## THE AMNESTY AND ITS EXCLUSIONS

We were useless. They said it was unjust to waste bread on us.
—Rahman Hamid Nader of Darbarou village, Taqtaq,
on his release from Nugra Salman prison

Early on the afternoon of 6 September, just after midday prayers, the Revolutionary Command Council announced on the radio that it had declared "a general and comprehensive amnesty for all Iraqi Kurds . . . both inside and outside of Iraq," with the sole exception of "the traitor al-Talabani . . . because of his willful and repeated violations of law and order, even after he was granted opportunities to reform his ways." Ali Hassan al-Majid was infuriated by the amnesty, he later told aides, but went along with it as a loyal party man.[1]

The optimists among the peshmerga believed that the amnesty came as the result of outside pressure, that the regime of Saddam Hussein had been compelled to back down by the international reaction to revelations that chemical weapons had been used during the final Anfal. Such outrage as there was over the Badinan attacks was not a significant contributing factor to the amnesty. The most scathing comments, and those likely to have had the greatest influence on Iraq, came from U.S. Secretary of State George Shultz. These comments, however, were not made until 8 September, a full two days after the amnesty had been declared.[2] It is clear from the Fifth Corps report on the final Anfal that the decision to declare a general amnesty was made because Baghdad was convinced by 6 September that the peshmerga forces had been crushed. In the words of the press release that accompanied the amnesty, "These [traitorous] Kurds had relinquished control of their cities and villages to Khomeini's troops, but God foiled their evil plans."[3]

The next day, 7 September, the presidential cabinet issued an additional order granting Ali Hassan al-Majid and the Northern Bureau of the Ba'ath Party special powers to facilitate the return of refugees from Turkey, where their stories had been causing Iraq considerable embarrassment and annoyance, despite the best efforts of the Turkish government to minimize the tragedy.[4]

The refugees would be allowed to return only at two approved entry points, where special reception camps would be set up. One was the Ibrahim Khalil international bridge outside Zakho. The other site was "to be determined by the First Army Corps with all due swiftness." After processing by a newly constituted Returnee Reception Committee (Lajnet Istiqbal al-'A'idin), which would operate under Ba'ath Party control, the refugees would be assigned to camps. There they would have the responsibility of building their own homes. The plot allocated to each family would become their property free of charge after five years, "on condition that the family receive a favorable assessment by the party and security authorities of its conduct from the point of view of loyalty."[5]

Once the assignment to a mujamma'a had been made, the Kurds who returned under the amnesty would not be allowed to move. They were obliged, in fact, to sign or affix their thumbprint to a sworn statement that read: "I, the undersigned ( . . . . ) testify that I live in the governorate of ( . . . . ), in the section of ( . . . . ), residence number ( . . . . ), and I recognize that I will face the death penalty should the information indicated be false, or should I alter my address without notifying the appropriate administration and authorities. To this I affirm my support."[6]

The refugees were granted only until 6:00 P.M. on 9 October, barely a month, to "return to the national ranks." Anyone who surrendered to the government after this grace period had expired would be taken into military custody and handed over to the Ba'ath Party's Northern Bureau Command—for what purpose it was not stated.[7]

A flurry of other decrees followed, for although the regime spoke of a general amnesty, it by no means intended that all Kurds should escape further punishment. First, on 8 September, the Revolutionary Command Council decreed that any amnestied Iraqi Kurds who had been affiliated with the armed forces, the domestic security services, or the jahsh were henceforth discharged and barred from reenlisting as volunteers.[8] The authorities were also worried that those "returning to the national ranks" would offer fertile soil for any attempt at reorganization by the peshmerga, even if the saboteurs seemed, for the time being, to present no further threat. Accordingly, Ali Hassan al-Majid resolved that it was necessary for those who benefited from the amnesty to have their civil rights radically curtailed and their activities strictly monitored. "Kurdish citizens shall be treated by the same standards applied to any other Iraqi citizen insofar as their rights and duties are concerned," the Northern Bureau ordered, "with the exception of those Kurds who benefited from the amnesty decree 736 of 8 September 1988."

These shall not be treated on an equal footing with other Iraqis in terms of rights and duties, unless they can effectively match good intentions with proper conduct and demonstrate that they have ended all collaboration with the saboteurs and that they are more loyal to Iraq than their peers who have benefited from the above-mentioned amnesty decree.

In dealing with such cases, the following parameters shall apply:

1. These Kurds shall not be entitled to be nominated for membership in the National Assembly (Al-Majlis al-Watani), the Legislature (Al-Majlis al-Tashri'i), the People's Councils (Majlis al-Sha'ab), the Municipal Councils (Majlis al-Baladiya), or mass organizations.

2. Those Kurds who took advantage of the amnesty decree shall not be entitled to sell, buy, or lease state lands or concerns for which ownership is attributed to the state. Nor shall they be entitled to enter into any contract with any state organ or to engage in private business, whether as professionals or workers, until a period of two years has elapsed since their return to the national ranks.

3. The competent authorities will monitor the behavior of those who benefited from the amnesty decree and will determine their inclinations through the placement of thorough and diligent informers in their midst.[9]

In its attempt to understand the thinking of the few "saboteurs" who survived, Amn scrutinized a communiqué in which the Kurdish opposition-in-exile gave its response to the general amnesty decree.[10] Kurdish propagandists were presenting the decree as a victory, Amn reported; further, it had been issued, according to Amn, "to try to absorb part of the resentment inside the country and to ease the worldwide campaign of protest." In the wake of its crushing of the Kurds, the regime no doubt found this show of bravado amusing. "The subject has been brought to the attention of Struggling Comrade Ali Hassan al-Majid, secretary general of the Northern Bureau," the Amn report concluded, "and his excellency's view of the matter was this: that those who betray Iraq or remain abroad should no longer be entitled to keep their nationality."[11]

Guards broke the news of the amnesty to the women and children at the Dibs army base and the Salamiyeh prison, to the old people who survived the summer in Nugra Salman, and to the last groups of prisoners who remained at the Popular Army camp of Topzawa. Refugees in Iran and Turkey learned of the amnesty from Baghdad Radio and reported by the thousands to army border posts. According to former field officers in Badinan, the order came down instructing them no longer to kill their prisoners.[12] Even fighters returning from Iran were not mistreated at the border. One group of former peshmerga who turned itself in at the military base at Piramagroun, close to the destroyed PUK headquarters at Sergalou, was briefly questioned before being released. "We were asked about the size of our forces, the kinds of weapons we used, and our reasons for fleeing to Iran. They asked us what we wanted. I answered that we were Kurds and that we wanted our rights. The government gave us one document to get us through the checkpoints and another that gave us permission to be in the new mujamma'at where we had been assigned to live."[13]

One group, however, seems to have been singled out for a harsher welcome. These were the draft dodgers and deserters who had eluded capture in the mountains, warding off starvation by eating wild grasses and the crops that had been left in the fields of abandoned and bulldozed villages. Some of these Kurds were returned to their old units and detained for as long as five months, in the custody, ironically, of the same army that had Anfalized their families and destroyed their homes. One group of sixty deserters from the Shwan area surrendered to the army in Kirkuk after four months on the run. Each man was given a letter to his old military unit and detained at that unit's base. "We were put in small overcrowded rooms with no space to sleep and very little food, and soldiers and officers beat me with cables," said Rezgar, a young man who was imprisoned at the army's Khaled camp, outside Erbil. From here, he was transferred to a training camp in the city, where he spent weeks being drilled and listening to lectures from a Kurdish officer on the virtues of the Ba'ath Party. "'What good is the Ba'ath Party?' we asked. 'If the Ba'ath Party is so good, where are our families and our villages?' They had no answer to this." After two months the men were released, but not before the army confiscated 10 dinars (then $30) from each of them, "for the rebuilding of Fao," the scene of the costliest battle of the Iran-Iraq War.[14]

### DISPERSAL OF THE CAMP SURVIVORS

For the inmates of Topzawa, Dibs, and Nugra Salman, the regime used two principal dispersal points and some secondary ones. Most of the detainees were abandoned either in Suleimaniyeh city or in nearby Arbat. A few were taken on as far as Chamchamal, where they were eventually resettled in the new Shoresh camp, or to Kalar, where their final home would be the camp of Sumoud. One old woman from the Taqtaq area reported being left off a little closer to her former home, at a government building in Dukan. Officials there asked her only a few questions. Had her sons been peshmerga? They wanted to know. "No," she replied, "they are with the government."

"Al-hamdu lillah," the men replied. Thanks be to God.

"Stand in line, you criminals," a guard snapped at the several thousand elderly inmates who had survived the rigors of Nugra Salman. "You must remember this experience forever, and you shall never think of doing anything against our leader, Saddam Hussein. You have been granted amnesty." The Amn guards registered their names once more and began to sort everyone into different groups. It was time to get rid of these useless people by dumping them in the cities, the loathsome Lieutenant Hajjaj was heard to remark.[15]

The prisoners were released from Nugra Salman at weekly intervals. Convoys of vehicles arrived every Saturday and took them away in fearful and crying groups of about five hundred at a time. Occasionally, army IFAS were used, sometimes windowless military transports of the kind used for the mass execution victims, but more often large civilian buses that were "open and pleasant" vehicles with seats, accommodating fifty or sixty people each. The lame, the blind, and the infirm were the first to be allowed to leave. If a person was sick or ailing, then his or her entire family was let go from Nugra Salman at the same time.

The final releases from "the pit of Salman" were not complete until well into November. One woman who left at the end of October said that many of those who remained were originally from the Qara Dagh or Halabja areas.[16] The greatest mystery, however, surrounds the two large groups of women and children from southern Germian who had been brought there from Dibs; the first after about six weeks, the second not until August. Numbering about five hundred in all, they were held in separate quarters at Nugra Salman and forbidden to have any contact with the elderly prisoners. During their detention, dozens reportedly died of starvation and disease.

The survivors of this group were the last to be released from Nugra Salman, with the exception of three old men from the Kifri area of southern Germian who refused to go until their daughters went too. "When I was released [in November]," said a teenage girl from Omerbel, "there was no one left there. We were the last ones."[17] Yet some of the group were never accounted for, such as two adult women and four children from the village of Benaka (nahya of Tilako). Their disappearances added to the already immense weight of tragedy that struck this part of southern Germian in the wake of the third Anfal.

After release from Nugra Salman, the first stop was sometimes Topzawa, sometimes Samawah. Sometimes the buses and their Amn guards traveled north stopping in both places. Many of those who were processed through Topzawa had the unnerving experience of passing once more through the same building (in some cases spending a night in the same cell) that had housed them on their outward journey several months earlier. Others had their names taken one more time at the Kirkuk office of the Ba'ath Party. Some of the deportees were issued with new identification papers that bore the words "Affected by Anfal Operations."[18]

At Samawah, the nearest town to Nugra Salman, the newly released prisoners stayed anywhere from an hour to a week. The fittest of them paused only briefly to have their names registered yet again. Those who were sick were "treated very kindly" by army personnel in an empty school or in the wards of an old military hospital. Everyone was cleaned up; the old men were shaved. "We looked like monsters," commented an old man from the nahya of Aghjalar, "We had to be made presentable."[19] After the privations of Nugra Salman, the diet was almost too rich. There was meat, fruit, and rice. "They wanted to show that the government was treating us well," remembered a middle-aged man from the Qara Dagh region. "We were given medicine and good food, like chicken and fish. The guards told us we had to sing and enjoy ourselves. The government is nice, they told us; it is going to set you free."[20]

On arrival at Suleimaniyeh and Arbat, there was one final name check. Fingerprints were taken, release papers signed. In the provincial capital some of the prisoners were taken to a security building "like a big hospital," where friendly city residents tossed food over the high walls. Others ended up at the Suleimaniyeh soccer stadium, where the huge crowds were divided into groups according to their nahya of origin and told that they were free to go, free to go anywhere but to their home villages (which, in any case, no longer existed). Anyone who strayed into the prohibited areas, one group was warned, would "be taken in a helicopter to heaven and dropped to the ground, or executed without trial."[21]

At the Ba'ath Party office in Arbat, the message was the same. Here, a few prisoners were asked to fill in questionnaires about their family members and issued with new papers. "Do you know why you were released?" one Ba'ath "comrade" asked a man from the Kalar area. "Because God saved me," the man answered. After a brief ritual questioning of this sort, the deportees were told that they should proceed to the "modern villages," the mujamma'at, such as Sumoud and Bayinjan, where they would be given good housing.

The few who were driven on to Chamchamal had a somewhat different experience. There, the newcomers were received by the *qaym maqam,* the civilian head of the qadha of Chamchamal. There were the usual harsh warnings: "They told us not to go to the villages, it was forbidden. We could not go beyond the paved highway. If they found us out there, we would be punished."[22] New housing would be made available in local camps, such as Shoresh and Benaslawa. What was more significant, however, was that the prisoners could not go free until local citizens vouched for them and agreed to take them temporarily into their homes. In some cases these guarantees were demanded for prisoners in groups of four. There was no shortage of guarantors: the residents of Chamchamal distinguished themselves once more, as they had during the April protest to free the Anfal prisoners, by their spontaneous display of generosity toward their fellow Kurds.

## THE MUJAMMA'A OPERATION OF DISENFRANCHISEMENT

The survivors of Anfal ended up in more than a dozen camps, according to their place of origin. Those from the southern part of Germian gravitated above all to Sumoud, the large camp outside the town of Kalar. Most people from northern Germian found their way to Shoresh (meaning revolution), on the outskirts of Chamchamal. Those from the Lesser Zab Valley were relocated mainly in Benaslawa and Daratou, on the plain south of Erbil. The harshest fate of all awaited the tens of thousands of survivors of the final Anfal in Badinan, who were left on the barren earth north of Erbil.

Sumoud and Shoresh both existed in rudimentary form a year before Anfal, having been originally designed to house the relocated inhabitants of the 1987 program of village clearances in Germian and the Erbil plain. As Anfal swept through these areas in 1988, many fleeing villagers found refuge in the two camps, though without official permission. After the September amnesty, they were enormously expanded to house the survivors. According to estimates of the Kurdish administration, the population of Sumoud by 1992 had grown to fifty thousand, 85 percent of whom were Anfalakan. Shoresh was even larger. Subdivided into four geographic areas, it housed sixty thousand people, including the entire population of the former district center of Qader Karam, who were brought there after the town was bulldozed in May 1988. Fully 70 percent of those housed in Shoresh were Anfal survivors.[23]

The word *housed* may be misleading since all that the new arrivals received from the Ba'ath government was a piece of paper giving them nominal title (subject to good behavior) to a small plot of land and, in a few cases, a bare cement floor. "Build your house," a former inmate of Nugra Salman was told when he was released in Kalar. "But how could I build?" he asked HRW/Middle East rhetorically. "I had no children, no son, no food, no money, no mattresses."[24] Gradually, however, two squalid townships came into existence, with rough cinder-block homes, electric power, lines, and running water. The camps were controlled by police and army posts, and no one could venture beyond the perimeter without an official pass.

To this arrangement there was no alternative. The villages and their adjoining farmlands were prohibited areas, on pain of death. Iraqi government files contain many references to individuals and groups of people executed after being found in these areas in the post-Anfal period. Residents of the towns left standing were warned over loudspeakers that anyone sheltering Anfalakan would be punished. The sweeps extended to the cities, especially Suleimaniyeh. Most, if not all, of the families in the camps had lost their male breadwinners, and there was no compensation for the lives, homes, and property that had been destroyed and pillaged. There was also no food without ration cards. Entitlement to these was based on the 1987 census. Each person's card, stamped with the seal of the Ba'ath Party, was marked with the name of the village and nahya of residence. They could only be obtained by registering as a resident of one of the camps or by the time-honored means of bribery. Some residents of the mujamma'a of Ber Hoshter were reportedly told by Ba'ath officials that they would receive food and other privileges if they joined the ruling party.[25] Those who did so found that the promise was an empty one.

Many Anfalakan also found it impossible to obtain new identity documents, without which there could be no public sector employment, no education for children, and no access to health care or other government services. According to an Anfal widow who was shuttled between the camps of Shoresh and Jedideh Zab:

> When I went to look for a job, I was told that Anfal families were not allowed to work. At the school, I was told that Anfal families could not register their children. At the hospital, we were denied treatment for the same reason. I wanted to get identification cards for my children, but the authorities were not allowed to issue them. At the school they told me I needed a citizenship card for the children. They sent me to Chamchamal and Erbil, and from there to Baghdad, to the secretary general of Amn. I finally got a letter saying my husband was lost in Anfal, but this was less of a help than a hindrance. It marked me. The police station at the Jedideh Zab camp told me this letter should make things easier for me, but when people saw it I was always turned down.[26]

Half a dozen encampments (for want of a better word) straggled across the barren, windswept shrubland northeast of the city of Erbil. At a Northern Bureau meeting on 7 September, Ali Hassan al-Majid decided to have the survivors of the Badinan campaign trucked to this inhospitable area from the prison at Salamiyeh, the fort at Dohuk, the smaller army posts at Atrush and Aqra, and from the Turkish border, where they had now begun to arrive in response to the previous day's amnesty. The largest single contingent was to be left, in many cases in the dead of night, on a patch of wasteland near the camp of Baharka. The site came to be known as Jezhnikan, after a nearby Kurdish village destroyed in an earlier army campaign. Over time, the twin settlements of Baharka-Jezhnikan, housing 4,241 families, effectively merged into a single huge camp.[27]

There was nothing there to welcome the new arrivals, just bare earth, thorn bushes, and guard towers with machine guns. It was September, and while the days still brought fierce heat, the nighttime chill heralded the approach of winter. There was no protection from the elements. "They gave us nothing, we had to sleep on the ground, we were starving," said a man who came to

Baharka.[28] With no infrastructure, no food or water, and no housing or shelter, it was clearly a matter of complete indifference to the planners of Anfal whether these deportees lived or died, and the camp guards frequently told them as much.

Yet most of them survived as the result of a prodigious private voluntary relief effort. The Kurdish citizens of Erbil were the first to help, bringing food, water, tea, sugar, and blankets to the Anfalakan, often at great personal risk. In time they were helped by relatives of the camp inmates, those who survived Anfal because their place of residence was a town or a mujamma'a. The first volunteers were fired on as they tried to approach Baharka and Jezhnikan across the open scrub; later they were detained by soldiers, questioned, and beaten. In the end, however, the authorities turned a blind eye to the relief operation, perhaps because they feared the spread of disease from the camps.[29]

By the end of the year, epidemics were rife. There were outbreaks of typhoid and hepatitis, as well as the more routine, but still deadly, scourges of influenza and dysentery. Despite the best efforts of the people of Erbil, many of the camp residents failed to make it through that first autumn and winter.[30] Many of those who died were children, many from villages in Dohuk governorate that had been attacked by chemical weapons. Villagers from Tilakru, Warmilleh, and Warakhal all reported burying many of their infants in Baharka, and one elderly woman from Gizeh, herself injured in a poison gas attack, lost three small grandchildren in Jezhnikan. They were Zana Muhammad Sharif (age two), Nahida (age two), and her brother, Saman Abd-al-Rahman (age four).[31]

For the first few months the deportees lived in makeshift shelters of blankets or plastic sheeting on a crude framework of wooden stakes or poles. During this time the only solid structures were the guard towers and the offices of Amn and Istikhbarat. As victims of Anfal, the camp residents were not able to obtain building loans from the state real estate bank. After about a year, however, they were able to build more substantial homes thanks to the cheap sale or outright donation of cinder blocks from a local factory. Gradually, the camps began to take on the semipermanent appearance of dozens of other camps that the Iraqi regime had built during earlier waves of Kurdish resettlement. At first no one was allowed to leave the camps for more than an hour a day, and then only with a permit. After three months these rules were relaxed, and the Ba'ath Party issued passes allowing people to travel to Erbil to shop and, eventually, to work. Some able-bodied teenage boys and elderly men managed to find jobs as laborers on construction sites, although most families remained without any significant source of income.

Free to move outside the camp, many of the women journeyed to Erbil to inquire after their missing husbands and brothers. The police and officials at the governorate gave them the runaround: "We have no information. . . . Perhaps in a couple of days. . . . Don't worry, they are on their way." The more persistent women were referred to the authorities in Dohuk, Mosul, or Baghdad. Yet there was never any news, and none of their men was ever seen again.

By the summer of 1990, with government control of Iraqi Kurdistan fully restored, the inmates of Baharka-Jezhnikan were told that they were free to leave. There was no possibility of returning to their home villages, which were now rubble. Many accepted the alternative of resettlement in one of the smaller camps in Dohuk governorate: Hizawa, Gri Gowr, Telkabber, and others, which were closer to their former homes in a Kurmanji-speaking area. Others stayed where they were, and two years after they arrived the government finally supplied the camp with water and electricity and opened primary and secondary schools. There, fifteen thousand Badinan deportees remained until the spring of 1991, when the Gulf War erupted, followed by a failed Kurdish uprising (*raparin*). As the uprising spread to the bleak camps on the Erbil plain, their inmates tore down the Amn post and the police station and took control of their own affairs for a few short days. Then the Republican Guard retook the camps and drove the Anfalakan of Baharka-Jezhnikan into exile in Iran, leaving them homeless and destitute once more.

## THE FATE OF THE CHRISTIANS AND YEZIDIS

Barely two weeks after the arrival of the first deportees at Baharka (testimonies suggest that the exact date was 23 or 24 September 1988) the official loudspeakers announced that some of the camp's inmates should present themselves at the police station without delay. Those singled out were either Assyrian and Chaldean Christians or members of the Yezidi sect of ethnic Kurds. What happened to these two groups remains one of the great unexplained mysteries of Anfal: a brutal sideshow, as it were, to the Kurdish genocide.

Despite Kurdish demands for autonomy, Iraqi Kurdistan is far from ethnically homogeneous. Although its minority populations have declined sharply in the twentieth century as a result of massacres, flight, and religious conversion, the region is still home to three important groups. In addition to the Yezidis and Assyrians (and their Catholic subgroup, the Chaldeans), there is an important Turkoman concentration in the mixed city of Kirkuk and several neighboring towns. With the exception of male deserters and draft dodgers, the Turkomans have long lived in government-controlled areas and have sometimes had tense relations with the Kurds. The Assyrians and Yezidis are distinctly different cases, and despite violent conflicts with the Kurds earlier in this century, the two groups have made common cause with Kurds since the 1960s, sharing a common legacy of oppression under the regime in Baghdad.

The Assyrians, who number more than a million, are one of the oldest

Christian communities in the Middle East. Most now live in the cities, and Mosul, Dohuk, and Erbil all have large Christian populations, as does the resort town of Shaqlawa. By the time of Anfal, their once large rural presence had dwindled to a handful of villages in the mountains of Badinan. These were attractive places, with pretty churches, neatly laid out gardens and orchards, and sophisticated irrigation systems. Those Christians who live in Iraqi Kurdistan speak Kurmanji as well as their own Aramaic dialects. Although they are not ethnic Kurds, they wear Kurdish clothes. Yet the regime officially classified them as Arabs in the 1977 census, a designation that many Assyrians and Chaldeans indignantly rejected. "Saddam Hussein calls us Arabs unfairly," one Chaldean Christian told HRW/Middle East, pointing indignantly to the head scarf he was wearing, just as any Muslim Kurd wears.[32] Having taken an active part in the Kurdish movement for years, Assyrians and Chaldeans are sometimes referred to in everyday parlance as "Christian Kurds."[33]

The Yezidis are a different matter. As Kurmanji-speaking ethnic Kurds, they belong to a syncretist sect that worships the Peacock Angel (Malak Tawus) and are sometimes incorrectly spoken of as devil worshipers.[34] In northern Iraq, the Yezidis are mainly concentrated on the hilly plains that stretch from the southern edge of the Badinan Mountains to the Tigris River to the north of the city of Mosul, areas that are also home to many Assyrian Christians.

This pattern of settlement left the Yezidis and Christians prey to early Iraqi campaigns of village destruction, and it left them prey to Anfal too. Several thousand Yezidis were displaced from their homes in Jabal Sinjar, west of Mosul, in early 1973. Along with their Muslim Kurdish neighbors, many Yezidis and Christians in the Sleivani and Sheikhan areas were removed from their villages during the Arabization campaign of the mid-1970s. The border clearances of 1977 destroyed a dozen Christian churches in Badinan, some of them more than a thousand years old.[35] Yet more Yezidis were removed from their homes and resettled in camps to make way for the construction of the gigantic Saddam Dam on the Tigris in 1985. It is apparent that Ali Hassan al-Majid had nothing but contempt for the Yezidis. "We must Arabize your area," he snaps at an unnamed official from Mosul in a tape recorded meeting during the Anfal campaign. "And only real Arabs—not Yezidis who one day say that they are Kurds and the next [say] that they are Arabs. We turned a blind eye to the Yezidi people joining the jahsh in the beginning, in order to stop the saboteurs from growing. Apart from that, what use are the Yezidis? No use."[36]

Al-Majid seems to have little more regard for the Assyrians, and the first stage of his 1987 program of village clearances leveled several Christian villages in the north. The destruction of the village of Bakhtoma that April was vividly described to HRW/Middle East by an Assyrian priest in Dohuk:

I was told that they would destroy Bakhtoma because they had already destroyed most of the surrounding villages. It was around noon when I went to the church of St. George to remove the furniture, but Iraqi army tanks and bulldozers were already beginning to roll into the village. I was the last one to pray in the church. After finishing my prayers, I removed the furniture to take it with me to Dohuk. It was a very sad day. The Iraqi soldiers and army engineers put the equivalent of one kilo of TNT at each corner of the church. After five minutes, they blew up the building and then went on to demolish every house in the village. Later they paid me compensation of 3,000 dinars. I went to the head of the Ba'ath Party in Dohuk to ask why they were destroying our villages. He replied, "You are Arabs, and we decide what you should do. That is all there is to it." I left his office then. What could I say?[37]

In Anfal there was not even the hope of compensation, and Assyrian villages like Kani Balaf (in the nahya of Berwari Bala), Mezeh (Sarseng), and Gund Kosa (al-Doski) were burned and bulldozed along with those of their Muslim Kurdish neighbors. Some of the people from these villages took to the mountains together with fleeing Kurds. Hundreds more sought refuge in Turkey. All waited where they were until they heard news of the amnesty of 6 September, at which point they surrendered. A few days after the amnesty a large contingent of Christian and Yezidi refugees crossed the Khabour River in Turkish buses and gave themselves up to the Iraqi army at the border post of Ibrahim Khalil. The Istikhbarat officers monitoring the repatriation asked the Yezidis and Christians to identify themselves and then ordered them to form a separate line off to one side. They said only that the men were to be returned to their army units if they were deserters and that the women and children would be sent back to their homes. The Muslim Kurds who were present were given a piece of paper, marked "To be sent to Erbil"; the Assyrians and Yezidis left empty-handed. The Kurds were at a loss to explain this, but assumed that their neighbors were being shown special favor.[38]

After surrendering under the amnesty, the Christians and Yezidis were sent to Dohuk, as everyone else was. Most of the group were Yezidis, according to a witness who saw them there, and they occupied six rooms on the second floor of the fort, segregated from the Muslim Kurdish prisoners. Word of the new arrivals spread rapidly, and relatives who heard the news rushed to Dohuk in an attempt to visit them. Isho, an elderly Chaldean Catholic from the village of Mezeh, came to inquire about his four sons. None of them was a peshmerga, although three were deserters and the other a draft dodger. It was a fruitless visit. Isho learned that all the Christian and Yezidi men had been taken away the day before in nine sealed vehicles. It was the last time they were seen alive. The women and children and the elderly, meanwhile, after a single night in Dohuk, were bussed to the barren camps of Baharka and Jezhnikan.

There, after about two weeks, came the curious call that the Christians and Yezidis should report to the police station or the camp's Ba'ath Party office. Istikhbarat officers drove through the camps to broadcast the announcement. The agents were thorough: they followed the announcement by delivering the message individually to each family, which huddled in its makeshift "shade," a shelter consisting of some stakes holding tree branches over them. It seemed there was nothing to fear, especially when an Assyrian priest repeated the request. "You are going to be taken back to the places where we took you from," an Istikhbarat agent said. "We are going to take you to your men," said another, a choice of phrasing that may have ironically conveyed the brutal truth.

At the police station, names were read out and checked off against a master list. One witness recalled that Istikhbarat then ordered those gathered to separate into three groups: Christians, Yezidis who had surrendered in Dohuk governorate, and Yezidis who had turned themselves in to the army at Aqra, in the neighboring governorate of Nineveh. This last distinction made some people suspicious, and several of them lied about their place of capture, lining up with those who surrendered in Aqra.[39]

Other residents of the camp said they watched enviously as the Yezidi prisoners waited by the main gate for the minibuses they believed would take them to their homes in the Sheikhan area. A few days later, a single khaki-colored military bus arrived, accompanied by an army officer and nine or ten soldiers, to pick up twenty-six people from the Assyrian Christian village of Gund Kosa. Now only a handful of Christians remained, along with the Yezidis who surrendered in Aqra, and these people stayed in Baharka-Jezhnikan until the summer of 1990, when the restrictions on movement were lifted. None of those who was bussed from the camps ever reached their homes, and none was ever seen in the camps, such as Mansuriya (Masirik) and Khaneq, that were set aside for relocated Christians and Yezidis. The inescapable conclusion is that they were all murdered. An Assyrian priest interviewed by HRW/Middle East said that he had assembled a list of 250 Christians who disappeared during Anfal and its immediate aftermath.[40]

Isho, the elderly Chaldean man from Mezeh village, embarked on a long and anguished search for his four missing sons. He wrote a petition to President Saddam Hussein, but received no reply. He begged Amn and Istikhbarat agents at the Baharka camp to tell him what could have happened to his sons. They answered that the four would not have been covered by the 6 September amnesty, since it applied only to ethnic Kurds (although evidently not to Yezidis). "If we had known that," the old man replied bitterly, "we would never have surrendered." At the risk to his own life, he visited the fort at Dohuk, only to be told that the Christian and Yezidi men had already been taken away to an unknown destination.

Although the old man's petition to the president went unanswered, it did trigger, unknown to him, an internal inquiry by military intelligence. The results of that Istikhbarat investigation came to light during HRW/Middle East's analysis of the captured Iraqi documents, which shed light on the chain of command of the Anfal operation (see chapter 13). They do not, however, explain why the Christians and Yezidis disappeared, particularly after an amnesty was in force.

One plausible explanation is this: these obstinate minorities had refused to be part of the national ranks, as defined by the Iraqi authorities. To aggravate their crime, they also refused to accept the regime's designation of their ethnicity. Not only did they want to be treated as Kurds, they acted as bad Arabs. Accordingly, they were considered traitors on two counts and punished accordingly.

# 12

## THE AFTERMATH

With God's help, we have managed to eliminate from our beloved North the saboteur factions and collaborators with the enemy. The situation in the Northern Region now calls for certain measures commensurate with this new phase.
    —Communiqué from Ali Hassan al-Majid's Northern Bureau, November 1988

As the experience of the Yezidis and Christians suggested, the general amnesty of 6 September was not the end of the Anfal story. As we shall see, there were continued mass executions of prisoners captured before the amnesty. The Ba'ath Party's Returnee Reception Committee continued to function until at least February 1989, relocating the families of "saboteurs" to camps on the Erbil plain.[1] In addition to the sworn residence statements mentioned earlier, "returnees to the national ranks" were also to undertake: (1) to live in housing assigned to them and not to change their address; (2) not to take part in any saboteur activity; and (3) to "stand for their country," on pain of punishment as stipulated by law.[2]

The new mujamma'a of Ber Hoshter, to the north of the city of Erbil, was opened for returnees on 27 November 1988,[3] and the resettlement of the families of suspected peshmerga in nearby Girdachal went on for at least another six or seven months after that.[4] The regime appears to have set up a special Pursuit (or Follow-up) Committee (Lajnet al-Mutaba'a) to enforce the terms of the returnee program, and a flurry of orders from Amn and other agencies exhorted the security forces to a greater vigilance of the camps. Amn also issued arrest warrants for anyone who left the mujamma'at without permission or otherwise violated the terms of their resettlement. In at least one case, the Erbil governorate's Committee to Fight Hostile Activity (Lajnet Mukafahat al-Nashat al-Mu'adi) also appears to have revived a pattern more characteristic of the 1970s in relocating individual Kurdish families in southern Iraq.[5]

By year's end, the tone of urgency in government documents was somewhat diminished, replaced by a tone of wary confidence. "With God's help," began an order from Ali Hassan al-Majid's Northern Bureau, "we have managed to eliminate from our beloved north the saboteur factions and collaborators with the enemy."

The situation in the Northern Region now calls for certain measures commensurate with this new phase, taking precautions against any new method to which the remaining saboteurs may turn—those who will try to create pockets of sabotage from which to carry out acts that will inspire their sympathizers, and give the impression to their masters abroad that they still possess footholds in our nation's soil and are capable of undertaking acts of sabotage. There is no doubt that, from now on, we will not find a group of saboteurs that is large in size, or that operates out of fixed bases, or that launches large-scale operations. Instead what we may find are small mobile groups of saboteur elements numbering no more than ten or fifteen. These groups would then wait to gauge the level of our response to their acts. If the reaction is normal and routine, then they will redouble their activities, broaden their base and undertake larger operations in graduated phases. They would also organize their internal structures in such a way as to keep in touch with some of their friendly elements who may have benefited from the amnesty decree.[6]

Al-Majid clearly felt that he faced a delicate dilemma. On the one hand, he could not afford to appear lax, in case this emboldened the peshmerga. To prevent this, he ordered draconian measures for the security apparatus. "Force and just harshness" must be used in the struggle. "There shall be a prompt and decisive response to any incidents that may occur, with the scale of the response being out of proportion to the scale of the incident, no matter how trivial the latter may be."

On the other hand, as far as the economic life of Iraqi Kurdistan was concerned, "What is called for is a departure from emergency measures, because the continuation of the economic siege gives the impression that we are still nervous about the situation." The blockade of the north would be relaxed slightly, the document concludes, although there would still be restrictions on the sale of gasoline, a blockade on the sale of certain foodstuffs, and a continued ban on any sale of food outside the camps. Any mujamma'a found to be involved in smuggling food to "the seats of sabotage" would immediately have its food rations terminated.[7]

Now that the rural population had been removed, there would also be a new census, or subcensus, to determine the numbers of those who were not registered in the 1987 census in the Autonomous Region.[8] By the following spring planting season, the regime was even prepared to countenance the resumption of modest farming activities in the Kurdish countryside. On 9 April 1989, the

Northern Bureau Command issued order 3335, which modified the ban on farming in the prohibited areas. At least in principle, these lands could now be worked once more by their owners (although not by amnestied returnees) or leased for agricultural use if they were the property of the state.

In practice, however, little changed. There would be no rebuilding of what had been destroyed. "The prohibited areas have been demarcated, and agriculture may not be pursued there," Amn reminded its branches. "Nor shall there be [any] human presence in them, owing to their effect in the military and security sphere and their location in the third phase [of village clearances]."9 Clause 5 of Northern Bureau Command directive SF/4008, ordering the summary killing of anyone found in the prohibited areas, remained in force.10 Having eradicated much of its Kurdistan bread basket, Iraq would be more reliant then ever on food imports and generous agricultural credit from abroad, notably the United States and Australia.11

Farmers would be allowed to work their lands only if they agreed to act as informers for Amn about any suspicious activities in their area. Indeed, in February 1990, Amn proposed to tighten these restrictions even further. Agriculture should be permitted, the security agency suggested to the Fifth Army Corps, only if the farmer in question were fully trusted by the authorities and in addition pledged not to build any fixed structure and to refrain from working at night.

## CONTINUED VILLAGE CLEARANCES

Only a few hundred villages remained intact in the three governorates that make up the Kurdistan Autonomous Region. According to a survey prepared by the Ministry of Reconstruction and Development of the new Kurdish government, 673 villages were still standing in the three governorates of Erbil, Suleimaniyeh, and Dohuk; 4,049 had been destroyed. Of those that remained, two-thirds were concentrated in the environs of Erbil city, Makhmour, and Aqra, areas that had been excluded altogether from Anfal.12

Yet there was no guarantee of lasting security for the minority of villages that had survived the Anfal campaign. On 15 April 1989, order 3448 of the Northern Bureau authorized the "evacuation and rounding up" of an unspecified number of villages belonging to the Bradost and Dolamari tribes in order to make way for a new dam on the Greater Zab River at Bakhma, an idea that had been in the works since the 1950s. The Bradost and Dolamari had been loyal to the government, but their location, in an area where the territory once controlled by the PUK abutted the traditional strongholds of the KDP, was now a liability. The Bakhma impoundment, in addition to its economic advantages, would drive a permanent strategic wedge between these two rebellious regions.13

Just a few miles to the south of the Bradost and Dolamari settlements, another fourteen villages were demolished in a joint army-Amn sweep in December 1988, and their inhabitants deported to the nearby camp of Basirma. This time the stated pretext was not the Bakhma Dam project but continuing counterinsurgency operations against any lingering pockets of peshmerga resistance.[14] One of the villages affected was Serkand Khailani, a relatively large place of nearly a thousand people. It had survived Anfal, but army troops now stormed it with artillery, helicopters, and ground forces, as well as units of Kurdish agents, the Mafarez Khaseh.[15] In the wake of the assault, Serkand Khailani was razed, and most of the villagers arrested. Everyone was taken to Shaqlawa, where they spent the night confined to IFAs at the army base, and from there to Basirma; everyone, that is, except for five people who were taken away by Amn in a separate jeep. They included the wife, brother, and teenage daughter of the village elder, or mukhtar.

The headman himself was picked up by Amn in a separate incident early in 1989. He was detained for seven months at Amn's Erbil headquarters and repeatedly tortured: beaten with a cable, suspended from a hook on the ceiling, soaked in water, and given electric shocks to the earlobes. At frequent intervals, cellmates were taken out to be executed. Yet curiously, during the long sessions of interrogation that the mukhtar endured, the five disappeared villagers of Serkand Khailani were mentioned only in passing. They were saboteurs, he was told, and he would never see them again. After seven months, without a word of explanation, the headman was released. At about the time he reached the Basirma camp, he received two documents from the census and sanitary department of the Ministry of Health in Erbil. They were death certificates for the two men who had disappeared. The date they bore was 20 February 1989; the cause of death was given as "execution by firing of bullets." No word was ever received about the fate of the three women, although documents describing their execution were reportedly found by the peshmerga during the uprising of 1991.[16]

## CONTINUED MASS KILLINGS: YUNIS'S STORY

Murder, in other words, including mass execution, continued to be a fundamental tool of the regime in its dealings with the Kurds, even though Anfal was now over and most of the countryside was uninhabited. Anyone found in a prohibited area was likely to be killed, as was anyone suspected of peshmerga activity in the few villages that were spared. Some of these killings were ordered by the Ba'ath Party's Northern Bureau, and Ali Hassan al-Majid appears to have kept a close personal eye on the elimination of prominent saboteurs. A handwritten note from September 1988 from the director of the Shaqlawa office of Amn conveys al-Majid's compliments to the agents responsible for the liquidation of a Communist Party cadre and the burning of his body: "Well done!" the Northern Bureau chief writes. "May God bless them for their faith and loyalty."

Some executions were decreed by Saddam Hussein himself, others by the Revolutionary Court, and still others by special military tribunals.[17] Many individual death certificates and other official documents bear witness to these executions. An August 1989 report from Amn Suleimaniyeh, for example, enumerates eighty-seven executions since 1 January of that year. Many were people picked up in prohibited villages. One was a literature teacher executed for teaching his students the Kurdish language in Latin script.[18]

Most crucially, there continued to be mass executions of people who were captured during the Anfal campaign but remained alive in custody at the time of the 6 September amnesty. Some were killed even after surrendering during the five-week amnesty grace period, their crimes recorded in official documents as suspected members of or collaborators with an illegal organization, such as the PUK, the KDP, or the Islamic Party.[19] HRW/Middle East was also able to find two survivors of these postamnesty mass killings.

Yunis was a nineteen-year-old peshmerga who fought with the PUK in the battle of Sergalou and later in the Balisan Valley during the sixth Anfal. Cut off from his main peshmerga force near Akoyan by Iraqi troops, he hid for a while with relatives in the town of Khalifan. He was persuaded by rumors of an amnesty, however, to surrender to Amn in the town of Sadiq about the middle of August.[20] The local Amn office speedily transferred him to the agency's headquarters in Erbil, where he shared a large cell with about a hundred other prisoners, a mix of peshmerga, deserters, and Anfalakan from the Koysinjaq area. Yunis was interrogated and tortured intermittently for another three weeks.

One day at the beginning of September, Amn guards assembled the prisoners, stripped them of their possessions, and loaded them into a single large civilian bus. It was so crowded that the men had to sit on each other's laps. Their destination was the Popular Army camp on the outskirts of Dibs, which they reached at about 7:00 that evening. The prisoners received two daily rations of stale bread and water. Each day there were further rounds of questioning by plainclothes agents, also Amn men, Yunis guessed. Then, on 6 September, guards told them that there had been a general amnesty and that they would be released.

Yet nothing changed. The daily interrogation sessions continued, together with brutal forms of torture. Beatings with a length of electric cable were part of an everyday routine. The interrogators also devised two other standard torments. One was to fill a plastic bag with water and ice cubes, suspend it from the ceiling, pierce it with a pin, and allow the freezing liquid to drip on to the forehead of the prisoner, who was tied to a bedframe beneath. This went on for up to twenty minutes each time; after ten minutes, the pain was acute, and the prisoner would thrash on the bed in a vain attempt to evade the icy drip. The ice-water treatment alternated with the application of extreme heat. The interrogators would slide a hot electric heater under the prisoner's bed for four or five minutes at a stretch, causing painful burns to the lower back.

These torments were the worst that Yunis personally had to endure. One day, however, just before the amnesty was announced, he and the other prisoners from Erbil watched through the windows of their cells as three men accused of being internal peshmerga, that is, peshmerga active in the cities, were brought into the courtyard below. The men were blindfolded, made to stand on chairs, and tied to posts in the yard, arms raised above their heads. The chairs were then kicked away, leaving the prisoners' feet dangling a couple of feet from the ground. Next, guards attached one end of a string to an empty gas container and the other to each prisoner's scrotum. When the signal was given, the guard would drop the gas cylinder, ripping out the man's testicles. Within half an hour, all three were dead.

A few days later the guards entered Yunis's cell, made a head count of the prisoners and told them that they were to be transferred. By now their numbers had swelled to about 180, including new arrivals—as before, a motley assortment of peshmerga, deserters, and ordinary civilians. Each man was blindfolded and stripped of his identification papers and had his hands tied behind his back. The prisoners were then loaded into six windowless vehicles with benches at the rear and a separate driver's compartment, of the same sort, in other words, as those described by survivors of the earlier mass executions near Ramadi. They left Dibs at about 7:30 P.M., just before sunset. It was the evening of 14 September, according to Yunis, and the general amnesty had been in force for eight days.

The buses turned left out of the camp gate, drove along a paved surface for a few minutes, and then turned right onto a dirt road. As the bus bumped along this track, Yunis managed to work his hands free and loosen his blindfold. After about an hour the convoy came to a halt, and the guards began to pull the prisoners out through the rear door. When it was Yunis's turn, they saw that his hands were no longer tied. The guards pushed him to the ground and kicked him viciously. Over the top of his blindfold, Yunis could see a uniformed officer walk over to him and raise his hand. There was a sharp blow to the base of his skull with a heavy metal object, and Yunis felt himself falling forward. The last thing he knew before he lost consciousness was the touch of his fingers on another human face.

When he came to, he found that his lower body was covered with sand. He saw now that he was in a narrow trench, twenty yards long, one yard across and two deep. As he took stock of his surroundings, he heard the sound of a bulldozer approaching, and a fresh load of dirt was dumped into the trench next to him, throwing up a large cloud of dust. In the dust and darkness, Yunis scrambled free, away from the buses, the bulldozer, and the voices of the guards. In the distance, to the east, he could see fires, which he guessed were the oil fields of Kirkuk.

He ran in the direction of Kirkuk until he reached a paved road. Hearing the sound of an engine, he jumped out to flag it down, but as the sound grew nearer he realized that it was an army IFA truck accompanied by a jeep; he flung himself down by the roadside before the drivers could spot him in their head-lights. Before long a civilian car stopped. The driver, a fellow Kurd, was wearing the uniform of the Popular Army, but Yunis was too exhausted to care, and to his relief the man drove him to Dibs without asking too many questions. From there, Yunis eventually rejoined his fellow peshmerga in Iran.[21]

## CONTINUED MASS KILLINGS: HUSSEIN'S STORY

"Hussein" presents a very different case. A year younger than Yunis, he was sympathetic to the peshmerga cause, as indeed most Kurds were, but was not politically active himself. At the time of Anfal, he and four companions found work as carpenters in towns and camps around Erbil. On 26 November 1988, they were working on a house in the village of Shiwarash, which had escaped destruction during the 1987 campaign on the Erbil plain, when four or five pick-ups and jeeps pulled up, filled with members of "security and the organization," in other words, Amn and the Ba'ath Party. The five young men were bundled into the vehicles and driven first to party headquarters in Khabat. As they approached their next destination, Hussein heard church bells ring. From this he concluded that they were in Einkawa, a Christian suburb of Erbil.[22]

Here they stayed for three days, handcuffed and blindfolded with their cum-merbunds. They were given no food or water and were forbidden to leave their cell, even to urinate. An electric light burned day and night, while a team of interrogators, headed by a man whom his colleagues referred to as Amn Lieu-tenant Ghassan, tried to get the five to admit to their connection to the PUK. The lieutenant played "good cop"; when his gentler methods failed, he transferred the prisoners to harsher colleagues. Each denial of PUK links brought a fresh round of torture. Hussein endured the *falaka,* in which the prisoner is beaten on the soles of the feet while seated with his legs in the air; he was hung from the ceiling by a rope tied to his handcuffs; if he passed out, he was revived by being burned with a lighted cigarette.

After three days of this, Hussein and his companions were taken to Amn headquarters in Erbil, where Yunis had been held three months earlier. There, each man was placed in an isolation cell that measured less than ten square feet.[23] Hussein counted the passage of nine days, the first seven filled with interrogation and torture. Again, there was the falaka; again, suspension from the ceiling. There were new tortures as well: the application of burning irons to his legs and neck, and electric shocks to the tongue and penis. The interrogators told him that if he confessed to his PUK ties, he would be released; if he denied them, he would be executed. He told them that he knew nothing.

On the seventh day, Hussein was forced to put his thumbprint to a piece of paper. He was still blindfolded, and the contents of the document were not read to him. With this, the questioning and the torture ceased, and two days later a guard opened the door of Hussein's cell to tell him that Saddam Hussein had decreed another general amnesty.[24] All the prisoners were to be freed. Hussein and his four friends were again placed in a common cell, handcuffed once more, and taken to a waiting vehicle. As they drove for an hour to two hours on a paved road and then another half hour on dirt, they could hear the guards discussing their fate. "Where are we taking them?" asked the first. "To the south," answered another. And then a third voice joined in: "They cannot live in the south." At that, the five men knew what was going to happen to them.

When they stopped, it was twilight and cold. "Sit down and don't move," the guards told the prisoners. "We are going to take your photographs." They sat cross-legged in a line, and almost at once the guards opened fire with automatic weapons. The first volley of shots missed Hussein, and he instinctively threw his head into his lap for protection. As he did so, a bullet from a second round of firing struck him in the right shoulder, passing right through the flesh. The impact knocked him forward into a deep ditch, and he could hear the bodies of the other four men tumbling in beside him. There was another burst of gunfire. When it was over, the executioners shoveled earth roughly on top of their five victims and went on their way.

Hussein, semiconscious, pushed aside the dirt, which had not fully covered him. He lay where he was for two hours as darkness fell. The grave, he saw now, was an abandoned and derelict well, its walls eroded by rainfall. He touched his friends to see if they were alive, but there was no response. Clawing his way upward over their bodies, he managed to pull himself out of the pit, leaving behind only his track shoes. It was cold and raining, and in the distance he could see two separate clusters of city lights. Closer at hand, perhaps two miles away, he saw the glow of a fire and struck out in that direction. Shoeless, and with his feet bruised and swollen from the falaka torture, it took Hussein all night to reach the house.

He guessed, wrongly, as it turned out, that he was somewhere near Kirkuk and called out in Arabic, "Family of the house!" (*ahl al-beit*). A man's voice answered, "Come on in!" (*tfaddal*). He knocked, and a woman opened the door. Seeing a young man barefoot and covered in blood, she started back in fear and beat her breast in pity. But the couple brought him a meal of water and tea and sheep's fat (*samneh*), and he told them the outlines of his story. As he talked, the woman fetched Arab clothing and a heavy Popular Army greatcoat to conceal the bloodstains from the wound in Hussein's shoulder. At daybreak the man took him to the door to show him where he was. The nearby highway, where Hussein could see electricity pylons and passing trucks, led in one direction to Mosul and in the other to al-Qayyara. The man explained that the lights that Hussein had seen in the night belonged to the Arab towns of Tharthar and al-Hadhar.[25]

Eventually, like Yunis, Hussein escaped to Iran. Some time later, Amn presented his mother with the young man's death certificate.[26]

## THE END OF THE "EXCEPTIONAL SITUATION"

When did Anfal reach its conclusion? The question can be answered in several ways. In a strict military sense, it ended with the victory over the KDP in Badinan and the announcement of the 6 September amnesty. From the point of view of the Iraqi public, it may be said to have ended on 1 October, when ritual celebrations of the victory were organized by the ruling Ba'athist Party.[27] As far as the logic of Anfal as a campaign of extermination is concerned, it certainly went on for several more months, at least until well into 1988.

Some might even argue that Anfal lasted until June 1989, for it was then that Iraqi troops destroyed the large town of Qala Dizeh, east of Dukan Lake. Qala Dizeh is an ancient settlement and a celebrated name in Kurdish history, for it was the target of a notorious bombing raid by the Iraqi air force on 24 April 1974 that left hundreds dead.[28] As a city, Qala Dizeh itself was exempt from the narrow logic of Anfal, but certainly not from reprisals or punitive action. Although parts of the city center were demolished in 1987, Ba'ath Party officials repeatedly assured the residents that they had nothing further to fear. The area around Qala Dizeh, which included the nearby town of Sengaser and the camps of Pemalek, Tuwasuran, and Jarawa—built for evacuees from the border clearances of the late 1970s—was also spared by Anfal. Although some villages were destroyed here in mid-1988, their populations had not been Anfalized.

Sandwiched between the depopulated Iranian border area and Dukan Lake, and in relatively flat terrain, the Qala Dizeh area had not harbored any significant peshmerga threat during Anfal, and the regime had been content to leave it alone. By the spring of 1989, however, it had become a glaring anomaly, the only sizable population center that remained so close to the Iranian border. Worse, the mountains to the east had become the principal regrouping point for the PUK as it struggled to reassert a presence inside Iraq, and on 22 March

1989, the RCC's Northern Affairs Committee ordered "maximum measures" against the area east of Dukan Lake.[29]

In late May, troops surrounded Qala Dizeh with tanks and heavy artillery and gave the townspeople a month to leave. They were to be moved "in the public interest," to "modern villages."[30] A number of choices were offered: trucks would take them either to Bazian, on the road to Suleimaniyeh, or to three new camps on the Erbil plain, Khabat, Kawar Gosek, and Daratou. It took the army engineers three weeks, beginning 1 June, to demolish Qala Dizeh, and they left nothing standing, not even the new electric power substation or the water-pumping station that the regime itself had built in 1987. On 24 June 1989, Qala Dizeh was officially declared a prohibited area.

Yet Qala Dizeh may best be seen, perhaps, as a postscript to Anfal, a return to the same logic of anti-Kurdish activities that had gone on for years. The best answer to our question may be that the logic of Anfal ended when the behavior of the Iraqi bureaucracy shifted into a perceptibly different gear. This is not the same as saying that it ended when the Iraqi regime stopped killings, deportations, or when the last village was burned and bulldozed. For killings, deportations, and scorched earth policies have been a feature of life under the Ba'ath Party for many years, and they continue to this day. However, by the spring of 1989, it is safe to say that the Iraqi regime felt that all the goals of Anfal had been met, and on 23 April the Revolutionary Command Council issued decree 271, in which the special powers conferred upon Ali Hassan al-Majid were revoked.[31] The sense that the Kurdish problem was now fully under control is further reinforced by Saddam Hussein's December 1989 decision to abolish the Northern Affairs Committee of the RCC, which had been in existence for more than ten years.[32]

With his task in Kurdistan complete, other duties awaited Ali Hassan al-Majid's singular talents, notably—after the August 1990 invasion—as governor of occupied Kuwait. "I would like to admit," he told Ba'ath officials gathered to welcome Hassan Ali al-Amiri, his successor as general secretary of the Northern Bureau, "that I am not the right person for the current stable situation. . . . I hope that the comrades in the North will not ask Comrade Hassan Ali to do things that he cannot do. Because that stage is over. It will no longer be allowed for a member of the party to have power over the army, because the exceptional situation has come to an end. These powers are not being withdrawn from Comrade Hassan Ali because he is not capable of the task, but because that stage has finished."[33]

Al-Majid was evidently well pleased with his efforts, not, he added, that the humanity of his motives should be doubted. "I cry when I see a tragic show or movie," he told his audience that day. "One day I cried when I saw a woman in a movie who was lost and without a family. But I would like to tell you that I did what I did and what I was supposed to do. I don't think you could do more than what I could do."

During another meeting with party officials, al-Majid was heard to remark that "what we have managed to do is something that the party and the leadership never achieved until 1987. Some of it was just the result of help and mercy from God. Nothing else." An unnamed party member chimes in to offer praise. "Only God can do more than you did. Otherwise you can do anything. This Ba'ath Party can do anything."[34]

# 13

## THE VANISHING TRAIL

These measures will have a deterrent effect because (a) the prisoners will vanish without leaving a trace; (b) no information may be given as to their whereabouts or their fate.
—*Nacht und Nebel Erlass* (Night and Fog Decree, Nazi Germany), modified version, February 1942

They have sunk into deep water. They were lost. We have no information about them.
—Elderly female survivor from Goktapa

Forced disappearance is the distinctive act of terror of the modern state. It immobilizes the survivor with doubt and fear, with unconsummated grief and mourning that is permitted none of the rituals of closure. The washing and clothing of the dead, the placing of the body with its face turned toward Mecca that is required of the devout Muslim, these acts were not possible for the disappeared of Anfal. In the case of those who were executed in captivity under the routine terror of the Ba'ath regime, a punctilious bureaucracy at least furnished the family with the legal proof of death. Yet for most of the Kurds who disappeared during Anfal, there was not even this.

Once the campaign was over, most of the survivors inhabited a netherworld of uncertainty. Women had lost their breadwinners, and Islamic law forbade them to remarry until seven years had passed since their husbands were missing. Although the stories of the firing squads were known and repeated, the Kurds' squalid resettlement camps were still swept by rumors of Anfalakan kept alive in secret jails in the desert, held as bargaining chips in some future round of negotiations between the regime and the peshmerga, or taken to other countries —Sudan, Yemen, and Jordan—to be used as slave labor.

Before the uprising of March 1991, while the Ba'ath Party still controlled Iraqi Kurdistan, few had the temerity to inquire after their lost ones, fearing that the same fate might await them or their surviving relatives. Aside from questions of security, few would have known how or where to start an inquiry within the labyrinth of the state bureaucracy: with the district head (*qaym maqam*)? the governor's office? the local police station? the mustashar? the Ba'ath Party? the army base? the dreaded Amn? Still, some did take the risk, and their searches, when pieced together with Iraqi government documents and the testimony of those who survived the camps, yield information about how Anfal worked. It appears to have been a highly compartmentalized operation, with each agency involved knowing only what it needed to know. Only a tiny circle at the heart of the Ba'ath Party machine was ever privy to the whole story about what happened to those who were Anfalized.

Some survivors came to learn the truth, but only in the most bald and unadorned terms. Rashid, a young shepherd from Chircha Qala, at the foot of Zerda Mountain, had managed to live through Anfal: by walking past the troops on the main road with his farm animals, he appeared to be a shepherd from town and not from a prohibited area. Yet he lost his mother, ten-year-old sister, six-year-old brother, and two aunts. Later he was drafted into the same army that had captured his family. A sympathetic Christian officer took a liking to Rashid and told him candidly to stop thinking about his relatives: "All the people from Anfal have been buried with bulldozers."[1]

Most, however, did not even discover this much. Nuri, an elderly man from the devastated village of Jelamort, in the Lesser Zab Valley, went to the office of the district head of Chamchamal to inquire after his missing son, daughter-in-law, and two-year-old granddaughter. The authorities registered their names and told him to come back after three days. When he returned, they said that the governorate could do nothing to help in this case. In fact, the official told Nuri, "I can do even less than you. You asked, but I am afraid to ask."[2]

Salim, a younger man from the Sheikh Bzeini tribal area, was away from his village when the army came. The troops captured his wife and eight children; the eldest was a boy of fifteen, the youngest a year-old girl. Some sympathetic jahsh from Salim's own tribe had tried bribing the soldiers, offering them 1,000 dinars ($3,000) for the freedom of each child. It was too late for this, the soldiers answered; the children had already been loaded into the trucks. After Anfal, Salim went on the track of every rumor. He went to Kirkuk, to Topzawa, and even to Nugra Salman. Amn arrested him three times for his persistence. On the last occasion they blindfolded him and warned him never to ask about his family again.[3]

Mahmoud Tawfiq Muhammad, the elderly head of the Jaff-Roghzayi tribe in one of the worst hit areas of southern Germian, refused to take no for an answer. Twenty members of his immediate family had vanished, most of them small children. Mahmoud was with them in the fort at Qoratu, but had lost track of them when the sexes were separated at Topzawa. After his own release from Nugra Salman, Mahmoud traveled to the home of Haji Ahmad Fatah, the Kurdish village elder (the mukhtar) who had been in charge of the Dibs camp. "I kissed his shoes and begged him. But I was told not to ask. 'You have nothing to do with it,' they told me. 'Go to Nugra Salman.'" All that the mukhtar would tell the old man was that the Dibs prisoners had been transferred, but he did not know, or would not say, where.

From Dibs, Mahmoud went to Erbil, where his personal connections enabled him to arrange a meeting with the head of Amn in that city. The security boss told him that the missing had been sent to a place called Ar'ar, an important border crossing point to Saudi Arabia and a resting place for pilgrims on their way to Mecca.[4] It was forbidden for anyone to visit or communicate with them. Mahmoud pleaded with the Amn chief, offering him 1,000 dinars for each person freed, but the man said it was impossible: "Only Saddam Hussein or Ali Hassan al-Majid could free them."

The civilian governor of Erbil said that he, too, was powerless. Despite Mahmoud's deferential gift of sheep, the Kurdish governor of Suleimaniyeh, Sheikh Ja'far Barzinji,[5] told much the same story: many prisoners, both men and women, were being held in Ar'ar in a facility that was serviced by Egyptian truck drivers in the interests of secrecy. Personally, he could do no more than Mahmoud. The affair rested in the hands of the president and his cousin. In Kirkuk, however, the information department of the Ba'ath Party's Northern Bureau told Mahmoud that Majid "had no time to meet me." In despair, he went back to Suleimaniyeh, where he approached a certain powerful Kurd who was known to be close to al-Majid and frequently entertained him in his home. The man agreed to intercede personally. "Majid swore by the Holy Qur'an that only Saddam Hussein and God could save the disappeared." Exhausted and dispirited, Mahmoud abandoned his search.[6]

## THE BA'ATH PARTY: THE ALPHA
## AND OMEGA OF THE ANFAL CAMPAIGN

Captured Iraqi documents corroborate such anecdotal evidence about the extreme extent to which power was concentrated during the Anfal campaign. Perhaps the most revealing case is that of four brothers, Chaldean Catholics, who disappeared from a Christian village near Gara Mountain in the nahya of Sarseng, in the wake of the final Anfal.[7] Their father "Isho," an influential local figure, was interviewed by HRW/Middle East in Erbil in July 1992 (see chapter 11). He explained that the family fled their village before Anfal reached them. His sons—three of them deserters and one a draft dodger—had surrendered to the army during the five-week grace period that followed the 6 September amnesty. They were last been seen by relatives who were able to visit them in the Nizarkeh fort outside Dohuk. After this sighting, Isho himself tried to visit the fort, but when he arrived a guard told him that all the Christians and Yezidis had been removed the previous day in sealed buses. In Baharka, Isho made inquiries with both Amn and Istikhbarat, demanding to know why his sons had not been brought to the camp with the rest of their family. As non-Kurds, he was told, they were not covered by the 6 September amnesty. They had no information about the young men's present whereabouts. Finally, the family wrote to Saddam Hussein himself, but they never received an answer.[8]

Six months after this interview, HRW/Middle East researchers happened upon the family's file in a box of documents from the Erbil regional office of Istikhbarat. The disappearance of Isho's four sons is the subject of a sequence of a dozen separate "secret and urgent" documents, beginning with a petition from Isho's sister-in-law to Saddam Hussein, dated 7 January 1989. She writes:

Mr. President, Commander-in-Chief (May God Protect and Guide Him): My heartiest greetings and great admiration for the builder of Iraq's glory and the realizer of victories over its despicable enemies:

I am the citizen M. . . . The four sons of my husband's brother are soldiers enlisted in the Southern Division. Upon your announcement of a general amnesty, they turned themselves in at Dohuk. Since that time, we have heard nothing of their fate.

Victorious and respected sir, please grace me with some knowledge of their fate.

Just as one knocks on the door of your justice, it opens onto the sweet smell of your compassion.

The petition is signed with the woman's fingerprint.

Since the case involved army deserters and draft dodgers, the presidential office referred it to military intelligence. It appears that Istikhbarat conducted a serious internal investigations into the affair and that it was genuinely unaware of what had happened to the four men. Although Istikhbarat's Northern Region headquarters complained angrily about the sloppiness of its Mosul and Dohuk offices and the contradictory quality of their reports, the initial facts of the case are quickly established. The four brothers are known to have surrendered to military units in Atrush on 10 September 1988, four days into the amnesty period, and Mosul Istikhbarat found no evidence that they "bore arms with the saboteurs." From there the prisoners were transferred to the party-run Returnee Reception Committee of Dohuk and detained, as their father already knew, in the Nizarkeh fort. Mosul reports that the Dohuk detainees were subsequently split into two groups. One was sent to a fort in the Daraman area, on the highway between Altun Kupri and Kirkuk; the other was transferred to Topzawa—the only reference to indicate that this Popular Army camp was being used for prisoners from the final Anfal in Badinan.

After this, the trail goes cold. Northern Region Istikhbarat dispatched agents to the Baharka-Jezhnikan camp to interview the family, as well as to each of the army forts along the Kirkuk-Erbil road. These inquiries yielded no fresh information. The Dohuk office might have been more helpful (as an Istikhbarat captain commented pointedly in his report to the Northern Region director) if it had been prodded by the ruling party. Three days later, however, on 14 March 1989, the director made his final report to Istikhbarat headquarters. The four men, he wrote, "were handed over to the [Returnee] Reception Committee of Dohuk governorate, which in turn handed them over to the Northern Bureau Command in Ta'mim [Kirkuk] governorate. We have no further information on their fate."9

Although Istikhbarat was clearly kept in the dark, it seems that even Amn, which wielded such enormous power over the lives of all Iraqis, was unaware of the final destination of those who disappeared during Anfal or surrendered to the authorities under the various amnesty decrees of 1988 and 1989. The archives of Amn headquarters in the governorate of Erbil, for example, are full of requests to local branches for information about hundreds of men, women, and children whose relatives inquired about their whereabouts.10 Eventually, as the survivors continued to knock on the door of the powerful security agency seeking "the sweet smell of compassion," Amn ordered a change in how its standard response to them would be worded. A handwritten Amn letter notes: "On 25 September 1990, the honorable director issued the following directive: The phrase 'We do not have any information about their fate' will replace the phrase 'They were arrested during the victorious Anfal operation and remain in detention.' The purpose of this is to be accurate in dealing with such an eventuality."11

Both Amn and Istikhbarat had to defer to the final authority of the Ba'ath Party's Northern Bureau on the matter of those who vanished. Evidence for this can be found, for example, in a communication from Amn Erbil that appears insignificant at first glance. Dated 26 August 1988, this is a brief note informing the agency's municipal office that two women were "returned [to Amn] by the Northern Bureau Command owing to the fact that they are not residents of areas that were included in the Anfal operations." Although both women were former residents of villages in the nahya of Taqtaq, which was decimated by Anfal, one had previously been relocated with her family to the city of Erbil and the other to the Qushtapa camp and were thus not subject to Anfalization. Conversely, it is clear, it would have been up to the Northern Bureau Command to dispose finally of anyone who *was* a resident of an area affected by Anfal.12

Decree 160 of 29 March 1987 had made it clear that Ali Hassan al-Majid was to enjoy full authority of the Revolutionary Command Council to orchestrate the efforts of the whole pyramid of other state and party agencies—military, civilian, and security—that played a role in Anfal (see appendix B). As the captured Iraqi documents and survivor testimonies indicate, it was the Ba'ath Party apparatus in the north, headed by al-Majid, that weighed in its hands the fate of each individual captured in the course of the campaign.

There remain many unsolved mysteries about the Anfal campaign. The identity of the uniformed men who made up the Anfal firing squads, for example, may forever remain a secret. Were they Amn agents? Members of the Republican Guard? Or were they, as seems more likely, "comrades" of the Ba'ath Party itself?[13]

Why were the women and children killed only in certain areas? Did their execution reflect patterns of combat and resistance, or was some other criterion used? Where are the graves of all those who died, and how many bodies do they hold? The answer cannot conceivably be less than fifty thousand, and it may well be twice that number. When Kurdish leaders met with Iraqi government officials in the wake of the spring 1991 uprising, they raised the question of the Anfal dead and mentioned a figure of 182,000—a rough extrapolation based on the number of destroyed villages. Ali Hassan al-Majid reportedly jumped to his feet in a rage when the discussion took this turn. "What is this exaggerated figure of 182,000?" he is said to have asked. "It couldn't have been more than 100,000"—as if this somehow mitigated the catastrophe that he and his subordinates had visited on the Iraqi Kurds.[14]

The identity of the executioners and the precise number of their victims may never be known, or at least not until the files in Baghdad can be opened. Whatever the answers to these lingering questions, there can be no doubt that the Northern Bureau of the ruling Ba'ath Party and its parallel command, headed by RCC member Taher Tawfiq, functioned as both the alpha and the omega of the Anfal operation. It was Ali Hassan al-Majid, Iraqi's present minister of defense, who gave the killers their orders.

Al-Majid appears almost defensive in talking about the Anfal operation with unnamed Northern Bureau officials in January 1989. "How were we supposed to convince them to solve the Kurdish problem and slaughter the saboteurs?" he asks them, alluding to the misgivings of senior military officers about the Anfal operation. In addition, he adds, what was to be done with so many captured civilians? "Am I supposed to keep them in good shape?" al-Majid asks. "What am I supposed to do with them, these goats? . . . Take good care of them? No, I will bury them with bulldozers." And that is what he did.

# EPILOGUE

In two separate shipments in May 1992 and August 1993, more than eighteen
metric tons of official Iraqi state documents captured by Kurdish parties in the
March 1991 uprising arrived in the United States for safekeeping and analysis.
An HRW/Middle East-led team has conducted research on these documents
since October 1992; by May 1994, approximately 70 percent of the materials
had been studied and catalogued. HRW/Middle East has now assessed the
provenance, physical condition, contents, and authenticity of these documents.
Because the project is ongoing, the findings are preliminary. (See appendix E,
facsimile documents in original Arabic, accompanied by English translations.)

Although separate documents obtained by western visitors to the Kurdish
region have been previously published, HRW/Middle East's documents project
constitutes the first attempt at a systematic analysis of a significant portion of
Iraqi state files. The project is part of a wider effort by HRW/Middle East to
provide evidence that the Anfal campaign by the government of Iraq against its
population of rural Kurds in 1988 amounted to genocide.

HRW/Middle East is currently working to bring a case of genocide before the
International Court of Justice at The Hague. The documents are crucial evidence in such a case. Other evidence consists of eyewitness testimonies collected by HRW/Middle East in northern Iraq in 1992 and 1993 and forensic
evidence obtained there by HRW/Middle East in collaboration with Physicians
for Human Rights. HRW/Middle East has been able to make important matches
between documentary and testimonial evidence—one confirming the other—
especially in relation to Iraq's repeated use of chemical weapons in 1987–88
against the Kurdish civilian population.

Most of the incriminating files originated in the offices of either the General
Security Directorate, Iraq's internal intelligence agency, or its secret police. The
holdings also include significant quantities of files from the Iraq's military
intelligence agency and local offices of the ruling Ba'ath Party. The Ba'ath
Party's regional headquarters in northern Iraq, the Northern Bureau in Kirkuk,
has been responsible for the implementation of the regime's policies against the
Kurds. Thus it is the Northern Bureau that had overall authority in the north for
the 1988 Anfal campaign.

The files being examined by an HRW/Middle East-led team primarily include memoranda, correspondence, arrest warrants, background information on suspects, official decrees, activity and investigation reports, logbooks, minutes of meetings, membership rosters, lists of names, census forms, and salary tables. By cross-referencing, the documents are connected in a vast and complex administrative web. Despite their variety, they display a remarkable consistency of style. The language is dry and formal, indicating rigid bureaucratic procedures.

Among the findings presented in this report are three key documents, two of which concern the Anfal campaign, and the third a plan of action against the insurgency in Iraq's southern marsh areas in 1989. The documents found in HRW/Middle East's research represent small pieces of a large puzzle. In addition to the three key documents, perhaps the most notable finding is the unequivocal evidence of Iraq's repeated use of chemical weapons against the Kurds. Likewise, there is an impressive documentary record of the incremental Iraqi campaign to raze all Kurdish villages and deport their populations.

Other documents cover a range of topics, including the Arabization campaign in the Kurdish areas, military operations in the war with Iran, the activities of the progovernment Kurdish militias, the Anfal campaign, and the political and human rights situation during and after the crisis over Kuwait. The documents reveal collective and extrajudicial punishments, summary executions, and illegal reprisals. Concerning the crucial years 1987–89, HRW/Middle East is confident that the evidence is sufficiently strong to prove its case against the Iraqi government as having the clear intent of committing genocide—in keeping with the language of the Genocide Convention of 1951.[1]

Together, the documents attest to the existence of a large bureaucracy that, by the nature of the policies carried out against the Kurdish population in the 1980s, was a bureaucracy of repression. Through the documents, Iraq's rulers in the Revolutionary Command Council, the Ba'ath Party, and the security apparatus speak with great clarity, even though their words are in the bureaucratic vernacular of civil servants in the dull routine of inflexible procedures. The documents contained in appendix E typify the cache captured by the Kurds of northern Iraq in the March 1991 uprising against the regime of Saddam Hussein.

Although HRW/Middle East's interest in the Iraqi documents is one of human and civil rights, the content of the documents also offers a singular vista of the inner workings of a sophisticated one-party police state. Much analysis remains to be done by other researchers on this aspect of the files. The documents are currently being recorded electronically. HRW/Middle East hopes to offer public access to a CD-ROM version when the work on the genocide case has been completed, possibly before the end of 1994.

The March 1991 uprising throughout the Kurdish regions of northern Iraq against the central government of President Saddam Hussein spread to all major Kurdish towns, including the important oil center of Kirkuk, which ceded control to the local population and Kurdish rebel parties. Within three weeks, however, Iraqi government troops, supported by helicopter gun ships, returned and crushed the revolt, sending more than a million civilians in desperate flight across the mountains to neighboring Iran and Turkey.

In early April, the allies in the war with Iraq during the Kuwait conflict, most prominently the United States, Britain, and France, intervened on behalf of the Kurds. They established a safe haven for the Kurds in an area of the Dohuk governorate and forced the Iraqi regime to establish a modus vivendi with the Kurdish rebel parties in the other parts of the Kurdish region. This permitted most of the population to return from the mountains to their homes.

An unstable arrangement between the central government and the Kurds, punctuated by small uprisings, lasted until the end of October 1991. Then, Iraqi troops, unable to assert central government control, withdrew unilaterally from most of the Kurdish areas, excluding the important city of Kirkuk. Since that time, Iraqi Kurdistan has been under the control of the Kurdish rebels and, following elections in May 1992, a Kurdish regional government.

These new realities provided outside observers, including those who monitor human rights, unprecedented access to northern Iraq.[2] In carrying out field research, HRW/Middle East, together with Physicians for Human Rights, exhumed mass graves in the area over a period of almost two years to investigate Kurdish claims of genocide by the Iraqi regime in the 1988 Anfal campaign. The consignment of Iraqi state files captured by the Kurds during the March 1991 uprising was a boon in this endeavor.

In the first hours of the revolt, Kurds stormed and took control of the offices of the Iraqi government and its agencies throughout the Kurdish region, including the various intelligence agencies and Ba'ath Party branches. Here large caches of official Iraqi state documents fell into their hands. The Kurdish rebel parties succeeded in moving most of these documents from the towns into the mountains before Iraqi troops returned to put down the uprising.

A little more than a year later, in May 1992 the Patriotic Union of Kurdistan agreed to send most of the documents that had come into its hands to the United States through a tripartite arrangement with HRW/Middle East and the U.S. Senate Foreign Relations Committee. Under the terms of the agreement, the Foreign Relations Committee made the documents official records of the U.S. Congress and stored them in facilities of the U.S. National Archives. For its part, HRW/Middle East agreed to lead the research of the documents for human rights purposes as well as the case before the World Court.

In August 1993, the Kurdistan Democratic Party entered into a similar arrangement with HRW/Middle East and the Senate Foreign Relations Committee, and a large part of its documents were also airlifted to the United States and stored with the PUK-captured documents. At the same time, a small consignment of six boxes of Iraqi state documents was sent to the National Archives by the Unity Party of Kurdistan, now defunct. The PUK cache consists of 14 tons of documents; the KDP cache 4.25 tons. The number of pages has been estimated at 4 million.

Since October 1992, an HRW/Middle East team has studied the Iraqi state files, which cover the period from the 1960s to the summer of 1991, with emphasis on the 1980s.[3] The captured documents give the administrative outlines of the Iraqi government's 1987–89 program to identify rural Kurds as a population to be subjected to increasingly severe penalties and, eventually, to be eliminated. The files clearly reveal the unprecedented concentration of power in Ali Hassan al-Majid, Saddam Hussein's first cousin and the current minister of defense, who, in his capacity as secretary-general of the Ba'ath Party's Northern Bureau in Kirkuk, became the architect of the Anfal campaign.[4] To date, no single master plan to exterminate the Kurds has, however, emerged in the collection.

In addition to evidence of intent, HRW/Middle East has searched for proof in the documents that genocide was in fact committed by the Iraqi government in 1988. Documentary evidence has been supplemented with testimonial and forensic findings collected in northern Iraq by teams from HRW/Middle East and Physicians for Human Rights in 1991–93. Finally, the team led by HRW/Middle East combed Iraqi state files for evidence of other violations of basic human rights. These include extrajudicial punishments, reprisals against the families of suspected Kurdish guerrillas, torture in detention, the use of chemical weapons, the large-scale destruction of homes and property, and forced relocation.

Virtually all the documents stored in facilities of the U.S. National Archives were captured in the three northern Kurdish governorates of Iraq: Dohuk, Erbil, and Suleimaniyeh, mostly from the three capital cities (bearing the same names) in these governorates. There is also a significant cache of files that came from the town of Shaqlawa in Erbil governorate, where they had been captured from the offices of Iraq's internal security apparatus, the Amn, by members of the PUK. Regrettably, the Kurds succeeded in removing only a small volume of documents from the town of Kirkuk in al-Ta'mim governorate, seat of the Ba'ath Party's all-powerful Northern Bureau, before Iraqi troops returned to suppress the uprising there just one week after it had erupted. Finally, the holdings in the United States include a smattering of documents from the towns of Tuz Khurmatu (Salah al-Din governorate), Khanaqin (Diyala governorate), Sheikhan, and Aqra (Nineveh governorate).

The vast majority of files in Kurdish hands originated in offices of the General Security Directorate (Mudiriyat al-Amn al-Ameh) in the towns of Dohuk, Erbil, Shaqlawa, and Suleimaniyeh. Amn, which fell under the ministry of the interior until 1989, from then on reported directly to the Office of the President. Amn has its headquarters in Baghdad, from which it guides the work of its main branches in each governorate. The Kurdish Autonomous Region (established by government fiat in 1974), which comprises the governorates of Suleimaniyeh, Erbil, and Dohuk and is based in the town of Erbil, has a special Amn office (referred to as the Security Directorate of the Autonomous Region) that reports directly to Amn headquarters on Kurdish matters.[5]

The holdings also include significant quantities of files from the general directorate of military intelligence (Mudiriyat al-Istikhbarat al-Askariyeh al-Ameh). The Istikhbarat falls under the direct authority of the Office of the President in Baghdad and asserts its authority in the nation through its regional headquarters (manthumat). Two of these affect the Kurds: the Northern Sector Istikhbarat, which is based in the town of Erbil and covers Nineveh (Mosul), and Dohuk and Erbil governorates; and the Eastern sector Istikhbarat, which is based in Kirkuk and covers al-Ta'mim, Salah al-Din, Suleimaniyeh, and Diyala governorates.

In the labyrinth of Iraqi intelligence agencies, there does not seem to be a clear division of labor; some agencies seem even to have been set up specifically to spy on the activities of other agencies. Generally, though, Istikhbarat deals exclusively with military matters, while Amn focuses on civilian matters. During the regime's counterinsurgency campaign against the Kurds in the 1980s, Istikhbarat was responsible for gathering military intelligence, involving activities by and against the armed guerrillas who were based in the countryside or in Iran. If armed men were captured by the army during military operations, they were invariably handed over to Istikhbarat for questioning. It seems, though, that even civilians arrested by the army ended up with Istikhbarat rather than Amn. In contrast, Amn operated in the towns and hunted down civilian members of the Kurdish parties, officially referred to as the internal organization (*al-tanzim al-dakheli,*), or urban underground. Amn might also accompany army units during actions against villages because of its specialized knowledge and expertise, and persons captured during such missions might end up in the hands of either Amn or Istikhbarat.

The Iraqi state files also comprise documents from local offices of the Ba'ath Socialist Arab Party (Hezb al-Ba'ath al-'Arabi al-Ishtiraki). Technically, these are not government files since the Ba'ath Party is independent of the state, and its structure remains strictly separate from that of state institutions. Nonetheless, Iraq has been ruled by the Ba'ath Party since 1968, and for all practical purposes the party, through its secretary-general, Saddam Hussein, has the final word on all major issues affecting the country. The party has a mass membership, extending throughout public institutions, the armed forces, places of work, educational institutions, and local communities. Party membership is an Iraqi citizen's ticket to job promotion, but the reverse is also true: once special efforts are made to recruit a particular person, refusal to join may trigger the loss of that person's job. In higher education, the situation was worse in the 1980s: to continue one's studies beyond a bachelor's degree was impossible if the student was not also a Ba'ath Party member.

The Ba'ath Party maintains its ideological grip on Iraq through its regional bureaus. The one affecting the Kurds is the all-powerful Office of the Organization of the North (Maktab Tanzim al-Shimal), the "Organization" being the Ba'ath Party based in Kirkuk, here referred to as the Northern Bureau. The function of this office has been to implement and even formulate the regime's policy in the Kurdish areas, especially during the mid to late 1980s. Under its secretary general in 1987–89, Ali Hassan al-Majid, the Northern Bureau drafted and directed the campaign to crush the Kurdish insurgency and thus became directly responsible for the murder of tens of thousands of Kurdish civilians. The Kurdish parties claim that some of the most incriminating documents and audiotapes obtained by HRW/Middle East were taken directly from al-Majid's home in Kirkuk. Although HRW/Middle East has seen no files that originated in the office of the Northern Bureau, it has found original Northern Bureau documents in Amn and Istikhbarat files.[6]

The cache of Iraqi documents analyzed by an HRW/Middle East-led team also includes a sprinkling of files from the following agencies (or original items of correspondence from these agencies found in files belonging to other agencies):

- The Presidential Cabinet of the Republic (Diwan Ri'aset al-Jumhuriya), the Office of the President, whose executive orders are habitually signed by the office's secretary (individual items of correspondence only).
- The Northern Affairs Committee (Lajnet Shu'oun al-Shimal) of the Revolutionary Command Council (Majlis Qiyadet al-Thawra) in Baghdad, which oversees the RCC's policy in the Kurdish areas (individual items of correspondence only).
- The command of the Office of the Organization of the North (Qiyadet Maktab Tanzim al-Shimal), a small but powerful office based in Kirkuk that coordinates activities between the RCC's Northern Affairs

Committee and the Northern Bureau (individual items of correspondence only).

- The Central Intelligence Apparatus (Jihaz al-Mukhabarat al-Markeziyeh) in Baghdad, Iraq's foreign intelligence agency, whose northern branch is based in the town of Tikrit, with smaller branches in Suleimaniyeh and other towns (individual items of correspondence only).
- The National Defense Contingents (Afwaj al-Difa' al-Watani), the progovernment Kurdish militias, based usually in the tribal areas from which they recruit their members (complete files).
- The National Defense Corps Command (Qiyadet Jahafel al-Difa' al-Watani), the command of the progovernment Kurdish militias, which had five regional headquarters in the north (complete files).
- The Popular Army (al-Jaysh al-Sha'abi), a militia largely made up of "volunteers," created to support the army by staffing guard posts at government facilities, and other tasks (complete files).
- The commands of regular army divisions, including the First Corps (Faylaq al-Awwal) in Kirkuk and the Fifth Corps (Faylaq al-Khames) in Erbil (complete files).
- The Command of Oil Protection Forces (Qiyadet Quwat Himayet al-Naft), a special army division charged with the protection of the town of Kirkuk and surrounding oil fields (complete files).
- The Security Committees (al-Lajnet al-Amniyeh), small but powerful regional committees that combine representatives of the local government, armed forces, and security agencies in a single forum to coordinate security policy and are based in the various governorate and district capitals. They served as executive agencies of the regime in the Kurdish areas during the 1980s; they were abolished after Anfal, and then reinstituted during the crisis over Kuwait (complete files).
- The Committees to Fight Hostile Activity (Lajnet Mukafehet al-Nashat al-Mu'adi), committees similar in conception to the Security Committees but operating at a local level (complete files).
- State-controlled popular organizations, like the Youth Union, Student Union and Women's Union (complete files).
- Local government offices, such as the local Department of Health (complete files).
- Kurdish "parties" set up by the regime to create the impression of Kurdish opposition to the guerrilla organizations. They include the Kurdistan Revolutionary Party (al-Hezb al-Thawri al-Kurdistani) and the Kurdistan Democratic Party (al-Hezb al-Dimuqrati al-Kurdistani).

The latter should not be confused with the KDP currently headed by Mas'oud Barzani (complete files).

Finally, the store of documents also includes files of local Iraqi police headquarters. More often than not, police documents deal with such mundane matters as common crimes, traffic accidents, car licensing. The police do not appear to have had a significant, if any, role in the counterinsurgency campaign, either in the countryside or in the urban areas.

In addition to documents written and signed by officials from these agencies, files found in their offices also often contain photocopies, carbon copies, and handwritten copies of correspondence and memoranda from officials in other towns. These are of special interest when they include, as they regularly do, decisions from the country's senior leadership. HRW/Middle East has found, for example, many copies of official decrees that were issued by Iraq's highest legislative authority, the Revolutionary Command Council (Majlis Qiyadet al-Thawra), under the signature of its chair, Saddam Hussein. It has also found copies of documents from the Special Security Apparatus (Jihaz al-Amn al-Khas), an internal intelligence organization based in Baghdad and run by Saddam Hussein's son Qussay, which spies on the other intelligence organizations by planting agents in their midst, and the National Security Council (Majlis al-Amn al-Qawmi) in Baghdad, an advisory group of security experts chaired by Saddam Hussein.

Aside from small bags of audiocassettes, photographs, rubber stamps, a pair of handcuffs, a collection of military maps of northern Iraq, and three reels of film,[7] Iraqi state files consist entirely of written documents. Other materials the Kurds claim to have captured, including more audiocassettes, photographs, and videotapes, have also found their way to the West but do not form part of the material currently stored in facilities of the U.S. National Archives.

The documents examined by an HRW/Middle East-led team are largely memoranda, correspondence, arrest warrants, background information on suspects, official decrees, activity and investigation reports, logbooks, minutes of meetings, membership rosters, lists of names, census forms, and salary tables. These are kept in file folders, ring binders, or bound ledgers and logs. The folders are most often held together with shoe strings, and pieces of related correspondence are usually gathered together with pins (rather than paper clips) and sometimes staples. Most of the documents are handwritten, but some, especially those written by senior authorities, are typewritten. In many cases, a typewritten version of a piece of correspondence is attached with a pin to the same letter in handwriting, the latter being the draft passed by an official to a secretary for typing and mailing.

The physical condition of the documents reflects the circumstances under which they were obtained in March 1991 and often varied from town to town. At the start of the mass uprising, Kurdish civilians and guerrillas overran buildings that housed government offices and state agencies. In some cases, heavy fighting preceded the takeover, and in others the occupants surrendered without attempting to defend themselves. As a result, some buildings were torched and burned to the ground in the heat of battle, while others sustained little or no damage.

In Suleimaniyeh, in the early days of the uprising, the civilian population engaged heavily armed Amn officers ensconced in their agency's headquarters in a violent battle that left scores dead or wounded. Part of the building sustained fire damage, and as a result some of the documents that survived bear burn marks. Other documents were trampled in the melee or read and then discarded by civilian looters, left exposed to rainy spring weather. Only later did members of the parties attempt to gather up scattered files and transfer them to hastily established offices (and later yet, to strongholds in the mountains). The physical quality of the documents captured in Suleimaniyeh is therefore often dismal: they include crumpled, rolled up and torn sheets of paper, sometimes stuck together, with ink streaked across the page owing to prolonged exposure to moisture. In contrast, documents originating in the town of Shaqlawa are generally immaculate, reflecting the takeover there of government offices by disciplined groups of guerrillas who were clearly under orders to protect the files they found and removed.

In areas where the Kurdish guerrillas were not immediately present, civilians often carried documents home with them. Many Kurds were looking for files about themselves, in order to learn who had provided information about them to the government and what incriminating information might be in Amn's possession. Usually they held on to their own files while scattering the others in their possession.

Some of the files in civilian hands were retrieved after calls from the Kurdish leadership to turn them in to party offices. Yet, even today, many documents are suspected to exist in the homes of individual Kurds. Some of these HRW/ Middle East has been able to inspect on site. Because of these circumstances, HRW/Middle East has no definitive way of ascertaining the total volume of the documents captured from the Iraqi government. Indeed, it cannot confirm that most of the captured documents were transferred to the United States, even though it has reason to believe that this is the case. It is clear that the Kurdish parties have kept at least some of the documents, usually those that refer directly to Iraqi infiltration of their ranks and include the names of Kurds who at one stage or another acted as agents or informers for the central government. Other files may also have stayed in northern Iraq.

The Iraqi documents analyzed by HRW/Middle East display a remarkable

consistency in style. The language is numbingly dry, the format rigidly formalistic. A standard format is: "Regarding the memorandum from the office of —
—— [ref. no.] of [date], as transmitted to us by cable, labeled Confidential and Personal, from the upper command [ref. no.] on [date], decree [no,] of [date] has been canceled. Please be informed of this and act accordingly. With regards." Written thus, the documents bespeak the daily tedium of career civil servants closely adhering to established bureaucratic procedure.

The all-pervasive Iraqi bureaucracy manifests itself in another fashion: through the simple mechanism of referencing, the documents are linked to one another in a far-ranging administrative web. Official decrees are issued from on high and passed down the ranks to the lowliest Amn officers in the various branches by means of memoranda and cables. Reports were then generated on the actions taken according to directives, and these reports were sent back up the hierarchy, triggering new memoranda, new instructions, and new reports. All decrees are numbered, as is each piece of written communication. Most memoranda make reference to preceding correspondence and orders issued in years past. In the absence of a computerized index system, this extensive network was doubtless managed by diligent civil servants endowed with sharp memories, able to place documents in the right subject files, and store them in a logical fashion in local offices. Institutional memory must have been a prized talent among Iraqi bureaucrats![8]

In a fashion, the meticulous cross-referencing that is characteristic of the Iraqi documents simply reflects the complexity of daily life in a sophisticated modern state. At another level, though, the mere fact that not a single document stands alone, that every reported action can be related back to an earlier decree, attests to a deliberate strategy by civil servants and other agents of the state to be absolved of all personal responsibility for any possible violations of the rights of others committed in the name of the party, the revolution, and the republic. The Amn officer stalking the streets of Salah al-Din, for example, first wants his superiors to know that the summary execution he carried out against a "saboteur" had been ordered from higher up and, second, that he did in fact carry out the order.

A military intelligence document of March 1988 offers a telling example of this. It discusses the injuring of two shepherds (one of whom was a member of the progovernment Kurdish militia, colloquially known as the jahsh) by an army unit. Their crime: to be found in the prohibited areas with their herd. The document explains: "The orders issued regarding that subject forbid shepherding or moving about in the areas prohibited for security reasons. The unit then opened fire on them."[9] Clearly, as directives stream down in a steady flow, those who carry out the orders revert accountability for their actions back onto the shoulders of central power.

The complexity of the bureaucratic web, the repetition down the ranks of orders from on high, the resulting multiplication of key documents in local offices throughout the Kurdish region, and the determination of Iraq's medium and lower-level officials to prove that directives were actually carried out—in short, the completeness and sophistication of the Iraqi archives—have an important, unintended consequence. Together they emphasize that the documents are a credible, authentic expression of the state's actions against the Kurds.

Apart from dealing with strictly administrative matters, the Iraqi state files captured by the Kurds describe in great detail Iraqi policy and practice regarding the Kurds in the 1970s and 1980s. They include research studies, instructions, decrees, arrest orders, execution orders, daily and monthly reports, death certificates, minutes of meetings, and a great amount of correspondence linking the various documents and thus keeping the bureaucracy of repression in motion.

Although HRW/Middle East in its study of the documents focused on the crucial 1987–89 period—the tenure of Ali Hassan al-Majid as secretary general of the Ba'ath Party's Northern Bureau—it has strong evidence of flagrant abuses of human rights as well as the racial animus that was to inform the 1988 Anfal operation throughout the period covered by the documents. In its view, the evidence is sufficiently strong to prove a case of genocidal intent.

Most notable, perhaps, among HRW/Middle East's findings is the unequivocal evidence of Iraq's repeated use of chemical weapons against the Kurds: documents that report on specific air and artillery attacks carried out by Iraqi forces with chemical agents against Kurdish villages in 1987 and 1988. These documents match in precise detail testimonial and forensic evidence collected by HRW/Middle East in northern Iraq in 1992. The documents are crystal clear, for example, on the issue of culpability for the chemical attack on Halabja on 16 March 1988, in which some five thousand Kurdish civilians were killed. Although some writers in the United States continue, inexplicably, to insist that the attack was carried out by both Iraqi and Iranian forces,[10] the Iraqi state documents, which report widely on Iranian military actions, make no reference to an Iranian gas attack on Halabja at all. Instead, they refer to the occupation of Halabja by Iranian troops and rebel forces belonging to the Patriotic Union of Kurdistan and to the subsequent "Iraqi chemical attack on Halabja."[11] In an explicit case, an Istikhbarat document states that "as a result of the bombing by our planes and our artillery on the area of Halabja and Khurmal, approximately 2,000 enemy forces of the Persians and agents of Iran were killed."[12]

Although HRW/Middle East has found many references to chemical attacks, most have not been explicit. For reasons that remain unclear, Iraqi bureaucrats most often refer to chemical attacks either indirectly, by reporting that Kurdish sources have accused the Iraqi government of having carried out a chemical attack,[13] or euphemistically, by referring to Iraqi "special attacks" (*hujoum al-khaass*) or attacks with "special ammunition" (*'etaad al-khaass*).[14] There are two ways in which HRW/Middle East has been able to establish that the special attacks were in fact chemical attacks. First, it has matched the documentary evidence of specific special attacks with testimonial evidence of particular chemical attacks. The matches are numerous and unambiguous. In a document from early April 1988, for example, Istikhbarat speaks of a recent attack on Halabja with special ammunition.[15] Second, some of the documents themselves establish the link between special attacks and the use of chemical agents by stating, for example, that the KDP obtained five hundred gas masks as a precaution against special attacks.[16]

HRW/Middle East was also able to unearth an impressive documentary record on the incremental Iraqi campaign to raze most Kurdish villages and even some towns. This campaign began in earnest with the border clearances of 1977–78, was then extended to all areas under government control in 1987, and culminated with the elimination of most remaining villages in 1988. Their populations were forcibly resettled in government-controlled camps, deported to southern Iraq for periods, or, in the notorious Anfal operation, they disappeared.[17]

The documents detail the various orders that were issued—often on a village-by-village basis—by the country's political leadership to its military forces, the progovernment Kurdish militia, and the security police charged with carrying out destruction and relocation. The documents also show how these orders were implemented, with what level of efficiency, what obstacles occurred during the operation, who participated in it, and whether there were casualties among the local population and Kurdish guerrillas who resisted. There were requests from village leaders to spare their villages, citing special circumstances, such as a long history of cooperation with the regime; there are documents with instructions from the country's senior officials (the Northern Bureau in Kirkuk) that order the army to make exceptions for villages belonging to certain tribes that had consistently proved their loyalty to the regime by organizing its young men in militias. HRW/Middle East also found arrest warrants for hundreds of persons wanted by the authorities for having left the camps without official permission.

The Iraqi campaign against the Kurds was essentially and originally a counterinsurgency campaign, one that eventually escalated to a level that grossly violated the rules of war and vastly exceeded military necessity. In the end, it led to the deaths of tens of thousands of noncombatant civilians at the hands of government forces. The documents are full of references to the Kurdish guerrillas, who are referred to as the saboteurs (*al-mukharrebin*), their plans, meetings, movements, and the names of their relatives living in areas under government control. They also include actions undertaken against them by army forces and the secret police, their arrest and execution, the deportation of their first-order relatives, and the demolition of their homes.[18] The files contain interrogation records, court orders, and death certificates provided by local hospitals. They include petitions by families to be permitted to return from the Arab regions of southern Iraq, where they had been transported in mass deportations in previous years to areas of their birth, as well as letters from those seeking information from authorities about the fate of relatives who disappeared after an army sweep of their areas.

There are documents that speak of punishments for those who dared to change their officially registered ethnicity from Arab to Kurd. There are other documents that list the means by which Arabs should be enticed to move to the predominantly Kurdish city of Kirkuk, whose surrounding district contains Iraq's most significant deposits of oil. There are policy statements concerning Iraq's small Turkoman population, as well as the Yezidis, a non-Muslim sect whose members consider themselves Kurds (and are considered by Muslim Kurds to be Kurds), but who have been designated by the regime as Arabs.[19] There are also documents about the Eastern Orthodox branch of Assyrians and Chaldeans, both ethnic groups adhering to the Christian religion, who have similarly been defined as Arabs by the regime.

The documents show how the policy toward minorities evolved over time: a Ba'ath Party file on a Chaldean soldier in the Iraqi army includes documents from 1982 in which the man is said to be an ethnic Chaldean; from 1985, in which he is said to be Arab-Chaldean"; and from 1990, by which time he was referred to as Arab.[20]

The files contain ample references to the jahsh forces, the corruption that prevailed in their ranks, the benefits they received, the duties they often sought to avoid. There are also references to their usefulness as a repository of young Kurds unwilling to give their lives for their country in the war with Iran but prepared, as a lesser evil, to work with the authorities to counter the growth of the guerrilla insurgency in the countryside.

The files bring us up to the time of the Iraqi invasion of Kuwait in August 1990, the second war in the Persian Gulf, and to subsequent uprisings. These later files, however, are few and far between.[21] Nevertheless, HRW/Middle East has found a significant document from 1989 that outlines the government's policy in the southern marshes. Called the Plan of Action for the Marshes, it approves, among other things, a campaign of poisoning, burning of homes, and an economic blockade in the area.[22]

What is notably missing from the Iraqi state files analyzed by HRW/Middle East is any direct reference to either torture and rape in detention or the fate of the disappeared. This means that such documents either do not exist or were considered so highly classified that they were never distributed to the branches in the north, but instead were kept under lock and key in central headquarters.[23] HRW/Middle East must assume the latter. It is likely that the strongest evidence of genocide will be found only in the event of a change of government in Baghdad and the opening up of security archives there. Yet HRW/Middle East has found documents that suggest what may have happened with the people who disappeared and has matched them with the eyewitness testimonies from the Kurdish areas. They provide evidence that the people who have failed to return were indeed killed.[24]

In addition, the regime has made an effort to disguise some of its cruelest practices either by limiting the circulation of sensitive documents through a Top Secret classification; ordering the use of standard euphemisms, both in internal and public documents; [25] or ordering the suppression of important information.[26]

Examples of instructions to employ euphemismistic language in internal documents (but likely also in public statements) include a document of the Committee to Fight Hostile Activity in Shaqlawa, which orders substitution of the term *al-qura al-mazaleh* (removed villages) for the term *al-qura al-muhaddameh* (destroyed villages).[27] In a clear example of an attempt to hide the reality about the people who disappeared during the Anfal campaign from the public, an Amn document from 1990 makes reference to instructions to replace the text, "They were arrested during the heroic Anfal operations and remain under arrest," with, "We don't have any information about their fate."[28]

HRW/Middle East has found several documents that contain orders to suppress information that could expose secret police methods or that might reveal the names of the perpetrators of illegal actions. A conference of the Eastern Sector, Military Intelligence Directorate, for example, held on 11 February 1990 instructs subalterns "not to leak office secrets, especially those relating to the fate of the detainees in your custody."[29] An Amn document circulated just before the Anfal campaign cites an order from the Northern Affairs Committee of the Revolutionary Command Council: "Do not disseminate the text of the directives issued by senior authorities or mention their provenance. It is sufficient to disseminate the content of the directives with the words, 'The following has been decided . . . ,' in order to permit the respective authorities to take their regular position in issuing directives."[30]

A note of caution is necessary, though, concerning the credibility of the information contained in Iraqi state files. Agents of the security police and military intelligence, like their counterparts elsewhere, had a natural interest in exaggerating their accomplishments before their superiors. Thus, HRW/Middle East has found reports of Iraqi military feats and casualties inflicted on guerrilla forces that are not substantiated by field research. Likewise, the evaluation by

Ba'ath Party officials and Amn agents of the organization, activities, and morale of Kurdish rebels exposes real weaknesses in their understanding of their adversaries. The documents, for example, often understate the capabilities of the rebel parties in the 1980s. Not a single document should therefore automatically be taken at face value.

In contrast, documents relaying official instructions from senior authorities are of real importance since they demonstrate an express intent to carry out specific policies. To move from proving intent to proving event one must methodically combine several sources, including documents, testimonies, and forensic evidence, comparing the findings, and try to reconstruct the events that took place.

The bureaucracy of repression has evolved a distinct discourse, the purpose of which has been to criminalize the regime's opponents and their actions while justifying and even glorifying the regime's own exploits. This discourse is marked by various narrative devices: euphemistic terms are employed to describe obviously illegal acts while adversaries are assigned different epithets that build on Ba'athist political rhetoric, symbols of Arab nationalism, and a reinvented cultural and ethnic past. To understand the true content of the Iraqi state documents, a narrative road map is necessary.

During Anfal, specific actions against a targeted group were not spelled out again once an original decree had been circulated through the ranks, but was given stock phrasing whose meaning would have been clear to all. Directive SF/4008 of the Northern Bureau, for example, issued on 20 June 1987, gave instructions to execute persons aged 15–70 who had been arrested in the prohibited areas; subsequent memoranda, sometimes referring to unspecified Northern Bureau instructions, then simply stated the need to carry out the "necessary measures" (*narjou ittikhad ma yalzem*).[31] Thus, a 1988 letter from the Command of the Oil Protection Forces in Kirkuk to the Security Directorate of al-Ta'mim Governorate states: "We are sending to you the families—their numbers are given below—who surrendered to our forces in the area of Sofi Raza on 15 April 1988. Please take the necessary measures against them, according to the directives of the Northern Bureau, and acknowledge their arrival."[32] As this document shows, mundane, sanitized bureaucratic language is employed to describe truly horrifying events.

Iraq's war against Iran is referred to as Qadissiyet Saddam, or Saddam's Qadissiya, a name that evokes the first, victorious battle between the Muslims and Persians in the seventh century. The word *Anfal* refers to an even earlier battle won by the first Muslims, also against "unbelievers," in 624 A.D. Since early 1988, army desertion has been termed an indecency under the law. The areas that fell under rebel control in the 1980s are called prohibited areas (*manateq mahdoureh amniyan*).[33] The deportation of Kurds from their villages to government-controlled resettlement camps is referred to as the amalgamation (*tajmi'*) and relocation (*tarhil*) of the villages to modern villages (*qura 'asriyeh*) or new cities (*mudun jedideh*). Ridding an area of rebels is hailed as purification (*tathir*).

The Kurdish guerrillas, widely known as peshmerga in Kurdish (literally, those who face death) are never referred to as such; they are routinely designated as saboteurs (*mukharrebin*). In contrast, members of the government-sponsored Kurdish militias are called fighters (*muqatelin*). Starting in 1987, anyone who refused to move out of the prohibited areas to the towns and camps was henceforth also referred to as a saboteur, whether or not he or she was a combatant. The parties to which the rebels belong, when named at all, receive the prefix "agent" (*'amil*) as in "the agent Kurdistan Democratic Party." A small Kurdish party set up by the regime is referred to as the *allied* Kurdistan Democratic Party (*halif*). More commonly, however, the rebel parties are referred to by completely different names: the Patriotic Union of Kurdistan is known in the documents as the agents of Iran (*'umala' Iran*), while the original Kurdistan Democratic Party is referred to as the offspring of treason (*salili al-khiyane*).

Persons, civilians as well as combatants, who voluntarily moved from the prohibited areas to areas under government control are referred to in the documents as returnees to the national ranks (*'a'edin lil-saf al-watani*). Before Anfal, this phrase meant that they were pardoned and could move into one of the modern villages. If, however, a "saboteur" belonging, for example, to the agents of Iran, did not abide by the regime's summons to "return to the national ranks," he would automatically be branded an outlaw, whose first-order male relatives would be subject to detention and whose mother and sisters might be "relocated" to "the area of the saboteurs" after they had been stripped of their Iraqi citizenship. Once resident in the prohibited areas, they all were subject to attack, arrest, and summary execution by the regime, a policy that found its apogee in the Anfal campaign.

Saboteurs who were defeated in combat, on the other hand, were considered to have surrendered (*salamu anfusahum*). Before Anfal, this usually meant that unless they benefited from an amnesty as army deserters (*harebin min al-khedmet al-'askariyeh*), they would be sent to their original army units for punishment.[34] From 1987 on, however, especially in the period after Ali Hassan al-Majid became secretary general of the Northern Bureau, many were killed following their "surrender." During Anfal, the regime's rhetoric could no longer keep up with events: the documents make it clear that even those who were said to have returned to the national ranks were handed over to the Security Directorate in Kirkuk. In all likelihood they were sent to their deaths from there.[35]

The Iraqi government has on at least three occasions over the past two years publicly challenged the authenticity of the documents analyzed by HRW/Middle East, claiming they are forgeries. HRW/Middle East rejects these accusations unequivocally. For the record, though, it may be useful to rebut the Iraqi government's allegations in detail.

On 5 March 1992, the Iraqi Mission to the United Nations in Geneva wrote to Max van der Stoel, special rapporteur of the United Nations Commission on Human Rights on Iraq, stating in part:

> With regard to the letters allegedly emanating from security departments at Sulaimaniya, Halabja, and elsewhere, we wish to point out that, during the disturbances, hostile bodies succeeded in obtaining stationery bearing the letterhead of those departments, which they used to forge letters ostensibly emanating from official bodies. Investigations have shown that those official letters were not issued by the departments referred to and the information contained therein is wholly fabricated. The manner in which one of these letters was drafted shows that it was written by a person with a poor command of the Arabic language, thereby confirming its spurious nature.[36]

Then, on 5 February 1993, the Iraqi Mission in Geneva referred to the documents in a note verbale to Van der Stoel as documents "allegedly issued by Iraqi authorities."[37] The note verbale included the official response by the government of Iraq on the matter of the documents:

> We wish to state that a number of falsified documents has been disclosed by unknown circles with a view to undermining Iraq's reputation, as part of the political and media [war] waged against it. Among those documents are the ones we received in connection with the events that, basically, took place during the Iran-Iraq War up to the July 1988 cease-fire.
>
> It is well known that Iraq's eastern and northeastern borders were scenes of military operations. It is therefore not possible to verify what went on during that period, especially with regard to the activities of those saboteurs who were fully cooperative with the hostile Iranian military forces.
>
> Regarding the documents that were sent to us, with the allegation that they are official documents—which in fact [they] are not—we wish to point out the following:
>
> 1. Following the all-out aggressive war that was waged against Iraq on 17 January 1990 [sic], the American, British, and French forces occupied vast areas in northern Iraq. By the force of weapons, the invading forces assisted the irresponsible elements and saboteurs in assuming control of the area. This foreign occupation of northern Iraq led to the absence of the state's official bodies. Government

departments with all their stores of printing machines, stationery, and official stamps bearing signatures of Iraqi officials fell in the hands of the saboteurs and American, British, and French forces of occupation. Moreover, many officials who worked in those departments fell under the mercy of the saboteurs['] gangs and carried out their orders.

2. All that has facilitated and will facilitate for the foreign powers and the saboteurs under their command the carrying out of large-scale forgery, including what has been so far disclosed of alleged documents and which may be disclosed in the future.

3. Furthermore, the violent and successive events that were imposed on Iraq during the Iran-Iraq War or during the aggression perpetrated by the allied forces against Iraq, along with the control by the saboteurs of the northern area and the preceding riots, have all inflicted damage and loss of most of the official documents in the northern area, rendering the competent Iraqi authorities unable to verify the validity of any information or claims requiring response.

Apart from the charge that they are fabrications, the key point in the Iraqi government's position on the documents is the admission that the events in the Kurdish areas in the spring of 1991 led to "damage and loss of most of the official documents" there. From this statement, two possible conclusions follow. If by "loss" is meant that the government lost the documents, or lost control of them, this would suggest that these same documents might well have survived the events in the north and could conceivably—and, indeed, would in all likelihood—be in the possession of someone other than the government of Iraq. If this is the correct interpretation, then the government's statement that most of its documents were lost would contradict its accusation that the documents the Kurds claim they captured are all forgeries. The government cannot have it both ways: either the documents represent a 4-million-page forgery on a scale unseen in history, or they are indeed the documents that the government has admitted losing. In the latter case, there can be little question as to the authenticity of these documents as a whole.

If, on the other hand, loss is meant to denote that the documents were irreparably damaged by fire or some other form of destruction, then the question arises, By what strange coincidence was it possible for several tons of stationery to survive the uprising relatively unscathed at a time when the government's undoubtedly vast inventory of written reports, correspondence, personal files, and other official documents completely perished?[38] Moreover, the Iraqi claim flies in the face of overwhelming testimonial evidence, collected by HRW/Middle East, that large holdings of written documents were found in and taken from government offices in all the major towns captured by the Kurds during the March uprising.

The special rapporteur, in his report to the forty-ninth session of the Commission on Human Rights in February 1993, pointed at a second contradiction in the various statements made by the Iraqi government on the subject of the documents. On 20 February 1992, the representative of the government of Iraq addressed the Commission on Human Rights, claiming that the documents were forgeries because "paper forms carrying the formal emblems" had fallen into "hands not qualified to use them" and that these documents were "written in bad Arabic, and it seems that they were drafted by people who do not master the language, a fact that confirms counterfeit."[39] In his reply, the special rapporteur made clear that, again, the Iraqi government could not have it both ways: either the documents were slipshod counterfeits produced by poorly educated Kurds, or they were forgeries made with mirror-image precision by captive government employees working under duress. HRW/Middle East and others who have examined the documents are wholly convinced that neither is the case.[40]

The following features support the argument that the documents are entirely authentic:

1. The sheer quantity of the holdings transferred to the United States: 18-¼ metric tons.
2. The variety and complexity of the material, both in form and content: The files include carefully maintained, bound ledgers containing codes or journal entries; thick folders comprising hundreds of chronologically organized pieces of correspondence carefully dated and numbered and referring to previous pieces of correspondence and official orders; personal files that offer detailed life histories of thousands of persons under investigation; and salary ledgers with carefully worked out calculations.
3. The nature of the material: The documents provide an extremely detailed view of the nature and scope of Iraqi intelligence operations in the Kurdish region over a period of thirty years (though most of the documents stem from the 1980–91 interval), *but few have self-evident value in human rights terms.* At least a third of the documents are entirely administrative in nature, chronicling the workaday world of government employees, with their constant demands for vacations, promotions, and appointments with senior officials. Some 50 percent of the documents relate to investigations of persons and events but offer no evidence of crimes. Only a small portion of the documents contain specific orders to undertake actions that would constitute clear violations of international law and human rights and

reports of such actions having been carried out. Most of the documents are completely useless to anyone interested in seeking legal action or redress against President Saddam Hussein's government, and it would be an act of sheer folly to try to recreate such an immense store of administrative paperwork merely to indict the regime.

There are other questions of a more logical nature: Why would forgers go to the trouble of manufacturing both handwritten and typewritten drafts of the same document, however innocuous in nature, and include even scribbled notes that must have formed the rudimentary outlines of these drafts if only the final, official, and signed versions could conceivably be used to bring charges against the regime? Why would they include documents that might potentially be a source of embarrassment to themselves, as, for example, the numerous references to the kidnappings for ransom of Kurds suspected of progovernment activity by Kurdish guerrillas? Why would they create large amounts of documents, only to then hold on to some of these themselves, claiming that these are of no significance to human rights organizations but had only an internal value for their own movement?[41]

These points suggest that a large-scale counterfeit operation would not only have been extremely unlikely but would have been completely impossible, especially taking into account the chaotic conditions that prevailed in northern Iraq after the March 1991 uprising. Iraqi forces succeeded in reconquering the area within three weeks, driving the Kurds into the difficult mountainous terrain along the borders with Iran and Turkey. In the wake of government announcements of an amnesty and promises of protection by the allied forces, Kurds began trickling back into the towns, most of which were now firmly under government control, in the late spring. The area remained under government control throughout the summer. Finally, at the end of October 1991, Iraqi forces withdrew voluntarily from most of the area, leaving the Kurds in charge of the major towns, Suleimaniyeh, Erbil, Dohuk, and the surrounding countryside.

Clearly, no large-scale counterfeit operation could have been staged until this date, if at all. Yet as early as November 1991 western visitors were able to inspect the enormous caches of documents held by the Kurds. HRW/Middle East itself inspected huge quantities of PUK-held documents in an abandoned school building in Mawat, near the Iranian border, in February 1992. Stored in grain sacks and ammunition boxes, they were covered with dust and showed no sign of having been disturbed in months.

To prove that any individual document is authentic is a more difficult, but by no means insurmountable, problem. First, the possibility exists to verify the age of the ink and paper used to produce the documents. If a case against the Iraqi government or its officials ever comes to court, such physical authentication would be helpful. Second, if the Kurdish parties themselves wished to indict the Iraqi regime, they would want to prove the regime's intent to commit genocide and crimes against humanity. In the absence of resources to manufacture large amounts of incriminating documents, it would be logical that they would draft a few documents that, by their explicit nature, would promptly be recognized as smoking guns. These would then be inserted into the captured files in such a way as to make it appear that they had always been there. In fact, the evidence HRW/Middle East has been able to collect so far is highly fragmented: it is incomplete and spread over an enormous number of files. Still, this evidence, however fragmentary, is remarkably consistent, and tiny bits of evidence in fact turn out to constitute the many small pieces of a gigantic jigsaw puzzle. The task of HRW/Middle East has been to assemble this puzzle. After examining some 70 percent of the documents, the evidence already shown is so compelling that the need for anyone to insert other smoking guns is obviated.

The two genuine smoking guns already found, both orders issued in 1987 by the Ba'ath Party's Northern Bureau under the signature of its secretary general, Ali Hassan al-Majid, are, in HRW/Middle East's view, authentic. HRW/Middle East has found multiple copies of these orders, sometimes with slight variations, in different boxes of varying provenance. The question this finding raises is, Why would forgers go to the trouble of manufacturing multiple copies of the same order when a single copy would have been enough to do the trick? and How would they have been able to distribute the copies throughout the files in various localities, sandwiching them chronologically between documents of similar but different content, while still maintaining the level of internal consistency these files invariably exhibit?

Frequent references to one of these key documents, the Northern Bureau's letter SF/4008, are made in later documents. Throughout the fall of 1987, in 1988 and even during 1989, by its blatant nature the order to kill all inhabitants aged 15–70 caught in the prohibited areas apparently filled unit commanders with uncertainty and hesitation because of its sweeping nature. The order therefore needed to be restated on several occasions, including in an evidently annoyed manner, by headquarters. The hesitation, the annoyance, and the numerous other nuances that mark the general narrative of the documents bespeak a complexity that would be impossible to falsify.

One should also ask why, if the Kurdish parties did actually produce fake smoking-gun documents and inserted them into state files, they did not produce clearer proof of the top authority's responsibility. Why do most of the documents originate in Amn and Istikhbarat offices if it is the Ba'ath Party that had final authority in the Anfal campaign? Moreover, some of the most egregious violations—rape and torture in prison and the mass killings of noncombatants arrested during the Anfal campaign—are either left unaddressed in the documents or are alluded to in indirect and obscure terminology.

Finally, there simply is no physical evidence in the rebel-controlled region of northern Iraq that the Kurds were at any time engaged in a logistic exercise of such monumental proportions. It would have been difficult to conceal such an enterprise, considering the direct and untrammeled access independent observers had to the area at the time.

There is not a shred of evidence that any one of the documents in the possession of HRW/Middle East was falsified, much less all 4 million of them. Apart from the government of Iraq, no one has claimed they were forged. To date, Baghdad has presented no evidence that the Kurds have done so.

# APPENDIX A

---

# THE ALI HASSAN AL-MAJID TAPES

The following are selected remarks by Ali Hassan al-Majid, secretary general of the Ba'ath Party's Northern Bureau, from meetings with senior Ba'ath officials in 1988 and 1989. Audiotapes of more than a dozen of these meetings were recovered from Iraqi government offices and from al-Majid's home in Kirkuk during the failed Kurdish uprising of March 1991.

1. Meeting with Northern Bureau members and directors of the Ba'ath Party headquarters in the northern governorates. The tape is dated 26 May 1988, but from context it appears to be from a meeting held in 1987.
[Response to a question about the success of the deportation campaign]

As a matter of fact, what we have achieved is something that the party and the leadership never managed to do until 1987. Some of it was just the help and mercy of God. Nothing else. Otherwise if you just go and conduct military exercises for the troops who were used in the campaign, you will have more casualties than we had. Imagine in such an exercise how many martyrs and casualties there would be! . . .

What happened? Are these the saboteurs? Are these the people you were afraid of? This is the reality of the saboteurs, and you have all these facilities and this capacity. They could not confront you. In the past they were confronting a division with just a few machine guns. This time they were just shelling us from far away with light artillery.

Some of you who were working here at the time when I arrived, so motivated with this duty, perhaps you said in your hearts, "Okay, wait a minute! Wait a minute! The people who were here before you said the same things and then didn't do anything!" Now you will be forced to take some action. All those years and the saboteurs still existed. At a time when we had this huge military! I swear to God it was not done in that way. All the Iraqi troops couldn't have done what we did. But this [deportation] hurts them. It kills them.

[Voice identified as Abu Muhammad: "Only God can do more than you. Otherwise you can do anything. This Ba'ath Party can do anything."]

The saboteurs watch the orders and directives. The orders are not that forceful. The previous ones were a hundred times stronger. But they were not combined with a belief on the part of those executing them. Now that exists. We said that at that date we would start to implement the deportation campaign. And we did it everywhere, with the help of God. The same day [in 1987] they captured Qara Dagh in retaliation.

Jalal Talabani asked me to open a special channel of communication with him. That evening I went to Suleimaniyeh and hit them with the special ammunition. [This presumably refers to the April 1987 chemical attack on the PUK headquarters in the Jafati Valley.] That was my answer. We continued the deportations. I told the mustashars that they might say that they like their villages and that they won't leave. I said I cannot let your village stay, because I will attack it with chemical weapons. Then you and your family will die. You must leave right now. Because I cannot tell you the same day that I am going to attack with chemical weapons. I will kill them all with chemical weapons! Who is going to say anything? The international community? Fuck them! the international community, and those who listen to them!

Even if the war with Iran stops and the Iranians withdraw from all occupied lands, I will not negotiate with him [Talabani] and I will not stop the deportations.

This is my intention, and I want you to take serious note of it. As soon as we complete the deportations, we will start attacking them everywhere according to a systematic military plan. Even their strongholds. In our attacks we will take back one-third or one-half of what is under their control. If we can try to take two-thirds, then we will surround them in a small pocket and attack them with chemical weapons. I will not attack them with chemicals just one day, but I will continue to attack them with chemicals for fifteen days. Then I will announce that anyone who wishes to surrender with his gun will be allowed to do so. I will publish 1 million copies of this leaflet and distribute it in the North in Kurdish, Sorani, Badinani, and Arabic. I will not say it is from the Iraqi government. I will not let the government get involved. I will say it is from here [the Northern Bureau]. Anyone willing to come back is welcome, and those who do not return will be attacked again with new, destructive chemicals. I will not mention the name of the chemical because that is classified information. But I will tell them that they will be attacked with new destructive weapons that will destroy them. So I will threaten them and motivate them to surrender. Then you will see that all the vehicles of God Himself will not be enough to carry them all. I think and expect that they will be defeated. I swear that I am sure we will defeat them.

I told the expert comrades that I need guerrilla groups in Europe to kill whoever they see from them [the saboteurs]. I will do it, with the help of God. I will defeat them and follow them to Iran. Then I will ask the *mujaheddin* to attack them there. [Following their expulsion from France in 1986, the People's Mujaheddin of Iran relocated to Iraq and came under the patronage of the Ba'ath Party.]


2. Meeting with members of the Northern Bureau and governors of the Autonomous Region of Iraqi Kurdistan, 15 April 1988.

By next summer there will be no more villages remaining that are spread out here and there throughout the region, but only camps. It'll be just like the hen when she puts the chicks under her wing. We'll put the people in the camps and keep an eye on them. We'll no longer let them live in the villages, where the saboteurs can go and visit them. Emigration from the villages to the city is necessary in the north of Iraq.

From now on I won't give the villagers flour, sugar, kerosene, water, or electricity as long as they continue living there. Let them come closer to me to hear me, so that I can tell them the things I believe and want in ideology, education, and common sense. Why should I let them live there like donkeys who don't know anything? For the wheat? I don't want their wheat. We've been importing wheat for the past twenty years. Let's increase it to another five years.

I will prohibit large areas; I will prohibit any presence in them. What if we prohibit the whole basin from Qara Dagh to Kifri to Diyala to Darbandikhan to Suleimaniyeh? What good is this basin? What did we ever get from them? Imagine how much we paid out and lost on those areas. How many good citizens are there among those people, and how many bad ones?

What went wrong? What happened? Thirty, twenty, twenty-five years of saboteur activity. Imagine how many martyrs we have! . . . Now you can't go from Kirkuk to Erbil any more without an armored vehicle. All of this basin, from Koysinjaq to here [Kirkuk]. . . . I'm going to evacuate it. I will evacuate it as far as Gweir and Mosul. No human beings except on the main roads. For five years I won't allow any human existence there. I don't want their agriculture. I don't want tomatoes; I don't want okra or cucumbers. If we don't act in this way the saboteurs' activities will never end, not for a million years. These are all just notes, but with the help of God we will apply them very soon, not more than a month from now. In the summer nothing will be left.

3. Meeting with unnamed officials, 1 August 1988.

Any Arab who changes his ethnicity to Kurdish is doing so to avoid serving in the army. This is a big problem. What shall we do about it? . . . Why did Mosul [governorate] register them as Kurds? We asked them to deport every Kurd who lives there and send them to the mountains to live like goats. Fuck them! Why do you feel embarrassed by them?

We deported them from Mosul without any compensation. We razed their houses. We said come on, go, go! But those who are already fighters, we tell them from the beginning that they must go and settle in the camps. After that we will tell them to go to the Autonomous Region. We will not get into any arguments with them. I will read the pledge for them, and they must sign it. Then wherever I find [passage inaudible], I will smash their heads. This kind of dogs, we will crush their heads. We will read the pledge for them: I, the undersigned admit that I must live and settle in the Autonomous Region. Otherwise I am ready to accept any kind of punishment, including the death penalty. Then I will put the pledge in my pocket and tell the Amn director to let him go wherever he wants. After a period of time, I will ask, where is he? They will tell me, here he is. The Ba'ath Party director must write to me saying that the following people are living in that place. Immediately I will say blow him away, cut him open like a cucumber.

Do you want to increase the Arab population with these bloody people? . . . We must Arabize your area [Mosul]—and only real Arabs, not Yezidis who say one day that they are Kurds and the next that they are Arabs. We turned a blind eye to the Yezidi people joining the fighters [jahsh] in the beginning, in order to stop the saboteurs from increasing. But apart from that, what use are the Yezidis? No use.

4. Northern Bureau meeting to review the campaigns of 1987 and 1988. The tape is undated, but is in a batch dated 21 and 22 January 1989.

The most dangerous stage of the threat to Iraq was between August 1987 and April 1988. It was a dangerous situation. We started to do serious work on the military front from 18 February to 4 September 1988.

All the successive commanders of the First Corps and the Fifth Corps: Lt. Gen. Nizar [al-Khazraji] and Sultan Hashem of the First Corps and Tali'a al-Durri, the martyr al-Hadithi, Muhammad and Ne'ama Fares and Ayad of the Fifth Corps. . . . All these men that I mentioned are commanders who have been serving in the north of Iraq since they were lieutenants. The first one among them to join the Ba'ath Party was Tali'a al-Durri.

When we made the decision to destroy and collectivize the villages and draw a dividing line [that is, the so-called red line] between us and the saboteurs, the first one to express his doubts to me and before the president was Tali'a al-Durri. The first one who alarmed me was Tali'a al-Durri. To this day the impact of Tali'a is evident. He didn't destroy all the villages that I asked him to at that time. And this is the longest-standing member of the Ba'ath Party. What about the other people then? How were we to convince them to solve the Kurdish problem and slaughter the saboteurs?

So we started to show these senior commanders on TV that [the saboteurs] had surrendered. Am I supposed to keep them in good shape? What am I supposed to do with them, these goats? Then a message reaches me from that great man, the father [Saddam Hussein], saying take good care of the families of the saboteurs and this and that. The general command brings it to me. I put his message to my head. [The sense conveyed in the Arabic phrase is that Saddam Hussein's wish is always al-Majid's command—but not, he goes on to say defensively, in this instance.]

But take good care of them? No, I will bury them with bulldozers. Then they ask me for the names of all the prisoners in order to publish them. I said, "Weren't you satisfied by what you saw on television and read in the newspaper?" Where am I supposed to put all this enormous number of people? I started to distribute them among the governorates. I had to send bulldozers hither and thither . . . [The tape is cut off in midsentence at this point.]

5. Meeting to welcome Hassan Ali al-Amiri, his successor as secretary general of the Northern Bureau, 15 April 1989

I would like to admit that I am not and will not be the right person for the current stable situation in the North. . . . For this current peaceful and stable situation, Comrade Hassan Ali is the right person. I am ready to come back and do whatever you think is necessary, though I would like to remain a member of the Northern Bureau.

I hope that the comrades in the north will not ask Comrade Hassan Ali to take administrative measures and do other things that he cannot do. Because that stage is finished. It will no longer be allowed for a member of the leadership to have power over the army, because the exceptional situation is over. These powers are not being withdrawn from Comrade Hassan Ali because he is not up to the task, but because that stage has now finished.

In my first meeting in April 1987 with the army corps commanders, Amn and police directors, governors and Ba'ath Party directors, we decided to deport all the villagers in order to isolate the saboteurs. We made it in two stages. The first stage started on 21 April and ran until 21 May. The second stage ran from 21 May to 21 June. From 22 June anyone who was arrested in those areas was to be killed immediately without any hesitation, according to the directives that are still in force.

In one of the meetings with the army chiefs of staff I was asked to postpone the campaign for a month by one of our best commanders. I said no, not even for one day. From now on our slogan will be to wipe out saboteur activity. That is our objective. That is the objective of this stage. Anyone who thinks he is not capable of implementing this must tell me now. One of the best commanders, the commander of the Fifth Corps, was reluctant, despite my providing him with more facilities than the First Corps. The result now is that the saboteurs are finished, and they had frozen 40 percent of Iraqi power.

When the [September 1988] amnesty was announced, I was about to get mad. But as a responsible party member I said okay. I said, probably we will find some good ones among them [the Kurds] since they are our people too. But we didn't find any, never. If you ask me about the senior officials of the Kurds, which ones are good and loyal, I will say only the governors of Erbil and Suleimaniyeh. Apart from those two, there are no loyal or good ones.

I cry when I see a tragic show or movie. One day I cried when I saw a woman who was lost and without a family in a movie. But I would like to tell you that I did what I did and what I was supposed to do. I don't think you could do more than what I could do.

I would like to speak about two points: one, Arabization, and two, the shared zones between the Arab lands and the Autonomous Region. The point that we are talking about is Kirkuk. When I came, the Arabs and Turkomans were not more than 51 percent of the total population of Kirkuk. [It is unclear here whether al-Majid is referring to the city or the governorate of Kirkuk.] Despite everything, I spent 60 million dinars until we reached the present situation. Now it is clear. For your information, the Arabs who were brought to Kirkuk didn't raise the percentage to 60 percent. Then we issued directives. I prohibited the Kurds from working in Kirkuk, the neighborhoods and the villages around it, outside the Autonomous Region. . . .

Kirkuk is a mixture of nations, religions, and doctrines. The people we deported from 21 May to 21 June—not one of them was from the prohibited areas. But they were under the control of the saboteurs, whether they were for them or against them.

# APPENDIX B

# THE PERPETRATORS OF ANFAL

## A Road Map to the Principal Agencies and Individuals

### THE REVOLUTIONARY COMMAND COUNCIL

The highest formal authority in Iraq is the ruling Revolutionary Command Council, headed by President SADDAM HUSSEIN. Although Saddam involved himself personally in the operational aspects of Anfal through the office of the president of the republic, supreme powers for handling Kurdish affairs between 1987 and 1989 were vested in his cousin, ALI HASSAN AL-MAJID.

### THE BA'ATH ARAB SOCIALIST PARTY

Anfal was a Ba'ath Party operation, commanded by the party's Northern Bureau, buttressed administratively by the Northern Bureau Command and the Northern Affairs Committee of the RCC. Under RCC decree 160 of 29 March 1987, the Northern Bureau's secretary general, Ali Hassan al-Majid, was given extraordinary powers over all other state, party, military, and security agencies. Al-Majid's co-signatory on Northern Bureau Command orders was TAHER TAWFIQ AL-ANI, secretary of the RCC's Northern Affairs Committee. Deputy Secretary of the Northern Bureau Command was RADHI HASSAN SALMAN.

Under al-Majid's command, the following were the other main agencies involved in Anfal:

The *Iraqi army and air force* (including commandos, special forces, chemical weapons units, and engineering corps): All field combat operations; village burnings and destruction; and mass transportation of detainees. The Iraqi defense minister at the time of Anfal was Gen. ADNAN KHAIRALLAH (later deceased). The army chief of staff was Brig. Gen. NIZAR ABD-AL-KARIM AL-KHAZRAJI. Most Anfal operations were handled by the Kirkuk-based First Corps (commander Lt. Gen. SULTAN HASHEM), and the Erbil-based Fifth Corps (commander Brig. Gen. YUNIS MOHAMMED AL-ZAREB).

259

Lieutenant General Hashem was also the field commander of the first Anfal operation; Brig. Gen. AYAD KHALIL ZAKI and Brig. Gen. BAREQ ABDULLAH AL-HAJ HUNTA commanded the second and third Anfals, respectively. The field commanders of other Anfals are not known.

*Republican Guard:* Elite combat operations during the first and second Anfals

*General Military Intelligence Directorate (Mudiriyat al-Istikhbarat al-Askariyeh al-Ameh):* Supervision of initial holding facilities, such as the Qoratu and Nizarkeh forts; some interrogation; matters affecting draft dodgers and deserters; field command of jahsh. Two of Istikhbarat's four regional commands played key roles in Anfal. The commander of Eastern Sector Istikhbarat was KHALED MUHAMMAD ABBAS; the commander of Northern Sector Istikhbarat was FARHAN MUTLAQ SALEH.

*General Security Directorate (Mudiriyat al-Amn al-Ameh) (including the special units of Kurdish agents known as Mafarez Khaseh):* Case-by-case intelligence gathering and surveillance of the population; interrogation of prisoners at Topzawa and other detention camps; supervision of informers; tracking down escapees and those sheltering them; monitoring of camps. The director of Amn for the Kurdistan Autonomous Region was ABD-AL-RAHMAN AZIZ HUSSEIN.

*Emergency forces (Quwat al-Taware'):* Units under Ba'ath Party command, including members of the jahsh, Amn, and police agents, in charge of urban intelligence, counterterrorism, and supervision of initial detention facilities in the city of Suleimaniyeh, and perhaps other locations

*National Defense battalions (Jahafel al-Difa' al-Watani, or jahsh):* Auxiliary role in combat operations; roundups and surrender of prisoners; guard duty at collection points

*Popular Army (Jaysh al-Sha'abi):* Guard duties at principal transit facilities (Topzawa, Dibs, and so forth)

Several interagency groups were in charge of discrete aspects of the Anfal operation and associated anti-Kurdish campaigns during 1987–89. Normally chaired by a Ba'ath Party official, most included representatives of Amn, the army's First and Fifth Corps and/or Istikhbarat, the Iraqi police, and civilian authorities. Notable were the following:

*Returnee reception committees (Lajnet Istiqbal al-A'idin):* Responsible for those "returning to the national ranks" under the General Amnesty between 6 September and 9 October 1988 and other later amnesties.

*Security committees (Lajnet al-Amniyeh)* and *Committees to Fight Hostile Activity (Lajnet Mukafahat al-Nashat al-Mu'adi):* Organized to combat the peshmerga at the governorate and local level respectively; and a number of ad hoc committees which monitored the economic blockade of the "prohibited areas," controlled food rationing and attempted to prevent smuggling.

*Follow-up committees (Lajnet al-Mutaba'a):* Charged with ensuring compliance with laws governing returnees, tracking down escapees and otherwise tying up the loose ends of the campaign.

In addition, some civilian ministries played supportive roles in Anfal. For example, the Agriculture Ministry harvested and disposed of the abandoned crop of 1988; the Finance Ministry administered the confiscated property of "saboteurs" and oversaw house demolitions; and the state real estate bank arranged loans for new housing in the camps.

## APPENDIX C

# KNOWN CHEMICAL ATTACKS IN IRAQI KURDISTAN, 1987–1988

Only those attacks that HRW/Middle East has been able to document through eyewitness testimony are listed here. The true figure may be considerably higher—the Middle East division has received many other unconfirmed reports and allegations of chemical weapons attacks during 1987–88. Based on field interviews, HRW/Middle East has determined that at least sixty villages, as well as the town of Halabja, were attacked with mustard gas, nerve gas, or a combination of the two.

| No. | Date | Location | Means | Deaths |
|-----|------|----------|-------|--------|
| 1. | 4-15-87 | Sergalou-Bergalou | Air | Not known |
| 2. | 4-15-87 | Gojar Mountain, Mawat | Rajima[a] | Not known |
| 3. | 4-16-87 | Sheikh Wasan, Balisan | Air | 225–400[b] |
| 4. | 5-?-87 | Ja'faran (Qara Dagh) | Rajima | — |
| 5. | 5-?-87 | Serko (Qara Dagh) | Air | — |
| 6. | 5-27-87 | Bileh, Malakan (village and valley) | Air | 1+ |
| 7. | 5–7-87 | Bergalou, Haladin, Yakhsamar, Sekaniyan, and surrounding areas (repeated attacks) | Air + Rajima | 7+ — |
| 8. | 2-?-88 | Sheikh Bzeini area | Air | — |
| 9. | 2-?-88 | Takiyeh, Balagjar | Air | — |
| 10. | 3-16-88 | Halabja | Air | 3,200–5,000 |
| | | **First Anfal (Jafati Valley)** | | |
| 11. | 2-23-88 | Yakhsamar | Rajima | 5 |
| 12. | 2-23–3-18-88 | Sergalou, Bergalou, Haladin, and neighboring villages and mountains (constant attacks) | Air + Rajima | Not known |
| 13. | 3-22-88 | Shanakhseh | Air | Up to 28 |

*(continued)*

## APPENDIX C (*continued*)

| No. | Date | Location | Means | Deaths |
|-----|------|----------|-------|--------|
| | | **Second Anfal (Qara Dagh)** | | |
| 14. | 3-22-88 | Sayw Senan | Rajima | 78–87 |
| 15. | 3-23-88 | Dukan | Rajima | Not known |
| 16. | 3-24-88 | Ja'faran | Rajima | — |
| 17. | 3-24-88 | Masoyi | Helicopter | — |
| 18. | c.3-30-88 | Zerda Mountain (Qara Dagh) | Rajima | — |
| | | **Third Anfal (Germian)** | | |
| 19. | 4-10-88 | Tazashar | Air | 15–25 |
| | | **Fourth Anfal (Lesser Zab Valley)** | | |
| 20. | 5-3-88 | Askar | Air | 9 |
| 21. | 5-3-88 | Goktapa | Air | 154–300 |
| | | **Fifth, Sixth, and Seventh Anfals (Shaqlawa-Rawanduz)** | | |
| 22. | 5-15-88 | Wara | Air | 37 |
| 23. | 5-23-88 | Seran; Balisan, Hiran, and Smaquli Valleys | Air | 2+ |
| 24. | 5-26-88 | Akoyan, Faqian, and Rashki Baneshan Mountain | Rajima | — |
| 25. | 7-31-88 | Malakan, Seran, Garawan; Balisan, Hiran, Smaquli, and Benmerd Valleys | Air | 13+ |
| 26. | 8-8–8-26-88 | Balisan Valley and adjacent areas (constant attacks) | Air | Not known |
| | | **Final Anfal (Badinan)**[c] | | |
| 27. | 8-24-88 | Zewa Shkan | Air + Rajima | Not known |
| 28. | 8-25-88 | Birjinni | Air | 4 |
| 29. | 8-25-88 | Tilakru | Air | Not known |
| 30. | 8-25-88 | Gelnaski | Air | — |
| 31. | 8-25-88 | Tuka, Barkavreh | Air | 14–15 |
| 32. | 8-25-88 | Warmilleh, Bilejaneh | Air | — |

(*continued*)

**APPENDIX C** (*continued*)

| No. | Date | Location | Means | Deaths |
|-----|------|----------|-------|--------|
| | | **Final Anfal (Badinan)ᶜ** | | |
| 33. | 8-25-88 | Ikmala, Heseh, Khrabeh | Air | 3–6 |
| 34. | 8-25-88 | Ruseh, Nazdureh | Air | 1+ |
| 35. | 8-25-88 | Berrabareh | Air | — |
| 36. | 8-25-88 | Swareh, Spindar, Avok, Sidara (south side of Gara Mountain) | Air | 2+ |
| 37. | 8-25-88 | Mergeti, Bawarkeh Ka-vri, and other villages (north side of Gara Mountain) | Air | Not known |
| 38. | 8-25-88 | Gizeh, Rodinya, Shirana, and other villages (center of Gara Mountain) | Air | 9+ |
| 39. | 8-25-88 | Baluka | Air | Not known |

ᵃTruck-mounted multiple-barrel artillery

ᵇThe dead include two busloads of adult men and teenage boys who subsequently disappeared from Amn captivity

ᶜThe fatality statistics for the final Anfal refer only to on-site deaths; they exclude later deaths from the effects of chemicals

The Iraqi regime appears to have used chemical weapons for at least four complementary purposes:

1. To attack base camps and main-force concentrations of Kurdish peshmerga. This strategy accounts for many of the attacks on the Jafati Valley (first Anfal), the Qara Dagh area (second Anfal), the Balisan and Smaquli valleys (fifth, sixth, and seventh Anfals) and Zewa Shkan (the final Anfal);
2. To harass and kill retreating peshmerga as Anfal progressed. Attacks of this sort include those on Shanakhseh (no. 14), Zerda Mountain (no. 19), Tazashar (no. 20), and the Shaqlawa-Rawanduz area (nos. 26 and 27);
3. To inflict exemplary collective punishment on civilians for their support for the peshmerga. The most dramatic case is the bombing of Halabja after the seizure of the town by peshmerga and Iranian revolutionary guards. Others include the 1987 attacks on Sheikh Wasan

and Balisan (no. 4), the Anfal attacks on Sayw Senan (no. 15), and Goktapa (no. 22);

4. To spread terror among the civilian population as a whole, flushing villagers from their homes to facilitate their capture, relocation, and killing. The opening of almost every phase of the Anfal campaign was marked by attacks of this sort, but they were most apparent in the final Anfal in the Badinan region, where more than thirty villages were bombed simultaneously along an east-west strip on the morning of 25 August 1988.

Although a distinction between these different aims is helpful in understanding the tactical thinking behind the Iraqi campaign, it is without meaning in legal terms. Chemical weapons are by nature indiscriminate, and their use is outlawed under any circumstances.

## APPENDIX D

# SAMPLE MASS DISAPPEARANCES DURING ANFAL, BY REGION

Shown here is the pattern, not the scale, of civilian disappearances and presumed mass killings during each phase of the Anfal campaign. Only a fraction of the numbers lost during Anfal are listed here—only those who were reported by name or by precise numerical count during more than 350 HRW/Middle East field interviews with survivors.

### First Anfal

No meaningful figures exist, and there is no evidence to suggest the mass disappearance of civilians. Recorded fatalities from four villages—Haladin, Sergalou, Qara Chatan (nahya Surdash), and Maluma (nahya Kareza)—seem to refer to deaths from bombing, shelling, chemical attacks, exposure, and cold.

### Second Anfal

| Nahya | Villages | Total Disappeared | Men | Women | Children | Unspecified |
|---|---|---|---|---|---|---|
| Qara Dagh-Serchinar[a] | 9 | 56 | 32 | — | — | 24 |
| Qara Dagh-Serchinar[b] | 5 | 103 | 23 | 27 | 17 | 36 |
| Total | 14 | 159 | 55 | 27 | 17 | 60 |

[a] Villages whose inhabitants fled to Suleimaniyeh
[b] Villages whose inhabitants fled to Germian

### Third Anfal

| Nahya | Villages | Total Disappeared | Men | Women | Children | Unspecified |
|---|---|---|---|---|---|---|
| Qader Karam[a] | 13 | 148 | 129 | — | — | 19 |
| Qader Karam[b] | 8 | 208 | 110 | 6 | 27 | 65 |
| Qara Hanjir | 1 | 3 | 3 | — | — | — |
| Qara Hassan | 1 | — | — | — | — | — |
| Altun Kupri | 1 | 8 | 8 | — | — | — |

(*continued*)

## APPENDIX D (continued)

### Third Anfal (continued)

| Nahya | Villages | Total Disappeared | Men | Women | Children | Unspecified |
|---|---|---|---|---|---|---|
| Sengaw<sup>c</sup> | 9 | 196 | 60 | 11 | 21 | 104 |
| Tilako | 7 | 200 | 17 | 27 | 69 | 87 |
| Kalar<sup>d</sup> | 1 | 200 | 6 | 2 | 3 | 189 |
| Serqala | 2 | 82 | 6 | 3 | 10 | 63 |
| Peibaz | 5 | 273 | 24 | 22 | 54 | 173 |
| Total | 48 | 1,318 | 363 | 71 | 184 | 700 |

[a] Areas where no combat is reported in army documents
[b] Areas of combat (Gulbagh Valley, Tazashar southward)
[c] The heaviest pattern of mass disappearances from Sengaw appears to reflect paths of flight—either into southern Germian or toward Chamchamal through the Gulbagh Valley
[d] The figure is an approximation, but the witness reported that almost all those who disappeared were women and children

### Fourth Anfal

| Nahya | Villages | Total Disappeared | Men | Women | Children | Unspecified |
|---|---|---|---|---|---|---|
| Aghjalar | 10 | 155 | 47 | 29 | 79 | — |
| Shwan | 7 | 68 | 43 | 9 | 16 | — |
| Taqtaq | 5 | 162 | 22 | 11 | 16 | 113 |
| Total | 22 | 385 | 112 | 49 | 111 | 113 |

### Fifth, Sixth, and Seventh Anfals (Nahyas Khalifan, Rawanduz, Harir)

| Nahya | Villages | Total Disappeared | Men | Women | Children | Unspecified |
|---|---|---|---|---|---|---|
| Total | 5 | 123 | 59 | 7 | 6 | 51 |

### Final Anfal

| Nahya | Villages | Total Disappeared | Men | Women | Children | Unspecified |
|---|---|---|---|---|---|---|
| Sarsenga | 17 | 189 | 189 | — | — | — |
| al-Doski<sup>a</sup> | 7 | 175 | 175 | — | — | — |
| Zawita<sup>a</sup> | 1 | 1 | 1 | — | — | — |
| al-Guli<sup>a</sup> | 2 | 30 | 30 | — | — | — |
| al-Sindi<sup>a</sup> | 3 | 42 | 42 | — | — | — |
| Berwari Bala<sup>a</sup> | 2 | 40 | 40 | — | — | — |
| Amadiya<sup>a</sup> | 1 | 9 | 9 | — | — | 9 |
| Nerwa Reikan<sup>a</sup> | 3 | 155 | 155 | — | — | — |

(continued)

## APPENDIX D (continued)

### Final Anfal (continued)

| Nahya | Villages | Total Disappeared | Men | Women | Children | Unspecified |
|---|---|---|---|---|---|---|
| Sarseng[b] | 3 | 86 | 11 | 13 | 26 | 36 |
| al-Doski[b] | 1 | 34 | 11 | 11 | 3 | 9 |
| Berwari Bala[b] | 1 | 6 | 4 | 2 | — | — |
| Deralouk[b] | 1 | 17 | 6 | 2 | 9 | — |
| Nerwa Reikan[b] | 1 | 7 | 2 | 2 | 3 | — |
| All[a] | 36 | 632[c] | 632 | — | — | — |
| All[b] | 7 | 150 | 34 | 30 | 41 | 45 |
| Total | 43 | 782 | 666 | 30 | 41 | 45 |
| Grand Total | 132 | 2,767 | 1,255 | 184 | 359 | 869 |
| As % | | 100.0 | 45.4 | 6.6 | 13.0 | 35.0 |

[a]Kurdish villages

[b]Christian/Yezidi villages

[c]Includes 5 boys aged 12 or 13

## APPENDIX E

# ORIGINAL ANFAL DOCUMENTS

HRW/Middle East's sample of the documents captured by the Kurds of northern Iraq in the March 1991 uprising against the regime of Saddam Hussein include the two main smoking-gun documents as well as documents that are less significant for legal purposes against the government of Iraq but are nonetheless helpful in showing the methodology and routine character of a bureaucracy of repression in action.

Most of the nine documents included here have been translated in full; some have been excerpted to feature essential information. Editorial comments by HRW/Middle East appear in brackets. In translating, an accurate sense of Arabic idiom has been favored over a literal translation where no equivalent exists in English. For dates, the Iraqi system of day/month/year has been observed.

The documents were originally published by Human Rights Watch in February 1994 in *Bureaucracy of Repression: The Iraqi Government in Its Own Words* and retain the same document numbers.

ـ برقية سرية فورية ـ

وقت الإنتاء ويومــــه

الى / مديرية امـــن الاقــــــــــام

من / امـــــن اربـــــــــل

١٩٨٨ / ٨ / ٢١

النسخ٠/ ير٠ره/١ / ٦٩ / ١٢١/ علمنا ما يلـي ( ٠ )

١٠ هنـاك عنـاصر التحقت بافواج الدفاع الوطني من الشبـن الذين غيروا قوميتهـــــم
من العـوبـة الى الكرديـة والساكنيـن محافظة نينـوى ٠٠

٢٠ نسب الرفيق النـاضـل علي حسن المجيـد مسؤول مكتب تنظيم الشمال بـــــــد م
دورهم جميعـاً ويرحلـون الى المجمعـات السكنيـة في محافظتنا ولايعوضـــون
نهائيـــــا ٠٠٠

للاطـــلاع واتخـــاذ ما يلـــزم وأعز ـــــا ا

٥٤٤٥
١٩٨١/٩/١

مديرامن محافظة اربيـــــل

٢١/ح

بسم الله الرحمن الرحيم

سري وشخصي

مقــر

اللجنة الامنية في شقلاوه

العدد / امن / ٥٥

التاريخ ٥ / ٤ / ١٩٨٧

الى / محافظة اربيل اللجنة الامنية

الموضوع / محضر اجتماع

نرفق طيا محضر اجتماع اللجنة الامنية
اقضاء شقلاوه المنعقد بالساعة ١٩٠٠ يوم الاربعاء ١ / ٤
يرجى التفضل بالاطلاع .

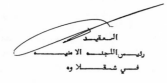

العقيد
رئيس اللجنة الامنية
في شقلاوه

نسخة الى : /

قيادة قوات الخاصه والابرعين / للتفضل بالاطلاع وطيا نسخه من المحضر
نائب قائمقام شقلاوه .
الفرقه الحزبيه في شقلاوه .
مديريه شرطه شقلاوه .
مديريه امن شقلاوه .

للتفضل بالاطلاع وطيا نسخه من محضر
الاجتماع .

سري وشخصي

محضر اجتماع اللجنة الأمنية بالساعة ١١٠٠
يوم الاربعاء / ١٩٨٧/٤/١

١٠ اجتمعت اللجنة الأمنية في قضاء شقلاوة بالساعة ١١٠٠ يوم الاربعا
وطبقا لــ توجيهات السيد العام لرؤساء اللجان الامنية والمسؤلين الاداريين
في الاقضية والنواحي من خلال اجتماعهم بالساعة ١١٠٠ ليـوم الاربعا
في ديوان المحافظة قدارست اللجنة الامنية المواضيع التالية :ـ
أ ـ القرى المحظورة امنيا ـ

اولا ـ ان القرى المحظورة امنيا هي القرى التي تقع خارج الخطا ٢ حمايسوى من
التطبيقات العسكرية .
ثانيا ـ ان القرى هذه اصبحت ملجأ للمخربين وقـ واعد انطلاق لهم للقيام
باعطيبات التخريبيــة داخـل المدن والقصبات ومناطـق استراحـــ
ازرميـم ومصادر تموين لهم بالمأكـل والمشرب والملبس .
ثالثا ـ تقترح اللجنة الامنية للاسباب اعلاه العاطفه على ازالــ كافة القرى
المحظورة امنيا وتفكــيل ساكنيهـــا .
ب ـ القرى غير المحظورة ـ امنيـا

ان هناك الكثير من القرى الغير محظوره امنيا خاصه القريبة مــن
المدن والقصبات يتخذ هذا المخربون كمصدر لمواد التموين او طريـق
مرور في الذهاب والاياب بما يقـدمية بحسن مكانهـا من صاعـد ازمـــ
التخريب طبيعة تقتـرح اللجنـة الامنيـة طلبــا :ـ
اولا ـ انذار سكان القرى الغير محظوره امنيا بتغييره على كافـــ
اشكال التعمـــاون ومهمـــا كانـتالاسبـاب لزمـرة التخريـب .
ثانيا ـ معاملة القريه الغير محظوره امنيا كالقريه المحظوره امــ
في حالتــ عدم تنفيـذ مابوود في (اولا) اعـلاه .
٢٠ كتاب محافظة اوميل اللجنة الامنية البي والخمسين ٨٧٠ فــ ١٥/٢
وكتاب محافظة ايضك اللجنة الامنية السي والخمسن ١٠٤٠ فــ ٢٨/٣
تقيبرح اللجنة الامنية اولا على قبول الدواجن البسو عليها
بالكتب اعلاه للاسبـاب التاليـــ :ـ
أ ـ ابما اصبحت ملجأ للمخربين وهي تشكـل سقطه انطلا ق لهم لقـرب هذ
الحقـول من قصبـــة شقـلاوه كـما تفكـل منطقه استراحه استراحـه لهم ليـلا .

سري وشخصي

ب. قيام أصحاب الحقول بتقديم المواد الغذائية والوقود للمعرضين وهم
مؤمنين من ذلك محافظة على منطلقاتهم بسبب بعد المسافة عنهم

د. إبقاء هذا المعتقلين على التنقل ... اللقاء في ... مع تنظيماتهم
الداخلية

ج. تشكيل مجلس لتحميل المواد المهمة ...

. تم وضع خطة للقضاء على ظاهرة التهريب في القصبة.

. تم مناقشة العميل ... وقوع حادث ... قطع الصومعة
وتم القرار في ما يلي :-

أ. يتم الاتصال اللاسلكي بين رئيس اللجنة الأمنية وأعضاء اللجنة ... ت.

ب. يتم القرار في العميل اللاسلكي لمعالجة ... ث.

٥. ناقشت اللجنة الأمنية موضوع طلبات تأمين الحماية الكاملة لحركة
الاصطياف لهذا العام وقد حافظ كافة الفقرات في القطاع الأمني
للعام السادس لم تتعرض اللجنة لتطوير الأمن من قبل نسبة إلى الطلبات
الضرورية وضرورة ذلك أن الأماكن ... لتخصيص طلع جيش شعبي
ليشكل نقطة تأمين داخلي للتعبئة وحماية المرافق السياحية
والحكومية ... من مركز القضاء. وحمايته الجوية متوفرة حالياً

<br>

العقيد     المقدم     العقيد     المقدم     السيد     الرائد

مدير أمن شقلاوه  مدير شرطة شقلاوه  أمين سر فرقة شقلاوه  قائم قام شقلاوه  رئيس اللجنة الأمنية
لقضاء شقلاوه

سري وشخصي

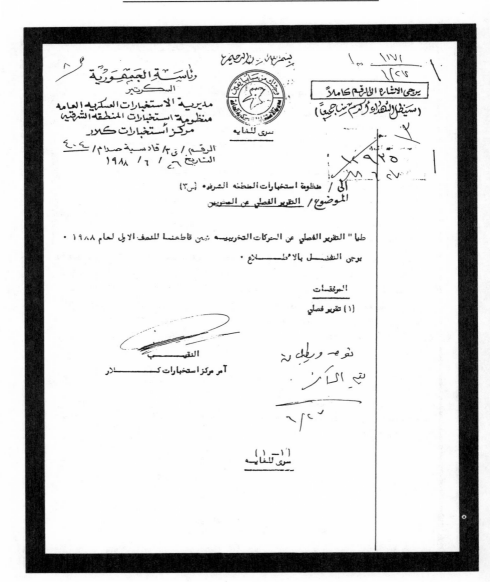

بسم الله الرحمن الرحيم

يرجى الاشاره الى الرقم كاملاً
(سينقل الشهداء و كرمت مناجيعاً)

رئاسة الجمهورية
السكرتير
مديرية الاستخبارات العسكرية العامه
منظومة استخبارات المنطقة الشرقية
مركز استخبارات كلار

الرقم / ق٢ قادسية صدام /
التاريخ  /  / ١٩٨٨

الى / منظومة استخبارات المنطقه الشرقيه (س٣)
الموضوع / التقرير الفصلي عن المتورين

طيا " التقرير الفصلي عن الحركات التخريبيه ضمن قاطعنا للنصف الاول لعام ١٩٨٨ .
يرجى التفضل بالاطـــــلاع .

المرفقات
(١) تقرير فصلي

النقيب
آمر مركز استخبارات كـــــلار

نوصى وربطك به
قم الكا

٢/٢

(١-١)

سـرى للغـايه

ب. خلال شهر آذار ١٩٨٨ قامت طائراتنا بقصف مقرات زمر التخريب في قريتي سيوان ( ٤٥٩٦ )
وللكجار ( ٤٢٩٤ ) وتوجيه ضربه كيماويه نتج عنها قتل ( ٥٠ ) مخرب وجرح ( ٢٠ ) مخرب آخر

ج. بالساعه ١٩١٥ يوم ٦/١٩ قام شخص مجهول الهويه بقذف رمانه يدويه على دار المواطن
صالح محمد عزيز في قضاء كلار — محلة بنكرد ولم تحدث خسائر في الدار .

١٢ . العمليات الخاصه

لا زلنا بصدد متابعتها

١٣ . الاستنتاجات

آ . لوحظ اعتماد المخربين على تنظيماتهم الداخليه للقيام باعمال تخريبيه داخل المدن .

ب . قيام النظام الايراني بابداء كل المساعدات اللازمه لكافة الحركات التخريبيه في المنطقه
الشماليه بخق احتضانها والتأمير على قواتنا الباسله واضعافها ١

ج . لوحظ قيام مخربي بؤلاء ايران السماح لافراد الحد والايراني الدخول الى الاراضي العراقيه
وتخصيص فارز لحمايتهم بغيـة استطلاع المناطق المهمه وتصويرها .

د . لا يزال المخربين يستخدمون هويات وعدم تعرضات صادره من افواج الدفاع الوطني لتنفيذ
مآربهم الدنيئه .

هـ . قيام مخربي عملاء ايران بالانفتاح على باقي الحركات التخريبيه ومحاولة توحيد صفوفهم ضذ
السلطه الوطنيه في العراق .

١٤ . المقترحـات

آ . متابعة عناصر التنظيمات السريه للمخربين بغية القاء القبض عليهم ومنعهم من ايصال
المعلومات الى المخربين .

ب . زرع الانشقاقات بين الحركات التخريبيه بغيـة الوصول الى حالة التصادم والتنافر فيما
بينهم .

ج . مواصلة القيام بعمليات عسكريه لضرب تواجد المخربين اينما كانوا والقضاء عليهم .

د . وضع ضوابط صارمه فيما يتعلق بهويات افواج الدفاع الوطني للحد من استخدامها من
قبل العناصر المشبوهه والزام ضباط استخبارات تلك الافواج مسؤولية سوء استخدامها .

هـ . تشجيع المخربين عن طريق ذويهم بالعوده الى الصف الوطني وكسبهم الى جانب السلطه
الوطنيه .

و . مواصلة طائراتنا العموديه باستطلاع طرق تسلل المخربين باستمرار للحد من نشاطهم
وشـل حركتهم في المنطقه .

يرجى التفضـل بالاطــــلاع .

النقيــــب
كفـاح علي حسـن
آمر مركز استخبارات كـــلار

( ٦ )

سـرى للغـايه

باسم الشعب

مجلس قيادة الثـــورة

رقم القرار / ١٦٠

تاريخ القرار / ٣ / ٢٩ / ١٩٨٧

قـــــرار
_____

استنادا الى احكام الفقرة (ٲ) من المادة الثانية والاربعين ، والفقـــرة
(ٲ) من المادة الثالثة والاربعين من الدستور ، وتنفيذاً" لما تقرر في الاجتمــاع
المشترك لمجلس قيادة الثورة والقيادة القطرية لحزب البعث العربي الاشتراكــي
المنعقد في ١٩٨٧/٣/١٨ •

قرر مجلس قيادة الثورة بجلسته المنعقدة في ٢٩ / ١٩٨٧/٣ مايلي :ــ

اولا • يقوم الرفيق علي حسن المجيد ، عضو القيادة القطرية لحزب البعـث
العربي الاشتراكي ، بتمثيل القيادة القطرية للحزب ومجلس قيادة الثـورة
في تنفيذ سياستهمـا في عموم المنطقة الشمالية وبضمنها منطقة كردستان
للحكم الذاتي بهدف حماية الامن والنظام وكفالة الاستقرار فيهـا وتطبيـق
قانون الحكم الذاتي في المنطقة •

ثانيا • يتولى الرفيق عضو القيادة القطرية ، لتحقيق اهداف هذا القرار ، صلاحية
التقرير الملزم لجميع اجهزة الدولة المدنية والعسكرية والامنية ، وبوجـه
خاص الصلاحيات المنوطة بمجلس الامن القومي ولجنة شؤون الشمـال •

ثالثا • ترتبط الجهـات التالية في عموم المنطقة الشمالية بالرفيق عضو القيـادة
القطرية وتلتزم بالقرارات والتوجيهـات الصادرة عنه التي تكون واجبـة
التنفيذ بموجب هذا القرار •

١ــ المجلس التنفيذي لمنطقة كردستان للحكم الذاتـــــــــــــي •

٢ــ محافظو المحافظات ورؤساء الوحدات الادارية التابعـــــــــــــين
لوزارة الحكم المحلـــــــي •

۲

٣ـ اجهزة المخابرات وقوى الامن الداخلي والاستخبارات العسكرية .

٤ـ قيــــادات الجيــــش الشعـــــــــي .

رابعا . تلتـزم القيادات العسكريـة في المنطقة باوامـر الرفيق عضو القيـــادة القطريـــة بكل ما يتصـل بـ ( اولا " ) من هــذا القـرار .

خامسا . يعمل بهذا القرار من تاريخ صدوره وحتى اشعار آخـر، ويتـوقــف العمل بالاحكام القانونيـة التي تتعارض واحكام هــذا القـــــــرار .

صــدام حســين

رئيس مجلـس قيادة الثـــورة

سرية فورية /١٢/١/

من /فن ١/ ر /ٽ/ا د /

الى /فني /٢٤/٢٧/٢٨/٢٤/٣٦/٢١/يي جحد و /٢١/ ق٤٤/قق حن /موا تعفل ١/القبوا تا لاولى
الرقم /٤١١٨//٠/ رسالة مبا/دة مشتب تنظيم الشما لسرية /٢٤٥/في /٦/٨/٠/تضب
ما يلى فى ضوء الاجتماع انذ يا شعقد بتا ريخ /١٩٨٧/٩/٦//٠/وشرا سه الرفيق
على حسن المجيد امين سرمكتب تنظيم الشما ل /١/٠//٠/تقوم اللجا ن الامنية فى
انمها دثا ت النشا لية بتفد يم جرد /يعوا ل ل المخربين على ا ن ينجز خلا النفتره صن
/٦/ الى/٩/١٥//٠/ ويبا شر فدرا /نتا ك ق من الجرد بترحيل تلك العوا ل ل المسا طق
توا جد د ويءم /٠/صن المخربين /عدا الكرجوز معكم بين سنه /١٢١/دا خل الرسنه /٥٠١/
دا حل /٠/ فيتم جرد مويستشنى من ك كرة الجراءات العوا ل ل التى لها شعدا ء
او صفقودين او اسرى ا ر مستحيق او مدا تنون فوة لترلج الد فا ع الوطن فذ لك مدة
انحا له يتم شرحين لازم نغد الجا المخربين /٢/٠//٠/ يبا شر بعقد ندوات جمل عية //
جما هيرية وا جتماعا ت ادارية /يجرى خلا نها الحد يث عن هفية عملية التعذا ب
الطم /السنا ت ة الها م النذ تشر ا جرا ء ة فى /١٩٨٧/١٠/١٢//٠/ ويو ء كد علي ا يما حا ن /
عن لا يشا رك فى العمدية بد ون عذر مشروع بقف قد عرا فنيه / تما سيعتبر من الها ربين
سن الجيش ويبيعن بحذ ف را رمجى /مجنس فيا دة النوره / التمرقم /١٧٧/ فى /٨/٢٦/٠/
/٢/٠/لا تنس عودة انها ربين سن المخربين بد ونا سلحتهم اعتبا را من /٦/٩/٠/الى
/١٧/ /٠/و بعد /١٠/١٧/ ذتنبل عودتهم حتى وا نجلبوا ا سلحتكم /٠/شرجوا لا طلا ع /
وا نفا د ما ينزم وا علا منا ٠٠٠٠٠/

الى السيد.٠٠                      الاءعم                      /٢١

حزب البعث العربي الاشتراكي    امة عربية واحدة

القطر العراقي      ذات الرسالة.خالدة

قيادة فرع اربيل

قيادة شعبة صلاح الدين

العدد ٦٠/٢٦٨٨

التاريخ ١٩٨ / ٧ / ٩ / ١٢

الى /قيادة فرع اربيل

م/ محضر اجتماع

....................

تحية رفاقية :-

بتاريخ ١٩٨٧/٩/١٢ قد عقد قيادة و شعبه صلاح الدين اجتماعاً استثناء في مقر قيادة و شعبه صلاح الدين وذار اجتماع والرفيق ماشور شهاب احد امين سر قيادة والشعبه وحضره الرفاق اعضاء قيادة والشعبه وتداول الاجتماع ما يلـــي :-

١) كتاب قيادة وفرع اربيل ١١٥٢٥/٣٤ في ١٩٨٧/٩/١٨ قرار اطلعت قيادة الشعبه طرى مضمون الكتاب اعلاه وتوصي بما عدا الرفيق عدنان حمدان طوان / عضو فرقه كهمستجي بمبلغ ٢٠٠ مائتان وخمسون دينار لحد وديه راتبه ولكونه صاحب عائلة كبيره .

٢) اطلعت قيادة و الشعبه على كافه استمارات جرد وتقييم عوائل المخربين الوارد ه من قيادة والفرق ويعد عقب كافه الاستمارات توصي قيادة والشعبه ما يلـــي :-

اولا :- حجز وترحيل افراد عوائل المخربين حسب الضوابط الوارد ة والبناء كتاب قيادة والفرع الرقم ١١٥٤٠/٣٨ في ١٩٨٧/٩/٩ ورقبه قيادة و مكتب تنظيم الشمال الرقم ٤٣٥ في ٢ / ٩ ١٩٨٧ وعددها (( ١١١ )) عائله من العوائل التي ليس لديها شهيد - اسير - مفقود - عسكري مقاتل افواج ال دفاع وطني - مقاتل في الجيش الشعبي

ثانيا :- ترحيل والد و المخرب او شقيقته الكبرى حسب الضوابط الوارد ة ورقبه قيادة و مكتب تنظيم الشمال وعددها (( ١٠٣ )) من العوائل التي لديها شهيد - اسير - مفقود - مقاتل عسكري - مقاتل افواج دفاع وطني - مقاتل جيش شعبي .

ثالثا :- اسقاط الجنسيه العراقيه وحجز الاموال المنقوله وغير المنقوله للعوائل الملتحقه حزب التخريب مع كافه افراد العائله وعددها (( ٨٤ )) اعتباره .

للتفضل بالاطلاع مع التقد يـــر .

و دمتم للنضــال

الرفيـــق      ماشور شهاب احمد

امين سر قيادة و شعبة لاح الدين

نسخة منها الى

الرفاق اعضاء قيادة والشعبه المحترمون / للتفضل بالاطلاع . مع التقديـــر

— صورة الكتـــــاب —

قررت رئاسة ديوان الرئاسة مايلـــــي : ـ

١) ان لا يكون التعميم باسماء الاشخاص الصادر بحقهم الحكم الجماعي وانما يكتب
منفــرداً .

٢) ان تعطى درجة كتمان عاليه الى الوثائق التي سيجرى التعميم فيها لمثـــــل
هذه الوثائـــــق .

راجين اتخاذ مايلزم والعمل بموجبـــــه .

موقع / ٠٠
ع / وزيـر الداخليـــــه .

_____

بسم الله الرحمن الرحيم                    الامن العام
سري وشخصي وعلى الفور     مديرية امن محافظة اربيــــل
                                       العدد / ش م ن ٥ / ١٤٢١٩
                                       التاريخ / ٦ / ١١ / ١٩٨٧
الى / كافة مديريات امن الاقسام وشعب السياسيه
م / الوثائق السريـــه

_____

اعلاه صورة كتاب وزارة الداخليه ـ مديرية الامور السريه والسياسيه المرقم / ١٧٩٠٣
في ١٥ / ١٠ / ١٩٨٧ ـ للعمل بموجبه رجـــــاءً .

رائد الامن
ع / مدير امن محافظة اربيـــــل

بسم الله الرحمن الرحيم

قـيـادة
قوات حمـايـة النفط
الاركان العامه
الاستخبارات
العدد/ ٦٩ >
التاريخ/ ١١ نيسان ٨٨

لسدادة حرب والمادة حق    سرى للغايه

الى/ مديرية أمن التأميم

الموضوع/ ارسال عوائل

ترسل لكم العوائل المدرجه اسمائهم في القائمه المرفقه والذين سلموا
انفسهم لقطعاط العسكريه يوم ٢٨ نيسان ٨٨٠
نرجو احتفاظ ـ بهم بصدد هم حسب مكتب تنظيم الشمال واعلامنا بالاستلا م٠

المرفقات
ـــــــ

( ١/١ ) قائمه تتضمن (٢٠٧) اسم

العميد ق غ الركن
بارق عبدالله الحاج حفظه
قائد قـوات حمـايـة النفط

نسخه الى/
ـــــ

قيادة فل ١ (ش آ ف ـ آ س) طيا نسخه من القائمه ٠ يرجى التفضل بالاطلاع ٠
ف آس ما الشرقيه / طيا نسخه من القائمه ٠ نرجوا الاطلاع ٠

( ١ ـ ١ )
سرى للغايه
ـــــــ

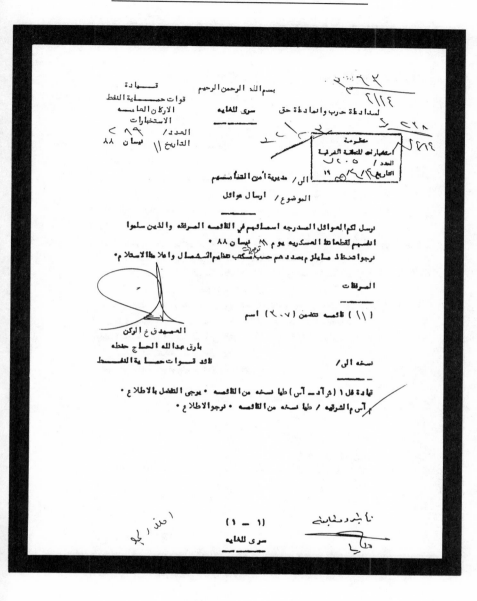

بسم الله الرحمن الرحيم

سري وشخصي

لجنة كاظم قره داغ
( الاستخبارات )

العدد / ٦ م ٦ /١٢٨
التاريخ / ٢١ /٥/١٩٨٨

السري / كافة الوحدات
الموضوع / ازالة القرى

كتاب فسل / ١ سري وشخصي ٢٠٨ في ٢٥ ايار ١٩٨٨
المبلغ الينا بكتاب قيادة اللواء الاول سري وشخصي ١٧ في ٢٨ مايس ١٩٨٨
تجـب ما يلــــــي :ـ

١ . وبه تم اطلاعنا تشير الى وجود قرى وبور عشائشه لم تتم ازالتها بالشكل المطلوب حتى الآن
في المناطق المحددة ادناه ، وانني مستلها عمليات الازالـــــــــل .

٢ . تحسب الاسراع بعملية تهديم وازالة كافة القرى والدور المتفرقة اعلاه بالسرعه ما يمكن واعطاء
الموضوع اسبقيه اولى ضمن سقف زمني لا يتجاوز ١٠ حزيران ١٩٨٨ .

٣ . ستقوم زمر من استخبارات القيافي واستخبارات القياده ، بتحقى القرى التي لم تتم ازالتها .

٤ . نوجهو تزويدنا بقائمة بتمكن احد اليآت اخرى للموضوع ، وليد الموضوع ، وانني لم تتم ازالتها حتى الآن
وتقديم احتياجكم من الجهد الهندسي اللازم لمساعدتكم في ازالتها على ان بمكننا ما مطلوب اعلاه بعد
مأمور وخلال ٤٨ ساعة لاهمية الموضوع .

٥٠ نوجـو المتابعة واطلاعنا بالاستلام .

نسخة الى /

العقيد
مهندس السيد عادل حميد
لجنة كاظم قره داغ

جرى عبد الحسن ١/ ٠٠

السيد المدير المحترم
تحية وتقدير

بتاريخ ٥ / ٩ / ١٩٩٠ أمر السيد المدير المحترم بالتوجيه بأن :-
تكون عبارة ( لم تتوفر لدينا معلومات عن مصيرهم )
بدلاً عن عبارة ( وقبض عليهم في عمليات الأنفال البطولية ولا زالوا
محجوزين حالياً ) .

لغرض أن تكون دقيقين في التعامل مع هذا الحالات .

طرحت في الموقع
التجمع G

العلي
١٤ / ١٠ / ١٩٩٠

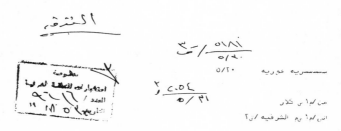

الشرقيه

سمسسرنه حربيه        ٥/٢٠

من لوا ى كلار

الى لوا م الشرقيه /٦٢

الرقم/٨٦٠/ قلعه شيروانه /١/٠٠٠٠٠/ بالسسساعه ٠٧٠٠ يوم ٥/٢٦ خرجت فوه
مرتبه من ف ١ نمى/٤٤٤ مع قوه من ف ١٠٠ وفا١٥١ دو زايد رعيب من ب٢ خمع
العباس بامره امر ف ١ نمى/٤٤٤ نتفتيش غابتش خوبجو / ٢٥١٢ / وشيخ لنكر
/٢٢٢٢/ حيث تم القاء القبى على اثنان من المشتبه بهم من القوميه العربيه /١/٠
/ المدعو حميد حمودى داود وبصحبته بندفيه كلاشنكوف المرقمه /٨١٦٠٦٦١/ ٢/٠
/ المدعو خليل ابرهيم يوسف بدون بندفيه بدون سلاح /٠/ عادت القوه بدون
حادث /٠/ يرجى الاعلاع

المرسل /ان يعلى/

نمستلم /امن موفق

الموقعت /٢٠٤٥

سريه و فوريه ١٢ــ وقت الانشاء ‏ ويومــــــــــ

٨٨/٥/٢١ ‏ ٤٤٢٠

من / م ا س م الشرقيـــــــه

الى / م ا س كــــــــــلار

رقم المنشى٠٢/ق/٣/٢٠ / (٠) رسالتكم السريه والثوريه ٨٦٠ في ٣٠/ ٥/ ٠٠ نرجو تزويدنا

باُفاد اتهم بالسرعه الممكنـــــــه واعـــلامنا ٠

القـــــــــــد م

بدء/ مدير منظومة استخبارات المذاقه الشرقيـــه

سريه فوريه

رئاسة الجمهورية
السكرتير
مديرية الاستخبارات العسكرية العامة
منظومة استخبارات المنطقة الشرقية
مركز أستخبارات كلار

سري

الرقم / ٨ / قادسية صدام / ٢٦١
التاريخ ٥ / ٦ / ١٩٨٨

المعلومة
أستخبار المنطقة الشرقية
الوحدة
التاريخ ١٩٨٨/٦/٧

الى / منظومة استخبارات المنطقه الشرقيه (ش ٣)
الموضوع / ايصال اقـــلاده

رسالتكم سريه فوريه ش ٢/ ق ٣/ ١٦٧٣ في ٧/٣١ ايار ١٩٨٨
طيا القادة المدعوين خليل ابراهيم يوسف و حميد حمودي داود المشــار اليهما برسالتكم
اعلاه حيث ان اوراق القادة تمت جم استعمالها طبق الاصل من قبل مــــــ ٤٤٤ ٠
برجـــــى التفضـــل بالاطـــــلاع ٠

المرفقـــــات
(٢) القاده طبق الاصل

التقيـب
امر مركز أستخبارات كــلار

تأشير المادة التم منظ

سري

بتاريخ ٢٩/٥/١٩٨٨ واثناء خروج قوة من وحدتنا لتفتيش غابات كوخو الجذور
امنياً تم القاء القبض على المدعو حميد حمودي داود لدخوله الى المناطق المحذورة امنياً
وبناء على ذلك أجري التحقيق التالي مع المذكور .

س: ماهو اسمك وعمرك وعملك واين تسكن ؟

ج: اسمي حميد حمودي داود عمري ٣٠ سنة عملي فلاح أسكن قرية القلعة العربيه .

س: لما ذا قمت بالدخول الى المناطق المحذورة امنياً ؟

ج: قمت بالدخول الى تلك المنطقة بحثاً عن الماء لكوني أملك قطيعاً من الاغنام والى الحرف
بأمر المنطقة محذورة امنياً للرعاي اسكن قرية القلعة العربيه القريبه من المنطقه
وقد دخلت تلك المناطق بحثاً عن الماء لعرضهم ارواح الاغنام لوجود نهر في تلك المنطقه
واني كنت اعتقد بأن الدخول الى تلك المناطق محرم محرم فقط على الاشخاص من القوميه
الكرديه وليست على الاشخاص العرب الذي عربي عربي القوميه .

س: عثر بحوزتك لدى القاء القبض عليك على بندقيه كلاشنكوف بين لنا اسباب هذا التقديم
وبيع عائديتها ؟

ج: البندقيه التي تم ضبطها معي هي تعود الى المنظمه الحزبيه في هلولاء والتي تما مت بتسليح جميع
رجال قريتنا للدفاع عن القريه في حالة تعرض علار ايري عليها واني احملها معي عندقيامي
برعي الاغنام لغرض الدفاع عن نفسي عندحدوث اي طارئ .

س: هل لديك علاقه مع علار ايرا اوأي تنظيم معادي ؟

ج: كلا . لاتوجد لدي أي علاقه مع تنظيمات علار ايرا أو أي تنظيم معادي وقدم
تسليحي من قبل الجهات الحزبيه لغرض الدفاع عن القريه في حالة تعرضها نذي الطاري .

س: هل لديك اقوال أخرى ؟

ج: كلا . هذه اقوالي واعترف بصحتها .

المدعو
حميد حمودي داود
يسكن كوخي / قريه القلعه العربيه

[Document 2]
Confidential and Urgent Message
Date and Time of Issuance:

31/8/1988
To:     Security Directorates of the Branches
From:   Security of Erbil

Ref.:   Sh.S.5//13069//

We were informed as follows:

1. There are elements from the Shabak [tribe] who joined the National Defense Battalions and who changed their ethnicity from Arab to Kurd and are residents of Nineveh governorate.
2. The Struggling Comrade Ali Hassan Al-Majid, head of the Northern Bureau, has ordered the destruction of all their houses and their deportation to the resettlement camps in our governorate. They will absolutely not be compensated.

For your information. Take whatever measures are necessary, and keep us informed.

[Signature]
Colonel of Security
Director of Security of Erbil Governorate

[Handwritten]   This should be circulated.
[Signature]
1/9
[Handwritten]   2445

1/9/1988
[Handwritten]   31/b

[Although the Iraqi government encouraged Kurdish tribes to change their stated ethnicity to Arab, the reverse practice was firmly punished, especially after 1988. The Shabak had always considered themselves to be Kurdish before the October 1987 national census, when some altered their self-designation to Arab under official pressure. The regime accused the Shabak tribe of choosing to be Kurdish so that its members would be able to join the progovernment Kurdish militia and thus not be sent to the front in the war with Iran. Now that the war had ended, in August 1988, the regime had its hands free to take revenge. MEW]

(MEW Ref.: 45/5-B)

[Document 6]

In the Name of God, the Merciful, the Compassionate

*Confidential and Personal*

Headquarters of the Security Committee in Shaqlawa
Ref.:     /Security/55
Date:     5/4/1987

To:       The Security Committee of Erbil Governorate
Re:       *Minutes of Meeting*

Enclosed are the minutes of the meeting of the Security Committee of Shaqlawa district, held at 1900 on Wednesday 1/4. Please be informed.

[Signature]
Colonel
The head of the Security Committee in Shaqlawa

cc.   Command of Division 45 / For your information. Enclosures:
Minutes of the meeting
District Administrator of Shaqlawa
Party Division of Shaqlawa
Police Directorate of Shaqlawa
The Security Directorate of Shaqlawa / For your information.
Enclosures: Minutes of the meeting

*Confidential and Personal*

[Handwritten]   1440
_____

9/4
_____

*Minutes of the Meeting of the Security Committee at 1900*
*on Wednesday 1/4/1987*

1. The Security Committee of Shaqlawa district held a meeting at 1900 on Wednesday according to the directives of the governor to the chairs of the Security Committees and the administrators of the districts and subdistricts in his meeting with them at 1100 on Wednesday in the governorate's cabinet. The Security Committee studied the following subjects:

a. *The Villages Prohibited for Security Reasons*

First: The villages that are prohibited for security reasons are those villages located outside the protective cover of the armed forces.

Second: Those villages have become havens for the saboteurs and reconnaissance centers for sabotage activity inside the towns as well as resting areas for their bands and a source of food, drink, and clothing fo them.

Third: For the above reasons, the Security Committee suggests that agreement be reached on the total elimination of all the villages that are prohibited for security reasons.

b. *Villages Not Prohibited for Security Reasons*

There are many villages that are not prohibited for security reasons, especially those that are close to the towns. The saboteurs use these as a source of supplies and a path to go back and forth. Some of their inhabitants provide assistance to the bands of saboteurs. The Security Committee therefore suggests the following:

First: Warn the inhabitants of the villages that are not prohibited for security reasons to prevent all types of assistance to the saboteurs for whatever reason.

Second: The villages that are not prohibited for security reasons are [to be] treated the same as the villages that are prohibited for security reasons if they do not implement the first [paragraph] above.

2. [Concerning] the letter of the Security Committee of Erbil governorate, Confidential and Personal, ref. 870 of 15/3, and the letter of the Security Committee of Erbil governorate, Confidential and Personal, ref. 1040 of 28/3, the Security Committee suggests the elimination of the poultry farms mentioned in the above letters, for the following reasons:

   a. They have become havens for the saboteurs and reconnaissance centers because these farms are close to the town of Shaqlawa and have [thus] become places for their [the saboteurs'] nighttime rest.

   b. The owners of these farms provide food and fuel to the saboteurs, and they are forced to do so in order to protect their property because the army bases are far away.

   d. [sic]. The saboteurs used these farms to meet with [members of] the internal organization [the guerrillas' underground network].

   c. [sic]. They have become stations for the loading of smuggled supplies during the night.

3. A plan has been prepared to eradicate the phenomenon of smuggling in the district.

4. A plan of action has been discussed in the event that an incident takes place in the sector of [our] jurisdiction. The following has been decided:

a. Communication will be established at once between the chair of the Security Committee and the members of the committee.

b. A decision will be made to act at once to deal with the incident.

5. The Security Committee discussed the matter of the necessity to ensure the complete protection of tourism during the year. It also discussed the holes in the protective cover during the past year. The committee then discussed the [military] force that is available and that which is required. It reached the conclusion that it is absolutely necessary to charge a section of the Popular Army with the creation of an internal security parameter for the town and the protection of tourist and government facilities in the center of the district [the town of Shaqlawa].

[5 signatures]

| Major | Lt.-Col. | Mr. | Mr. | Colonel |
|---|---|---|---|---|
| Director of Security, Shaqlawa | Director of Police, Shaqlawa | Secretary of Shaqlawa Division | District Admin- istrator, Shaqlawa | Chair of Security Cte in Shaqlawa district |

---

[The meeting held in Shaqlawa in essence constituted a rehashing of instructions received from the governor of Erbil, who in turn, according to the regular chain of command, would have received his orders from the Northern Bureau. The first item of discussion offers the key to understanding how a counterinsurgency campaign was allowed to become a campaign of genocide: in order to fight the rebels, most of rural Kurdistan was declared prohibited, and the villages in these areas were marked for destruction regardless of whether the inhabitants actively participated in the insurgency or in any other way offered support to the rebels. In the 1987 campaign of village destruction, all villages that the military forces were able to reach were destroyed. Significantly, they included a large number of villages that were *not* located in areas designated as prohibited. The next stage was Anfal, in which the remaining villages were destroyed and their inhabitants detained and killed, again regardless of whether or not they themselves belonged to the rebels. MEW]

(MEW ref.: 70/10-J)

[Document 9]
[Cover letter]


In the Name of God, the Merciful, the Compassionate
[Emblem of Iraqi Military Intelligence]

[In frame] Please refer to the full number

The Martyrs Remain More Generous Than All of Us

President of the Republic
Secretary
The General Directorate of Military Intelligence
Subdirectorate of Military Intelligence, Eastern Sector
Intelligence Center of Kalar


*Confidential and Personal*

Ref.:   Q.3/Qadissiyat Saddam/404
Date:   26/6/1988

                        [Stamp, partly illegible]        ref.: 12935
                                                  date: 27/6/1988

To:   Subdirectorate of Military Intelligence, Eastern Sector (Sh.3)
Re:   *Quarterly Report about the Saboteurs*

Enclosed is the quarterly report about the saboteurs' movements within our sector during the first half of 1988.

Please be informed.

Enclosures: 1 quarterly report

                        [Signature]
                        Captain
                        Director of the Intelligence Center of Kalar

[Handwritten]   To be shown, and ask the other centers.
                 27/6
                        (1 of 1)
                    *Confidential and Personal*

[Excerpt of quarterly report. Only the marked area on page 6 of the report has been translated here.]

*Top Secret*

b. During the month of March 1988, our aircraft bombed the headquarters of the sabotage bands in the villages of Saywan (4,596) and Balakajar (4,294) in a chemical strike. This resulted in the death of 50 saboteurs and the wounding of 20 other saboteurs.

c. At 1915 on 19/6, an unknown person threw a hand grenade at the house of the citizen Saleh Muhammad Aziz in Kalar district, Bengird neighborhood. There were no casualties or damage to the house.

[Etc.]

[Signature]
Captain
Kifah Ali Hassan
Director of the Intelligence Center of Kalar

(6)

*Top Secret*

[This document contains the first, but by no means only direct reference in the Iraqi state files to a chemical attack carried out by Iraqi forces. The attack in question took place, according to eyewitnesses interviewed by HRW/Middle East in the summer of 1992, in the Qaradagh area on 22 March 1988 at the beginning of the second Anfal operation. The casualties, which local inhabitants put at between 78 and 87, were almost all civilians as the rebels had their bases outside the two villages mentioned here. (Note that Saywan is referred to as Sayw Senan by the Kurds.) The numbers in parentheses following the villages are the coordinates given to them by the military. HRW/Middle East has seen maps that list all the villages by number rather than by name. (For further information on the chemical attack in the Qaradagh area, see *Genocide in Iraq*, chap. 4.) MEW]

(MEW ref.: 2123/5-C)

[Document 13]
In the Name of God, the Merciful, the Compassionate
[Emblem of the Iraqi Republic]

In the Name of the People
Revolutionary Command Council
Number of the decree: 160
Date of the decree: 29/3/1987

## DECREE

In accordance with the provisions of article 42, paragraph (a), and article 43, paragraph (a), of the constitution, and in order to execute what was decided in the joint meeting of the Revolutionary Command Council and the regional command of the Ba'ath Party on 18/3/1987,

The Revolutionary Command Council decided in its meeting on 29/3/1987 the following:

First: Comrade Ali Hassan al-Majid, member of the Regional Command of the Ba'ath Party, will represent the Regional Command of the Party and the Revolutionary Command Council in implementing their policies in all of the northern region, including the Autonomous Region of Kurdistan, in order to protect security and order and guarantee stability and the implementation of the autonomy law in the region.

Second: Comrade [al-Majid], member of the Regional Command, will have authority over all the state's civil, military, and security apparatuses to carry out this decree, in particular the authorities of the National Security Council and the Northern Affairs Committee.

Third: The following authorities in the northern region fall under the comrade's authority and must implement all the decisions and directives issued by him, as by this order:

1. The executive committee of the Autonomous Region of Kurdistan.
2. The governors and the heads of the administrative units under the ministry of local government.
3. The foreign intelligence apparatus, the internal security force, and military intelligence.
4. The commands of the Popular Army.

Fourth: The military commands in the region must respond to the comrade, member of the regional command, concerning everything pertaining to the first paragraph of this decision.

Fifth: This decree goes into effect on the date it is issued until further notice, and any regulations contradicting this decree are suspended.

[Signature]
Saddam Hussein
President of the Revolutionary Command Council

---

[Revolutionary Command Council decree 160 of 29 March 1987 contains the all-important order authorizing Ali Hassan al-Majid to take charge of all affairs in northern Iraq. In it Saddam Hussein spells out the extent of al-Majid's authority over all other security, military, and civil organs. It was immediately after the appointment of al-Majid that the chemical attacks against Kurdish civilians began and the campaign of village destruction went into high gear. Decree 160 was revoked on 23 April 1989 through Revolutionary Command Council decree 272 (MEW ref.: 82/4-E), after al-Majid had completed his job: He had defeated the Kurdish insurgency by erasing almost all the Kurdish villages from the map and killing most of their inhabitants during the Anfal campaign. MEW]
(MEW ref.: 42/5-L)

[Document 16]
*Part 1*
[Handwritten]    171
————Security
15/9/87
[Handwritten]    184

————

C

Urgent and confidential /12/9/
From: First Corps / R./Sh.I.D./
To: Division 24 / 27 / 28 / 34 / 36 / 39 / Command of the National Defense
Corps Forces 1 / Division 44 / Division H.N. / Headquarters of First Corps / the
First Forces
Ref.: 4198

[Concerning] the confidential letter of the Northern Bureau Command, ref.
/435/ of 8/9, the following has been decided:

In view of the meeting that was held on 6/9/1987, led by Comrade Ali Hassan
al-Majid, general secretary of the Northern Bureau:

1. The security committees in the northern governorates must submit a
   survey of the families of saboteurs. This must be done during the period 6/9 to 15/9. Immediately after the completion of the survey, the
   deportation of these families to the areas where their saboteur relatives are must be initiated, except for the male [members], between
   the ages of 12 inclusive and 50 inclusive, who must be detained. The
   families that have martyrs, missing persons, prisoners of war, soldiers, or fighters in the National Defense Battalions [among their
   sons, husbands, and fathers] are excluded from these measures. In
   this case, only the mother must be deported to the side of the saboteurs.
2. Public and administrative meetings must be held. In these meetings,
   the importance of the census, which it was decided will be held on
   17/10/1987, must be pointed out. Be certain to clarify that anyone
   who does not participate in the operation [the census] without a reasonable excuse will lose his Iraqi-ness [that is, his citizenship] and
   will be considered to be an army deserter, and [in this case] Revolutionary Command Council decree 677 of 26/8 will apply to them.
3. The return of the saboteurs without their weapons is not acceptable
   between 6/9 and 17/10. After 17/10, their return is not acceptable
   even if they bring their weapons.

Please be informed, take the necessary measures, and let us know.

[Handwritten] R.A. [Chief of Staff]
 Please be informed and disseminate
 16/9 [initialed]
[Handwritten] The commander
 Please be informed
 Approve for dissemination
 16/9 [initialed]
[Handwritten] I.S. [military intelligence]
1. To be disseminated
2. Put together the responses as soon as possible and inform the First Corps
[Handwritten] It has been disseminated.
 16/9

*Part 2*

One Arab Nation with an Immortal Message

The Socialist Arab Ba'ath Party
Iraq Region
Erbil Branch Command
Salah al-Din Section Command

Ref. :60/2648
Date: 12/9/1987

To: Erbil Branch Command
Re: Minutes of Meeting

Comradely Greetings:

On 12/9/1987, the Salah al-Din Section Command held an extraordinary meeting at the headquarters of Salah al-Din Section Command. Comrade Ashour Shahab Ahmad, the secretary of the Section Command, chaired the meeting. The comrades, members of the section command, attended the meeting. The meeting addressed the following [issues]:
1. The letter of Erbil Branch Command, ref. 34/11521 of 18/9/1987 [*sic;* date must be wrong], decision [*sic*]. The section command studied the contents of the above letter and suggests to help Comrade Adnan Hamdan Alwan,

member of the Koysinjaq Division [of the Ba'ath Party], [by giving him] 250 Iraqi dinars because he has a limited salary and a big family.

2. The section command studied all the survey and evaluation forms of the families of saboteurs that arrived from the division commands. After checking all the forms, the section command proposes the following:

First: To detain and deport members of the saboteurs' families according to the regulations included in the letter we received from the branch command, ref. 38/11540 of 9/9/1987, and the message of the Northern Bureau Command, ref. 435 of 7/9/1987. There are 111 families [according to the survey] that do not have a martyr, prisoner of war, soldier, fighter in the National Defense Battalions, or fighter in the Popular Army [among their male members].

Second: To deport the saboteurs' mothers or their oldest sisters in accordance with the regulations contained in the message of the Northern Bureau Command. There are 103 families that have a martyr, prisoner of war, missing person, soldier, fighter in the National Defense Battalions, or fighter in the Popular Army [among their male members].

Third: To strip the families that joined the saboteurs with all their family members of their Iraqi citizenship and to confiscate their movable and immovable property. There are 82 forms.

Please be informed. With regards.

Keep up the struggle.

> [Signature]
> The Comrade
> Ashour Shahab Ahmad
> Secretary of the Salah al-Din Section Command

[Handwritten]     I was informed / For keeping
> [Signature]
> 14/9

cc: The comrades, respected members of the section command / Please be informed. With regards.

---

[These two documents highlight an important policy announced in the fall of 1987 and subsequently implemented. The Iraqi population census of 1987 (the census is held every ten years) became a key event in the buildup to the Anfal campaign. As is clear from paragraph 2 of the first document, all those who failed to register in the census would lose their Iraqi citizenship. In reality, this meant that all persons living in the prohibited areas were excluded from the census; to be registered they would have had to move from their ancestral villages into government-provided housing in one of the resettlement camps. Needless to say, few people were prepared to leave their land and homes (essentially denying themselves their livelihood) just to be included in the census. The result was that they were stripped of their citizenship and overnight became virtual outlaws living on their own land. At this time, when Iraq was at war with Iran, to be considered an ex-Iraqi, a traitor to the Iraqi cause, was particularly dangerous. During Anfal the people who had failed to register in the census were rounded up and killed. (Note that an amended version of RCC decree 677, mentioned in paragraph 2, is included as document 19 in *Bureaucracy of Repression*.)

Paragraph 1 of the first document highlights another important policy: that of deporting the wives, mothers, and children of alleged guerrillas to the prohibited areas. They, too, were stripped of Iraqi citizenship and subsequently became victims of Anfal. As the document shows, some exceptions were made for families that had at least one member in the Iraqi armed forces or the progovernment Kurdish militias. The second document shows how this policy was being carried out with meticulous care by local Ba'ath Party officials (see also document 20 in *Bureaucracy of Repression*). MEW]

(MEW ref.: 56/52-A and 2192/5-A)

[Document 18, Main document]
The head of the presidential cabinet has decided as follows:

1. The names of persons who are subject to a collective judgment must only be disseminated in separate memoranda.
2. Such memoranda, when disseminated, should be accorded the greatest secrecy.

Please take whatever measures are necessary and act accordingly.

Signature/ ..

The Dep. Minister of Interior

---

[Cover letter]

In the Name of God, the Merciful, the Compassionate

General Security
Directorate of Security, Erbil Governorate
Secret, Personal, and Urgent

Ref.:    Sh.S.5/14314
Date:    1/11/1987

To:    All Directorates of Security Branches and Political Sections
Re:    Secret Documents
The above is a copy of the interior ministry's memorandum—Directorate of Secret and Political Affairs—ref. 17903 of 15/10/1987. Please act accordingly.

[Signature]
Major of Security
The Dep. Director of Security, Erbil Governorate

[Handwritten]        3423

8/11
[Signature]
To be disseminated

---

[This document is extremely important because it makes clear that there was a group of people that henceforth were subject to a collective judgment, and it tries to cover up this important information by ordering separate files for victims of the policy. The date on the document tells us what is about to take place: Issued in October 1987, around the time of the population census, this document signals the beginning of the policy against all those in the prohibited villages who failed to register in the census. Anfal started four months later, and during the Anfal campaign persons were sorted for deportation and execution based on their place of capture (the prohibited villages) rather than as a result of an individual judgment following interrogation and trial. Each person arrested during Anfal was therefore briefly questioned about matters of personal status, place of residence, and so on.]

(MEW ref.: 70/4-A)

[Document 23]
[Handwritten]     603
                  Sh.3
                  14/4

In the Name of God, the Merciful, the Compassionate

We Seek Justice, Not War
Command
Oil Protection Forces
General Staff
Intelligence
Ref.: 289
Date: 11 April 1988

                              *Top Secret*
[Handwritten]     238
                  ——— Q.2
                  14/4/88
[Handwritten]     321
                  Sh.3 [Signature]
[Stamp]           Subdirectorate of Military Intelligence
                  Ref.: 7205
                  Date: 14/4/1988
To:     Directorate of Security of al-Ta'mim
Re:     *Sending Families*

We are sending you the families that surrendered to our military forces on 11 April 1988 and whose names are on the appended list.

Please take the necessary measures according to the directives of the Northern Bureau and acknowledge receipt.

Enclosures: 11 lists with 307 names

                         [Signature]
                         Brigadier General Q.Kh. [Special Forces]
                         Bareq Abdullah al-Haj Hunta
                         Commander of the Oil Protection Forces
cc:   First Corps Command (Sh.Id. and Is.) [the administrative section and military intelligence]. Enclosed is a copy of the list. Please be informed.

M. Is. M. Eastern [subdirectorate of military intelligence, Eastern Sector].
Enclosed is a copy of the list. Please be informed.
[Handwritten] Mark for correspondence
   [Signature]
   15/4
   The Captain

(1 of 1)

*Top Secret*

---

[This may be one of the most important documents HRW/Middle East has found to date. Above, only the cover letter has been included. The remainder of the document offers a list of 139 families (or 307 individuals). There were several other similar lists in the same file, including hundreds of names. These lists have proved to be extremely significant because HRW/Middle East was able to match fifty-eight of the names listed there with the names of people who, according to the information obtained during field research in the Kurdish areas, never returned home after their arrest by the army during Anfal. Though fifty-eight is a relatively small number, it merely reflects the limited scale of HRW/Middle East's field research. Matching the names on the lists with the names collected systematically by Kurdish human rights organizations could prove to be a much more valuable corroboration of those who disappeared at government hands.

The importance of the lists goes further: Not only was HRW/Middle East able to make fifty-eight positive matches of names, it also found the names of three of the execution survivors it interviewed in the summer of 1992 (see chapter 9). Through the testimony of these three survivors, HRW/Middle East is now able to conclude with great certainty that virtually all the people named in the lists were in fact executed in 1988. The survivors mentioned several persons whose names appear on the lists as having been in their company at the time of the executions. This proof concerning their fate would confirm the nature of the "necessary measures" ordered by the Northern Bureau: in all likelihood the document refers to Northern Bureau directive SF/4008 of 20 June 1987.

The Iraqi government has yet to account for the persons it has admitted having arrested in 1988. MEW]

(MEW ref.: 2110/9-A)

[Document 26]

In the Name of God, the Merciful, the Compassionate

*Secret and Personal*

Qaradagh Section Command
([Military] Intelligence)
Ref.:    I.S./28/56
Date:    31/5/88

To:    All the Units
Re:    Elimination of Villages
[Concerning] the letter of the First Corps, Secret and Personal, ref. 208 of 25 May 1988, of which we were informed in the letter from the First Forces Command, Secret and Personal, ref. 97 of 28 May 1988, the following was decided:

1. The information we received makes clear that there are villages and separate houses in the prohibited areas that were covered by the Anfal operation but have so far not been eliminated as required.
2. It was decided to speed up the destruction and elimination operation for all the villages and scattered houses as soon as possible and to give this matter top priority within a time frame not exceeding 10 June 1988.
3. Groups of the Corps Intelligence and command intelligence will check the villages that were not eliminated.
4. Please provide us with the list that includes the coordinates of the villages, marked and unmarked, that have not yet been eliminated. Please state your engineering requirements so that we can help you in the elimination of these villages. This request should be hand-delivered to us within 48 hours because of the importance of the matter.
5. Please follow up and acknowledge receipt of this letter.

[Handwritten]        [Signature]
                     I was informed, 1/6

                                        [Signature]
                                        Colonel
                                        Fahmi al-Sayed Adel Rashid
                                        Qaradagh Section Commander

cc.
C.M.H. Abd-al-Hassan//..

[This military intelligence memorandum from the middle of the Anfal campaign, in May 1988, indicates that the destruction of all villages in the area of the second Anfal (which ended on 1 April) had not been completed on schedule. In dry bureaucratic language, the fate of Kurdish villages is decided here. None survived. MEW]

(MEW ref.: 234/9-A)

[Document 29]

To the Honorable Director:

Greetings

On 25/9/1990, the Honorable Director issued the following directive:

The phrase, *We do not have any information about their fate,* will replace the phrase, *They were arrested during the victorious Anfal operation and remain in detention.*

The purpose of this is to be accurate in dealing with such an eventuality.

[Signature]

Director of Security

Officer N.M.R.

[Handwritten] It was raised in the monthly conference

[Signature]

Political Officer

18/10/1990

---

[This order indicates that after Anfal the regime absolved itself of all responsibility for those who had been arrested during the Anfal campaign. Government offices were besieged by people wishing to know what had happened to their relatives, and this was the official response from the government that had arrested and killed them: "We have no information about their fate." MEW]
(MEW ref.: 102/7-A)

[Document 39]
*Part 1*

[Handwritten] 5181
                    30/5-Q3

Confidential and urgent 30/5

[Handwritten] 2054
                    31/5-Q3

[Stamp] Directorate of Eastern Sector Intelligence
Ref.:     9616
Date:     30/5/1988

From:   M.IS. Kalar [Intelligence Directorate of Kalar]
To:     M.IS.M. Eastern / Sh3 [Directorate of Eastern Sector Intelligence]

Ref. /860, Qala'at Shirwana 1/ . . . . . /. / At 0700 on 29/5 a force consisting of
F 1 [= Brigade 1] L.M.Sh./444 with a force of F 100 and F 151, and also a
detachment of S 3 K.M.A al-'Abbas, led by the commander of F 1 L.M.Sh./444,
went to search the two forests of Kulajo / 2513 / and Sheikh Lenkar / 2223 / and
they arrested two suspects who are of Arab ethnicity: /1/ the so-called Hamid
Hamoudeh Da'oud, who carried a kalashnikov rifle no. 8160631; /2/ the so-
called Khalil Ibrahim Yousef, without a weapon. The force returned with no
incidents. Please, for your attention.

Transmitter: N.Dh. Ali
Recipient: N.Dh. Muwaffaq
Time: 2045

[Handwritten]   Q3
                Send them a message to provide us with their statements
                [Signature]
                121 D.

[Handwritten]   Take the proper measures according to the instructions of the
                director
                [Signature:]
                31/5
                Captain

*Part 2*

[Handwritten]    2386
                 31/5-Q3

*Confidential and Urgent*

Time of writing: 2230
Date of writing: 31/5/88

[Handwritten]    862
                 1/6-Q3

From:   M.IS.M. Eastern [Directorate of Eastern Sector Intelligence]
To:     M.IS. Kalar
Ref:    Sh3/Q3/9673

Concerning your confidential and urgent letter ref. 860 of 30/5. Please provide us with their statements as soon as possible and inform us.

[Signature]

Lt.-Colonel
For/Director of the Directorate of Eastern Sector Intelligence
Karim Mayes
31

Confidential and urgent

---

*Part 3*

*In the Name of God, the Merciful, the Compassionate*

[Framed] Please state the full number
The Martyrs Will Always Be Purer Than Us

Presidency of the Republic
Secretariat
General Directorate of Military Intelligence
Directorate of Eastern Sector Intelligence
Intelligence Center of Kalar

[Stamp]   Directorate of Eastern Sector Intelligence
          Ref.: 11417
          Date: 6/6/1988

*Confidential*

Ref.: Q3/Qadissiyat Saddam/361
Date: 5/6/1988

[Handwritten]    1131
                 6/6-Q3

[Handwritten]    596
                 6/6-Q3

To:      Directorate of Eastern Sector Intelligence (Sh.3)
Re:      *Transfer of Statements*

Concerning your confidential and urgent letter Sh3/Q3/9673 of 31 May 1988, enclosed are the statements of the so-called Khalil Ibrahim Yousef and Hamid Hamoudeh Da'oud, who were referred to in your letter. The originals of their statements were photocopied at the headquarters of L.M.SH.444. Please, for your attention.

Enclosed:
        (2) original statements

[Signature]
Captain
Commander of the Intelligence Center of Kalar

[Handwritten]
        Authorize only water for them
        [Signature]
        Captain

*Confidential*

*Part 4*

*[Statement]*

On 29/5/1988, when a force of our unit went to search the forests of Kulajo that are prohibited for security reasons, they arrested the so-called Hamid Hamoudeh Da'oud on the charge that he entered the areas that are prohibited for security reasons. The following interrogation was therefore conducted with the above-mentioned:

Q1: What is your name, your age, your occupation, and where do you live?
A:  My name is Hamid Hamoudeh Da'oud. My age is 53 years. My occupation is farmer. I live in the Arab village of Qala'a.

Q2: Why did you enter the areas that are prohibited for security reasons?

A: I entered that area searching for water because I own a herd of sheep. I know that the area is prohibited for security reasons, but I live in the nearby Arab village of Qala'a and I entered that area searching for water in order to give [the sheep] water because there is a stream in that area and I thought that entering those areas was prohibited only for people from the Kurdish ethnicity and not for Arab people, and I am of Arab ethnicity.

Q3: When you were arrested, a kalashnikov rifle was found with you. Tell us the reasons for having a rifle, and to whom does it belong?

A: The rifle that was found with me belongs to the Party Organization [i.e., the Ba'ath Party] of Jalula who have given rifles to all the men in our village to defend the village in case of attack by the Agents of Iran [i.e., the PUK]. I have it with me when I am shepherding for self-defense in case of emergency.

Q4: Do you have any relations with the Agents of Iran [the PUK] or any other hostile organization?

A: No, I have no relations with the Agents of Iran or any other hostile organization, and I was armed by the Party Organization in order to defend the village in case of an emergency.

Q5: Do you have anything else to add?

A: No. This is my statement, and I declare that it is the truth.

The so-called
Hamid Hamoudeh Da'oud
Resident of [subdistrict of] Koks / the Arab village of Qala'a

[Stamp]
Directorate of Eastern Sector Intelligence
Intelligence Center of Kalar
Ref.: / original
Date:
[Signature]

---

[The above four documents were found together in a file from the time of the Anfal operation. Although the Anfal had ended in the Kalar area in April 1988, army units continued to search the area at the end of May because many villagers were still suspected to be at large. During one such sweep, the army arrested two Arab shepherds who were in clear violation of standing orders banning "all human and animal presence" in the prohibited areas. The news was promptly transmitted to the headquarters of Military Intelligence in Kirkuk. But unlike in the case of Kurdish detainees, Kirkuk asks only for the statements of the two men to be sent. Nothing in the file indicates that anything else happened to the two men—again, unlike their Kurdish brethren, who were systematically sent to Kirkuk for processing and then killed. The above documents therefore highlight the ethnic character of the Iraqi genocide. MEW]

(MEW ref.: 2368/6-B)

# NOTES

## INTRODUCTION

1. *Ba'ath* translates as "revival." Because of common usage in English, we refer here simply to the Ba'ath Party. The regional command is the leading organ of the Ba'ath Party in Iraq. It forms part of the Arab Ba'ath, which fell under the leadership of founder Michel Aflaq until the latter's death in 1990, when Saddam Hussein replaced him.

2. A derisive Kurdish term for the National Defense battalions, the word *jahsh* means "donkey foals."

3. *Saboteurs* is the term commonly applied by the Iraqi regime to the Kurdish guerrillas and their civilian sympathizers.

4. As defined in the Convention on the Prevention and Punishment of the Crime of Genocide (hereinafter the Genocide Convention), 78 UNTS 277, approved by GA Res. 2670 on 9 Dec. 1948, entered into force 12 Jan. 1951.

5. Hilberg, *Destruction of the European Jews,* 267.

6. Although the Yezidis, a syncretic religious sect, are ethnic Kurds, the Assyrians and Chaldeans are a distinct ancient people in their own right.

7. Al-Majid has served variously over the past five years as secretary general of the Ba'ath Party's Northern Bureau, as interior minister, governor of Iraqi-occupied Kuwait in 1990, and as defense minister.

8. Rural Kudrish men carry personal weapons as matter of tradition, regardless of their politics.

9. Other mass graves have been found elsewhere in Kurdish-controlled territory containing the remains of Amn executions before, during, and after the Anfal period.

## CHAPTER 1: BA'ATHISTS AND KURDS

1. Braidwood, *Prehistoric Investigation in Iraqi Kurdistan.*

2. The definitive work on the Kurds is *Agha, Shaikh, and State* by Martin Van Bruinessen. For a general historical and cultural overview, see Izady, *Kurds.* A useful brief summary is McDowall, "Kurdish Question," esp. 24–30.

3. Izady, *Kurds,* 117, gives the following figures: Turkey 13.65 million, Iran 6.6 million, and Iraq 4.4 million.

4. According to Izady, Kurds made up 25 percent of the Iraqi population in 1980, compared to 21.3 percent in Turkey. By 1990, he estimated the figures were 23.5 percent and 24.1 percent, respectively. Other estimates are much lower, putting the Kurds at only 16 or 17 percent of the Iraqi population.

5. The Kurds, however, unlike other national liberation movements, were never able to count on consistent Soviet support.

6. Since the revolution of 14 July 1958, there have been four regimes in Baghdad:

the military government of Abd al-Karim Qasem and the "Free Officers" (1958–63); the first regime of the Ba'ath Arab Socialist Party (Feb.–Nov. 1963); the governments of the Arif brothers and Abd al-Rahman al-Bazzaz (1963–68); and the second Ba'ath regime (1968 to the present). Saddam Hussein, one of the leaders of the July 1968 coup, has been president of Iraq since 1979. The best general work on the period is Farouk-Sluglett and Sluglett, *Iraq since 1958*. Other useful studies include Marr, *History of Modern Iraq,* and CARDRI, *Saddam's Iraq*.

7. Books on the Iran-Iraq War have routinely echoed the unsubstantiated report that both sides used chemical weapons in Halabja. This notion originated in a study for the U.S. Army War College: Pelletiere, Johnson, and Rosenberger, *Iraqi Power and U.S. Security in the Middle East*. It is repeated in a later book by Pelletiere, a former U.S. intelligence officer, *The Iran-Iraq War*. This strongly pro-Iraqi work comments, "On May 23 [sic], in fighting over the town, gas was used by both sides. As a result scores [sic] of Iraqi Kurdish civilians were killed. It is now fairly certain that Iranian gas killed the Kurds" (see pp. 136–37).

The supposed factual basis for this conclusion is that the Halabja victims had blue lips, characteristic of the effects of cyanide gas, which Iraqis were not believed to possess. Cyanide gas, a metabolic poison, would indeed produce blue lips, but this is far from being a specific indicator of its use. Nerve agents, which are acetylcholinesterase inhibitors that cause respiratory paralysis, would also turn the lips of victims blue (HRW/ME interview with Dr. Howard Hu, Harvard School of Public Health, 13 May 1993). On Iraq's proven use of nerve agents against the Kurds during Anfal, see below, n.10.

8. The Kurdish researcher Shorsh Resool, author of a study of the destruction of Kurdish villages *(Destruction of a Nation),* has assembled a list of the names of some 3,200 people who died in the Halabja attack. More impressionistic estimates have ranged as high as 7,000.

9. The most frequently cited figure of 65,000 derives from Galbraith and Van Hollen, *Chemical Weapons Use in Kurdistan*. Tens of thousands also sought refuge in Iran, either fleeing directly from Iraq or after passing through Turkey.

10. See Galbraith and Van Hollen, *Chemical Weapons Use in Kurdistan*. The February 1989 report by PHR, *Winds of Death,* concluded that the injuries of refugees examined in Turkey were consistent with exposure to sulfur mustard (yperite). However, PHR noted, "Eyewitness accounts of deaths beginning within minutes of exposure . . . cannot be explained by mustard gas alone." The mystery was laid to rest in April 1993 when research on soil samples from the village of Birjinni, the site of a 1988 chemical weapons attack, showed the presence of trace elements of the nerve agent GB, also known as Sarin. See PHR and HRW, "Scientific First."

11. The Convention on the Prevention and Punishment of the Crime of Genocide, 78 UNTS 277, approved by General Assembly resolution 2670 on 9 Dec. 1948, entered into force 12 Jan. 1951. The convention defines genocide as "acts committed with intent to destroy, in whole or in part, a national, ethnical, racial, or religious group, as such." For a general discussion of the issues, as well as a series of case studies, see Chalk and Jonassohn, *History and Sociology of Genocide,* and Fein, *Genocide Watch*.

12. The findings of these missions are contained in two HRW/ME and Physicians for Human Rights reports: *Unquiet Graves* and *Anfal Campaign in Iraqi Kurdistan*.

13. Although the U.S. Defense Department has expedited the research of the documents by assigning technical staff to the Iraqi Kurdistan project, HRW/ME and the PUK jointly retain full control of the archive.

14. Hilberg, *Destruction of the European Jews*, 8.

15. Amn, whose technical functions are roughly equivalent to those of the U.S. Federal Bureau of Investigation, originated in the mid-1960s in a secret unit of the Ba'ath Party known as al-Jihaz al-Khas, the "special apparatus." Its code name was Jihaz Haneen, the "instrument of yearning." Saddam Hussein personally supervised the restructuring of the secret police that gave Amn its present name and functions in 1973. See Makiya, *Republic of Fear*, 5–6, 12–13.

16. The Iraqi regime may have selected this sura to legitimize its war on the Kurds by invoking a battle between two regular armies and against a numerically stronger adversary. Makiya's article "Anfal" is an extract from his book *Cruelty and Silence*. His visit to northern Iraq also formed the basis for a report by the British filmmaker Gwynne Roberts, "Saddam's Killing Fields," broadcast on BBC television in January 1992, and in the United States on CBS's *60 Minutes*, 23 Feb. 1992, and PBS's *Frontline*, 31 Mar. 1992.

Two other overviews of the Anfal campaign have been published: Bonner, "Always Remember," and Miller, "Iraq Accused." Miller's article deals in some detail with the progress of HRW/ME's Iraqi Kurdistan documents project.

17. Arberry, trans., *Koran Interpreted*, 198.

18. Indeed, the July 1970 Provisional Constitution stated that "the populace of Iraq is formed of two principal nationalities, the Arab and the Kurdish. This constitution shall recognize the national rights of the Kurdish people and the legitimate rights of all minorities within the unity of Iraq." The Iraqi government's view of the autonomy issue is set forth in *Settlement of the Kurdish Problem in Iraq* (Government of Iraq).

19. Again, interestingly, it was a census that defined the geographical extent of the 1988 Anfal operation. See the comments of Ali Hassan al-Majid on the size of the Arab population in Kurdistan, app. A, 353.

20. According to Sluglett and Sluglett, *Iraq since 1958*, 172, Iraqi oil revenues, a mere $575 million in 1972, rose to $1.84 billion in 1973 and $5.7 billion in 1974.

21. The Israeli scholar Amazia Baram, in his fascinating book *Culture, History, and Ideology in the Formation of Ba'thist Iraq, 1968–89* (pp. 61–62), shows how much of this administrative reform illustrated the party's desire to relate Iraq's modern history to the glories of antiquity. Most striking is that the province of Diwaniya was renamed Qadissiya—after the decisive battle between the Arab and Persian armies in A.D. 635. The Iran-Iraq War of 1980–88 was officially referred to as "Saddam's Qadissiyah."

22. As McDowall puts it in "Kurdish Question," this was "autonomy by ultimatum."

23. Speech of 24 Sept. 1973, in Saddam Husain, *Current Events in Iraq*, 17–18, cited in Makiya, *Republic of Fear*. There is also some evidence that the Ba'ath Party harbored a general racial hostility against the Kurds for their kinship with the Persians. According to Makiya, for example (p. 17), the Iraqi government publishing house Dar al-Hurriyya circulated a pamphlet in 1981 entitled *Three Whom God Should Not Have Created: Persians, Jews, and Flies* and written by Saddam Hussein's father-in-law, Khairallah Tulfah, a former governor of Baghdad. According to Tulfah, Persians are "animals God created in the shape of humans"; Jews are a "mixture of the dirt and leftovers of diverse peoples"; and flies are a trifling creation "whom we do not understand God's purpose in creating."

24. A helpful guide to the scale of these village clearances is Resool, *Destruction of a Nation*. Resool's figures, which HRW/ME regards as highly reliable, list 369 villages

destroyed or depopulated in the northern part of Iraqi Kurdistan and another 154 in Diyala governorate.

25. For example, a directive from the headquarters of the General Security Director-ate, dated 4 May 1985 and coded K3/34478, expresses concern over Kurdish migration to the city of Kirkuk (in Al-Ta'mim governorate). The document orders that no change of residence in the governorate of Al-Ta'mim will be allowed "until the Northern Affairs Committee [of the Revolutionary Command Council] and security circles have given their opinion. This is in order to carry out a secret investigation of the person and the reasons for his [sic] taking up residence in the above-mentioned governorate."

26. HWR/ME interview, Qushtapa camp, 3 May 1992.

27. Reported in the *Times* (London), 27 Nov. 1975, as cited in Van Bruinessen, "The Kurds between Iran and Iraq," 27.

28. HWR/ME interview, Qushtapa camp, 4 May 1992.

29. Resool, *Destruction of a Nation,* gives the following figures: 336 villages de-stroyed in Suleimaniyeh (26 in 1977 and 310 in 1978); 120 in Erbil governorate (79 in 1977 and 41 in 1978); and the remainder scattered in the governorates of Dohuk and Diyala. Additional testimony gathered by HWR/ME speaks of 124 villages destroyed around the town of Qala Dizeh; and of 260–265 villages destroyed in the entire governor-ate of Suleimaniyeh.

30. *Al-Thawra,* 18 Sept. 1978, cited in Van Bruinessen, "Kurds between Iran and Iraq," 24.

31. The Northern Affairs Committee is the source of numerous Iraqi government documents that HWR/ME has examined. It is also referred to as the "Higher Committee for Northern Affairs" in Makiya, *Republic of Fear,* 24. The Kirkuk-based Special Investi-gations Committee, according to a former Iraqi military intelligence officer interviewed by HWR/ME, consisted of four members—one each from the Ba'ath Party, the General Security Directorate, Military Intelligence, and the foreign intelligence organization.

32. Other resettlement camps—*Urdugakan* in Kurdish, or *Mu'askarat* in Arabic, were built during the 1975 Arabization campaign to house newly arrived Sunni Arabs from the south. This was especially true of areas on the plain north of Dohuk that was formerly occupied by the Kurdish Sleivani tribe.

33. Idris died of a heart attack in 1987; Mas'oud Barzani remains the supreme leader of the KDP.

34. HWR/ME interview, Qushtapa camp, 4 May 1992.

35. There is some evidence that the Barzani men were kept alive in captivity for at least a year before eventually being killed. One *Mukhabarat* file contains a sequence of thirty-nine presidential decrees issued in 1983, numbered 998 to 1036, listing individuals who were sentenced to death in "cases of a special nature." Later correspondence is appended, and one handwritten comment asks, "Are any of the above-mentioned persons who have been sentenced to death in our custody?" The reply, also handwritten, and dated 9 Apr. 1985, says, "None of the above-mentioned persons who have been sen-tenced to death are in our custody, *with the exception of the Barzani group who were living in our area prior to their detention*" (emphasis added).

According to a surviving Barzani tribesman interviewed by HWR/ME in Salah al-Din on 18 Mar. 1993, some of the Barzani women and children were again rounded up by government officials in 1986, trucked to the Turkish border, and ordered to leave the country. After remaining on the border for some time, they returned to Qushtapa, and it appears that no further action was taken against them. A series of proposed measures against the surviving Barzanis, including stripping them of their Iraqi citizenship, is detailed in Istikhbarat correspondence from January 1986, which reports a ruling by the Northern Affairs Committee of the Revolutionary Command Council (NAC letter 6740, classified Confidential and Personal and dated 16 Jan. 1986).

36. *Al-Iraq*, 13 Sept. 1983.

37. See, e.g., Van Bruinessen, *Agha, Shaikh, and State*, 28, 231–32.

38. For general background, see Sluglett and Sluglett, *Iraq since 1958*, 187–190, and Van Bruinessen, *Agha, Shaikh, and State*, 31–32, 34–36. The picture was further complicated by the presence in these areas of smaller groups, including Iranian organizations, such as the KDP-Iran and Komala, an Iranian-Kurdish (Marxist-Leninist) rebel party, which were conducting guerrilla war against the regime in Teheran from Iraqi soil.

39. Kurdish is a member of the Iranian language group and has many dialects in addition to Sorani and Kurmanji. See Van Bruinessen, *Agha, Shaikh, and State*, 21–22, citing D. N. MacKenzie, "Origins of Kurdish," 68–86.

40. By now Iraq had used chemical weapons several times against Iranian troops, but it is probable that the Penjwin offensive marked their first use on Iraqi soil. See Cordesman and Wagner, *Iran-Iraq War*, 514, and generally 506–18.

41. HWR/ME interview with Nawshirwan Mustafa Amin, Washington, D.C., 2 May 1993.

42. Marr, *History of Modern Iraq*, 307.

43. The epithet is in such common use that it has lost much of its pejorative force in the process. In the Kurmanji-speaking areas of the north, the Kurdish paramilitaries are also called *chatta*—brigands or bandits.

44. One former mustashar described a 1987 conversation with the head of Amn in Suleimaniyeh, a colonel by the name of Khalaf. "He told me that I must carry a gun for the government. He pressured me to join. He told me, 'You did not participate in the [Iran-Iraq] war; you must now become a mustashar.' He then told me, 'If you don't join, your identification card may be revoked.'" The later implications of this threat turned out to be grave, since during Anfal the correct identification card could be a matter of life or death. HWR/ME interview, Suleimaniyeh, 12 May 1992.

45. In general, Islamic law does not apply in Iraq, a secular state—although some elements of Islamic law have been incorporated into such domains as family law. Like the Anfal operation itself, however, this was an entirely characteristic attempt by the Ba'ath regime to legitimize its campaigns by wrapping them in the language of religion.

46. There are obvious parallels, for example, with Guatemala and Peru. See Americas Watch, *Civil Patrols in Guatemala* and *Peru under Fire*.

47. According to a dossier of destroyed villages compiled by the Kurdistan Reconstruction and Development Society (KURDS), Upper and Lower Besifki were destroyed in 1987 and Dergijneek in 1988. Both were in the nahya of Al-Doski.

48. Some villages had developed relatively sophisticated water-supply and irrigation systems, channeling rivers to their homes through mud-brick covered trenches called *karez*.

49. HWR/ME interview with Nawshirwan Mustafa Amin, Washington, D.C., 2 May 1993.

50. The tendency to describe the regime's opponents using insulting epithets was common. One seventeen-year-old who was executed by the regime was described in an

official Amn document, ordering the Suleimaniyeh morgue to dispose of his body, as a "fire-worshiper"—a derogatory reference to the ancient Iranian religion of Zoroastrianism.

51. This was another in the long line of broken promises to the Kurds, who were certainly not consulted in July 1988 when Teheran accepted the U.N. cease-fire resolution in the middle of the Anfal campaign.

52. HWR/ME interview with Nawshirwan Mustafa Amin, Washington, D.C., 2 May 1993.

## CHAPTER 2: PRELUDE TO ANFAL

1. The marshes have been the object of a vast engineering scheme designed to bring the rebellious south under the control of the central government in Baghdad. The regime's treatment of the Shi'a inhabitants of the south, including the *Ma'dan*, or Marsh Arabs, is detailed in the HRW/ME report, "Current Human Rights Conditions among the Iraqi Shi'a," March 1993.

2. The Northern Bureau is one of five regional bureaus of the Ba'ath, and is separate from the Northern Affairs Committee of the Revolutionary Command Council. Other party bureaus have responsibility for the south, the center, and the capital city of Baghdad. This division of Iraq into security zones is mirrored by the five-bureau organization of Amn and by military intelligence (Istikhbarat).

3. The family tree is shown in Henderson, *Instant Empire*, 87. Other notable cousins of Saddam's include the former defense minister, Adnan Khairallah, who died in a helicopter crash in 1989, and Hussein Kamel Majid, minister of industry and military industry.

4. HRW/ME interview with former mustashar, Zakho, 1 Sept. 1992. In 1989 al-Majid was appointed as minister of the interior, and then, after the August 1990 invasion, as governor of Kuwait. He is now Iraq's defense minister and continues to be implicated in actions of the grossest brutality. According to an eyewitness, Majid himself shot to death some 25–30 detainees in Basra prison on 3 or 4 Apr. 1991. The dead included six children. See HRW/ME, "Current Human Rights Conditions among the Iraqi Shi'a," 5 Mar. 1993.

5. The Iraqi army has seven regular corps in all. The term *special forces* requires some explanation. In the U.S. armed forces and others built on the U.S. model, these are light infantry forces designed to conduct such irregular missions as guerrilla warfare and covert operations. Iraq's special forces, in contrast, are mobile elite infantry units, armed with the best available weapons and often supported by tank battalions. Growing out of the Iran-Iraq War, they have been compared to the German *Stosstruppen* of World War I. See "Iraqi Order of Battle: Ground Troops," in *Desert Shield Factbook* (Bloomington, Ind.: GDW, 1991), 50–59.

6. The basic texts on the war include O'Ballance, *Gulf War;* Hiro, *Longest War;* Chubin and Tripp, *Iran and Iraq at War;* and Cordesman and Wagner, *Iran-Iraq War.* Most of these books share the defect of neglecting the temporary revival of Iran's fortunes in the final year and a half of the war, without which it is difficult to understand the relation between the first Gulf War and the Anfal campaign. A useful corrective is Jupa and Dingeman, *Gulf Wars,* 1–9.

7. The *basij,* or mobilization unit, comprised virtually untrained volunteers under

pasdaran supervision. They were integral to Iran's conception of an "Islamic warfare" that depended more on faith than on technology and conventional military skills. See Chubin and Tripp, *Iran and Iraq at War,* 42–49.

8. See, e.g., Cordesman and Wagner, *Iran-Iraq War,* 257.

9. The KDP and PUK eventually reached formal military and political agreements to collaborate in Nov. 1987, and in 1988 formed the Iraqi Kurdistan Front. Five smaller parties later joined the Front.

10. According to comments by Nawshirwan Mustafa Amin in an April 1987 interview with *Le Monde,* one option under consideration by the PUK was "the severance of Iraq into a number of small states: Shi'a, Kurdish, and Sunni." Cited in Baram, *Culture, History, and Ideology,* 127.

11. Cordesman and Wagner, *Iran-Iraq War,* 259–60. O'Ballance echoes this view but provides less detail.

12. Audiotape of a conversation between Ali Hassan al-Majid and unnamed Ba'ath Party aides, 22 Jan. 1989.

13. Ibid. For the full text, see app. A.

14. Special National Defense Forces General Staff (Operations) to Fifth Corps Command, Erbil: letter 28/573, dated 13 Apr. 1987 and classified Top Secret and Confidential. The town of Makhmour lies thirty-five miles southwest of Erbil.

15. Minutes of Shaqlawa Security Committee meeting, 4 Apr. 1987.

16. HRW/ME interview, Zakho, 24 June 1992.

17. HRW/ME interview, Choman, 23 Mar. 1993. Reportedly, there was also a chemical attack on 15 Apr. 1987 on the KDP headquarters in Zewa, a largely depopulated area close to the Turkish border.

18. The PUK had four malbands. The first, based in the Qara Dagh Mountains, was responsible for political and military affairs in the governorate of Suleimaniyeh; the second, in the Jafati Valley, was in charge of operations in Kirkuk (al-Ta'mim); the third and fourth, based in the Balisan Valley and the adjoining Smaquli Valley, shared responsibility for the PUK's work in Erbil. Later, the third and fourth malbands were merged; under the PUK-KDP unity agreements, a new fourth malband was opened in Zewa, the KDP headquarters on the Turkish border, to handle operations in the governorate of Dohuk.

19. Population figures for Balisan and Sheikh Wasan are derived from Resool's dossier of destroyed villages, although villagers interviewed by HRW/ME suggested that Balisan may have been even larger, with perhaps as many as 525 households. Officials of the United Nations High Commissioner for Refugees assume an average household size of seven persons in Kurdish villages.

20. Not coincidentally, the Iraqi intelligence agencies were mainly equipped and trained by their East German equivalents. It may well be that the files of the former *Staatssicherheitsdienst* (Stasi) will shed further light on this relation.

21. The symptoms described by villagers are generally consistent with the effects of mustard gas, although reports that some victims died immediately suggest that nerve agents may also have been used, since mustard gas, even in high concentrations, is not usually lethal for at least half an hour. See PHR, *Winds of Death.*

22. HRW/ME interview, Erbil, 16 Mar. 1993.

23. In an interesting, if indirect confirmation of the 16 May attack, an undated handwritten note from Amn Shaqlawa also mentions that sixteen Iranian revolutionary guards (pasdaran) were present during a bombing raid on the villages of Balisan, Sheikh Wasan, and Tutma. The pasdaran are reported to have "made fires that saved their lives"—a

reference that cannot conceivably apply to anything but an attempted defense against poison gas. A separate Amn Shaqlawa document in the same file, dated 20 May 1987, notes that three members of the PUK Politburo are reported to have been injured by gas during "the latest military attacks in Kurdistan."

24. These workhorse vehicles are ubiquitous in Iraq. They are commonly known simply as coasters and are referred to by that name throughout this text.

25. HRW/ME interview, Balisan, 30 Apr. 1992.

26. This is consistent with the procedures of an Iraqi firing squad, as recorded on a videotape that has been viewed by HRW/ME. Five prisoners in Kurdish clothes are blindfolded, tied to posts, and machinegunned with almost luxurious excess by a line of troops with Kalashnikov rifles. The firing continues long after it is obvious that the prisoners are dead. Even then, a uniformed officer delivers the coup de grace to each man with a pistol. There is a pause. Finally, another officer moves down the line, discharging his pistol into the fallen bodies. This particular execution was carried out in a public square in front of a large crowd and was greeted with applause from party and security dignitaries in the front row.

27. This account is based on HRW/ME interviews in Erbil, 23–25 Apr 1992.

28. The bodies of those who died in custody were exhumed from the Erbil cemetery in September 1991 and reburied in a ceremony that was recorded on videotape. In the course of later exhumations, Hamoud Sa'id Ahmad discovered the body of his own brother, who was killed by Amn in a separate incident in April 1988. Ahmad was interviewed by HRW/ME in Erbil, 25 Apr. 1992. For additional detail, see HRW/ME and PHR, *Unquiet Graves*, Feb. 1992.

29. HRW/ME interview with Sheikh Qader Sa'id Ibrahim Balisani, Balisan, 30 Apr. 1992.

30. A handwritten list of 103 dead and 48 injured villagers was given to HRW/ME in 1992 by the Inspection Committee of Oppressed Kurds, a human rights group in Erbil.

31. Amn Erbil governorate to Amn Shaqlawa, letter Sh. Sh./4947, dated 11 June 1987, and classified Secret. Exposure to mustard gas causes prolonged temporary blindness or vision impairment, and dozens of survivors interviewed by HRW/ME described being blind for at least a month after a chemical attack.

32. HRW/ME interview, Choman, 23 Mar. 1993.

33. Kandour is one of the five villages named in the Amn report on the 27 May attack. The others are Malakan, Talinan, and Upper and Lower Bileh.

34. The symptoms described by Kamal are entirely consistent with exposure to mustard gas.

35. There are two basic administrative divisions within each Iraqi governorate: the qadha and the smaller nahya. The nahya of Qara Tapa belongs to the qadha of Kifri. The examples of Narin and Zerdow are drawn from an HRW/ME interview, Benaslawa camp, 7 July 1992.

36. Middle East Watch interview, Suleimaniyeh, 23 July 1992.

37. Audiotape of a meeting between Ali Hassan al-Majid and senior Ba'ath Party officials, Kirkuk, 26 May 1988.

38. June 1987 statement by a "returnee to the national ranks," found in Amn files.

39. Since few villages were destroyed in the Shaqlawa area at this time, other than those in the Balisan Valley, it is possible that this may refer to the dumping of the survivors of the chemical attack at Alana.

40. The power structure of the Ba'ath Party is complex, and a full grasp of the chain of

command in the anti-Kurdish campaigns depends on understanding the nuances that distinguish several overlapping groups. As a national branch of the Ba'ath Arab Socialist Party, the Iraqi Ba'ath has a regional command—of which Ali Hassan al-Majid had been a member since 1986. Within Iraq, the highest executive body is formally the Revolutionary Command Council, which did not include al-Majid, although in practice ultimate power is wielded by Saddam Hussein himself and a largely Tikrit-based group of loyalists from the military and security sectors, many of them related to the president. Al-Majid is a key member of this fraternity.

In turn, the RCC has regionally based committees, including its Northern Affairs Committee. Saddam Hussein was secretary of this committee at the time of the 1970 autonomy manifesto. In 1987–88, the post was held by Taher Tawfiq, who as an RCC member was technically al-Majid's superior, although the temporary special powers granted to al-Majid under decree 160 superseded this. Al-Majid himself was secretary general of the Ba'ath Party Northern Bureau. To complicate matters further, the Northern Bureau *Command* was a parallel but separate entity under Taher Tawfiq. The Northern Bureau and Northern Bureau Command are clearly distinguished as necessary in the text.

41. Northern Bureau letter S. Sh./18/2396, 6 Apr. 1987.

42. Northern Bureau Command letter 1/2713, 10 Apr. 1987.

43. The principle of collective implication in executions, including an insistence that party members form part of the firing squads, is a well-established element of Ba'ath Party rule. The most notorious example of this was the televised purge of two dozen senior Ba'ath officials and military officers, including several members of the Revolutionary Command Council, in July 1979, a month after Saddam Hussein had assumed the presidency. In front of a room full of their peers, the condemned men made ritual confessions on charges of treason and were then whisked away to be killed. A tearful Saddam implored—and thus effectively ordered—other senior Ba'athists to take part in the execution squad. See Makiya, *Republic of Fear,* 70–72. Also Mallat, "Obstacles to Democratization in Iraq," which differs from Makiya in other important respects about the nature of the Ba'ath's exercise of power.

44. This exemplary collective punishment, according to a former resident interviewed by HRW/ME in Halabja on 11 June 1992, was meted out in retaliation for an antigovernment demonstration. Some 1,500 homes were reportedly destroyed.

45. By now it appears that the two phases originally envisioned (21 Apr.–20 May and 21 May–20 June) have been collapsed into a single operation. In this order, the "second stage" is clearly intended to begin on 21 June.

46. Northern Bureau Command letter reference 28/3726, dated 6 June 1987 and classified Highly Confidential and Personal. This document is reproduced in "Report on the Situation of Human Rights in Iraq," 77.

47. Northern Bureau Command directive 855, classified Confidential and Personal for addressee only, 29 Dec. 1987.

48. This is only one of numerous copies of directive SF/4008, which HRW/ME found in Iraqi government files, addressed to different agencies. It is a pre-Anfal memorandum, our second smoking-gun document about the Iraqi regime's policy toward the Kurds, and sets the framework for the Anfal campaign of 1988 by turning the prohibited areas into free-fire zones; by ordering the arrest, interrogation, and summary execution of all those aged 15–70 found in the prohibited areas; and by giving permission to the progovernment Kurdish militias to keep everything they might seize in those areas, not only light weapons but also personal belongings, thereby giving true meaning to the word *Anfal,* or

"spoils." The instruction, in para. 5, to summarily execute all those between the ages of 15 and 70 who were detained by the military forces was so blatant that it caused confusion in the ranks, and the Northern Bureau was forced to repeat it on several occasions to remind the soldiers of their duties. During Anfal, the order was generally observed. Documents from that period show that all the people from the villages in the prohibited areas were rounded up and sent to the authority of the Security Directorate in Kirkuk, whose agents were asked to carry out the "necessary measures" according to the directives of the Northern Bureau. We know from eyewitness testimonies that from there, most were taken away and killed (MEW ref.: 93/1-B).

49. The document here refers to the jahsh, whose ranks had been greatly expanded in the period immediately following Ali Hassan al-Majid's appointment, according to an HRW/ME interview with a former mustashar, Zakho, 30 Aug. 1992. This clause of decree SF/4008, with its reference to booty, may offer some hint of the connection between the coming campaign and the concept of Anfal in the Qur'anic sense. Army documents reviewing the Anfal campaign make further reference to the approved role of the jahsh in seizing booty.

50. Northern Bureau Command letter 3321, 6 July 1988, cited in Amn Suleimaniyeh circular to all security directorates (number illegible), 16 July 1988.

51. This letter also urged that "saboteurs should be dealt with strongly, like the Iranian enemy." Amn Erbil governorate to all branches, letter Sh. S.1/13295 of 15 Oct. 1987, classified Secret and Personal "to be opened by addressee only."

52. Letter 542, classified Secret and Confidential and dated 30 [month illegible] 1988, from Suleimaniyeh governorate Committee to Fight Hostile Activity to all local Committees to Fight Hostile Activity.

53. It is mentioned, for example, in a letter from the Special Office of the Army Chief of Staff to Second Corps Command, RAJ/1/13/1/5033 of 14 June 1985; order 4087 of 22 Dec. 1986 from the Security Committee of Erbil governorate; and communiqué 4151 of the RCC Northern Affairs Committee, dated 15 June 1987.

54. The only exception was for "families that comprise martyrs [i.e. those killed in battle], missing persons, captives, soldiers or fighters in the National Defense Battalions [jahsh]. In those instances, only the mother is to be expelled, together with any subversive sons." The summary conclusions of the 6 Sept. meeting are included in a cable, reference 4350, dated 7 Sept. 1987, from the Northern Bureau to all regional security committees. These instructions evidently received wide distribution. HRW/ME has also found a second version of this document, in the form of a letter, 2/237, classified Secret, Urgent, and Immediate and dated 19 Sept. 1987, from the Shaqlawa district security committee to a number of local party and police agencies. Although in other respects identical, it gives the ages of those to be detained as "17 to 50." Whatever the final regulation on minimum age may have been—12, 15, or 17—it is apparent from survivor testimonies that the separation of those to be killed during Anfal depended less on birth certificates than on a quick visual inspection of the prisoners.

55. Amn Erbil to Erbil Police Directorate, letters 9475 and 9478, 16 and 17 Sept. 1987, classified Secret. The 44 families are broken down as follows: Agents of Iran (PUK)—22; Offspring of Treason (KDP)—7; Treacherous Communist Party—8; Socialist Party—3; unknown affiliation—4.

56. RCC decree 10 of 3 Jan. 1988 modified some aspects of decree 677 but maintained this clause intact. Both were signed by Saddam Hussein as chair of the Revolutionary Command Council. Two additional comments are pertinent here. First, the census gave

the regime a means of detecting deserters, a perennial problem for the Iraqi military. Second, and more important, it specified that the executions of deserters would be carried out by agents of the Ba'ath Party itself—a hint, perhaps, of the identity of the executioners during the Anfal campaign.

57. HRW/ME interview, Naser camp, 28 July 1992. The existence of a subsidized food system was a key element of the national economy during the Iran-Iraq War and a significant source of political control for the regime.

58. Northern Bureau Command, letter 1216, dated 18 Oct. 1987, classified Secret and Confidential, to all security committees and security directorates in the governorates of the autonomous zone and the governorates of Diyala and Salah al-Din.

59. A copy of the findings of Tawfiq's committee on the blockade was found attached to a letter from the head of the economic section of the Interior Ministry, Erbil, reference 248, dated 14 Nov. 1987.

## CHAPTER 3: FIRST ANFAL

1. HRW/ME interview with former Haladin resident Hakim Mahmoud Ahmad, Piramagroun camp, 27 July 1992.

2. The PUK, together with the Iraqi Communist Party, the Socialist Party of Kurdistan, and several Iranian parties, had formerly been based in Nawzeng, the "Valley of the Parties," some distance to the north. See Van Bruinessen, *Agha, Shaikh, and State,* 39. They were driven out in 1983, however, when the Iranian army attacked and the Iraqis moved in to retake the area. The Jafati Valley housed contingents of the Iranian KDP and Komala parties, in addition to the PUK.

3. Again, these symptoms suggest that a nerve agent such as Sarin was used here.

4. Confirmation of the Iraqi regime's intent to use chemical weapons and the peshmerga having obtained gas masks is contained in a document in the captured Iraqi archives. Classified Urgent and Secret, it is a telegram from Major Sa'di Mahmoud Hussein, commander of Zakho District, dated 22 June (year omitted, but from the context almost certainly 1987), reference AS/3/4181, and addressed to "Commander (A)." It reads: "[With reference to the] letter of the command of the 38th Force, Secret and Urgent, no. 14665 on 20 June, we have learned the following: 4,000 gas masks arrived at the First Branch of the descendants of treason [the KDP] to guard themselves against poison gas, and the saboteurs will wear them when we use chemical materials to attack [them wherever they are concentrated]. Please check the accuracy of this information and take all necessary measures."

5. These notes are drawn from a lengthy series of secret cables on conditions in the Sergalou and Qara Dagh areas sent to the Security Directorate of the Autonomous Region from Amn Suleimaniyeh. The cables are dated 25 Jan.–19 Mar. 1988.

6. HRW/ME was given various dates for the opening of the Sergalou campaign, ranging from 22 to 26 Feb. 1988; from the Defense Ministry order cited here, it seems apparent that the correct date is 23 February. In field interviews, both peshmerga combatants and ordinary villagers differed wildly in their recollection of dates, even for crucially important events.

7. Defense Ministry legal department circular to the Interior Ministry, Q2/236/6300, dated 23 Feb. 1988.

8. HRW/ME interview, Goktapa, 2 June 1992.

9. The Republican Guard began as a politically reliable paramilitary force made up of three brigades from President Saddam Hussein's Tikrit district. Over time, it expanded into a heavily mechanized elite corps, twenty-five divisions strong. It is easy to recognize Republican Guard troops in the field because of their camouflage uniforms and their distinctive red triangular shoulder patches.

10. This figure was given to HRW/ME by Aras Talabani, a senior PUK official and nephew of party leader Jalal Talabani. Interview, Zakho, 12 Apr. 1992.

11. Secret cable signed "security colonel," Amn Suleimaniyeh to Amn Autonomous Region, 4610, 25 Feb. 1988.

12. HRW/ME interviews, Zakho, 14 Mar. and 6 Apr. 1993.

13. Ibid., Piramagroun camp, 30 July 1992.

14. Ibid., 27 July 1992.

15. The lower figure was cited by former PUK officials; higher estimates were given by villagers interviewed by HRW/ME.

16. HRW/ME interview, Piramagroun camp, 27 July 1992.

17. Amnesty decrees were long a favorite tactic of the Ba'ath regime. It was vital, however, for citizens to know whether they were dealing with a genuine amnesty announced through official channels. The rumor of an amnesty could have devastating effects; fleeing civilians and peshmerga were often lured into government traps during the Anfal campaign by spurious offers of amnesty, local as well as general. Not until 6 Sept. and the completion of the military campaign was a genuine amnesty offered. See chap. 11.

18. Jupa and Dingeman (*Gulf Wars*, 5–6), believe that Iraq fired as many as 182 enhanced-range SCUD-B missiles in a fifty-two-day assault, starting 29 Feb. 1988. Developed with the help of East German and Brazilian engineers, these souped-up Scuds were capable of reaching the Iranian capital, 340 miles from the Iraqi border.

19. According to this report, "The official explained that Iraq's confidence that it could repel a major offensive would demonstrate to Iraq's allies that Iran had no hope of breaching the country's defenses. Moreover, the world would be reminded, he said, that the war is a volatile flashpoint requiring a major diplomatic effort to bring it to an end." *Washington Post,* 2 Mar. 1988.

20. On the razing of the Kani Ashqan neighborhood, see the document cited earlier.

21. Secret cable exchange from Amn Suleimaniyeh to Autonomous Region Amn headquarters, 6–16 Mar. 1988.

22. The two parties to the Halabja ruse gave differing accounts of the relative strength of the forces involved. Although Iran played up its own participation, PUK sources interviewed by HRW/ME claimed that the seizure of Halabja was a joint peshmerga operation, which the Iranians joined in large numbers only after the 16 March chemical attack. Neither version can be regarded as wholly reliable.

23. Among the many Iranian offensives of the war, the designation of Val-Fajr carried special weight. In February 1983, Val-Fajr 1 was Iran's first land assault on Iraqi territory; Val-Fajr 8 and 9, in February 1986, resulted in the seizure of the Fao Peninsula and the simultaneous occupation of mountain areas near Suleimaniyeh, bringing Iranian forces close enough to shell that city. See Cordesman and Wagner, *Iran-Iraq War,* 159, 219–24.

24. Both cities contain important Shi'a shrines: Najaf is the burial place of the Imam Ali, and Karbala of the Imam al-Husayn. The question asked by the pasdaran says

something about their naïveté. Both cities are situated well to the south of Baghdad—that is, several hundred miles from Halabja.

25. HRW/ME interview with former municipal employee, Halabja, 8 May 1992.

26. Secret Amn cable, unnumbered, to Autonomous Region Amn headquarters, 16 Mar. 1988.

27. HRW/ME interview, Halabja, 17 May 1992.

28. The symptoms described by survivors are consistent with those from exposure to both mustard gas and a nerve agent such as Sarin.

29. Resool lists these villages among those destroyed in the border clearances of 1978. Daratfeh appears as a village of thirty households in the nahya of Biyara; Lima and Pega, hamlets of eight and twelve houses respectively, are in the nahya of Sirwan.

30. This reportedly occurred in every one of the nahyas and qadhas that were demolished during the campaigns of 1987–89. By way of comparison, see HRW/ME's analysis of the targeting of Iraq's electrical system during the 1991 Gulf War (Operation Desert Storm), in HRW/ME, *Needless Deaths in the Gulf War,* 171–93. In Halabja and Sayed Sadeq, of course, the evident intent was to make the towns uninhabitable. Both were subsequently declared part of a prohibited area.

31. The Iranian forces in Halabja had managed to bury an estimated three thousand victims of the 16 March chemical attack in mass graves under a thin layer of dirt in the camp of Anab. Four years later, the corpses were still there, and they were beginning to pollute the local groundwater.

32. Amman *Sawt al-Sha'b* in Arabic, 25 Mar. 1988, in FBIS, 25 Mar. 1988.

33. HRW/ME interview, Suleimaniyeh, 20 May 1992.

34. See, e.g., "The Cries of the Kurds," *Time,* 19 Sept. 1988, and "Rebel Kurds Say They Are Ready to Strike at Iraq," *Washington Post,* 24 Jan. 1991, both of which cite the figure as 4,000; Kendal Nezan, "Saddam's Other Victims—the Kurds," *Washington Post,* 20 Jan. 1991 (5,000); Isabel O'Keeffe, "Flanders Fields Revisited," *New Statesman and Society,* March 1989 (5,500); "Massacre by Gas," in *The Kurds: A Minority Rights Group Profile,* 1990 (6,000); and "Hitler-Style Genocide Threatens the Kurds," *Observer,* 7 May 1989 (7,000).

35. This figure was reached by the Kurdish researcher Shorsh Resool.

36. Letter 297 of the Northern Bureau Command, 15 Mar. 1988. These instructions were conveyed to Suleimaniyeh Amn (Chamchamal, Sayed Sadeq, and Darbandikhan) in an unnumbered letter from Eastern Region Military Intelligence, dated 18 March and classified Confidential and Personal.

37. By the same logic of Anfal—perverse yet utterly consistent—villagers from the Halabja region who returned to their homes in the prohibited areas after the chemical attack were later Anfalized. Thus, twenty families who were found by Iraqi troops in the village of Tawella (nahya of Biyara) when the army retook this area in July 1988 reportedly were all arrested and have since disappeared. HRW/ME interview with a former resident of Tawella, Suleimaniyeh, 27 Mar. 1993.

38. Baghdad *Voice of the Masses,* in Arabic, 19 Mar. 1988, in FBIS, 21 Mar. 1988, 23.

39. The various forces named correspond to divisions of the Iraqi army. The first, of course, is named for the Battle of Badr in A.D. 624, which is the subject of the Qur'anic sura of al-Anfal. Lieutenant General Hashem was later in command of Iraqi forces during Operation Desert Storm and negotiated the terms of the Iraqi surrender on 3 Mar. 1991 with allied commander Gen. Norman Schwarzkopf.

40. Baghdad *Voice of the Masses,* in Arabic, 19 Mar. 1988, in FBIS, 21 Mar. 1988, 22–23.

## CHAPTER 4: SECOND ANFAL

1. From a sequence of secret cables from Amn Suleimaniyeh to Amn Autonomous Region headquarters: 1754, 25 Jan. 1988; 5474, 6 Mar. 1988; and 5860, 9 Mar. 1988. The second cable also states that sixty members of the "Treacherous Iraqi Communist Party" were present in Balagjar.

2. This witness also claimed that the pasdaran's weaponry included U.S.-made HAWK antiaircraft missiles, the type supplied to Teheran in the course of what came to be known as the Iran-contra affair. HRW/ME interview, Bayinjan camp, 21 Mar. 1993. PUK officials deny, however, that any HAWKs were present inside Iraq and say that they had only SAM-7s. They also claim that the main function of the Iranian Revolutionary Guards was to conduct reconnaissance and intelligence missions.

3. Amn Suleimaniyeh to Amn Autonomous Region headquarters, cables 6631 of 16 Mar. 1988 and 6739 of 17 Mar. 1988. Despite the dates, from other references in these documents to pasdaran activities in and around Halabja, it is apparent that both reports were prepared by agents who were unaware of the 16 March chemical attack.

4. Although a second witness gave the date of the Sayw Senan attack as 18 March, the later date seems more credible since the witness specifically referred to Nowroz falling on the previous day. All dates given by witnesses should be treated with caution: although the Kurds use a 365-day solar calendar, the months do not correspond precisely to those of the Gregorian calendar. On the Kurdish calender and the traditional celebration of Nowroz, see Izady, *Kurds,* 241–43.

5. HRW/ME interview, Naser camp, 30 July 1992.

6. Not to be confused with the larger town of Dukan to the north of Suleimaniyeh.

7. HRW/ME interviews, Ja'faran village, 6 June 1992.

8. The army's day-to-day movements are detailed in a sequence of sixteen handwritten Amn cables contained in the file "The Purification of Qara Dagh Operation, [illegible] Darbandikhan." The documents, classified secret and urgent, cover the period 23 Mar.–1 Apr. 1988, when Amn announced the capture of Takiyeh and Balagjar.

9. HRW/ME interview, Bayinjan camp, 21 Mar. 1993.

10. Ibid.

11. HRW/ME interview, Suleimaniyeh, 1 Apr. 1993.

12. HRW/ME interview, Bayinjan camp, 19 Mar. 1993.

13. Confidential letter from Amn Autonomous Region to Amn Erbil governorate, 2 Aug. 1988. The text reads, "Please take note of our telex 9887 of 20 July 1988 and inform us whether the persons who are the subject of the communication came from the fighting basin."

14. HRW/ME interviews, Bayinjan camp, 21 Mar. 1993, and Naser camp, 26 Mar. 1993.

15. A "secret and urgent" telegram from Amn Darbandikhan, no. 9507, 5:40 P.M. 1 Apr. 1988, reports the seizure of "four bases of the saboteurs and agents of Iran, along with a base of the guards of Khomeini the impostor and a base of the saboteurs of the Iraqi Communist Party." With these army victories, the military aspect of the second Anfal was essentially complete.

16. HRW/ME interview with a former resident of Sheikh Tawil, Bawanur camp, 28 Mar. 1993.

17. HRW/ME interview, Naser camp, 28 July 1992. Akram, in fact, later passed army lines and checkpoints along the way, but he never abandoned his goats; this may have saved his life. HRW/ME was told several stories of draft-age men being spared—especially in the southern Germian area—if they were tending their farm animals at the time of Anfal.

## CHAPTER 5: THIRD ANFAL

1. The town of Peibaz, on the main road from Kalar to Darbandikhan, is also known as Bawanur—"Father of Light"—in honor of a holy man buried there and whose shrine is said to emit light each Friday evening.

2. HRW/ME interview with former PUK commander in Germian, Suleimaniyeh, 28 Mar. 1993.

3. HRW/ME interview, Bayinjan camp, 19 May 1992. By this time, of course, there was absolutely no incentive for draft dodgers to turn themselves in, given the recent decrees establishing the death penalty for desertion. Public and even televised executions of deserters were commonplace.

4. HRW/ME interview, Suleimaniyeh, 25 July 1992.

5. A "secret and urgent" field report from Eastern Region military intelligence to the Northern Bureau, for example, describes a dawn raid on 26 April on the abandoned village of Kilar. Three armored companies of the 444th Infantry regiment encircled the village to search for "families that had infiltrated the village as a result of the Third Anfal Operation." All the fighting in this sector had ended at least a week earlier.

6. There are reliable reports of a chemical attack on the village of Tazashar (nahya Qader Karam). For details, see below, this chapter. HRW/ME has also received unconfirmed reports of a gas attack during Anfal on Khalo Baziani (Qara Hassan).

7. These cables, generally headed "Umala Iran Synopsis," are dated 9–27 Apr. 1988. They were found bound together in a folder whose cover bears the handwritten title, "The File on the Third Anfal Operation (Qader Karam Sector), 9 April 1988." For all its detail, it is apparent that this is far from a comprehensive file on the Germian theater. Most of the documents originate with Kalar Military Intelligence or the Second Army Corps and describe operations in the southern part of Germian. A handful from Tuz Khurmatu and Chamchamal Istikhbarat report on actions farther to the north. Some of these documents are reproduced in the 19 Feb. 1993 report on Iraq by the Special Rapporteur of the U.N. Commission on Human Rights (UNCHR, 102–17).

8. Second Corps cable 10724 of 14 Apr. 1988, describing the actions of the Kifri column. "After occupying the village of Aziz Qader, the force inside the village found nothing but furniture inside homes and documents and pictures of saboteurs and the charlatan Khomeini. It was burned."

9. Kalar Istikhbarat cable 10687 to Eastern Region Istikhbarat, 13 Apr. 1988; Second Corps cable 11386 to Northern Bureau Command, 21 Apr. 1988.

10. Amn Kalar, secret and urgent cable 19442, 20 Aug. 1988. The order to "isolate prohibited areas from tilling and burn them" was given by Northern Bureau communiqué 3821 of 3 July 1988.

11. The task force was made up of the 65th Brigade of the Special Forces, supported

by the 58th and 200th National Defense Battalions (jahsh). Tuz Khurmatu Istikhbarat cable 10340, 10 Apr. 1988. The cable complains that another jahsh unit, the 25th, had "withdrawn from the task, having failed to carry out its mission." Such complaints of the shortcomings of the Kurdish militia occured frequently in these cables.

12. Paragraph 4 of Northern Bureau Command directive SF/4008 of 20 June 1987.

13. HRW/ME interviews with former residents of Warani, Benaslawa camp, and Suleimaniyeh, 19 Apr. and 12 May 1992.

14. According to numerous witnesses interviewed by HRW/ME, it was a common practice for peshmerga and ordinary villagers to tune in to frequencies used by the armed forces. One PUK commander in Germian was unsure whether chemicals were used in Tazashar, but eyewitness accounts, together with frequent references in other interviews, offer persuasive evidence that such an attack did occur. HRW/ME interviews with former residents of Sheikh Hamid, Bayinjan camp, 19 May 1992; Kani Qader Khwaru, Suleimaniyeh camp, 25 July 1992; and a second interview with Sheikh Hamid residents on 19 Mar. 1993. It is also possible that there was a second chemical attack on 10 April. A sheep farmer in the nearby village of Talau reported that peshmerga survivors fled in that direction and were bombed by aircraft at about midnight. According to this man, the chemicals killed ten people in Talau. HRW/ME interview, Daratou camp, 18 Apr. 1992.

15. Tuz Khurmatu Istikhbarat cable 10334, 10 Apr. 1988.

16. HRW/ME interview, Bayinjan camp, 19 May 1992.

17. General Bareq, a "hero of al-Qadissiyah," (the Iran-Iraq War), was now in charge of a Special Forces detachment guarding the Kirkuk oil fields. Other witnesses also reported sighting him at Glazerda Mountain during the second Anfal. According to a former Iraqi police chief, Bareq was also the commander of military campaigns against Shi'a dissidents in the south in the mid-1980s. (HRW/ME interview with Hamdi Abd-al-Majid Gilli, Suleimaniyeh, 24 July 1992.) Bareq was reportedly executed in 1991 on suspicion of being involved in a plot to overthrow President Saddam Hussein.

18. Cable 10488 from Chamchamal Istikhbarat to Eastern Region Istikhbarat headquarters, 11 Apr. 1988. There are unconfirmed reports of one chemical attack in this sector against the village of Khalo Baziani.

19. HRW/ME interview with a former inhabitant of Ibrahim Ghulam, Suleimaniyeh, 28 June 1992.

20. The Zangana are one of the largest nonconfederated tribes in Kurdistan, with settlements on either side of the Iran-Iraq border. The Jabari were not protected during Anfal by the pro-regime stance of their two mustashars, Sayed and Adnan Jabari. For general information on Kurdish tribes and tribal confederacies, see Izady, *Kurds*, 74–86.

21. Both quotations are from HRW/ME interviews with a former inhabitant of Hanara, Suleimaniyeh, 21 May and 28 June 1992.

22. HRW/ME interviews, Jedideh Zab camp, Erbil, 2 May and 16 July 1992.

23. HRW/ME interview, Suleimaniyeh, 21 May 1992. Many of the most hated mustashars, including Tahsin Shaweis himself, later changed sides and joined the peshmerga during the March 1991 uprising, creating a further twist in the complicated road map of Kurdish politics.

24. HRW/ME interview with a former PUK commander who took part in the Gulbagh Valley fighting, Kalar, 30 Mar. 1993. The fall of Upper and Lower Gulbagh was reported in Chamchamal Istikhbarat cable 10488, 11 Apr. 1988.

25. HRW/ME interview, Suleimaniyeh, 21 May 1992.

26. One of the most feared of the mustashars, Sheikh Mu'tassem was the brother of

Sheikh Ja'far Barzinji, a Saddam Hussein loyalist who was governor of Suleimaniyeh and later became chair of the official executive council of the Kurdistan Autonomous Region.

27. HRW/ME interview, Suleimaniyeh, 12 May 1992.

28. For a sense of these regional patterns, see app. D..

29. A U.S. Defense Mapping Agency map of this sector, sheet 5060 III, shows the villages of Penj Angushti Haji Muhammad, Penj Angusht–i Haji Muhammad Agha, and Penj Angushti Sheikh Mustafa. Such multiple naming is common in rural Iraqi Kurdistan.

30. HRW/ME interviews with former residents of Hassan Kanosh and Drozna, Shoresh camp, and Suleimaniyeh, 9 May and 28 June 1992. Resool lists all these villages among a total of sixty-seven destroyed in the nahya of Sengaw during Anfal.

31. The general's full name is not given. The Kifri column was made up of troops from the 417th and 444th Infantry regiments, supported by the 100th, 131st, and 197th National Defense battalions. Kalar Istikhbarat cables 10212 and 10238 to Eastern Region Istikhbarat, 9 Apr. 1988.

32. HRW/ME interview with PUK regional commander, Suleimaniyeh, 1 Aug. 1992, supporting details provided by an interview with a former inhabitant of Omerbel, Banaslawa camp, 7 July 1992.

33. Aliyani Taza is reported as having been "burned and destroyed" at 8:30 A.M. on 13 April in secret and urgent cable 10687 from Kalar Istikhbarat to Eastern Region headquarters, 13 Apr. 1993.

34. HRW/ME interview, Aliyani Taza village, 30 Mar. 1993. Identity of informant concealed at subject's request.

35. Cable 10468 from Kalar Istikhbarat to Eastern Region Istikhbarat headquarters, 11 Apr. 1988.

36. HRW/ME interview, Sumoud camp, 20 May 1992.

37. The officer is identified in cable 10212 from Kalar Istikhbarat to Eastern Region Istikhbarat headquarters, 9 Apr. 1988.

38. HRW/ME interview, Sumoud camp, 20 May 1992.

39. Cable 10687 from Kalar Istikhbarat to Eastern Region Istikhbarat headquarters, 13 Apr. 1988.

40. The story of Taymour—for a long time the only known survivor of an Anfal execution squad—has been widely reported. The account given here is from an HRW/ME interview, Sumoud camp, 29 July 1992.

41. Villagers from other parts of southern Germian were reportedly funneled toward the town of Maidan, on the far side of the highway.

42. The army recorded the exact time of the burning of Hawara Berza as 5:27 P.M. on 17 April. Cable 11180 from Kalar Istikhbarat to Eastern Region Istikhbarat headquarters, 19 Apr. 1988.

43. HRW/ME interviews, Sumoud camp, 20 May 1992.

44. HRW/ME interview, Sumoud camp, 20 May 1992. Several other witnesses name Fatah Beg as the commander of jahsh forces in this area; according to one, he was from the Bagzada branch of the Jaff tribe.

45. Northern Bureau Command letter 297, 15 Mar. 1988.

46. HRW/ME interview with a peshmerga who fought at Sheikh Tawil, Kalar, 31 Mar. 1993.

47. This euphemistic terminology continued to crop up in official communications

during the Anfal period, even though many of those captured were now to be killed rather than resettled. Cables 10780 and 10915 from Second Corps Istikhbarat to Northern Bureau Command and other agencies, 15 Apr. 1988. Bustana, it should be recalled, was the site of the surrender in late March of people fleeing from the village of Omer Qala as a result of the second Anfal operation in Qara Dagh.

48. Cable 11386 from Second Corps Istikhbarat to Northern Bureau Command and other agencies, 21 Apr. 1992.

49. Several survivors told similar stories about Sheikh Mu'tassem, including this witness from the village of Kani Qader Khwaru. HRW/ME interview, Suleimaniyeh, 25 July 1992.

50. HRW/ME interview with a former resident of Khidr Reihan, Shoresh camp, 1 July 1992.

51. Letter of 2 May 1988, reference L. Sh. D/397, classified personal and secret, from the secretary of the National Security Council to the Interior Ministry, Office of the Minister, with copies to the Northern Affairs Committee of the Revolutionary Command Council and to the General Security Directorate. The National Security Council is a high-level advisory group headed by President Saddam Hussein. The letter also warns that "underground cells of the PUK" may organize an antigovernment demonstration in Kalar to protest the fact that "saboteurs who returned to the national ranks along with their families" were being detained. "Returning to the national ranks" continues to appear in army documents reporting the capture of civilians during Anfal operations. The National Security Council's 2 May warning clearly implied that Kurdish villagers had begun to suspect that the term had now become a euphemism concealing a more sinister intent.

52. HRW/ME interview with a former resident of Sheikh Hamid village, Bayinjan camp, 18 May 1992.

53. HRW/ME is aware of other groups being spared, either because a bribe was paid or from some other private arrangement with a local official, but neither appears to have happened in this case.

54. HRW/ME interview, Erbil, 12 Sept. 1992.

55. The destruction of Qader Karam was described to HRW/ME by a former resident; interview in Shoresh camp, 29 June 1992. In April 1988, according to this witness, Shoresh was merely an open field, and those relocated there built their own homes under the supervision of a government engineer.

56. HRW/ME interview, Erbil, 12 Sept. 1992.

57. Ibid., Shoresh camp, 1 July 1992.

58. A similar partial escape did occur the following month in the town of Koysinjaq during the fourth Anfal, but on a much smaller scale.

59. HRW/ME interview, Suleimaniyeh, 12 May 1992. After the Chamchamal revolt, the authorities carried out house-to-house searches for those who had eluded the Anfal dragnet. It did not take a revolt to provoke this treatment. Similar searches were conducted in Kirkuk, Suleimaniyeh, Tuz Khurmatu, and the large Sumoud camp, outside Kalar in southern Germian. All witnesses concur in identifying those who performed the searches as agents of Amn.

60. HRW/ME interview, Suleimaniyeh, 1 Apr. 1993.

61. HRW/ME interview with a family from the nahya of Naujul, Benaslawa camp, Erbil, 19 Apr. 1992.

62. Makiya, "The Anfal," 55.

63. HRW/ME interview with a villager from Karim Bassam, Sumoud camp, 20 May 1992.

64. HRW/ME interview, Zammaki camp, 24 July 1992.

65. Ibid., Sumoud camp, 29 July 1992.

66. Northern Bureau Command directive SF/4008, 20 June 1987.

67. The remark was overheard by a villager during a conversation between a military officer and a mustashar named Sa'id Agha in the village of Garawan (nahya Rawanduz). HRW/ME interview, Garawan, 29 Apr. 1992.

68. HRW/ME interview with former mustashar Muhammad Ali Jaff, Suleimaniyeh, 11 May 1992.

69. HRW/ME interview, Bayinjan camp, 18 May 1992. This witness was from Galnaghaj, a village destroyed in early May during the fourth Anfal, but the essential details in her account were repeated in many other testimonies on different stages of the Anfal campaign.

70. Zils were an earlier Soviet model of the East German–manufactured IFA army truck, and the term is commonly used by Kurds to refer to either—even though by the time of Anfal, IFA's were more widely used. In this book, these vehicles are referred to as IFA's.

71. HRW/ME interview, Suleimaniyeh, 21 May 1992.

72. In other words, as had happened initially during the well-known deportations of the Barzanis and others in the 1970s.

73. HRW/ME interview with Muhammad Ali Jaff, Suleimaniyeh, 11 May 1992.

74. HRW/ME interview with a former resident of the Daoudi village of Warani, Suleimaniyeh, 12 May 1992.

75. HRW/ME interview, Suleimaniyeh, 12 May 1992.

76. A handwritten December 1986 letter from the Northern Affairs Committee of the Revolutionary Command Council reports on the destruction of three villages but approves a First Army Corps recommendation to spare others because their inhabitants were members of the jahsh.

77. HRW/ME interview, Sumoud camp, 20 May 1992.

78. A memorandum from Amn Suleimaniyeh, dated 11 July 1988, appears to confirm this new policy. This document reads in part:

"Comrade Ali Hassan al-Majid, Member of the Regional Command and Secretary General of the Northern Bureau, has announced the following:

1. The saboteur who turns himself in and hands over his weapon and who is returning from areas that have not been included in Anfal operations until now, will be granted amnesty for all crimes, including those of delinquency and flight [from military service].

2. *The saboteur returning without a weapon from those areas not included in Anfal operations will be pardoned* for the crimes of affiliation with a saboteur group and of delinquency and flight" (emphasis in original).

3. There is nothing barring the enlistment of the aforementioned in the National Defense Battalions [the jahsh]."

79. HRW/ME interview with former mustashar, Suleimaniyeh, 30 June 1992.

## CHAPTER 6: FOURTH ANFAL

1. "The following has been deemed appropriate," reads a communiqué from Amn Suleimaniyeh to the agency's local office in Chamchamal: "All persons who surrender in the theater where fighting took place during the First, Second, and Third Anfal Operations shall be sent to the security directorates with an explanation regarding the political stance of each in order to take the necessary measures [word illegible]" (communiqué 2827, 4 May 1988).

2. This, in addition to the emphasis on the place of capture, is the particular significance of the Amn correspondence cited in chap. 4, n.13. The governorate office of Amn in Erbil has evidently found it necessary to appeal to the agency's headquarters for a ruling on what to do with particular individuals in its custody.

3. Resool, *Destruction of a Nation,* calculates that two hundred villages were destroyed in this sector during Anfal, with a total population in excess of 35,000. On the basis of numerous HRW/ME interviews with survivors, a disappearance rate of 30 percent seems conservative. HRW/ME hopes to prepare a comprehensive statistical survey that will allow for a more precise estimate of the numbers who died or disappeared as a result of Anfal.

4. Redar is the town in the center of the nahya and tribal area of Shwan, and the two names are often used interchangeably.

5. This account of the PUK withdrawal is based on HRW/ME interviews with two former peshmerga commanders in Suleimaniyeh and Kalar, 28 and 30 Mar. 1993.

6. See Jupa and Dingeman, *Gulf Wars,* 6-7.

7. HRW/ME interview, Bayinjan camp, 18 May 1992.

8. The 1958 land reform did away with these old patterns of ownership. Abd-al-Qader Abdullah Askari continued to be acknowledged, however, as the effective leader of the village of Goktapa.

9. HRW/ME interviews with former residents of Askar and Haydar Beg, Askar village, 2 Aug. 1992.

10. HRW/ME interview, Suleimaniyeh, 1 Aug. 1992.

11. HRW/ME was given the names of thirty-eight people in two families who died in the attack. More than half of these were children. Interviews with Abd-al-Qader Abdullah Askari and other former residents, Daratou camp and Goktapa village, 20 Apr. 20 and 24 May 1992, respectively.

12. HRW/ME interview, Suleimaniyeh, 4 July 1992. As a result of his official contacts, this relative—who as a city resident was unaffected by Anfal—was granted permission to return to Goktapa after the attack to search for members of his family.

13. Handwritten daily report 8184 from (signature illegible), First Corps commander, to Army Operations Headquarters, 4 May 1988.

14. Handwritten daily field report 19/8179 from First Corps commander to Army Operations Headquarters, 5:00 A.M., 5 May 1988.

15. Handwritten daily report 8276 from First Corps commander to Army Operations Headquarters, 6 May 1988.

16. These are merely the villages from which HRW/ME was able to interview survivors. According to Resool, *Destruction of a Nation,* 75 villages in the nahya of Aghjalar were destroyed during the fourth Anfal, along with 24 in the nahya of Koysinjaq center, 52 in the nahya of Taqtaq, and 61 in the nahya of Redar. Army documents speak of 138 villages "burned, destroyed, or purified" during the fourth Anfal. As in the case of

the third Anfal, these lists include most of the villages whose survivors reported mass civilian disappearances to HRW/ME.

17. Handwritten daily report 8280 from First Corps commander to Army Operations, 6 May 1988.

18. HRW/ME interview, Koysinjaq, 22 Apr. 1992. This witness supplied the names of eleven men who disappeared from the village of Darbarou.

19. HRW/ME interview, Taqtaq, 24 Apr. 1992.

20. Ibid., Erbil, 23 Apr. 1992.

21. Ibid., Bayinjan camp, 18 May 1992.

22. Like Chamchamal in the third Anfal, Koysinjaq was the target of massive house-to-house searches to locate survivors of the fourth Anfal. Many people disappeared as a result of these Amn sweeps.

23. HRW/ME interviews, Erbil, 7 and 8 July 1992.

24. Handwritten daily report 8276 from First Corps commander to Army Operations Headquarters, 6 May 1988. This phase of Anfal also seems to have sucked in some people who were not its direct targets. One curious case concerns a driver and two porters—one a twenty-five-year veteran of the Iraqi police named Khasraw Khidr Sa'id—in the town of Koysinjaq. Sometime in early May, the three men were approached in the bazaar by an Amn agent and three members of the jahsh of Qasem Agha. They ordered the men to accompany them, saying only that they had some belongings that needed to be moved. Khasraw Khidr Sa'id's family later heard that the three men were taken to the village of Kanibi, just across the river from Goktapa.

Three days later the former policeman's family received a message through a guard at the Topzawa camp, to say that the man had been arrested. (Topzawa's crucial role in Anfal is described in detail in chap. 8.) Beyond this, the family dared not approach the authorities for fear that they too might "disappear." This was the last word they received from any of the three men, who then vanished.

Then, in January 1992, they learned that Khasraw Khidr Sa'id's name had appeared on a document pasted to the wall of a local mosque. The paper turned out to be a transmittal order from the Erbil office of Amn to the morgue at the city's Republic Hospital. The letter (no. 10160) was classified Confidential and dated 29 June 1988—six weeks after the porter's disappearance. It ordered the hospital to bury and provide death certificates for four "saboteurs," including Khasraw Khidr Sa'id; the list also included the name of Hassan Muhammad Hassan Mawloud, the Koysinjaq driver abducted with him. The name of the second captured porter appeared on a similar document posted on another part of the mosque wall. Four days later, the family of Khasraw Khidr Sa'id obtained his death certificate from the Erbil Hospital. It listed the cause of death as execution. This case strongly suggests that Amn may have forced civilian bystanders to play an auxiliary role in the removal of the property and effects of villagers during the fourth Anfal and then killed them to preserve the secrecy of the operation.

25. HRW/ME interview, Benaslawa camp, 7 July 1992.

26. Ibid., Daratou camp, 20 Apr. 1992.

27. Note, however, that the amnesty did not put an end to their troubles. The sixty deserters were sent back to their army units, where at least some were beaten and mistreated before finally being released. HRW/ME interview with Ilenjagh villager, Taqtaq, 24 Apr. 1992.

28. Although a chemical weapons attack on this area was not mentioned by any other sources and is not included in any of the PUK and KDP listings of such attacks, the details

of this account are persuasive. On all other matters, the witness was extremely credible. HRW/ME interview, Daratou camp, 15 July 1992.

29. In the nahya of Aghjalar. Rahman was evidently unaware that other army units were simultaneously laying waste to this area in the wake of the chemical attack on Goktapa.

30. HRW/ME interview with former resident of Goktapa, Bayinjan camp, 18 May 1992.

31. HRW/ME interview, Suleimaniyeh, 1 Aug. 1992.

32. Ibid., Koysinjaq, 26 Apr. 1992.

33. Hashem notes that on 5 May, "forty-one persons . . . from various villages came to our mobile base at Shwan"; on 6 May, four men and one woman "were detained in the prohibited village of Turki." Both groups were "sent on to the Amn administration of Ta'mim governorate." Handwritten reports (numbers illegible) from First Corps commander to Army Operations Headquarters, 6:00 A.M., 6 May 1988, and 7:00 A.M., 8 May 1988.

## CHAPTER 7: FIFTH, SIXTH, AND SEVENTH ANFALS

1. Losing ground rapidly after the loss of Fao, Iran attempted a final offensive in the south on 13 June 1988, but it was contained by Iraqi forces. Simultaneously, the Iraqi army's First Corps—which had handled the fifth, sixth, and seventh Anfal operations in the area south of Rawanduz—recaptured strategic mountain peaks that the Iranians had been holding in the north. See Jupa and Dingeman, *Gulf Wars,* 8; on the overall military situation in June 1988, see also Cordesman and Wagner, *Iran-Iraq War,* 384–90.

2. HRW/ME interview with a PUK peshmerga, Galala camp, 23 Mar. 1993.

3. The territory of the two Garawans, like much of this area, had been a thorn in the regime's side for a long time. An Amn report dated 22 Apr. 1987 (that is, less than a week after the chemical attacks on Sheikh Wasan and Balisan, a few miles away) speaks of an attempt—presumably unsuccessful—by a joint force of army, police, Amn, and Ba'ath Party Special Forces to raze the villages of Upper and Lower Garawan. Amn Shaqlawa to Amn Erbil, letter 5614, classified secret and confidential and dated 22 Apr. 1987.

4. See chap. 1.

5. HRW/ME interview, Wara, 24 Mar. 1993.

6. Ibid., Garawan, 29 Apr. 1992.

7. Ibid., Ramhawej village, 18 July 1992.

8. Swara Agha was reportedly a former PUK member who had surrendered and made his own separate peace with Baghdad, promising that areas under his control would stay neutral. HRW/ME interviews with villagers from Akoyan and Garawan, 28 and 29 Apr. 1992, respectively.

9. HRW/ME interview, Garawan, 29 Apr. 1992. It remains a mystery why those who surrendered in Gulan were spared while people from the same villages who surrendered to the army at Julamerg were sent to the Anfal camps. The difference may be explained by the clemency of a local army commander.

10. Julamerg lies a little to the south of the town of Khalifan at the head of the Alana Valley. It was near here, on the banks of the Alana River, that the survivors of the Sheikh Wasan and Balisan chemical bombing of April 1987 were abandoned by Amn.

11. Julamerg survived intact until 3 Sept., when it was destroyed, according to tele-

gram 4799 from Amn Shaqlawa to Amn Erbil, 3 Sept. 1988, alluding to the "purification" of the Alana Valley by the army's 37th Division.

12. According to survivors, this list ran to 267 villagers from Bileh (secret and confidential telegram 1130 of 3 June 1988, from Amn Sadiq to Amn Erbil). "FQ 45" appears to refer to the army's 45th Division (firqa), based in Khalifan. This report is one of a sequence of forty-two Amn telegrams giving daily field updates on the period 3 June–18 Sept. 1988. These papers make it possible to reconstruct in some detail the course of the fifth, sixth, and seventh Anfals—as well as providing a glimpse of the evident frustration of the First Army Corps as it attempted to "purify" these recalcitrant areas of "saboteurs."

13. HRW/ME interview, Ramhawej village, 18 July 1992.

14. Burning may not be the same thing as demolition. It is worth noting that Resool lists the date of destruction of the two Garawans, as well as the neighboring villages of Akoyan and Faqian, as 28 Aug. 1988. He also lists many villages in these sectors as not being destroyed until December 1988. This is the case, for example, with eleven villages in the nahya of Salah al-Din and eight in the nahya of Harir (both qadha of Shaqlawa). See also chap. 12, n.14.

15. This appears to have been a frequent practice. For example, an extensive file of Amn and army documents dated 18–22 Aug. 1988 indicates that many of the villages occupied during the third and fourth Anfals—including the sites of such important clashes as those at Sheikh Tawil and the Chemi Rezan Valley—were not destroyed until several months later. This campaign also destroyed any crops, vehicles, and stores that remained, with the goal, as one document put it, of "removing any signs of life" in the Anfal areas. Amn Kalar, secret and urgent cable 19442, 20 Aug. 1988.

Similarly, even while the fourth and fifth Anfals were under way, other military units were burning scores of villages in the Qala Dizeh area, to the east of Dukan Lake, where there were no hostilities at the time. This parallel campaign of village destruction was described to HRW/ME in an interview with a survivor from the village of Binowshan, 23 May 1992. The villages, however, were not considered part of the Anfal operation.

16. HRW/ME interview, Garawan, 29 Apr. 1992.

17. From, respectively, secret and urgent Amn telegrams 1333 (Sadiq to Erbil), 3215 (Shaqlawa to Erbil), 1293 (Sadiq to Shaqlawa), 3550 (Shaqlawa to Erbil), and 12233 (Erbil to Shaqlawa).

18. *New York Times,* 22 June 1988.

19. HRW/ME conversation with PUK officials, Washington, D.C., 2 May 1993. Documents obtained through the Freedom of Information Act by HRW/ME and the National Security Archive throw scanty light on this contentious issue.

A Defense Department cable dated 19 Apr. 1988 notes that "an estimated 1.5 million Kurdish nationals have been resettled in camps . . . approximately 700–1,000 villages and small residential areas were targeted for resettlement . . . an unknown but reportedly large number of Kurds have been placed in 'cowcentration' [sic] camps located near the Jordanian and Saudi Arabian borders . . . [and] movement by the local population throughout the north has been severely restricted." The long section that follows that text is heavily deleted.

A second Defense Department cable, dated 15 June 1988, makes reference to Talabani's visit to the United States and reports on a new Iraqi offensive against Iranian forces in Kurdistan. It also makes a clear allusion to the fifth Anfal: "The offensive, if confirmed, follows sweeps against Kurdish and Iranian positions in both V and I Corps that have continued for about two weeks. Iran and the Kurds have accused Iraq of using chemical weapons in the operations."

20. In view of the chronology that follows in the chapter, this date is evidently incorrect.

21. The 'Id al-Adha, in the Muslim calendar, occurs sixty-nine or seventy days after the first day of the 'Id al-Fetr, which is the close of Ramadan. In 1988, when Ramadan began on 17 April, this would have fallen on 25 July.

22. Security Council Resolution 598, adopted 20 July 1987, called for an immediate cease-fire to be monitored by U.N. observers. The full text is contained in Hiro, *Longest War*, 309–10.

23. HRW/ME interview with a former mustashar, Suleimaniyeh, 30 June 1992.

24. All these extracts are taken from the sixty-page report from the Fifth Army Corps commander to the Command of the Staff of the Army, "Analysis: Final Anfal Operation, for the Period 28 August to 3 September 1988," dated 25 Dec. 1988 and coded H2/2422.

## CHAPTER 8: THE CAMPS

1. Amn Suleimaniyeh to Amn Autonomous Region Headquarters, letter 25163 of 29 Oct. 1988. Unfortunately, no time period is indicated, making it impossible to extrapolate the total of those who passed through Topzawa during the Anfal campaign. The Popular Army was founded in 1970 as a party-controlled militia that would provide the Ba'ath cadre with basic military training and act as a counterweight to the regular armed forces. Despite its nominal strength of 250,000, the Popular Army was largely ineffective as a combat force in the Iran-Iraq War; its most important role was to guard buildings in the cities in the absence of the regular army.

2. HRW/ME interview with Abd-al-Qader Abdullah Askari, Goktapa, 24 May 1992.

3. HRW/ME interview, Sumoud camp, 20 May 1992.

4. These officers may have been from Istikhbarat, given the demonstrated role of military intelligence in overseeing the initial transit camps. See chap. 3. They may equally well have been from Amn, which uses the same ranks as the military. (HRW/ME interviews with Abd-al-Qader Abdullah Askari and a survivor from the village of Zijila [nahya Shwan], Taqtaq, 24 Apr. 1992.)

5. HRW/ME interview, Sumoud camp, 20 May 1992.

6. Ibid., Benaslawa camp, 21 Apr. 1992.

7. These sessions appear to have followed a standard "information form" used by the Iraqi security agencies. HRW/ME has found many examples of this form among official files.

8. HRW/ME interview, Erbil, 12 Sept. 1992. One survivor did recall a more extensive interrogation, in which he was asked not only whether he was a saboteur, but to which party he belonged, whether he knew any saboteurs, had relatives who were saboteurs, had any relatives living abroad or who had been executed, and whether he was an army deserter (HRW/ME interview, Shoresh camp, 1 July 1992). Both these men were among the handful of execution survivors located by HRW/ME. For their full stories, see chap. 9.

9. HRW/ME interview with a survivor from the Jabari village of Mahmoud Parizad, Shoresh camp, 9 May 1992.

10. Taymour has been interviewed many times by journalists and human rights delegations visiting Iraqi Kurdistan. See, e.g., HRW/ME and Physicians for Human Rights,

*Unquiet Graves;* Taymour is also the subject of a chapter in Makiya, *Cruelty and Silence,* 151–99.

11. HRW/ME interview with Taymour Abdullah Ahmad, Sumoud camp, 29 July 1992.

12. After Topzawa, Abd-al-Qader never again saw his two sons, Omed and Latif, or his daughter-in-law Fahima. HRW/ME interview, 24 May 1992.

13. A letter from Amn Shaqlawa, ref. Research/11408, 31 Dec. 1987, refers to a Northern Bureau directive of 13 Dec. 1987 to the effect that "it is completely prohibited for bearded people to have access to the center of the governorates and other towns for any reason whatsoever, unless permitted by the proper authorities."

14. HRW/ME interview, Sumoud camp, 20 May 1992.

15. Ibid., Benaslawa camp, 19 Apr. 1992.

16. Most members of Amn are drawn from Ramadi, Tikrit, and Samarra, a triangle of Sunni-dominated towns west of Baghdad, the heartland of Saddam Hussein's political support.

17. HRW/ME interview, Daratou camp, 18 Apr. 1992.

18. HRW/ME interviews, Ramhawej village, 18 July 1992; Rawanduz, 5 May 1992; and Khalifan and Basirma camp, 24 Mar. 1993.

19. The nahya of Kalar in southern Germian was included in the third stage of Anfal. Thousands of villagers from the Kalar area were brought to Topzawa in early and mid-April, but this is the only case reported to HRW/ME of their being taken there any later. The witness offered no explanation of what had happened to them during the three months since the third Anfal. HRW/ME interview, Halabja, 8 May 1992.

20. The supposition must be that Faraj was released under the general amnesty of 6 Sept. 1988. By this reckoning, he would have been brought from Suleimaniyeh to Topzawa on or about 16 July. The Bayinjan camp was used to resettle the survivors of several phases of Anfal. Two other testimonies suggest that its other main purpose was to rehouse returning refugees from the Halabja attack. HRW/ME interviews, Halabja, 8 and 15 May 1992.

21. HRW/ME interview, Benaslawa camp, 6 July 1992.

22. Ibid., Shoresh camp, 9 May 1992.

23. Ibid., Chamchamal, 19 Sept. 1992.

24. HRW/ME interviews, Rawanduz, 28 Apr. 1992; Shoresh camp, 9 May 1992; and Zammaki camp, 24 July 1992.

25. The town of Dibs lies in an area of Iraqi Kurdistan that is still controlled by the Baghdad regime. Neither the Gumbat cemetery nor the old children's cemetery was therefore accessible to HRW/ME for an independent forensic examination.

26. HRW/ME interview with a woman from Omerbel village, Kifri, 30 Mar. 1993.

27. HRW/ME interview, Shoresh camp, 29 June 1992. The witness's nieces were from the Gulbagh Valley, from which a significant number of women were reported to have disappeared.

28. These figures are based on interviews with twenty-one former inmates of Nugra Salman, as well as a former Iraqi military officer with first-hand experience of the prison. The interviews included seventeen men, aged 45–83, and four women, aged 50–60. Asked to estimate the total prison population, a dozen witnesses gave figures ranging from 5,000 to 11,000. Two gave much higher figures, which HRW/ME has discounted. With the exception of deaths and new arrivals, the population of Nugra Salman remained stable until the general amnesty of 6 Sept. 1988.

29. One witness also told of Arab prisoners being held in the basement of Nugra

Salman, wearing distinctive white *dishdashas;* this could not be corroborated in other interviews.

30. HRW/ME interview, Zarayen camp, 28 July 1992. Anfal, of course, cannot explain the disappearance of these young men from Suleimaniyeh, since Halabja was not included in the operation. Their disappearance may be taken, rather, as part of the routine practice of terror by the Iraqi security forces. Later press reports suggest that some younger people from Halabja may also have disappeared from Nugra Salman. "Halabja Wounds Still Open Years after Gas Attack" (*Reuter's,* 7 Mar. 1993), cites the case of a woman from Halabja who has not seen her four children, aged 10–24, since they were interned there.

31. HRW/ME interview, Erbil, 23 Apr. 1992.

32. Ibid., Ja'faran, Qara Dagh, 11 May 1992.

33. The Iraqi monarchy was overthrown in a military coup on 14 July 1958. Its main architect was Brig. Abd-al-Karim Qasem, who subsequently became prime minister.

34. There are persistent, if somewhat contradictory, reports of a basement level at Nugra Salman, from which the sound of weeping and screams could be heard. A former Iraqi infantry officer who visited the prison before Anfal said that this basement was entered through a heavy barred trapdoor with a double lock. The space beneath was approximately two meters high—just enough for a prisoner to stand up. The officer also described a punishment cell at Nugra Salman, built "like a bird cage, with only enough room to sit down." HRW/ME interview, Erbil, 26 Apr. 1992.

35. Ramadan, the ninth month of the Muslim calendar, is a time of fasting, from sunrise to sunset. After sunset, meals tend to be more lavish than at other times, and the rations given to the inmates of Nugra Salman—assuming they were intended to be eaten in the evening—may be taken as a sign of relative lenience by the authorities toward the elderly. (By the same token, of course, if these foods were offered during daylight hours, they could be construed as a mockery or as a test of the Kurds' Muslim faith. The context, however, seems to make this explanation unlikely.)

36. Although Abd-al-Qader's estimate here may be high, his figures in general appeared to be unusually reliable, especially where the numbers of deaths at Nugra Salman were concerned.

37. Other witnesses said that the ration was only two samoun a day—one at 10:00 A.M. and the other at 10:00 P.M. It may be that this varied from time to time.

38. The dinar is made up of 1,000 fils; 50 fils are 1 dirhem, and 20 dirhems equal 1 dinar.

39. HRW/ME interview with a woman from Qala village (nahya Naujul), Benaslawa camp, 20 Apr. 1992.

40. The only exception to this harsh behavior was when the guard was a Shi'a Muslim. Witnesses described the Shi'a (including even Shi'a military officers commanding troops during Anfal operations) as having shown the Kurds numerous small kindnesses.

41. One witness queried this and thought Hajjaj was an army officer. The same witness identified the "head of the prison" as a man named Sa'id Hama but was unable to specify to which agency he belonged. There was a general and understandable confusion among witnesses when it came to identifying particular government agencies by their uniforms or other visible signs. At Nugra Salman, as at Topzawa and the earlier processing centers, witnesses variously identified their oppressors as being from Amn, Istikhbarat, the regular army, and police.

42. HRW/ME interview, Erbil, 23 Apr. 1992.

43. Ibid., Sumoud camp, 20 May 1992.

44. One even more lurid account spoke of a large group of single women being kept apart from the other prisoners and regularly raped by Amn agents. One of these women reportedly killed herself with a knife as a result. The rape of female detainees in Iraq has been well substantiated elsewhere and is known to have been recorded on videotape. HRW/ME did not succeed, however, in speaking to any witnesses or victims of rape at Nugra Salman. Remember that the Kurds are reluctant to talk to outsiders about matters involving sexual abuse.

45. The description strongly suggests that an original purpose of these posts would have been for the use of firing squads. Prisoners can be seen tied to similar posts in captured videotapes of the execution of Kurdish prisoners.

## CHAPTER 9: THE FIRING SQUADS

1. Muhammad's story is based on an HRW/ME interview with him on the site of Aliyani Taza village, 30 Mar. 1993.

2. Ar'ar, an Iraqi-Saudi border post and a way station for pilgrims traveling to Mecca, was mentioned in several interviews as a site for internments and mass executions during Anfal. A guard at Nugra Salman, for instance, told an elderly detainee that Kurdish prisoners from Anfal were being held there.

3. Again, there are minor discrepancies in the witnesses' estimates of the size of the convoy. The various figures given to HRW/ME would suggest that it contained 1,000–1,500 prisoners.

4. The reference may have been to either the high proportion of Republican Guards from Mosul, or to the fact that the majority of Kurds sentenced to death by the Revolutionary Court were executed in Mosul.

5. *Ayat al-Kursi*, "the Throne," is verse 255 of the second sura of the Qur'an. It reads in full, "God: there is no god but He, the Living, the Everlasting. Slumber seizes Him not, neither sleep; to Him belongs all that is in the heavens and the earth. Who is there that shall intercede with Him save by His leave? He knows what lies before them and what is after them, and they comprehend not anything of His knowledge save such as His will. His Throne comprises the heavens and the earth; the preserving of them oppresses Him not. He is the All-high, the All-glorious." Arberry, *Koran Interpreted,* 65.

6. The old shepherd was presumably one of the thousands of Iranian Kurds relocated from their border villages after the Iraqi army's occupation of portions of Iran's Kermanshah province in 1980. The location described by Mustafa is strongly suggestive of a camp called Al-Tash, outside Ramadi, which once held as many as 30,000 people. According to the International Committee of the Red Cross, which had access to this camp, 12,000–15,000 prisoners remained there in mid-1992. HRW/ME interview, Geneva, 14 July 1992.

7. She was therefore probably a victim of the Arabization campaign of the mid-1970s. Khanaqin lies in the extreme southeastern part of Iraqi Kurdistan, in the Arabized section of Diyala governorate.

8. Ibrahim and Omar, the remaining two survivors of the massacre in the bus, also made it back to Kurdistan. For both men, the ordeal was not yet over. Ibrahim, who like Ozer and Mustafa passed through the camp of Iranian Kurds on his way to Ramadi, was

recaptured as a deserter in Baghdad and passed through a series of military jails before taking refuge with a contingent of jahsh in Suleimaniyeh. Omar spent a further period in hiding in Kurdistan before eventually surrendering to the army in September, after the general amnesty. He was forced into another stint in the military and sent to serve in Kuwait (as was Ozer) after the August 1990 Iraqi invasion. He deserted for the last time three days before the beginning of the air war in January 1991.

Anwar Tayyar, who had been on the same bus as Ozer, Ibrahim, and Omar, also escaped from the execution site and was seen in late May or early June by peshmerga who were hiding out in the Qader Karam area. He sustained four flesh wounds during the shooting in the bus and had been left for dead. After the encounter near Qader Karam, Tayyar disappeared for good. The last peshmerga to see him alive speculated that he either starved to death or was captured by the army and killed. HRW/ME interview with former PUK commander, Kalar, 30 Mar. 1993.

9. The directive, it should be recalled, stated that "all persons captured in those [prohibited] villages shall be detained and interrogated by the security services, and those between the ages of 15 and 70 shall be executed after any useful information has been obtained from them." See chap. 2.

10. Saddam Hussein's fascination with al-Hadhar is detailed in Baram's *Culture, History, and Ideology,* 53–54. Al-Hadhar may also be the site referred to by a former Zakho mustashar interviewed by Neil Conan of National Public Radio in the United States. This man spoke of twelve thousand Kurdish men being executed at an unknown site in August 1988 after being imprisoned in Mosul. (Conan's interview is cited in Makiya, *Cruelty and Silence,* 144.) There are also persistent but unconfirmed reports of mass Anfal graves near Ar'ar on the Iraqi-Saudi border, and in Diwaniyah and Naseriyah governorates in southern Iraq.

11. See, e.g., HRW/ME and Physicians for Human Rights, *Unquiet Graves,* 23–25; and Makiya, *Cruelty and Silence,* chap. 5. Taymour has also been featured extensively in television reports, including "Saddam's Killing Fields," on CBS's *60 Minutes,* 23 Feb. 1992.

12. Although Taymour referred to the executioners as soldiers, he had no specific recollection of their uniforms, and it is much more likely that the men belonged to another agency, such as the Ba'ath Party or Amn.

13. Taymour, in fact, lost twenty-eight relatives in Anfal. In addition to his father, mother, and three sisters, they included his uncle Omar Ahmad Qader; his aunt Ayna Ahmad Qader, her husband, Hama Sa'id Mohi-al-Din Abd-al-Karim, and their three young children; his aunt Mahsa Muhammad Mahmoud and her nine children; an unmarried aunt, Hamdia Muhammad Mahmoud; his uncle Osman Muhammad Mahmoud, his wife, Amina Ali Aziz, and four of their fourteen children. HRW/ME interview with Taymour Abdullah Ahmad, Sumoud camp, 29 July 1992.

## CHAPTER 10: FINAL ANFAL

1. Cordesman and Wagner, *Iran-Iraq War,* 3, calculate that there were 450,000–730,000 Iranian and 150,000–340,000 Iraqi deaths. These figures are based on unclassified CIA estimates.

2. The Battle of Muhammad, the Prophet of God, was the Iraqi drive to remove Iranian troops from the mountainous northern front in mid-June 1988.

3. Zareb, *Analysis: Operation End of Anfal,* 39.

4. Ibid., 1.

5. While the PUK had regional commands (malband), the KDP had four branches, or *lak,* which handled both political and military affairs. Zewa Shkan housed the first lak; the second lak, based in the Smaquli Valley, handled operations in Erbil governorate; the third, in the Qara Dagh village of Ja'faran, ran KDP affairs in al-Ta'mim (Kirkuk) governorate; and the fourth, in the Chwarta area, was responsible for Suleimaniyeh. The KDP also had special units known as the Barzan Forces in Hayat (nahya Mergasur). HRW/ME interview with Hoshyar Zebari, Washington, D.C., 7 June 1993.

6. Among Kurdish tribes, aghas are the secular leaders, and sheikhs the religious leaders. The definitive work on the subject is Van Bruinessen, *Agha, Shaikh, and State.*

7. Van Bruinessen, "Kurds between Iran and Iraq, 27.

8. Sherzad, "Kurdish Movement in Iraq, 1975–1988," 138.

9. The army estimated that the KDP itself had between 1,800 and 2,000 fighters in Badinan, divided into a half-dozen local committees. In addition to the KDP, there was a unit of 250–300 PUK peshmerga in the valley of Zewa Shkan, close to the Turkish border and northeast of the summer resort of Amadiya; 200–220 combatants of the Iraqi Communist Party; and 70 "saboteurs" of the Kurdistan Popular Democratic Party of Sami Abd-al-Rahman, a KDP breakaway group. The KDP continues to dispute the accuracy of the army figures. According to senior KDP officials, the organization's combat strength on the eve of Anfal was 8,000, with an additional 36,000 villagers formally registered as members of the civilian "backing force." HRW/ME interview with Hoshyar Zebari, Washington, D.C., 7 June 1993.

10. Zareb, *Analysis,* 2.

11. Ibid., 32.

12. Ibid., 33.

13. HRW/ME interview, Dohuk, 10 June 1992.

14. Ibid., Gund Kosa village, 5 Sept. 1992; see also the 1987 government recommendations on tightening the economic blockade, chap. 2.

15. HRW/ME interview, Kwaneh camp, 29 Aug. 1992.

16. Since the 1930s, Turkey and Iraq had frequently cooperated in suppressing Kurdish dissent. In 1982, the two governments signed an agreement authorizing Turkey to send its armed forces into Iraq in pursuit of rebel Turkish Kurds or in joint operations with the Iraqi army against Iraqi Kurdish peshmerga. See the *Economist,* 18 June 1983.

17. According to surveys by KURDS.

18. HRW/ME interview, Dohuk, 4 Sept. 1992.

19. Ibid., Zakho, 1 Sept. 1992.

20. Even in internal communications, the Iraqi government evidently treated the matter of its chemical weapons with the utmost secrecy. Letter Sh. 5/19299 from the Amn director of the governorate of Erbil to all branches, 17 Dec. 1988, classified secret and personal for addressee only, reads: "Pursuant to the memorandum from the Honorable Office of the President, 4/4/11/44154 of 4 December 1988, a decision has been taken to give all memoranda that contain information about the production of chemical weapons the highest degree of secrecy. Take all necessary measures, keep this memorandum to yourself, and sign for its receipt."

21. One mustashar did allege that chemical artillery was used against the village of Warmilleh, but the testimony could not be confirmed in interviews with residents. HRW/ME interview, Zakho, 1 Sept. 1992.

22. There have also been persistent rumors about Iraq's use of biological weapons, including reports of mysterious and localized outbreaks of disease in peshmerga-controlled areas. At least one document proves that the Iraqi army possessed stockpiles of such weapons. In highly confidential and personal letter H1277, 8 Aug. 1986, Erbil District Commander Gen. Abd-al-Wahab Izzat instructed all units in his area to carry out a half-yearly stocktaking of all biological and chemical agents in their possession.

23. Galbraith and Van Hollen, "Chemical Weapons Use in Kurdistan," 1, 42. Their list appears to include villages that were affected by wind-borne gas from other locations. A persistent difficulty in documenting Iraqi chemical attacks lies in distinguishing primary sites from other places that suffered secondary effects; the list (pp. 323–27) includes only proven primary targets. This is not only a problem of methodology; it is also the most vivid illustration of the indiscriminate character of these weapons.

24. Soil samples from Birjinni were collected on 10 June 1992 by a forensic team assembled by Physicians for Human Rights and HRW/ME. They were subsequently analyzed at the Chemical and Biological Defence Establishment of Great Britain's Ministry of Defence at Porton Down and found to contain trace evidence of the nerve gas GB and mustard gas. See the PHR-HRW statement "Scientific First."

25. A full account of the chemical attack on Birjinni is contained in MEW-PHR, *Anfal Campaign,* 31–44.

26. HRW/ME interview, Gri Gowr camp, 27 Aug. 1992.

27. HRW/ME interviews, Hizawah camp and Zakho, 1 Sept. 1992.

28. HRW/ME interview, Warmilleh village, 31 Aug. 1992.

29. Ibid., Batufa, 9 April 1993.

30. Ibid.

31. Several HRW/ME interviews produced strikingly similar lists of the villages attacked with chemicals along Gara Mountain: to the northern side, Bawarkeh Kavri, Birozana, Dehukeh, Drisheh, Geyrgash, Havintka, Kavna Mijeh, Mergeti, Mijeh, and Spindar Khalfo; on the mountain itself, Baluti, Garagu, Gizeh, Goreh, Ikmala, Razikeh, Rodinya, Sarkeh, Shirana, Zarkeh, and Zewa Shkan; and on the southern side, Avok, Spindar, Swareh, and others.

32. HRW/ME interview, Dohuk, 10 June 1992.

33. HRW/ME interviews, Jezhnikan camp, 3 May 1992, and Sarseng, 11 Apr. 1993.

34. HRW/ME interview, Dohuk, 6 June 1992.

35. Ibid., 2 June 1992.

36. Ibid., Amadiya, 29 Aug. 1992. According to this fighter, the helicopter attacks included the renewed use of chemical weapons.

37. Zareb, *Analysis,* 39.

38. It is clear that a very serious incident occurred either in the Bazeh gorge, through which thousands of civilians fled in an attempt to cross the main Zakho-Baluka road, or in nearby Bazeh village, a peshmerga headquarters. During their interviews with refugees in Turkey in September 1988, Galbraith and Van Hollen spoke with two people who reported witnessing a massacre of about 1,300 people, including women and children, in Bazeh village. According to these accounts, the victims were machine-gunned and then buried in mass graves dug by bulldozers. Filmmaker Gwynne Roberts interviewed two teenage refugees in Turkey who claimed to have witnessed a chemical attack on the Bazeh gorge in which "more than three thousand" people died. According to one of these witnesses, "thousands of soldiers with gas masks and gloves" entered the gorge the next day, dragging the bodies into piles and setting fire to them. HRW/ME interviews in Bazeh

and surrounding villages, however, turned up no recollection of such an event four years later. Neither were there any reports of significant deaths or disappearances of women and children that might have occurred during an attack such as those described. Exactly what took place at Bazeh remains an enigma.

39. HRW/ME interview, Dohuk, 7 Sept. 1992.

40. HRW/ME interviews, Jezhnikan camp, 3 May and 13 July 1992.

41. HRW/ME interview, Amadiya, 29 Aug. 1992. In *Analysis*, Zareb acknowledges the problem of frequent vehicle breakdowns.

42. There is a brief account of conditions at the fort in Mangesh in MEW-PHR, *Anfal Campaign*, 58.

43. According to a dossier compiled by KURDS, 310 villages were destroyed in the Dohuk governorate during the final Anfal. The internal Iraqi army figure for the total number of males taken into custody during the final Anfal, including "saboteurs" who surrendered or were captured, is 3,063. The pattern of male disappearances from villages surveyed by HRW/ME suggests that the total numbers may be higher.

44. Note that at least some of the Dohuk prisoners were subsequently transferred to Topzawa, which remained in operation to the very end of the Anfal campaign.

45. HRW/ME interview, Zakho, 24 June 1992.

46. The commander himself is extremely unlikely to have been under orders to kill all those he apprehended, regardless of age or gender, since there are no documented instances of this occurring. If this report of his comments is accurate, he may have had in mind what would happen later to those he handed over into the custody of Amn and Istikhbarat. HRW/ME interview, Khaneq camp, 27 Aug. 1992.

47. In a curious footnote to this story, the families were detained after the 6 September amnesty by Amn, which sent them on by way of the fort at Dohuk to the camp of Baharka, which was entirely in line with the bureaucratic logic of Anfal. HRW/ME interview, Hizawa camp, 1 Sept. 1992.

48. The story of this village is told in considerable detail in MEW-PHR, *Anfal Campaign*, esp. 12–29, 45–52.

49. There was some debate among the villagers as to whether all the members of this group had been carrying weapons when they surrendered. See MEW-PHR, *Anfal Campaign*, 45–47.

50. The sloppiness of the Koreme execution was remarkable in itself. Even more surprising was the fact that one of the six who survived, a thirty-four-year-old man, was wounded by the gunfire but removed to the hospital in Mangesh the next day by a jahsh unit. He was treated there and eventually transferred to the fort at Dohuk—which he also, inexplicably, survived. See MEW-PHR, *Anfal Campaign*, 51–52.

51. According to Ba'ath Party membership forms found in the Iraqi government archives, merely concealing prior membership in another political party constituted grounds for the death penalty.

52. These four later disappeared from the fort at Dohuk, according to an HRW/ME interview, Dohuk, 9 June 1992.

53. This account is based on the testimony to relatives of one of the eight men. He was wounded in the shooting, escaped temporarily to a nearby jahsh post in the camp of Qadish but was later handed over by his fearful family to Amn in Sarseng. From there he disappeared. The seven men who died were Muhammad Saleh Abd-al-Qader (b. 1938), Serdar Sa'id Muhammad (b. 1957), Mustafa Abd-al-Qader Mustafa (b. 1926 or 1928), Suleiman Sha'aban Checho (b. 1956), Adel Muhammad Khaled (b. 1961), Ramadan

Ahmad Hamou (b. 1968), and Hamid Ahmad Hamou (birthdate unknown). The temporary survivor was Banjin Mustafa Abd-al-Qader (b. 1966). The full names of the twenty-seven executed in Koreme are given in MEW-PHR, *Anfal Campaign,* 50.

54. Zareb, *Analysis,* 17–19.

55. Ibid., 16.

56. Ibid., 17–19.

57. Ibid., 27.

58. Ibid., 38–39.

59. Ibid., 39.

60. Ibid., 57–60.

61. HRW/ME interview, Jezhnikan camp, 3 May 1992.

62. Ibid., Telkabber camp, 28 Aug. 1992.

63. Apart from a handful who reportedly died of disease and starvation, the elderly prisoners survived Nizarkeh. So, by a curious quirk, did at least two younger men who were confined with the elderly because of their injuries. One was the wounded survivor of the execution squad at Koreme; the other was a man suffering from the effects of the poison gas attack on Warmilleh, the only adult male from that village to survive. HRW/ME interviews, Koreme and Warmilleh villages, 30 May and 31 Aug. 1988.

64. HRW/ME interview, Jezhnikan camp, 3 May 1992.

65. The witness identified two of the peshmerga as Muhammad Taher Musa, aged 25, from Zewa Shkan village (Sarseng), and Lazgin Omar, aged 20–22, from Ikmala village (Mangesh). HRW/ME interview, Bateli, Dohuk, 12 June 1992.

66. HRW/ME interview, Dohuk, 4 Sept. 1992.

67. Ibid., Kwaneh camp, 29 Aug. 1992.

68. One witness described the blue vehicles as being "as long as buses, but not looking like buses," with a single small window high up on one side, near the driver's compartment. This witness saw between seven and ten of these buses leaving the fort each day for several days. HRW/ME interview, Dohuk, 4 Sept. 1992.

69. HRW/ME interview, Bateli, Dohuk, 12 June 1992.

## CHAPTER 11: THE AMNESTY AND ITS EXCLUSIONS

1. Iraqi News Agency, as reported in *Al-Thawra,* 7 Sept. 1988. The amnesty was turned into law two days later by Revolutionary Command Council decree 736 of 8 Sept. 1988. Other, broader amnesties were also decreed in the immediate post-Anfal period. On 30 Nov. 1988, Revolutionary Command Council decree 860 announced "a comprehensive and general amnesty" for all "persons who have engaged in dissident political activities and subsequently gone into hiding." On 28 Feb. 1989, RCC decree 130 declared a general amnesty for all Iraqis who had fled the country, although again "with the exception of the traitor Jalal al-Talabani and agents of the Iranian regime." Al-Majid's comments on the amnesty are from an audiotaped meeting held on 15 Apr. 1989.

2. At its noon briefing on 8 September, after Shultz had met with the Iraqi minister of state, Saadoun Hammadi, the State Department described Iraq's use of chemical weapons against the Kurds as "unjustifiable and abhorrent" and "unacceptable to the civilized world." See HRW/ME, *Human Rights in Iraq,* 108–10.

3. *Al-Thawra,* 7 Sept. 1988.

4. Two versions of the document spelling out al-Majid's powers over refugee reset-

tlement have come to light. One, apparently the original order, is unclassified letter Q/1509 from the Presidential Office of the Iraqi Republic to various departments, 7 Sept. 1988. The other is secret and confidential letter Sh. 3/13631 from Amn Erbil to all security directorates in the governorate, 12 Sept. 1988.

5. Letter Q/1509 from the presidential office of the Iraqi Republic to "[illegible] Deputy Commander in Chief of the Armed Forces, Respected Defense Minister, Respected Interior Minister, and Ali Hassan al-Majid, Respected Secretary General of the Northern Bureau," 7 Sept. 1988.

6. HRW/ME has examined many files of these sworn statements, duly filled in by returnees and dated at various times in September and October 1988. The documents also bear the signatures of representatives of the civil administration, the police, security, and intelligence agencies and the local Ba'ath Party branch.

7. This procedure is spelled out in two documents, both issued by the local office of Amn in Shaqlawa: letter to the Ba'ath Party's Returnee Reception Committee, 7 Oct. 1988, and letter 5823 to all police stations, 11 Oct. 1988.

8. The reader might imagine that this would hardly constitute punishment for a Kurd. Entry into the military, the jahsh, or the security forces, however, had always been seen as an option that offered economic benefits as well as immunity from the regime's anti-Kurdish activities. The prohibition was therefore a blow to Kurdish aspirations as well as a further erosion of the civil rights of the Iraqi Kurdish minority. These modifications to the amnesty were set forth in Revolutionary Command Council decrees 737 (8 Sept. 1988) and 785 (29 Sept. 1988).

9. Secret and confidential letter 14951 from the secretariat of Amn for the Autonomous Region to Amn Suleimaniyeh, 23 Nov. 1988, citing instructions of the Northern Bureau Command.

10. The organization in question here is the Political Command of the Iraqi Kurdistan Front *(Al-Qiyadeh al-Siyasiyeh lil-Jabha al-Kurdistaniyeh al-Iraqiyeh)*, a seven-party body (later eight) dominated by the PUK and the KDP.

11. "Reactions to the General Amnesty for the Kurds": secret and confidential letter Sh.S. Sh. 3/5089 from Amn Chamchamal to all security directorates, 18 Oct. 1988.

12. HRW/ME interview, Zakho, 24 June 1992.

13. Ibid., Taqtaq, 24 Apr. 1992.

14. Ibid.

15. HRW/ME interview, Erbil, 23 Apr. 1992.

16. Ibid., Zarayen camp, 28 July 1992.

17. Ibid., Kifri, 30 Mar. 1993. This account of the southern Germian women in Nugra Salman also draws on interviews in Basirma camp, 24 Mar. 1993; Suleimaniyeh, 1 Apr. 1993; and Zakho, 8 Apr. 1993.

18. HRW/ME interview, Benaslawa camp, 20 Apr. 1992.

19. Ibid., Erbil, 23 Apr. 1992.

20. Ibid., Ja'faran, Qara Dagh, 11 May 1992.

21. Ibid., Erbil, 23 Apr. 1992.

22. Ibid., Taqtaq, 24 Apr. 1992.

23. These figures were provided by Jawhar Nameq, speaker of the new Kurdish Parliament, who was elected in May 1992. HRW/ME interview, Erbil, 18 June 1992.

24. This man last saw his two sons, aged 11 and 13, in detention in Tikrit. He also lost fifteen other members of his family in Anfal. HRW/ME interview, Suleimaniyeh, 12 May 1992.

25. HRW/ME interview with former resident of Ber Hoshter, Zarayen camp, 28 July 1992.

26. HRW/ME interview, Jedideh Zab camp, May 2, 1992.

27. The decisions of the Northern Bureau meeting are reported in an Amn Erbil letter dated 16 Sept. 1988. It reads, "It is possible to house the families returning to the national ranks in the new towns of our governorate, up to a maximum of 12,714 families, to be distributed among the following new towns: Jezhnikan 4,241; Girdachal 2,794; Ber Hoshter 2,314; Shakholan 2,387."

28. HRW/ME interview, Dohuk, 2 June 1992.

29. This at least was the view expressed to HRW/ME by a number of Kurdish doctors in Erbil who had entered Baharka and Jezhnikan clandestinely at the end of 1988, by which time epidemics were a serious threat.

30. An HRW/ME–Physicians for Human Rights forensic team investigated the Baharka-Jezhnikan cemetery in June 1992 and took measurements of 85 graves of camp inmates. Of these, 71 were judged to be under adult age. For a full discussion of the team's methodology, see MEW-PHR, *Anfal Campaign*, 65–70, 92–95.

31. Several survivors said that 20 children from Tilakru had died in the camps, as well as 30 from Warmilleh and 33–40 from Warakhal. In the first two cases, the effects of exposure to chemical weapons may well have been a contributing factor. The MEW-PHR forensic team exhumed the remains of three infant girls in the Baharka-Jezhnikan cemetery; each showed signs of severe malnutrition, disease stress, or both. See MEW-PHR, *Anfal Campaign*, 68.

32. HRW/ME interview, Erbil, 7 July 1992.

33. The Iraqi Christians had their own peshmerga organization, the Assyrian Democratic Movement (ADM), which was a full member of the Kurdistan Front. According to a PUK commander interviewed by HRW/ME, the ADM had 100–150 men in arms. Christians also had 5 seats reserved for them in the 105-seat Kurdish parliament elected in 1992.

34. The Peacock Angel is a divinity that may be associated with the Christian Satan, although it shares none of Satan's evil attributes. See Van Bruinessen, "Kurdish Society, Ethnicity, Nationalism, and Refugee Problems," 37, which cites T. Menzel, "Ein Beitrag zur Kenntnis der Jeziden," in H. Grothe, ed., *Meine Vorderasienexpedition, 1906, 1907*, vol. 1 (Leipzig: Hiersemann, 1911). See also the chapter on religion in Izady, *Kurds*, 131–66.

35. From a list prepared by Shorsh Resool and published as an appendix to his 1990 report, *Destruction of a Nation*.

36. Ali Hassan al-Majid, tape recorded conversation with unnamed Ba'ath officials, Kirkuk, 1 Aug. 1988.

37. HRW/ME interview, Dohuk, 19 June 1992.

38. This separation procedure at the Ibrahim Khalil bridge was described by several witnesses. HRW/ME interviews, Dohuk, 3 and 5 Sept. 1992.

39. The lie was a judicious one, for the separation of the Yezidis suggests that the regime's intent was to cause to disappear only those who had been captured within the theater of operations covered by Anfal, which territory ended at the edge of Nineveh governorate. This same logic—which reflects bureaucratic rigidity rather than clemency—is evident in Iraqi government documents dealing with the treatment of captured civilians. For example, secret letter Sh. 2/12809 from Amn headquarters in the governorate of Erbil, 26 Aug. 1988, says that two (nàmed) individuals detained in the Anfal theater were "returned by the Northern Bureau Command owing to the fact that

they are *not residents of areas that were included in the Anfal operations*" (emphasis added).

40. HRW/ME interview, Dohuk, 10 June 1992. In the course of a dozen interviews with Christians, Yezidis, and other survivors of Baharka-Jezhnikan, HRW/ME assembled names of 98 people who had disappeared. This list comprises 64 Christians (25 men, 18 women, 12 children under age 16, and 9 of unknown age and sex), and 34 Yezidis (4 men, 9 women, and 21 children). Several of those who disappeared were infants of less than 1 year; the oldest was a woman of 85.

## CHAPTER 12: THE AFTERMATH

1. The minutes of the Ba'ath Party's Returnee Reception Committee meeting on 1 Feb. 1989 refers to the relocation of a saboteur's family in the Ber Hoshter camp. The minutes of another meeting of the committee, dated 13 Sept. 1988—a week after the declaration of the general amnesty—resolve that "people who used to live in areas controlled by the saboteurs are to be treated as saboteurs," and notes that returnees are to be transferred to the camps by the Iraqi Police and the [Erbil governorate's] Committee to Fight Hostile Activity.

2. Sworn statements to this effect, bearing various dates in late 1988, were found among files recovered from Ba'ath Party offices in Erbil.

3. Undated Ba'ath Party letter found in Iraqi government files in Erbil.

4. This was reported to HRW/ME by a family from the village of Gelnaski, one of the principal KDP headquarters in Badinan, whose son was reportedly executed after surrendering under the amnesty. HRW/ME was shown a grave at Dohuk that supposedly contained the young man's body. It lay in an unmarked area outside the Dohuk municipal cemetery that appeared to contain approximately forty-five other graves. HRW/ME interview, Dohuk, 4 June 1992.

5. A series of instructions from the local Committee to Fight Hostile Activity in Shaqlawa indicates that five families from the Harir area, totaling thirty-seven people, were deported to the marshy southern governorate of Thiqar (formerly Nasiriyah) on 2 Jan. 1989 in vehicles supplied by the traffic directorate *(Mudiriyat al-Murour)* of the Erbil governorate. These people were accompanied by a regular Iraqi police officer, indicating that there was nothing secretive about the transfer.

An Amn Shaqlawa memorandum, dated 16 May 1989, also notes that the former residents of the destroyed village of Khirkhawa, who now live in camps, will be deported to the south if the "saboteurs" attempt to make contact with them.

6. These are extracts from the decisions taken at a meeting held on 8 Nov. 1988 and relayed to Amn chiefs in the Autonomous Region by a secret and confidential set of instructions from the region's security director, no. 14951, 21 Nov. 1988.

7. Ibid.

8. Plans for the subcensus are outlined in communiqué K/2/1/45508 from the Office of the President, 2 Dec. 1988. These in turn are conveyed in letter 548 from the Northern Affairs Committee of the RCC to the Ministry of Planning, 25 Jan. 1989.

9. The "third phase," in other words, clearly refers to the period since 22 June 1987 and continuing after the Anfal operation. This order is conveyed in letter 6271 from Amn Erbil to Amn Shaqlawa, 26 April 1989, and apparently classified.

10. This was true until at least July 1989, several months after the derogation of al-

Majid's exceptional powers. Erbil Committee to Fight Hostile Activity, confidential letter 3489 to Fifth Army Corps, 5 July 1989. The only exceptions to the rule were Amn informers and members of the Mafarez Khaseh, whose presence in the prohibited areas had to be coordinated in advance with the military. The exceptions are spelled out in Erbil governorate Amn letter Sh. 3/1524 to the internal security section of Fifth Army Corps Command, 13 Feb. 1990.

11. Between 1983 and 1988, Iraq acquired more than $2.8 billion in U.S. agricultural products under the Commodity Credit Corporation's (CCC) credit-guarantee program. In 1989, the Bush administration doubled the CCC program for Iraq, raising credits to a level exceeding $1 billion in 1989. In addition to credit guarantees, the CCC program included interest-free loans and direct sales at prices subsidized by the U.S. government. See HRW/ME, *Human Rights in Iraq,* 152.

12. Resool's figures (*Destruction of a Nation*) closely parallel those of the ministry. He cites a cumulative total of 3,839 villages destroyed since 1975. The villages that were spared include a hundred or so belonging to the loyalist Surchi tribe in the qadha of Aqra. On 28 Jan. 1988, on the eve of Anfal, the Shaqlawa Security Committee "pointed out that it will not object to the lifting of the security prohibition regarding these villages, since their population belongs to the Surchi tribe and most of them are volunteer members of the National Defense Battalions. Furthermore, these villages have been beyond the reach of the saboteurs, their inhabitants have not collaborated with them, and no confrontations have occurred in the region." Letter S T/17922 from Amn Erbil to Amn Shaqlawa, 21 Nov. 1988.

13. The Bakhma dam project was conceived originally as a small-scale irrigation and electricity-generating project. After the Ba'ath came to power in 1968, however, it grew more ambitious. Scheduled for completion in 1994, the dam remained only partially built by the time of the Kurdish uprising in March 1991, when its machinery was extensively looted and damaged. HRW/ME interview with a former administrator in the Erbil headquarters of the *Jahafel al-Difa' al-Watani,* or jahsh, Erbil, 7 July 1992.

14. These fourteen villages lay between the town of Khalifan and the Greater Zab River. Their names are listed in an Amn Erbil report of 11 Dec. 1988 as Faqian, Kulken Kolo, Madgerdan, Mingerdan, Daljar, Qalata Sin, Pir Marwa, Deremer, Serkand, Suka, Serkoz, Kuska, and Upper and Lower Jimkei. Resool, *Destruction of a Nation,* 65–67, lists nineteen villages in the nahyas of Salah al-Din and Harir destroyed in December 1988. Serkand Khailani is the only name that appears on both lists, and its story follows.

15. On the Mafarez Khaseh and other special jahsh units, see chap. 1.

16. HRW/ME interview, Basirma camp, 11 Sept. 1992. An internal Istikhbarat report on Serkand Khailani village of 1 Nov. 1988 notes that a number of Kalashnikov rifles were found in this man's home, concealed in a child's crib. Again, the matchup of documentary and testimonial evidence is striking.

17. Letter 25163 from the security director of the Suleimaniyeh governorate, dated 29 Oct. 1988, mentions executions ordered by the Ba'ath Party's Northern Bureau and by the Revolutionary Court. One former prisoner was brought before military court 23 in Erbil, a body with the power to impose the death sentence. In this case, the court's powers were superseded by "a special [execution] order from Baghdad." The man eventually escaped and was interviewed by HRW/ME in Khaneq camp on 27 Aug. 1992.

18. Secret and Confidential letter 19727 from the director of Amn Suleimaniyeh to the director of Amn Autonomous Region headquarters, 24 Aug. 1989.

19. Handwritten documents found in an Amn Erbil file.

20. Many Kurds in the Khalifan area surrendered prematurely as a result of these rumors. Another was a PUK peshmerga named Haydar Awla Ali Muhammad-Amin, whose arrest on 15 Sept. 1988 is referred to in an Amn document of 7 Sept. 1990. Haydar was persuaded to surrender to Amn by one Najma Grou, a leader of the Amn-controlled Kurdish Mafarez Khaseh. After this, he disappeared. In response to his wife's persistent requests for news, Najma Grou told her, "Go home. Your husband is no more." (HRW/ME interview, Galala camp, 23 March 1993.)

In an earlier interview in Sadiq, 18 July 1992, Yunis told HRW/ME that the only person he recognized in the group to be executed was a relative from Galala named Haydar Abdullah. Since Awla is a shortened Kurdish form of the name Abdullah, this was almost certainly the same man.

21. Ibid.

22. HRW/ME interview, Erbil, 14 July 1992.

23. HRW/ME accompanied Hussein to the former Amn building in Erbil on 14 July 1992, where he identified the room in which he had been detained.

24. The Revolutionary Command Council did in fact issue an amnesty decree on 14 December. Yet Hussein was convinced—and his chronology bears this out—that the date of his attempted execution was 8 December. Amnesties, as noted elsewhere, are a regular feature of life under the Ba'athist regime, and yet another was decreed on 29 Feb. 1989, this one for all those who had fled to Iran, with the exception of PUK leader Jalal Talabani.

25. This fact is of particular interest, since the archaeological site of al-Hadhar, south of Mosul, was mentioned several times as a mass execution site during Anfal. (See chap. 9.) Hussein's story is based on an HRW/ME interview, Erbil, 14 July 1992.

26. A third reported example of postamnesty killings involves Omar and Rahman, the two brothers from the Sheikh Bzeini area whose flight during the fourth Anfal is re-counted in chap. 6 and who were captured by the army in mid-June 1988. Another prisoner who was released under the 6 September amnesty saw them in jail at that time, still alive, but that is the last that was ever seen of them. (HRW/ME interview, Daratou camp, 15 July 1992.)

27. Yusef Rahim Rashid, a lawyer with the Kurdish Human Rights Organization (KHRO) told HRW/ME that he attended one such ceremony in Erbil.

28. The motive for the 1974 bombing was apparently the KDP's decision to reopen the University of Suleimaniyeh in Qala Dizeh. The university had been closed down by the regime that March.

29. RCC Northern Affairs Committee directive 1925 of 22 March 1989, signed by Abd-al-Rahman Aziz Hassan. These measures were to include the temporary deporta-tion to the south of families that had contact with the "saboteurs." The directive also insists that the "clear instructions" of Northern Bureau Command directive SF/4008 of 20 June 1987 should continue to be observed.

30. HRW/ME interviews with former residents, Qala Dizeh, 23 May 1992.

31. The RCC decree is conveyed in a circular from Amn Erbil to all section security directors, Sh 3/7604, classified Secret and Confidential, and dated 17 May 1989. The circular reads, "By virtue of the Revolutionary Command Council's decree 271 of 23 April 1989, it has been decided to abrogate RCC decree 160 of 24 March 1987 granting special authority to the comrade secretary general of the Northern Bureau."

32. RCC decree 771 of 3 Dec. 1989, signed by Saddam Hussein, revoking RCC decree 997 of 2 Aug. 1979.

33. Audiotape of a meeting between Ali Hassan al-Majid and unnamed officials, Kirkuk, 15 April 1989.

34. Audiotape of meeting between Ali Hassan al-Majid and unnamed officials, Kirkuk, 26 May 1988.

## CHAPTER 13: THE VANISHING TRAIL

1. HRW/ME interview, Naser camp, 26 March 1993.
2. Ibid., Erbil, 23 April 1992.
3. Ibid., Daratou camp, 20 April 1992.
4. On Ar'ar as a possible mass execution site, see chap. 9, n.10.
5. Sheikh Ja'far, it should be recalled, was the brother of the notorious Qader Karam mustashar, Sheikh Mu'tassem Barzinji. Sheikh Ja'far was also reportedly the main point of liaison between Ali Hassan al-Majid and the mustashars during the Anfal campaign.
6. HRW/ME interview, Sumoud camp, 20 May 1992.
7. All names and locations in this account have been altered or omitted to protect the witnesses.
8. HRW/ME interview, Erbil, 7 July 1992. Further information on this case was provided by additional interviews with former residents of the village.
9. Classified correspondence between Istikhbarat national headquarters, Northern Regional headquarters, and Dohuk and Mosul offices, 12 Feb.–14 March 1989.
Recall that the 6 September amnesty decree stipulated that anyone surrendering *after* October 9—not the case here—was to be taken into military custody and then handed over to the Northern Bureau Command.
10. The Amn requests examined by HRW/ME were issued between June and August 1989. They refer, however, to detentions and surrenders as far back as the second Anfal in April 1988.
11. Handwritten internal memo from the "Person in Charge of Political Affairs," Amn Erbil, 18 October 1990.
12. Amn Erbil to Amn municipal command, letter Sh2/12809, classified secret and dated 26 August 1988. This document is also an excellent illustration of both the meticulous bureaucratic procedures and the rigid logic of Anfal. Individual detainees were evidently evaluated on a case-by-case basis before a decision was made about their fate. Although it is noted that one of these two women is "politically independent" and the other a "housewife," it is not this that saves them but their place of residence. This appears to be the key to the logic of the whole Anfal operation.
13. This tentative conclusion is supported by two factors. One is the known subordination of Amn, Istikhbarat, and other agencies to the Ba'ath Party in all aspects of the Anfal campaign. The other is the frequent reference, in Revolutionary Command Council decrees and other documents, to the party as the agency responsible for executing draft dodgers and deserters—terms that became virtually synonymous, as we have seen, with anyone living in the prohibited areas of the Kurdish countryside.
14. This remark was reported to HRW/ME by Kurdish officials present at the meeting and has appeared in a number of press reports. See Makiya, "The Anfal," 58–59.

## EPILOGUE

1. Although outside observers have had unprecedented access to northern Iraq, it has not been without danger. After the Iraqi government lost control of its northern border crossings with Turkey, Syria, and Iran in 1991, it has considered the entry of persons into northern Iraq through these crossings to be illegal. Numerous attacks against representatives and facilities of the United Nations and nongovernmental organizations are believed to have been the work of agents of the Iraqi government.

2. In July 1993 HRW/ME published a report presenting the first overview on the 1988 Anfal campaign. This report, *Genocide in Iraq: The Anfal Campaign against the Kurds,* combines testimonial and forensic evidence from field missions to Iraqi Kurdistan in 1991–93 and documentary evidence garnered as of May 1993 to argue that the Iraqi government did indeed commit genocide against the Kurds in 1987–89.

3. In addition to establishing responsibility for the greatest of crimes—genocide—and creating a deterrent for other governments that might be tempted to engage in similar crimes, there are practical reasons for bringing a case before the World Court: the Kurds might receive court-ordered provisional measures of protection from the international community, Iraqi state reparations to victims, and a full accounting by the government of Iraq for those who disappeared in the Anfal campaign.

4. Neither Ali Hassan al-Majid's predecessor as secretary of the Northern Bureau nor his successor received the broad authority from the RCC that al-Majid had from 29 Mar. 1987 to 23 Apr. 1989. (See doc. 13, *Bureaucracy of Repression,* 64–67.) Before taking up his post at the Northern Bureau, al-Majid served as head of Amn from 1985 to 1987. In the early 1980s, al-Majid was the director of the office of the regional command of the Ba'ath Party. As such, he was the third-ranking Ba'athist official in Iraq after Saddam Hussein, the secretary general, and Izzat al-Durri, his deputy. Following his assignment in Kurdistan, al-Majid served as minister of the interior and as governor of Kuwait during the brief military occupation of 1990–91. Since 1991, he has been minister of defense.

5. Although by the rules of bureaucratic hierarchy the Amn offices of Suleimaniyeh, Erbil, and Dohuk governorates were supposed to report to the Amn office of the Autonomous Region (which, as the documents show, they often did), at times they reported directly to Amn headquarters in Baghdad.

6. Kurdish rebels held the town of Kirkuk for barely a week during the uprising. According to rebel sources, they failed to remove most of the documents they had captured in Kirkuk in time because they had not anticipated their quick defeat. Some of the files of the Eastern Sector Istikhbarat were saved, but files from the Northern Bureau apparently were not.

7. The three reels form part of a single film showing a famous Ba'ath Party meeting in 1979 shortly after Saddam Hussein's rise to power during which a coup plotter-turned-informer tells a large audience the details of a plot to overthrow the new president. Some of the conspirators are present in the audience, and at the mention of their names, Saddam Hussein orders them to leave the room at once. (All, including the informer, are known to have been executed.) At one point, following loud exclamations and applause in support of Saddam Hussein, the president, who has been calmly smoking a large cigar, is seen to be weeping. Iraqi exiles say that after 1979, the film was distributed widely among Ba'ath Party offices in Iraq and shown to selected audiences for propaganda purposes.

8. The documents captured in the Kurdish towns show no evidence that a

computerized file management system existed in the regional offices. It is likely, though, that the Baghdad headquarters of the various intelligence agencies were equipped with more sophisticated index systems. The only indication that there was any sort of organized file management in the governorates came in the form of a large number of standard-format index cards found in Amn offices. These cards invariably bear the person's name, date of birth, place of residence, occupation, and relevant "activity" (relevant, that is, to the work of the secret police), and they have a number that turns out to correspond to a file in that person's name. (Each personal file has the name of one or more persons written on its front cover.) Thus Amn was always able to find a person's file simply by looking up his or her name in the card index. There does not seem to have been a similar system for files of directives, correspondence, reports, or matters of a strictly administrative nature.

9. Letter from the Military Intelligence Directorate, Kalar, to the Military Intelligence Directorate, Eastern Sector (in Kirkuk), 7 Mar. 1988 (ref. 2228, MEW 2106/4-J).

10. See, e.g., Pelletiere, *Iran-Iraq War.*

11. One example is a telex message from the Military Intelligence Directorate in Suleimaniyeh referring to a videotape sold in several shops in Suleimaniyeh that showed "the Iraqi chemical attack on Halabja," 11 Apr. 1988 (ref. 10472, MEW 2107/2-A).

12. The document is a letter from the Military Intelligence Directorate in Suleimaniyeh, 27 Mar. 1988 (MEW 2106/4-I). The "agents of Iran," or PUK, had actually captured the town of Halabja with the help of regular Iranian forces a few days before the chemical attack. This document is typical of Iraqi documents that describe the campaign against the Kurds in the 1980s in that it conflates the civilian population of Halabja with Iranian troops and rebel forces. On the matter of chemical attacks, this same document also refers to an attack in the Qaradagh area in which fifty guerrillas were said to have been killed. HRW/ME knows from its interviews in the field that this was the chemical attack on the village of Sayw Senan on 22 Mar. 1988 (see doc. 9).

13. Such references are numerous. They usually concern reports by Amn on Kurdish accusations expressed before international fora, such as the United Nations. Amn invariably ordered reprisals against the families of those making the accusations who lived in Iraq. In 25 June 1987 letter, for example, the Amn directorate of Erbil governorate ordered the confiscation of the property of thirteen named Kurds whom it accused of having participated in a protest in front of the Iraqi embassy in London on 1 May 1987 against "Iraq's use of chemical weapons in the towns and villages in the north" (ref. Sh. S. 3/5666, MEW 70/10-F).

14. Although Iraqi bureaucrats clearly tried to avoid making direct references to chemical attacks, HRW/ME evidence shows that slips did occur. There may have been a general order forbidding them from using the term *chemical attacks* in direct reference to Iraqi forces. HRW/ME has so far found one document that orders assignation of the classification Top Secret *(darajeh 'aliyeh min al-ketman)* to documents that contain information about the production of chemical weapons. Memorandum from the Amn directorate in Erbil to Amn subdirectorates, 17 Dec. 1988; ref. S5/19299, MEW 91/25-A.

15. The document is a report prepared by the Military Intelligence Directorate, Eastern Sector, Kirkuk, distributed with a cover letter on 2 Apr. 1988 (MEW 2123/5-H).

16. One of these documents is from the Military Intelligence Directorate, Eastern Sector, Kirkuk, dated 19 June 1988 (MEW 2128/6-A). Note that Ali Hassan al-Majid himself, in a taped meeting in 1987, used the terms *chemical attacks* and *special ammunition* interchangeably.

One can also draw conclusions about Iraq's use of chemical weapons based on how often and when references were made to Kurdish rebels obtaining protective devices. It is clear from the documents that suddenly, in the spring of 1987, PUK and KDP began acquiring significant quantities of gas masks and vials with chemical antidotes. This was no coincidence: it occurred on the heels of what we know from testimonies to have been the first Iraqi chemical attacks against the Kurds at PUK headquarters at Bergalou-Sergalou (on 15 April) and on the villages of Balisan and Sheikh Wasan a day later. Moreover, HRW/ME has found references in the documents to Iraqi airstrikes that caused people to lose their eyesight. The only logical explanation for such a medical complaint would be that chemical agents were used.

17. The three periods mentioned here represent three distinct waves of village destruction. Yet villages were destroyed long before 1977 in Ba'ath-run Iraq and before the Ba'ath Party came to power in 1968. Many villages were destroyed in the Penjwin and Chwarta area during the 1980–88 Iran-Iraq War. Anfal village destruction continued even after the war, as the documents clearly show, and the large town of Qala Dizeh was destroyed, along with three adjacent camps, in the spring of 1989.

18. First-order relatives include parents, spouse, and children. It was mostly the women, children, and old men who were deported, while adult men were detained (see doc. 16).

19. See doc. 2.

20. File of Ghazi Shabo Ilia, Ba'ath Party, Einkawa, Erbil (MEW 2188/3-A, B, C).

20a. Fewer still are documents that speak of policies in other parts of the country.

21. There are a large number of files from the years 1990–91, but few deal with security matters. Beginning in 1989—after the Anfal campaign had been completed and the regime believed it had solved its Kurdish problem—there is a general decline in the number of documents dealing with security matters.

22. Report distributed by the Amn directorate of Erbil governorate, 30 Jan. 1989 (ref. S5/1657) and found by HRW/ME in a box of files originating in Shaqlawa, accompanied by a letter from the Amn directorate there acknowledging its receipt (MEW 32/1-B). The text of the document has been reproduced in full in UNCHR, *Report on the Situation of Human Rights in Iraq* (in accordance with commission resolution 1992/71; E/CN.4/1993/45, 19 Feb. 1993), 94–98.

23. HRW/ME knows from testimonies that torture is rampant in Iraqi jails and that rape in particular may be used as a method of intimidation. It is likely that these matters are not openly discussed by Iraqi bureaucrats for the simple reason that torture and rape are illegal under Iraqi law. Moreover, the regime's open acknowledgment of such practices, which affect families throughout the country and are not linked to a military campaign against a specific group of people, might stir tremendous unrest among the population.

There has been some discussion in the American media about the documentary evidence of rape in Iraq. Iraqi writer Kanan Makiya claimed in an article in the *Nation* on 10 May 1993 that the "General Security Organization" employs persons as professional rapists, offering a single document to substantiate this claim. The document in question is a printed index card with handwritten entries, bearing a man's name, profession, and activity. His profession is said to be "fighter in the Popular Army," and his activity is "violation of women's honor." Although there is no reason to doubt this particular card's authenticity, there is no evidence to suggest that the man mentioned on the card was in the employ of the Iraqi secret police at all, for any purpose. HRW/ME has found hundreds of identical cards in the Iraqi state files. All list the name of the person and his or her profession and activity. Many of the professions listed are jobs that are not in the government but in the private sector. The word *activity* is meant to refer to the main reason why Amn keeps a file on that person. Almost invariably the handwritten entry offers one of the following types of activities: being a saboteur, membership in one of the rebel parties, fleeing to Iran, "returning to the national ranks," being an army deserter, "arrested in Anfal operations," and "father was executed." The index cards do not constitute a record of employment by Amn, and in HRW/ME's view neither they nor any other Iraqi government document seen by HRW/ME provide a shred of evidence of the use of rape as a matter of state policy in Iraq. (See also n. 8 above.)

24. HRW/ME has found many documents, for example, on the mass detention of members of the Barzani tribe in 1983 who subsequently disappeared. Documents from around the same time ordered employers in Erbil to consider those Barzanis among their employees who were suddenly absent from their jobs as dismissed. Documents also attest to the arrest of thousands of persons and their transfer to Kirkuk during Anfal. Some of the names match the names given to HRW/ME of persons said not to have returned home after Anfal and even include three execution survivors interviewed by HRW/ME in 1992 (see doc. 23).

25. See sec. 8 of "A Narrative Road Map to the Discourse of Repression" for a full discussion of official euphemisms used in the context of the Iraqi government's campaigns in northern Iraq. Some phrasing is meant to conceal unpleasant realities from the public; at other times euphemistic language is used as propaganda to further the regime's ideological objectives.

26. See above, n. 14.

27. Letter from the Committee to Fight Hostile Activity in Shaqlawa, 4 May 1988 (ref. LM/135), referring to instructions from the Northern Bureau of 16 Apr. 1987 (MEW 92/1-T). This was at the height of the Anfal campaign and is therefore likely to reflect an attempt by the regime to conceal from the Kurdish urban population the far-reaching nature of the campaign in the countryside. During operations to relocate villagers to camps in previous years, the army often left the houses of villages unharmed, offering the population at least the hope of return. For the duration of Anfal, people were to be left with this illusion, probably to forestall a mass protest. Incidentally, a document from 1987, during the spring campaign of village destruction, instructs military intelligence agents to "use the term *amalgamation* for the deportation operation" (MEW 2126/1-S). Again, this change represents a softening of the rhetoric used in official documents. A year later, during the much more violent Anfal campaign, even the term *deportation* (and *removal*) had become acceptable.

28. From a memorandum signed by an Amn lieutenant that refers to instructions issued by "the respected Amn director"—most likely the head of the General Security Directorate in Baghdad—on 25 Sept. 1990 (MEW 102/7-A) (see doc. 29).

29. Contained in a letter of the Military Intelligence Directorate, Eastern Sector, 16 Feb. 1990 (ref. 168, MEW 2003/2-A). The order goes on to state, ominously: "If such a case is found, the punishment will be severe." The "fate of the detainees" refers to standard practice in Iraq not to notify families of the arrest of their relatives, at least not until after court sentencing.

30. Memorandum of the General Security Directorate, Baghdad, 10 Feb. 1988 (ref. Sh. 3 Q.2/8970), circulated by the director of Amn of Erbil governorate, 20 Feb. 1988 (ref. 2629, MEW 83/2-B). Although the desire to conceal the names of senior authorities is clear from this order, initially two interpretations of the officials' motivation are

possible: one is that they did not wish to be held accountable for deeds that would constitute clear breaches of international law, such as the mass killings that were about to take place; another (suggested by the ambiguous phrase, "Take their regular position") is that they did not want to be harangued by junior officers about the precise detail of directives. At the time of Anfal, official instructions proliferated at a dizzying speed, and some were so strong (e.g., the order to execute all persons 15-70 detained in the prohibited areas) that they sowed confusion and uncertainty in the lower echelons of the security apparatus. HRW/ME has found pieces of correspondence, for example, that ask for confirmation as to whether certain particularly severe orders should be implemented.

The argument against this second interpretation is that junior officials in any case would not be permitted to address senior authorities directly but would have to go through their immediate superiors in the regional offices. The issue addressed by the directive is thus more likely to be one of accountability for crimes.

31. Literally, "Please [under]take what is necessary."

32. Letter from the military intelligence section of the Command of the Oil Protection Forces (COPF), Kirkuk, 15 Apr. 1988 (ref. 337, MEW 2110/9-A). The arrests took place at the height of the third Anfal operation in the Germian plain. (See *Genocide in Iraq,* chap. 5.) COPF's leader was Maj. Gen. Bareq Abdullah al-Haj Hunta, who commanded Iraqi forces in the third Anfal operation. The security directorate in al-Ta'mim governorate (Kirkuk), is the last known place of detention of families arrested during Anfal. After that they disappeared. HRW/ME testimonies indicate that most were taken to sites in the western desert and killed. The document sports a slogan in the top right-hand corner: "We Seek Justice, Not War." At the bottom the numbers of detainees are given: 69 women, 100 children, and 10 men. (See also doc. 23.)

33. Literally, "security-prohibited areas," translated here usually as "areas prohibited for security reasons."

34. Draft dodgers (*mutekhallefin*) who "surrendered" were sent to the local army recruitment center.

35. See doc. 23.

36. U.N. General Assembly, *Situation of Human Rights in Iraq.*

37. Reproduced in UNCHR, *Report on the Situation of Human Rights in Iraq,* 52–53.

38. Not all the documents are written on stationery. The files include many handwritten letters and even notes scribbled on regular sheets of paper. This is particularly true for Amn and Ba'ath Party offices in smaller towns but not so much for Istikhbarat. The reason is not immediately clear. Perhaps it was an issue of cost since the stationery had to be brought in from one of the larger centers, or perhaps no need was seen to write interoffice correspondence on matters of a purely local nature on official stationery.

39. Permanent Mission of the Republic of Iraq to the U.N., *Response of the Iraqi Delegation,* 7.

40. Moreover, the documents are written in excellent Arabic, clearly the product of native Iraqis fluent in the Iraqi dialect. Moreover, the consistency of these documents indicates that they were undoubtedly written by bureaucrats, indeed, bureaucrats well versed in the official discourse of the Iraqi state apparatus.

41. PUK and KDP shipped most, but by no means all, of the documents in their possession to the United States for safekeeping.

# GLOSSARY OF ARABIC
# AND KURDISH TERMS

agha   The owner of large tracts of land, often entire villages. The aghas were endowed with considerable political power until they lost most of their property in the sweeping land reforms of the 1970s.

Ahl al-Haqq   A religious sect in Kurdistan

Amn   Security (as in Mudiriyat al-Amn al-Ameh, General Security Directorate)

anjuman   Village council in Kurdish villages controlled by the PUK

aqid   An officer with the rank of colonel; organization undetermined

basij   Mobilization unit

chatta   Bandit or brigand; derogatory term for jahsh in Badinan region

dishdashas   A man's robe (Iraq)

falaka   A form of torture, which involves beating the soles of the feet

fawj   A jahsh unit

firqa   An army division; also, a branch of the Ba'ath Party

hezi bergri   The PUK's local defense forces

intifada   The Arabic word meaning *uprising*

Istikhbarat   Military Intelligence

jahsh   Donkey foal; derogatory term for Kurdish National Defense battalions

jamadani   A Kurdish head scarf

kart   A guerrilla unit (PUK), comprising four to five mafrazeh

laq   Peshmerga Branch Command (KDP)

liwa'   An army brigade

Mafarez Khaseh   A special unit (Kurdish section of Amn)

mafrazeh   Smallest guerrilla unit (PUK)

maghawir   Commandos

maghreb   Sunset

mahkamat al-Thawra   The Revolutionary Court

majlis al-sha'b   Parliament

malband   Peshmerga regional command (PUK)

manateq mahdoureh   Prohibited areas

mujamma'a   Resettlement camp

mujaheddin   Muslim guerrilla fighters

mukhabarat   Foreign Intelligence Agency

mukhtar   Village elder

mullah   Prayer leader

mustashar   Adviser or consultant; Kurdish tribal commander of a jahsh unit

nahya   Administrative unit; district center, and the villages within its jurisdiction

naqib   An officer with the rank of captain in the Iraqi army

pasdaran   Iranian Revolutionary Guards

peshgiri   The PUK's local defense forces

peshmerga   "Those who face death"; Kurdish guerrilla fighters

qadha   The largest administrative unit within a governorate

qaym maqam   A district administrator

rajima   Truck-mounted multiple-barrel artillery, sometimes used to deliver chemical weapons

raparin   The Kurdish word for *uprising*

samneh   Sheep's fat

samoun   Pita bread

sharwal   Kurdish baggy pants

sunnah   'Path' of the Prophet Muhammad

sura   A chapter of the Qur'an

tahqiq   An investigation

teep   Basic PUK military unit within the malband, comprising five karts

vilayet   An administrative unit under the Ottoman Empire; a governorate in Iraq until 1975

# BIBLIOGRAPHY

Abdulghani, J. M. *Iran and Iraq: The Years of Crisis.* London: Croom Helm, 1984.

Americas Watch. *Civil Patrols in Guatemala.* New York: Human Rights Watch, August 1986.

———. *Peru under Fire: Human Rights since the Return to Democracy.* New Haven: Yale University Press, 1992.

Amnesty International. *Iraq-Children: Innocent Victims of Political Repression.* London: Amnesty International, 1989.

———. *Iraq: Executions.* London: Amnesty International, 1988.

———. *Iraq/Turkey–Iraqi Kurds: At Risk of Forcible Repatriation from Turkey and Human Rights Violations in Iraq.* London: Amnesty International, 1990.

———. *Torture in Iraq, 1982–1984.* London: Amnesty International, 1985.

Arberry, A. J., trans. *The Koran Interpreted.* New York: Collier, 1955.

Axelgard, Frederick. "A New Iraq." *The Washington Papers.* Washington, D.C.: Center for Strategic and International Studies, 1988.

Axelgard, Frederick, ed. *Iraq in Transition.* Boulder, Colo.: Westview, 1986.

Ayubi, Shaheen, and Shirin Tahir-Kheli, eds. *The Iran-Iraq War: New Weapons, Old Conflicts.* New York: Praeger, 1983.

Baram, Amazia. *Culture, History, and Ideology in the Formation of Ba'thist Iraq, 1968–89.* New York: St. Martin's, 1991.

———. "Qawmiyya and Wataniyya in Ba'thi Iraq." *Middle Eastern Studies* 19 (April 1983): 188–200.

Batatu, Hanna. *The Old Social Classes and the Revolutionary Movements of Iraq: A Study of Iraq's Old Landed and Commercial Classes and of Its Communists, Ba'thists, and Free Officers.* Princeton, N.J.: Princeton University Press, 1978.

———. "Class Analysis and Iraqi Society." *Arab Studies Quarterly* 1(3) (1979): 229–44.

———. *The Egyptian, Syrian, and Iraqi Revolutions: Some Observations on Their Underlying Causes and Social Character.* Washington, D.C.: Georgetown University Press, 1984.

———. "Iraq's Underground Shi'a Movements: Characteristics, Causes, and Prospects." *Middle East Journal* 35(4) (1981): 178–94.

Bonner, Raymond. "Always Remember." *New Yorker,* 28 Sept. 1992.

Chailand, Gérard. *People without a Country: The Kurds and Kurdistan.* London: Zed, 1982.

Chalk, Frank, and Kurt Jonassohn. *The History and Sociology of Genocide: Analyses and Case Studies.* New Haven: Yale University Press, 1990.

Chubin, Shahram, and Charles Tripp. *Iran and Iraq at War.* 2d rev. ed. Boulder, Colo.: Westview, 1991.

Committee against Repression and for Democratic Rights in Iraq (CARDRI). *Saddam's Iraq: Revolution or Reaction?* London: Zed, 1986.

Cooley, John K. "Conflict With the Iraqi Left." *Jerusalem Quarterly* 9 (1978): 131–44.

Cordesman, Anthony H., and Abraham R. Wagner. *The Lessons of Modern War.* Vol. 2, *The Iran-Iraq War.* London: Mansell-Westview, 1990.

Dann, Uriel. *Iraq under Qassem: A Political History, 1958–1963.* New York: Praeger, 1969.

*Desert Shield Factbook.* Bloomington, Ind.: GDW, 1991.

Fédération International des Ligues des Droits de l'Homme. *Iraqi Kurdistan: Fact-Finding Mission on the Human Rights Situation.* Paris, 1993.

Fein, Helen, ed. *Genocide Watch.* New Haven: Yale University Press, 1992.

Finkelstein, J. J. *The Ox That Gored.* Philadelphia: American Philosophical Society, 1981.

Gabbay, Rony E. *Communism and Agrarian Reform in Iraq.* London: Croom Helm, 1978.

Ghareeb, Edmond. *The Kurdish Question in Iraq.* Syracuse, N.Y.: Syracuse University Press, 1981.

Government of Iraq. *Settlement of the Kurdish Problem in Iraq.* Baghdad: Ath-Thawra Publications, [c. 1974].

Helms, Christine Moss. *Iraq: Eastern Flank of the Arab World.* Washington, D.C.: Brookings Institution, 1984.

Henderson, Simon. *Instant Empire: Saddam Hussein's Ambition for Iraq.* San Francisco: Mercury House, 1991.

Hilberg, Raul. *The Destruction of the European Jews.* New York: Holmes and Meier, 1985.

Hiro, Dilip. *The Longest War: The Iran-Iraq Military Conflict.* New York: Routledge, 1991.

Husain, Saddam. *On Current Events in Iraq.* London: Longman, 1977.

Ingrams, Doreen. *The Awakened: Women in Iraq.* London: Third World Centre, 1983.

Ismael, Tareq Y. *Iran and Iraq: Roots of Conflict.* 1st ed. Syracuse, N.Y.: Syracuse University Press, 1982.

Izady, Mehrdad R. *The Kurds: A Concise Handbook.* Washington, D.C.: Crane Russak, 1992.

Jawad, Sa'ad. *Iraq and the Kurdish Question, 1958–70.* London: Ithaca Press, 1981.

Jupa, Richard, and James Dingeman. *Gulf Wars: How Iraq Won the First and Lost the Second. Will There Be a Third?* Cambria, Calif.: 3W Publications, [c. 1991].

Kedourie, Elie. "Continuity and Change in Modern Iraqi History." *Asian Affairs* 62(2) (1975): 140–46.

Kelidas, Abbas, ed. *The Integration of Modern Iraq.* London: Croom Helm, 1979.

Khadduri, Majid. *Socialist Iraq: A Study in Iraqi Politics since 1968.* Washington, D.C.: Middle East Institute, 1978.

King, Ralph. *The Iran-Iraq War: The Political Implications.* London: International Institute for Strategic Studies, 1987.

Kreyenbroek, Philip G., and Stefan Sperl, eds. *The Kurds: A Contemporary Overview.* London: Routledge, 1992.

———. *The Kurds: A Nation Denied.* London: Minority Rights Publications, 1992.

MacKenzie, D. N. "The Origins of Kurdish." *Transactions of the Philological Society,* 1961.

Makiya, Kanan [Samir al-Khalil]. "The Anfal: Uncovering an Iraqi Campaign to Exterminate the Kurds." *Harper's Magazine,* May 1992.
———. *Cruelty and Silence: War, Tyranny, Uprising, and the Arab World.* New York: W. W. Norton, 1993.
———. *Republic of Fear: The Politics of Modern Iraq.* Los Angeles: University of California Press, 1989.
Mallat, Chibli. "Obstacles to Democratization in Iraq: A Reading of Post-Revolutionary Iraqi History through the Gulf War." Unpublished MS., 1992.
Marr, Phebe. *The History of Modern Iraq.* Boulder, Colo.: Westview, 1985.
Mattar, Faud. *Saddam Hussein: The Man, the Cause, and the Future.* London: Third World Press, 1981.
Middle East Watch. *Background on Human Rights Conditions, 1984–1992.* New York: Human Rights Watch, 1993.
———. *Endless Torment: The 1991 Uprising in Iraq and Its Aftermath.* New York: Human Rights Watch, 1992.
———. *Human Rights in Iraq.* New Haven: Yale University Press, 1990.
———. *Needless Deaths in the Gulf War: Civilian Casualties during the Air Campaign and Violations of the Laws of War.* New York: Human Rights Watch, 1991.
Middle East Watch and Physicians for Human Rights (MEW-PHR). *The Anfal Campaign in Iraqi Kurdistan: The Destruction of Koreme.* New York: Human Rights Watch, 1993.
———. *Unquiet Graves: The Search for the Disappeared in Iraqi Kurdistan.* New York: Human Rights Watch, 1992.
Miller, Judith. "Iraq Accused: A Case of Genocide." *New York Times Magazine,* 3 Jan. 1993.
Niblock, Tim, ed. *Iraq, The Contemporary State.* London: Croom Helm, 1979.
*The 1968 Revolution in Iraq: Experience and Prospects. The Political Report of the Eight Congress of the Arab Ba'th Socialist Party in Iraq.* January 1974. London: Ithaca Press, 1979.
O'Ballance, Edgar. *The Gulf War.* London: Brassey's, 1988.
Pelletiere, Stephen C. *The Iran-Iraq War: Chaos in a Vacuum.* New York: Praeger, 1992.
Pelletiere, Stephen C., and Douglas V. Johnson II, and Leif R. Rosenberger. *Iraqi Power and U.S. Security in the Middle East.* Carlisle Barracks, Pa.: U.S. Army War College, Strategic Studies Institute, 1990.
Permanent Mission of the Republic of Iraq to the United Nations Office in Geneva. *Response of the Iraqi Delegation to the Report Presented by the Special Rapporteur of the Commission on Human Rights in Iraq at the 48th Session.* Geneva, 20 Feb. 1992.
Petran, Tabitha. "Social Structures and Class Formation in Iraq." *Monthly Review* 32(7) (1980): 46–53.
Physicians for Human Rights (PHR). *Winds of Death: Iraq's Use of Poison Gas against Its Kurdish Population.* Boston: PHR, 1989.
Physicians for Human Rights and Human Rights Watch (PHR-HRW). "Scientific First: Soil Samples Taken from Bomb Craters in Northern Iraq Reveal Nerve Gas—Even Four Years Later." 29 Apr. 1993.
Price, David Lynn. "Baghdad: Return to the West?" *Washington Quarterly* 2 (Autumn 1979): 143–46.

Resool, Shorsh. *Destruction of a Nation.* April 1990.

Rubin, Barry. *The Politics of Terrorism.* Washington, D.C.: Foreign Policy Institute, School of Advanced International Studies, John Hopkins University, 1989.

Sherzad, A. "The Kurdish Movement in Iraq, 1975–1988." In Kreyenbroek and Sperl, eds., *The Kurds.*

Shikarah, Ahmed Abd al-Razzaq. *Iraqi Politics, 1921–41: The Interaction between Domestic Politics and Foreign Policy.* London: Laam, 1987.

Simon, Reeva S. *Iraq between the Two World Wars: The Creation and Implementation of a Nationalist Ideology.* New York: Columbia University Press, 1986.

Strok, Joe. "Oil and the Penetration of Capitalism in Iraq: An Interpretation." *Peuples méditerranéens—Mediterranean Peoples* 9 (1979): 125–52.

Supreme Defense Council. *Our Tyrannized Cities: Statistical Survey of Aggressions of Baathist Regime of Iraq against Iranian Cities and Residential Areas.* Teheran: War Information Headquarters, 1983.

Tarbush, Mohammed A. *The Role of the Military in Politics: A Case Study of Iraq to 1941.* London: Kegan Paul, 1982.

Tulfah, Khairallah. *Three Whom God Should Not Have Created: Persians, Jews, and Flies.* Baghdad: Dar al-Hurriyya, 1981.

Turner, Arthur Campbell. "Iraqi Pragmatic Radicalism in the Fertile Crescent." *Current History* 81(471) (1982): 14–17.

United Nations Commission on Human Rights (UNCHR). *Report on the Situation of Human Rights in Iraq.* (Prepared by Max van der Stoel, special rapporteur of the Commission on Human Rights.) New York: United Nations, 25 Feb. 1994.

United Nations General Assembly. *Situation of Human Rights in Iraq.* 13 Nov. 1992, 16. A/47/367/Add.1.

United States Senate. Peter Galbraith, *Kurdistan in the Time of Saddam Hussein.* Staff report to the U.S. Senate Committee on Foreign Relations, November 1993.

———. Peter W. Galbraith and Christopher Van Hollen, Jr. "Chemical Weapons Use in Kurdistan: Iraq's Final Offensive." Staff report to the U.S. Senate Committee on Foreign Relations, 21 Sept. 1988.

Van Bruinessen, Martin. *Agha, Shaikh, and State: The Social and Political Structures of Kurdistan.* London: Zed, 1992.

———. "The Kurds between Iran and Iraq." *Middle East Report.* July–August 1986.

# INDEX

MAF